SEXUAL MISCONDUCT
IN COUNSELING
AND MINISTRY

SEXUAL MISCONDUCT IN COUNSELING AND MINISTRY

PETER MOSGOFIAN, M.A.
AND
GEORGE OHLSCHLAGER, M.S.W., J.D.

Wipf & Stock
PUBLISHERS
Eugene, Oregon

Unless otherwise indicated, all Scripture quotations in this volume are from the *New International Version* of the Bible, copyright © 1983 by the International Bible Society. Used by permission of Zondervan Bible Publishers.

Those Scripture quotations marked RSV are from the Revised Standard Version of the Bible, copyrighted © 1946, 1952, 1971, 1973 by the Division of Christian Education of the National Council of the Churches of Christ in the U.S.A., and are used by permission.

Those Scripture quotations marked AMP are from The Amplified Bible, copyright © 1965 by Zondervan Publishing House and are used by permission.

In references to clients, all names and identifying circumstances have been changed to protect their privacy.

Wipf and Stock Publishers
199 W 8th Ave, Suite 3
Eugene, OR 97401

Sexual Misconduct in Counseling and Ministry
By Mosgofian, Peter and Ohlschlager, George
Copyright©1995 by Ohlschlager, George
ISBN 13: 978-1-60608-506-6
Publication date 2/20/2009
Previously published by Word, 1995

To Gale and Lorraine
for their love and encouragement;

And to all those who
have had the courage to face
their sexual brokenness
and trust God for their healing.

Contents

Preface

Don't tell me about your indigestion. "How are you?" is a greeting, not a question.

Ogden Nash

On many occasions as I (Peter) have been writing this book, the question about what I am writing has come up. For many people, my response to their query indicates that they would rather not know about my "indigestion." Most seem to hope that I am "just fine." Their response fits our belief that most people would rather not know that professional counselors and clergy sexually exploit people. Most people want to believe that this only happens rarely and is, in fact, being quickly eradicated. They especially don't want to consider that it could happen to them or to someone they love. Unfortunately, this is not so.

We have endeavored to write a book that exposes the breadth of the problem of sexual exploitation in counseling and ministry. Our hope is that by exposing the lie to the light, it will die back. We want our work to further the healing process that our nation and Western culture as a whole must undergo to recover from the proliferation of sexual abuse. Though this book is primarily intended to be read by Christians who are seeking ways to help in the healing process, we trust others will be interested in looking at this subject.

Though we are males, we hope, as a result of the many women we have treated in therapy, that we communicate the compassion we feel for all victims, the majority of whom are women. There is a lot of pain in the process of writing a book of this nature. It has not been fun to look carefully at the dark side of humanity.

We call all readers to consider carefully the central message of this book: If we do not deal honestly with our sexual sins as the church, we will come under such severe judgment that the AIDS epidemic will seem trivial in comparison. We have enjoyed sexual liberty far too much and avoided genuine sexual and personal intimacy. That road is far less traveled—this is not good.

The sexual misconduct crisis exposes significant portions of the church to be naked and ashamed. We hide. We fail. This is all to be expected. But without repentance and a serious turning from wrong, the church in America will soon come under severe persecution. Read on, and keep your rolaids™ handy!

BOOK PURPOSE AND OVERVIEW

Our purpose in this book is to help blow the flickering candles into a flame of light—to help drive the darkness out. We endeavor to give a full and clear picture of the sexual misconduct problem, to clarify direction in the search for godly solutions, and to bring hope and healing to victims and violators that is made known only by deeper relations with Christ himself. We intend to address the puzzling questions of how respectable Christian men violate sexual boundaries so easily and frequently. We explore what must be done in the church and the Christian counseling profession to challenge this plague and effectively change its course. Our desire is to communicate the redemptive hope of Christ to a church deeply troubled by a moral and ministerial plague unprecedented in recent history.

We have worked professionally for many years with both victims and violators as Christian therapists, mediators, and consultants. We have written this book primarily for counseling and mental health professionals, pastors and church staff, lay ministers, and leaders in the church. Others who will benefit from this work are church and human service administrators, supervisors, organizational leaders, lawyers and judges, policy and law makers, teachers and students, and members of various allied professions.

This book presents a comprehensive picture of sexual exploitation in counseling and ministry and the multiple ways to bring healing, prevention, justice, and restoration to victims, violators, and the larger church. At numerous places where more in-depth study is needed or desired, we have footnoted other resources for your use. In the second chapter we explore the socio-cultural roots of sex and violence, then construct a biblical theology of sexual misconduct prevention in chapter 3. We then tackle the subject of wrongful sex between counselors, ministers, and their adult victims. We outline the problem, present therapeutic and helping strategies for adult victims, and address the controversies surrounding homosexual misconduct, seductive clients, touch in counseling, recovered memories, false memories, and false allegations. Then we consider sexual abuse by counselors and pastors against children—including help for child victims.

The book then shifts to systemic issues, addressing Protestant and Catholic church policies and corporate practice regarding this trouble. We explore ways to facilitate the healing of congregations, the coincident victims of this plague. We then present rapidly changing developments in law and ethics. We outline ways to help and take action toward violators and define personal prevention measures in detail. We challenge the church and Christian counseling field to actively confront the sexual lies in our culture and develop comprehensive sexual abuse recovery programs. Finally, in the appendices, model church policies are provided; a proposal for national dispute-resolution ministry is made; and some key forms for practice are outlined.

Acknowledgments

Our thanks go first of all to Dr. Gary Collins, who has been our writing advocate. He believed in us and allowed us to influence him that this was a worthwhile project. Frankly, we wrote too much material for our first book in this series. Gary allowed us to persuade him that we could turn much of the extra material into a second book that would substantially address sexual misconduct issues. He has been a great source of encouragement to both of us.

Special thanks to our two collaborators in writing: Carol A. Carrell and Dr. Canice Connors. The two chapters they wrote make this a far better book, and we are blessed by their expertise and enthusiasm for this project. Working with them reminds us anew that God's people are a worldwide and diverse community, much larger than our familiar boundaries. Many thanks to Dr. Gerard Egan, Professor of Psychology at Loyola University in Chicago, for putting us in touch with Dr. Connors.

Thanks again to the people at Word Inc. for their help with this project. We are especially grateful for David Pigg, formerly Manager of Academic and Pastoral Publishing, for his efforts to publish this series. We thank David Moberg, Senior Vice President and Publisher of Word Bibles and Academic and Reference Works, and Terri Gibbs, Editor of Academic and Reference Works, for their work on this project. Thanks also to the library staffs at Humboldt State University and the general, research, law, and theological

libraries at the University of California at Berkeley, the Graduate
Theological Union at Berkeley, and Stanford University.

We thank Dr. Emil Authelet, who reviewed our manuscript, giving
us both helpful commentary and needed encouragement. Thanks
also to Joan Grytness for her expertise and encouragement. Many
thanks also to Rolly Anderson for his encouragement and perse-
verance with both of us—he truly is an exceptional Christian.

We are also thankful to our colleagues, staff, and Board at The
Redwood Family Institute. They have tolerated us and supported
us through yet another writing project. We are sure they are better
people because of it, but we will endeavor to be more graceful with
them from here on out.

Thanks also to church, family, and friends who prayed for and
supported us during this writing project. We couldn't have done
it without your help, prayer, and caring. We are also very grateful
to the people that let us tell their stories, so that in composite form
and actual case studies the reader could better understand the personal issues involved. Thanks for your courage!

Finally, our most sincere thanks goes to our wives and families
for putting up with yet another writing project with us. We had
hopes this would be less time-consuming than the first book. It
did not turn out that way, so to say we are indebted to you is a
great understatement. We owe you!

Peter and George
Eureka, California

PART I

The Sexual Revolution and the Church

Chapter One

Challenging Forbidden Sex

Sin arises when things that are a minor good are pursued as though they were the most important goals in life. If money or affection or power are sought in disproportionate, obsessive ways, then sin occurs. And that sin is magnified when, for these lesser goals, we fail to pursue the highest good and finest goals.[1]

Augustine

The daily news of the 1990s erupts too frequently with tragic stories of sexual misconduct in church, government, entertainment, business, and counseling professions. Television, newspapers, and newsmagazines regularly report forbidden sex by prominent professionals and clergy. The media orgy over the sexual troubles of Jim Bakker and Jimmy Swaggart still reverberate years after these incredible revelations. The troubles of the Roman Catholic Church are legion, with both tragedy and hope distilled in the allegations and their repudiations as false charges against Joseph Cardinal Bernardin.

The entire American scene is awash with reports of sexual scandal tied to names far more prominent than those in the church—President Clinton, Senator Packwood, Michael Jackson. Much of this pales, however, when compared to the sexual shame of church leadership caught in sexual misconduct. Few, if any denominations across Christendom are free of abusive clergy and devastated victims. The sexual revolution has come to the church and, instead of liberating it, is revealing the horror and pain of the sexual sin insidiously enslaving the culture-at-large. Churches are haunted with this tragedy across all fronts—from helping victimized congregants and wounded churches, to preventing forbidden sex and restoring ministers, to defending lawsuits and ministers and their overseers. Maintaining a Christian witness with integrity to society is increasingly difficult in this dark moral environment.

Sexual misconduct in society, in the church, and in the helping professions is big news because it is a big problem—not only in the number of victims and the severity of the harm, but in the adverse moral and ethical impact on the church and society. Consider these sweeping truths about forbidden sex in our modern culture. Nearly 90 percent of all misconduct is perpetrated by men against women and children—men who are usually middle-aged and successfully established in their marriage and careers. Sexual misconduct now comprises nearly 60 percent of all lawsuits and license revocation actions against all counselors in the United States, with plaintiffs prevailing in nearly 70 percent of these suits.[2] A 1985 *Los Angeles Times* poll showed that 27 percent of the women and 16 percent of the men in America were sexual abuse victims as children—a staggering thirty-eight million people nationwide.[3] Abuse was prevalent across all societal boundaries: rich, poor, and middle class; white and minority; educated and noneducated; and religious or nonreligious.

Historical Roots and Controversies

Concern about sexual contact in professional relations is ancient. The original code of medical ethics, the Hippocratic Corpus (compiled five hundred years before Christ)[4] held that, "The intimacy . . . between physician and patient is close. Patients in fact put themselves into the hands of their physicians, and at every moment he meets women, maidens . . . very precious indeed. So toward all these, self-control must be used." By the time it was translated to the Greek (referred to thereafter as the Hippocratic Oath), physicians were sworn to pledge, "I will abstain from all intentional wrongdoing and harm especially from abusing the bodies of man or woman. . . ." Early in the life of the church, Christian physicians rewrote parts of the Oath to conform to biblical ethics. "With purity and holiness I will practice my art. . . . Into whatever house I enter I will go into them for the benefit of the sick and will abstain from every voluntary act of mischief and corruption and further from the seduction of females and males. . . ."[5]

In contrast, the mental health professions closed ranks against sexual involvement with clients only at the close of the twentieth century—up to the 1970s the moral and professional landscape was indeed mixed. Although Sigmund Freud contributed some troubling theory to this problem (see chapter 2), on the root issue of therapist-patient sex he remained consistently opposed. Freud argued not so much against direct patient harm but against the harm to the patient transference.[6] In contrast, Carl Jung carried on a lengthy affair with a young woman who "fell in love" with him shortly after beginning her analysis at age nineteen. The relationship with Sabina Speilrein, who eventually extricated herself from Jung's misdeeds and went on to become a physician and psychoanalyst herself, still generates much rumor and controversy in the field.[7]

By and large, the psychoanalytic tradition sought to follow Freud's lead on this issue. Like many things in Western culture, however, the climate of prohibition began to change dramatically in the 1960s. Not only were alternative models of human behavior and psychotherapy being developed, but the human potential movement began to promote sexual touch as a tool for growth. Maslow asserted that sensitivity groups ought to experiment with "physical nudism. People would go away from there an awful lot freer, a lot more spontaneous, less guarded, less defensive. . . ."[8]

In time, there were voices from the psychodynamic school that began to question the taboo against touch, even erotic touch.[9] McCartney's 1966 article on "Overt Transference,"[10] in which he confessed to numerous incidents of erotic patient contact, and Shepard's book, *The Love Treatment*,[11] inflamed the sexual contact debate in psychiatry, in mental health generally, and in the society at large. In the 1970s, a plethora of sexual treatment techniques had developed that thoroughly confused the ethical treatment boundaries. In 1975 Schultz, promoting the value of eroticized transference, queried social worker's attitudes on the use of such things as: direct sex coaching, teaching masturbation, using sex surrogates, clinical prostitution, erotic body contact, infidelity therapy, group nudism, bisexual therapy, and therapeutic intercourse.[12]

During the 1970s numerous voices in the field began to counter this corrupting fascination with unethical sex in psychotherapy—the evidence of multiple harm was accumulating and available for review. Masters and Johnson shook up the annual meeting of the American Psychiatric Association (APA) in 1975[13] by asserting that therapist-patient sexual contact was tantamount to rape. Phyllis Chessler published her ground-breaking feminist treatise on *Women and Madness* in 1972, devoting an entire chapter to sex between male therapists and female clients. She described classic profiles of hysterical females and predatory males, charging that psychotherapy reinforced the patriarchal sexism of society by fostering "the violation of the incest taboo; i.e., the initial and continued 'preference' for Daddy, followed by the approved falling in love with and/or marrying of powerful father figures."[14]

Judd Marmor presented his now classic paper, "Some Psychodynamic Aspects of the Seduction of Patients in Psychotherapy" to the 1976 APA convention. In it he listed both situational and characterological factors in therapist-patient sex. The situational factors include (1) emotional intimacy—being alone with a client who is sharing her innermost thoughts; (2) the client's physical attractiveness; (3) the client's seductive and flirtatious behavior; and (4) the health of the therapist's marriage and sex life. Characterological factors include (1) the therapist's need to respond as the affectionate "parent"; (2) unconscious hostility toward women—the sadistic need to exploit, humiliate, and reject; (3) a Don Juan complex—reaction formation against masculine inadequacy or fears of homosexuality; and (4) defective superegos—remorseless psychopathic (now deemed sociopathic) personalities. He concluded, "When a therapist lends reality to a patient's eroticized fantasies of transference love, he fosters a serious confusion between reality and fantasy in the patient, with inevitable antitherapeutic results. I have yet to see a woman patient who became involved in an erotic relationship with a therapist who did not eventually end up feeling exploited and betrayed by him."[15]

FORBIDDEN SEX IN THERAPY AND MINISTRY

Various surveys on professional sexual misconduct over the past twenty years indicate that approximately 10 percent of all psychotherapists have engaged in sexual or erotic contact with their patients.[16] These studies also reveal that from 40 to 80 percent of abusing therapists have crossed forbidden sexual boundaries more than once; some of these repeat offenders have dozens of victims. While these figures are disturbing enough considering there are approximately five hundred thousand therapists nationwide, many believe these self-reported figures are too conservative. The discrepancies between reported abuse to authorities (very low) compared with reports to subsequent therapists (much higher) suggests the problem is far more extensive than these surveys indicate.[17]

Affirming this data is the explosive growth in sexual misconduct complaints and legal actions. During the 1976–1986 period of the American Psychological Association insurance trust study, sexual misconduct actions mushroomed from 9 percent early in the study to nearly 50 percent of all suits filed at the end of the study. The American Association of Marriage and Family Therapists reports a tenfold increase in ethical complaints over the past decade, from twenty per year to nearly two hundred at present, with two-thirds of these involving sexual misconduct charges.

Within the church, we hear all too familiar stories of clergy and counselors who have succumbed to this forbidden sex plague. The 1988 *Leadership* poll surveyed pastors and other subscribers to *Christianity Today*.[18] The findings reveal a pervasive and painful problem in Christian ministry, one that a pastor revealed "covers the greatest agonies of my life." Twelve percent of the pastors and 23 percent of the subscribers admitted to extramarital intercourse. Nearly a quarter (23 percent) of the pastors acknowledged some form of sexually inappropriate behavior while in ministry, and 39 percent believed that sexual fantasy about women other than one's spouse was acceptable. Among the people pastors were sexual with, 69 percent came from within their own congregations, *including 17 percent who were counselees.*

The High Cost of Sexual Misconduct

Recently, we counseled with a woman and her husband who sought help in resolving the traumatic impact of her long-repressed sexual abuse. More than twenty years ago, as a teen she had been sexually abused by her youth pastor. She told how she had managed to keep this memory isolated from reality by blaming herself for allowing the sexual contact. However, recent circumstances in her life had lead her to realize that this man had violated her. Unfortunately, the all too common twist is that this man is still recognized as a respected leader in a local church.

As counseling proceeded, she began to understand her struggle with men in authority and her lack of intimacy with God. The abuser has always been recognized in his community as a godly man of gentleness, wisdom, and kindness—a man one would least expect to have perpetrated this shameful betrayal on a young believer. During the time of abuse he maintained a pure and godly stature, becoming her trusted father figure, above reproach. Even though she did not initiate or invite this sexual behavior, she assumed (due to his standing in the church and his kindness toward her) that somehow she was causing him to act this way toward her. Only now in midlife, after much harm to herself and her marriage, is she rejecting the lie that he loved her and is facing the awful truth that he stole from her what was not his to take.

The costs to violators are also deep and long lasting. In a recent book on this subject with a chapter entitled "The High Cost of Ministerial Infidelity," Tim LaHaye asserts that a man *never fully recovers* from the weight of sexual betrayal.[19] As Gordon McDonald painfully reveals, "I am a broken-world person because a few years ago I betrayed the covenants of my marriage. For the rest of my life I will have to live with the knowledge that I brought deep sorrow to my wife, to my children, and to friends and others who have trusted me for many years."[20]

The offender's self-perceptions will never be the same, especially because of the difficulty of accepting God's forgiveness and forgiving one's self. The offender's marriage will never be the same. The Scriptures give a spouse the right to divorce because of adultery and its devastating effects. If a couple remains together, infidelity is not easily healed nor forgotten. The recovery from the betrayal, rage, and grief of this loss can be extremely difficult and is usually a perilous journey. As family and close friends face the crushing impact of the betrayal they are likely to suffer in significant ways. Children, and perhaps teenagers most of all, will be shaken to the roots and may never recover their faith, let alone recover from the other wounds of this betrayal.

The impact of sexual misconduct stretches far beyond the family unit. It is accurate to assert that all of Christendom pays a high price.[21] The Christian minister and counselor have a unique and vital role in the community of faith. When these helpers yield to sexual misconduct, all the members of the community suffer. This person who represented Christ has betrayed trust vertically—toward God—as well as laterally—toward God's people. The media are fed fresh stories they relish to report, and comedians have new fodder for their humor mills. The church and Christ are mocked, people withdraw their financial support, and ministries of evangelism, service to the poor, and social justice suffer as people consider the shameful examples of Christian leaders.

THE NECESSITY OF CHALLENGING FORBIDDEN SEX

We do not paint a dark picture to imply that sexual misconduct is sin beyond the reach of God's forgiveness. We believe that true forgiveness, complete healing, and full restoration is possible in the fullness of Christ. Instead, we reveal the truth of this tragedy to challenge the pervasive denial of this plague that now has infected a broad expanse of the church. Like our culture's denial of the pervasiveness and long-term harm of divorce, the church and the mental health professions have too long denied the evil of forbidden sex.

The heart of Christ, which longs for the salvation and healing of broken people (see Isaiah 61), is betrayed by forbidden sex in counseling and ministry. Offending Christian leaders who participate in forbidden sexual activities cause their victims serious harm at multiple levels. As one victim painfully stated, "I don't know if anyone can understand the guilt you feel. . . . You can never have a good day."[22] The systemic impact of abuse promises a ripple effect that resonates through the entire marital, family, friendship, and church network.

It is likely that erotic and sexual involvement with clients and congregants is one of the most difficult sins for counselors, pastors, and youth workers to prevent. This is because a universal dynamic comes into play whenever a less powerful person is dependent upon an esteemed person in a position of respected authority. The very factors that provide the atmosphere for healing and help to occur in counseling and ministry are the *same* factors that permit forbidden sex to occur—trust, privacy, neediness, power, vulnerability, transference, countertransference, attraction, and sexuality are normally involved in helping relationships.

The difference between helping and harming in counseling and ministry is *agape* love. *Agape* "is not self-seeking" and "does not delight in evil but rejoices with the truth" (1 Cor. 13:5, 6). Consistent with what Augustine stated, sin occurs when affectionate desire becomes disproportionate and obsessive, out of alignment with truth. When the truth of agape love is not our central pursuit, the risk of sexual wrongdoing increases in counseling and ministry. We will be taking a careful look at how this occurs and what we must do in order to prevent this harm from occurring and increasing in counseling and in the church.

The hopeful news is scant, but candles are being lit in the darkness. Some churches are beginning to address this problem seriously with right policies and just action in response to this wrong. Marie Fortune's work with domestic violence and her efforts with preventing sexual misconduct in Protestant churches are noteworthy. We applaud the recent church policies advocating for sexual abuse victim rights and protection, and for justice and restorative action toward violative ministers (see appendix A). Also heartening has been the compassion and integrity of Joseph Cardinal Bernardin in the face of false abuse charges. We cheered the Cardinal's vindication after his accuser dropped suit, admitting the fallacy of his recovered memories.

Cᴏɴᴄʟᴜsɪᴏɴ

The widespread problems of sexual misconduct may well be the Waterloo of the Western church. If the church does not declare a halt and take effective control of its erring ministers and counselors, the state will take control of the church and exact harsh punishment upon violators and the church at large. The moral integrity that empowers our witness for Christ will also be lost. We intend this book to help the church, its leaders, and Christian counselors in particular to avoid this otherwise likely outcome.

NOTES

1. Augustine, Bishop of Hippo, *The Confessions of St. Augustine* (Orleans, Mass.: Paraclete, 1986), quoted in *Christianity Today*, 23 November 1992, 41.

2. Daniel Hogan, *The Regulation of Psychotherapists: A Review of Malpractice Suits in the United States*, vol. 3 (Cambridge, Mass.: Ballinger, 1979); S. Fulero, "Insurance Trust Releases Malpractice Statistics," *State Psychological Association Affairs* 19, no. 1 (1987): 4–5; Laura Markowitz, "Crossing the Line: Who Protects Clients from Their Protectors," *The Family Therapy Networker* (November/December 1992): 25–31.

3. See the *Los Angeles Times* 25–26 August 1985. The national sexual abuse poll was summarized on page 1 on both days.

4. Translated by W. H. S. Jones in S. J. Reiser, A. J. Dyck, and W. J. Curran, *Ethics in Medicine—Historical Perspectives and Contemporary Concerns* (Cambridge, Mass.: MIT Press, 1977), 5.

5. F. Braceland, "Historical Perspectives on the Ethical Practice of Psychiatry," *American Journal of Psychiatry* 126 (1969): 230–37.

6. Sigmund Freud, "Observations on Transference-Love: Further Recommendations on the Technique of Psychoanalysis" in *The Standard Edition of the Complete Psychological Works of Sigmund Freud*, vol. 12, ed. J. Strachey (1915; reprint London: Hogarth Press, 1958), 158–71.

7. Aldo Carotenuto, *A Secret Symmetry: Sebina Spielrein Between Jung and Freud* (New York: Pantheon Books, 1982).

8. Abraham Maslow, *Eupsychian Management: A Journal* (Homewood, Ill.: R. D. Irwin, 1965), 160.

9. B. R. Forer, "The Taboo Against Touching in Psychotherapy," *Psychotherapy: Theory, Research and Practice* 6 (1969): 229–31; but see R. Robertiello, "Introgenic Psychiatric Illness," *Journal of Contemporary Psychotherapy* 7 (1975): 3–8.

10. J. L. McCartney, "Overt Transference," *Journal of Sex Research* 2 (1966): 227–37.

11. M. Shepard, *The Love Treatment: Sexual Intimacy Between Patients and Psychotherapists* (New York: Peter H. Wyden, 1971).

12. L. G. Schultz, "Survey of Social Workers' Attitudes and Use of Body and Sexual Psychotherapies," *Clinical Social Work Journal* 3 (September 1975): 90–99.

13. William Masters and Virginia Johnson, "Principles of the New Sex Therapy," paper delivered at the annual meeting of the American Psychiatric Association, 6 May 1975; see also "Principles of the New Sex Therapy," *American Journal of Psychiatry* 133 (1976): 548–53.

14. Phyllis Chesler, *Women and Madness* (San Diego, Calif.: Harcourt Brace, 1989), 138.

15. Judd Marmor, "Some Psychodynamic Aspects of the Seduction of Patients in Psychotherapy," *The American Journal of Psychoanalysis* 36 (1976): 319–23.

16. See N. Gartrell, et al., "Psychiatrist-Patient Sexual Contact: Results of a National Survey, I: Prevalence," *American Journal of Psychiatry* 143, no. 9 (1986): 1126–31; N. Gartrell, et al., "Reporting Practices of Psychiatrists Who Knew of Sexual Misconduct of Colleagues," *American Journal of Orthopsychiatry* 57 (1987): 287–95; Kenneth S. Pope, P. Keith-Spiegel, and B. G. Tabachnick, "Sexual Attraction to Clients: The Human Therapist and the (Sometimes) Inhuman Training System," *American Psychologist* 41, no. 2 (1986): 147–58.

17. See Gartrell, et al., "Reporting Practices," 287.

18. "Special Report: How Common Is Pastoral Indiscretion? Results of a Leadership Survey," *Leadership* 9, no. 1 (1988): 12–13.

19. See Tim LaHaye, *If Ministers Fall, Can They Be Restored?* (Grand Rapids: Zondervan, 1990).

20. Gordon McDonald, *Rebuilding Your Broken World* (Nashville: Oliver Nelson, 1988), xvii.

21. See 1 Corinthians 12:26.

22. Aric Press and Carolyn Friday, "Priests and Abuse," *Newsweek* 16 August 1993, 42.

Chapter Two

Love, Sex, and Power: The Dangerous Triangle

For although they knew God, they neither glorified him as God nor gave thanks to him, but their thinking became futile and their foolish hearts were darkened. . . . Because of this, God gave them over to shameful lusts.

Romans 1:21, 26a

Suddenly, in the midst of their fight, his wife screams at him and runs off crying. He stands there shaking and thinks to himself, "DARN IT! I am furious! My mind is cloudy and I feel such intense pain—I want to yell. How could she even think of refusing me? I want to grab her and shake her and force her to lie down. She doesn't have a choice, I must have my needs met. After all, I didn't marry her to be treated this way, spurned and ignored when I make advances. Too tired. Ha! Who does she think I am that she can refuse me and reject me like this? I need to make love, that's all there is to it!

I don't want to hurt her, but if she treats me like this, then I am going to make her submit to me. She wants to talk. Yeah, and I want to smash her mouth. I am hurting so bad right now, how can she ignore my needs? I can't stand this much longer, I need to have her close. I need to have sex with her, not talk. What's wrong with her, can't she see the pain she's causing me? I must have her, or I had better get out of the here before I hurt her—RIGHT NOW!"

PSYCHOTHERAPIST CLOÉ MANDANES SUGGESTS THAT HUMANS are caught in a dilemma between love and violence. Like the frustrated husband above, people struggle over whether to love, protect, and help each other, or to intrude, dominate, and control, doing harm and violence to others. The problem is compounded because love involves intrusion, domination, control, and violence, and because violence can be done in the name of love, protection, and help. The more intense love is, the closer it is to violence in the sense of intrusive possessiveness. Similarly, the more attached and dependent we are on the object of our violence, the more intense the violence.[1]

While agreeing with the thrust of Mandanes' thought, it seems more accurate to view these two primary forces as a struggle between love and power. Power struggles are common to every relationship and do not always include violence. This seems to be especially true of those relationships that mean the most to us, whether family members, spouse, or friends. Indeed, to understand the dynamics of sexploitation in counseling and ministry we must look at the issues of love, sex, and power. These three factors, which interact dynamically throughout all helping relationships, must be understood in order to help those who cross forbidden sexual boundaries either as victim or offender. Thus the issue of power differences in relationships of trust will be a central theme throughout this book. In this chapter, we will study these concepts as they impact forbidden sex and examine the interrelationship of their sociocultural, theological, and psychological dynamics.

OUR LOVE AFFAIR WITH LOVE

All you need is love, love; love is all you need.[2]

Humans are fascinated with love. Countless songs, poems, books, cards, letters, and dreams have expressed people's thoughts about and longings for love. Love is a central concern for virtually all people, including those who have been irretrievably wounded and fear loving. Love is powerful; love is disturbing. We cannot love another without being affected by that relationship. This is good when the relationship is going well but difficult to handle when it is not. Yet, even when we love and are loved, the reality of our mortality and possible separateness impinges on our full enjoyment of that love.

When we give ourself in love to someone, we give that person power over our life: power to hurt us or to bless us by action or inaction. Whatever that person's behavior, the one who loves must interpret the beloved's behavior. Often these actions are misinterpreted because of insecurities and perceptual difficulties. So we make efforts to love and to be loved, and we try to protect ourselves from revealing our fear of being hurt by that love. If I love you, will you hurt me or bless me? Like Adam and Eve, we want to run and cover ourselves. But we also want to be known.

The New Testament distinguishes three types of love: (1) *eros*, sexual or erotic love; (2) *phileo*, the love of friends; and (3) *agape*, unconditional love, as represented in God's love toward unredeemed persons. Each of these types of love has a valid and useful place in people's lives. For our purposes here, we will focus on *eros* to demonstrate how the perversion of erotic love impacts forbidden sex in helping relationships.

EROTIC LOVE

Human sexuality is caught between the awesome forces of love and power. That is why every relationship of trust involves some degree of struggle with the dynamics of love, sexuality, and power. Our sexual interest is aroused by special and eligible people in our lives. The sensual desire calls out to us to enjoy its fruit and does not differentiate whether the fruit is forbidden or sanctioned.

Our wounded or broken self (what the Bible metaphorically calls "the natural man" or "the flesh") cries out for fulfillment in another person. This is true because "sexuality involves a lot more than mere behavior. It includes a heartfelt yearning for connection with another."[3] This broken self, however, can see only the object of its desire; it does not make moral discernments. The sexual self cries out to be heard and fulfilled in this meeting with another person, forbidden or not. This yearning element of sexuality is intended by God—the longing and desire are fundamental to sexuality, even as God deemed it not good for man to be alone. After the Fall, however, the direction of this yearning became corrupted and misdirected—mankind since has imposed and abused this longing for sexual connectedness.

Men and woman are designed so that relationship with God is not by itself sufficient, but relationship with another person is also essential for discovering the self. The intention in the beginning was focused on discovery of the original self (see 1 Cor. 12:18, 22) but now also includes the painful discovery of the corrupted self. Because of God's beautiful design of male and female, there is a "dynamic sense of dissimilarity and similarity"[4] that draws man and woman into exhilarating discovery.

This yearning for the other can lead a person to a greater sense of completeness. The danger is that our sexuality, under the corrupted influence of the Fall, often masquerades as the whole yearning. Psychiatrist John White observes that, "A common pattern in marriage is for a man to be preoccupied with sex while his wife feels starved of affection. But the two, affection and sex, are meant to be one, to be so much a part of one another as to be indistinguishable."[5]

The road to mature love, however,—that which mines the depths and joys that God intends—is not a painless journey. Due to our emotional woundedness, entrapment in sin, and fear of intimacy, we often choose to avoid the painful road to maturity and accept the shortcut to illusory satisfaction. Many men and women forsake the depth and wisdom of *agape* love for the powerful siren call of *eros*'s quick fix. In the biblical metaphor, darkened in our understanding by our rejection of God's high call, we exchange our birthright for a warm meal. The deep and abiding satisfaction of agape love and transparent sexual intimacy in marriage is exchanged for the hot rush of increasingly empty and anonymous sex. Tragically, this emptiness and anonymity can deceptively consume the best years of marriage.

Perverted Sexuality

Lust is born when we confuse the Creator with the creation, when we make gods out of things that can be properly desired. Lust unleashed becomes an enslaving compulsion, an obsessive and single-minded pursuit that, if unchecked, reaps eventual destruction. Some of our more common lusts in Western culture include money, fame, food, drugs, beauty, romance, the avoidance of pain and death, perfect health, an upstanding name, a unique image, pretentious religion, the power to influence others, and sexual pleasure. Like a craving addiction, lust is difficult to admit as lust—as something destructive to life and relationships and offensive to God. Most often our lusts are justified as good and proper, or as something we cannot control. For some, the moral dilemma is well understood. So at the merest challenge to our materialism we can quote the verse that the love of money is the root of all kinds of evil—but WE don't love money that way, that is our neighbor's problem.

Blinded to the awful truth about our lusts, we pursue them as if the lie were true: we will be satisfied when we have enough of our deepest desires. Satan must laugh in God's face at this, because he knows better than we that our lusts can never satisfy. Unless redeemed and saved from our cravings, we will expend our entire lives pursuing things that hurt those around us and leave us desperately dissatisfied. Or worse, we will be forced to sink deeper into the lie that we are fulfilled by our compulsions. In the end we will blame the world around us for our failure to be complete when we are broken and embittered by the awful costs of pursuing false gods.

FROM LUST TO SEXUAL ADDICTION

Sexual lust becomes an idolatrous addiction when we cut off eros from agape and fixate on eros as the pleasurable escape from the stresses, anxieties, and pain of daily living. In his excellent book, *False Intimacy*, Harry Schaumburg asserts that, "Sexual addiction primarily stems from the sinfulness of the heart and a reluctance to be in a passionate, dependent relationship with God."[6] John White also understands the depraved digression of sexual lust:

> Ultimately, the craving leads to illicit and pathological forms of sex. The devil has achieved his aim. We fall into cravings that drive us into addiction to pornography, to masturbation, to excessive needs for sexual intercourse, heterosexual or homosexual, to child molestation, and every form of perversion. . . . Perverted sex is always diabolical. . . . As long as we crave it we are unable to relish the real thing. It needs the power of Christ to break the enchantment and restore what is lost.[7]

Without redemptive healing and renunciation of our deadly ways, sexual addiction evolves, melding sexual cravings with diabolical perversion and transforming sexual lust to a full-blown addiction. The four primary evidences of addiction are (1) compulsive, consuming behavior (the sex addict plans his or her life around sex or the love object of the moment); (2) loss of control (sexual thoughts are intrusive and the addict is unable to stop thinking about and craving sex); (3) harmful consequences (addiction is maintained even when the harmful outcomes pile up—sexual diseases, marital destruction, loss of vocation and reputation, financial ruin, and legal trouble); and (4) denial (the addict is a master at denial, minimization, self-justification, and blame-projection, refusing to accept the glaring facts of personal addiction even when the consequences have stung deeply).

All sexual perversions, including forbidden sex in ministry relations, begin in the mind as sexual fantasy. We should not be so amazed at the pervasiveness of sexual misconduct in the church when we consider how many pastors admit to fantasized sex with women other than their spouses (as shown in a *Leadership* survey).[8] Spurgeon held that, "Thoughts are the eggs of words and actions, and within the thoughts lie compacted and condensed all the villainy of actual transgressions."[9] Many in church leadership, it seems, have denied the power of this crucial relationship, co-opted by the world's view that fantasy is harmless fun. Control of sexual misconduct in the church is unlikely to be successful—and certainly will not be redeemed—without control of harmful sexual fantasy.

SEXUALLY CHARGED HELPING RELATIONSHIPS

Sexual interest is a factor in relationships that are based on either eros or agape. Relationships based on agape are much more likely to keep sexual purity for the sake of the other and for the sake of relatedness and obedience to God. Nevertheless, EVERY relationship of trust with a person in power (the counselor or pastor) gives that person numerous advantages over the person seeking help. One of these advantages involves the combination of sex and power. It is easy for the male person in power to misread the interest displayed by a female counselee as an interest in mating. This misinterpretation is especially likely when the male counselor himself is in a place of vulnerability due to illness, stress, poor self-care, grief, depression, anxiety, sexual lusts, or shallow yieldedness to God. Though this interest may start in an apparently innocent and nonsexual way, unless it is acknowledged and controlled it is an easy step to sexual arousal and physical intimacy with the counselee.

That is why it is imperative that our sexuality come under the dominion of the Father's will, if it is to be expressed in a manner that heals rather than harms. Our sexual drives and interests must be controlled and deferred in those relationships that are forbidden due to marital, moral, and professional-ethical vows. Counselors must know and practice what God says. Failure to do so creates unbelievable grief and profound harm, because decisions and actions based on momentary feelings create nothing but distance and harm. Only when we do what God commands can we reflect who He is and create healing.

One may know that the best choice for sexual relating is meant to occur in the marital context, where the whole of sexual joy can be celebrated. However, knowing the truth in one's head does not change or heal the broken self. Striving to be what one is supposed to be is a far cry from becoming what God intends when we are transformed from the inside out. Yet this inner transformation is readily resisted for a variety of reasons, perhaps especially because it means giving away our power to the Saviour and putting all our trust in His plans for our life.

THE DYNAMIC NATURE OF POWER AND AUTHORITY

Recently, two women shared their thoughts with us about relationships with pastors who violated their ministerial trust. One woman stated, "Whenever I think of God, Steve (the abusing pastor) is there." The other woman said, "To challenge him was to challenge God." There is an awesome attribution of power to people in positions of leadership, especially when those people are in positions that represent God.

POWER: THOUGHT, WORDS, DEEDS

In defining power, we conceive it on a continuum that includes thoughts, words, and deeds. In the simplest sense, power means the ability or capability to act. This basic definition includes the actual strength or force expended to do something, but the meaning of power also includes the right and capacity to exercise control, to influence, and even to have dominion over someone or something. Synonyms cover a range of words (including respect, influence, control, coercion, and domination) that move from a passive stance to actual manipulation. These words help us understand the awesome potential of power—a capacity or action that can be used for good or evil, to bless or to harm.

How do love, sex, and power become confused and conflicted? Certainly the emotional connection between those who love one another allows for potential abuse of power, leading ultimately to violence (in thought, word, or deed). Jesus considered violent thought the same as violent action in terms of its sin quality (cf. Matt. 5:21–22) with both to be judged harshly by God. Violence is a distortion of eros and an abandonment of agape. Misused power demands its own way, and that always leads to harm for those so oppressed.

ABUSIVE POWER IN WESTERN SOCIAL SYSTEMS

As it loses its moral anchor to genuine love, Western culture is experiencing increased sexual violence. This breakdown is facilitated by the increased divorce rate, which has set millions of children adrift without a visible model of faithfulness to their personhood and to their needs. As Western culture abandons its Judeo-Christian heritage and what that means to love, and as competent models for love become scarce, the societal focus increasingly shifts from care to pleasure. This shift gradually develops into a fixation on pleasure at any cost—caring for others becomes an intrusive and rejected nuisance. Pleasure becomes a sexual or material obsession that becomes more and more displeasing, creating confusion, frustration, and anger.

The pleasure obsession devalues others; it reveals a loss of empathy and a numbness toward human suffering. When combined with unresolved anger and hostility, the results are increased sexual violence. In this situation, eros must be restrained or it takes over and demands its own way no matter what the cost.[10] Not only is our society's loss of self-control seen in increased violence but also in the increased incidence of sexually transmitted diseases. People continue to engage in immoral sexual practices and intravenous drug use compulsively, even though they know it puts them in a high risk category of contracting AIDS and other diseases.

In addition, as men feel the loss of power and are increasingly angered by their inability to be sexually satisfied, increased violence is committed on children, including sexual, emotional, and physical abuse.[11] Recently, sports star Isaiah Thomas shared on a talk show how as a child he remembers that gang members respected young children and would not involve them in drug running. In the 1990s, however, those rules have changed, and children are not protected from this level of involvement, not even by their own parents in growing numbers of cases.

The Brave New American World. There was a powerful idealism in America between the end of the Second World War and the Vietnam War. We believed we would overcome evil by our will, our faith in God, the power to do good, and an economic and political might that remained largely free of the ravages of war. Our social activism attacked the problems of poverty, disease, racism, illiteracy, and lack of participation in the democratic order. Our psychology expressed an idealism that assumed we would discover how to understand, even to control, the dark side of human nature. For a time it seemed that our culture—that American the beautiful—was making good on its enormous promises.

With the Viet Nam war, the assassinations of the Kennedys and Martin Luther King, and the moral upheaval and social dislocation wrought by recreational drugs and free sex, things began to change in the 1960s. By the 1990s American idealism had come under strong attack. Today, the rise of a secular multiculturalism and the rejection of Judeo-Christian mores is systematic and active in the United States. It is not coincidental that a significant, even nation-threatening rise of violence and social demoralization is also taking place.

Some studies indicate that America today may be the most violent "civilized" nation on the earth. On a per capita basis, we are twenty times more violent than Western Europe and forty times more violent than Japan. A woman is twenty times more likely to be raped in America than she would be in England or Japan.[12] Without restraint, this demoralizing violence and its attendant social chaos spills over into all strata of society. Without a moral and spiritual transformation, the best of our culture may eventually be lost as a dynamic force for good.

Family and Social Systems. Family and social life is significantly influenced by these dynamics. Madanes has suggested four primary styles of relating that confuse the proper use of love and power. These styles represent dysfunctional uses of power in families and, to some degree, in social systems more generally.[13]

• Style 1: People who struggle for power and control over their own lives and over the love of others. The main emotion in this family or social system is fear. People are motivated mainly to satisfy selfish needs, so power is used for personal advantage and relationships are primarily exploitive.

• Style 2: People whose primary wish is a desire to be loved. "The wish to be loved and appreciated can bring out the best qualities in people, but it can also result in irrationality, selfishness, and harm. The main emotion among family members is desire. Needs never seem to be fulfilled and there is always frustration and discomfort."[14]

- Style 3: People who wish to love and protect others. This can also bring out the highest qualities, but it can also manifest intense manipulation and control. Intrusion and dominance are often justified in the name of love. Codependent care often leads children to learn to sublimate their wishes and focus instead on the fulfillment of others. The main emotion in these family members is despair.

- Style 4: People whose anger is unrestrained and who are openly violent with one another. The main emotion in this family "is shame because of what one has done, because of what one has refrained from doing, or because one cannot forgive."[15]

SYNTHESIS: LESSONS FROM RAPE

Rape is a growing, horrific, and controversial crime—a devastating trauma to its victims. Historically, the study of rapist's actions and understanding focused on their individual psychopathology and on classifying them according to the characteristics of the rapes themselves. The psychoanalytic literature emphasized the pathological mothering of rapists. However by the 1970s, influenced by the feminist critique, the mental health community began acknowledging the violence of rape, rather than focusing solely on the sexual nature of the crimes. In the influential typology by Nicholas Groth, rape was defined as an expression of either power or anger, in which sexuality is only the vehicle of expression.[16] This sociocultural perspective stood apart from the psychodynamic understandings of the power and anger motives.

Sociocultural and Feminist Analysis. The common thread of feminist analysis locates the cause for rape within the patriarchal and misogynist culture—men using coercive social structures to support and justify abusive power against women. Rape, in the radical feminist paradigm, is the acting out of these culturally sanctioned beliefs and images. That is, rapists are normal men doing what the normative culture prepares them to do. They conclude, then, that we will not find any meaningful psychological differences between men who do or do not rape. Furthermore, sexuality has all but been ruled out as the cause for rape, and the motive focuses exclusively on power and violence.

To the good, feminist and sociological analysis has focused on the horror of rape and corrected the overly individualistic assessment of dynamic psychology. From this perspective, much research was undertaken to demonstrate how the culture fosters beliefs and practices that lead to the exploitation of women. These include the objectification of women (in advertising, for example), the denigration of women via pornography, and the institutional oppression of women (as in the business world or by the legal system, for example).

We believe, however, the feminist critique has gone too far in its sociocultural attributions, failing to distinguish individuals from the gender (all men are guilty) and disregarding personal responsibility (patriarchal culture is the enemy). Some feminist authors have come to disregard any psychosocial explanation for rapist beliefs and behavior. As one author noted, "Adherents of the sociocultural etiology do not consider most rapists as sick and psychologically distinct from other groups of men."[17]

Though we agree that because of the universality of sin *all men are capable of abuse*, the charge that *all men are violent* grossly exaggerates. It is a blatant case of ideology shaping science—using data to support preconceived and passionate beliefs. The psychological research does show differences in men who rape versus those who do not. Furthermore, sexuality cannot be ruled out because gender is shown to be an important factor in the motivation for rape, and gender, while not the same as sexuality, cannot be divorced from sexuality. The effect of gender in rape and how gender is determined—to what extent it is biologically or culturally based—are key questions underlying the research on understanding why men and women relate as they do.

The Psychology of Rape. In the last twenty years there have been important advancements in the psychological understanding of sexual violence. In one study of rapists[18] the beliefs of fifteen unreported rapists were compared to those of a control group of nonrapists. Almost all of the rapes occurred with an acquaintance. The following observations were made about rapists.

Rapists made significantly more negative comments about their fathers and mothers than did nonrapists. Every nonrapist made more positive statements about his father and mother, but of the rapists six had more positive and four had more negative statements about their mothers.

Rapists described fathers as emotionally and physically distant. Most of these fathers were successful professionals whose work kept them from home for long periods of time. The worse the relationship with a father, the more the man expressed anger toward women, dominance over women, underlying power motivations, and hypermasculine attitudes.

In addition, those rapists whose fathers were more physically violent with them were more likely to become the most violent in raping women (three of every four men). In contrast, the nonrapists' fathers spent quality time with them, even though they were busy men. Their fathers also tended to be physically affectionate. This suggests that it is not gender per se that most critically influences rape. It is the quality of the intimacy and affection (and the lack of violence) in both same and cross-gender relations in families.

Another study of college rapists[19] demonstrated that the rapists were consistently afraid of being engulfed or consumed by women, so they felt they needed to protect themselves by dominating women. They saw women as potentially hostile and powerful adversaries who, in cold and heartless ways, would reject them after enticing them sexually.

This fear of rejection is consistent with Margaret Rinck's[20] central thesis that men abuse spouses because of their fear of abandonment. Robert Hicks, writing on a Christian perspective of the men's movement, also indicates that the fear of rejection is a major motivation for the way men relate to women.[21] In our work with ephebophiles, we have also observed the sense of powerlessness that draws men away from adult women and toward young pubescent girls and boys because they are vulnerable, less powerful, and available.

Freud's Troubled Contribution. In the sexual abuse of children, Sigmund Freud was the first to describe the psychological damage that resulted from incestuous relationships between fathers and daughters. Within a short time, however, arguably because of his complicity with the Viennese culture and its values, he refuted the seduction theory and its root acceptance of the reality of incest. Instead, he asserted a female hysteric hypothesis that denied incest—an explanation that was culturally plausible but nothing more than a scientific fairy tale. His complicity ushered in about seventy years of additional harm to children.

The psychotherapy movement, especially that of Freudian root, has possibly done more to collude with than to challenge rape and sexual violence. As Cloé Madanes aptly notes,

> Therapy developed as a worldwide movement during the transition from the elitist pseudomorality of the Victorian era

to the terrifying excesses of the fascist regimes supported by institutionalized religion. Perhaps historical contexts determined that therapy would be a humanism carefully divorced from the hypocrisy of religion and morality. . . . An exaggerated version of this view prevails today.[22]

This divorce of therapy from religion and morality is certainly one of the key reasons why misuse of therapeutic power occurs.

The psychological analysis of rape exposes the rapist's spiritual impoverishment, sexual brokenness, fear of rejection, and sense of powerlessness at the core of violence done to rape victims. These issues help explain why men in positions of power cross boundaries to invade the bodies of women; these men seek pleasure, meaning, and personal fulfillment at the risk of losing everything of true and lasting value. As Hicks explains, "Men feel powerless and end up acting out this feeling in a violent way."[23] For the wounded male, if identity and meaning cannot be achieved in a positive way, he will resort to what is exclusively male—using his penis to prove and affirm his power over women.

Power and Authority in Counseling and Ministry

Those who are in positions of authority in the church and professional counseling must respect the impact of their power on the lives of those they counsel, lead, and advise. "In addition to the power and authority given a pastor as a professional, the symbolic power of the pastor as religious leader magnifies the professional role. The minister is a physical representation of the whole community of faith, of the tradition, of a way of viewing the meaning of life, . . . and of God. The importance of this dimension should never be underestimated."[24]

Many of those who come to counselors and pastors for help, and some who work with pastors in ministry, are at risk for forbidden sexual entanglements because of their vulnerability and weaker position in the relationship. There are many factors that influence this power imbalance. Some of these are listed below:

1. *Some persons attribute God-like power to those from whom they seek help.* People place great confidence in counselors, pastors, and other church leaders to lead them out of trouble, comfort them in hardship, and advise them regarding important life and career choices. Marie Fortune observes that people "trust their pastor implicitly with the most important parts of their lives. . . ."[25]

2. *People seeking help are vulnerable, especially in relationships of imbalanced power.* People likely to be sexually violated by a helper are usually innocent victims of the violator's manipulation—the less powerful one is manipulated and harmed by the more powerful one. The victim is vulnerable, in a position of need, with lowered self-esteem, lowered defenses, and is often anxious, depressed, or grieving loss.

3. *People who come for help let their guard down in relationships of trust.* They let down their guard in this type of relationship because of the difficulty of the task they face and the need for solutions to help them cope. For example, a woman will only seek help from someone she trusts. To allow herself to share her deepest secrets, a woman has to make herself deliberately vulnerable. The greater the reputation of the professional and her confidence in him, the more readily a woman will let down her guard and trust the helper.

4. *Many people who are seeking help are readily compliant and open to suggestions from the one in a position of authority.* Vulnerable and needy people have not learned how to set firm boundaries with someone they respect, and when a boundary is violated, they are uncertain how to respond. They become paralyzed—unable to think or act constructively or at all—in this kind of crisis. Further, they can become dependent on the suggestions of the helper to resolve their confusion and fear.

5. *Therapeutic privacy can evolve into illicit secrecy.* One of the hallmarks of a counseling relationship is its confidential nature— the privacy needed to be honest and to struggle with those issues that would bring shame and condemnation if publicly disclosed. The victim may be easily persuaded that he or she must keep secret the illicit things that have occurred. This secrecy is often accepted by the victim, who cannot bear to admit to anyone else the shame and confusion over what has happened.

6. *Feeling fearful and confused, victims are at a distinct disadvantage in defending themselves.* They are often afraid no one will believe them if they accuse the professional who violated them. They fear the loss of their marriage, their moral reputation, and community respect. Normally, violators are well-respected, and victims struggle immensely to accept that anyone will believe their word over the reputation of the violator. Victims expect they will be accused of making false accusations—accusations assumed untrustworthy because of their mental disturbance or emotional distress. This expectation is often realized, whether true or not, as the accused professional counterattacks and defends against the charges.

7. *Counselor-client interaction may foster an illusion of strength or special status.* Sometimes, counseling relations develop quickly and powerfully; counselor and client like each other and the interaction becomes intimate and enchanted, with strong feelings of special status. Some counselors manipulate this dynamic by communicating how special the exchange is—detached from the normal rules of relationships. Clients may project an illusory strength that covers their wounds and the counselor mistakenly reads this as power to manage an affair.

8. *The differences in male and female psychology are an ever-present dynamic in counseling situations.* Men and women can and do perceive sexual signals and personal boundary violations quite differently. Thus a vulnerable male helper may misread a woman's enthusiastic response as a sign of sexual interest or minimize signals of resistance to his sexual advances. And a needy woman may compliantly accept male advances because she does not want to displease her helper. Others minimize violative behavior because, historically, most males have approached them this way and they have accepted this as the unavoidable price of male relationships.

9. *Ignorance about transference and countertransference dynamics can contribute to a power imbalance in a counseling relationship.* In a nutshell, both counselor and client project onto the other powerful emotions and unresolved conflicts from their respective histories. Clients and parishioners project onto counselors their anger, dependencies, fears, and, yes, their sexual seductiveness. Counselors countertransfer their own anger, fears, and needs onto those they help. The untrained, ignorant, immature, or vulnerable helper can easily misread these dynamics and attribute plausible but, usually, false meaning to their appearance.

CONCLUSION

Most of us are aware of Lord Acton's famous axiom that "power corrupts and absolute power corrupts absolutely." When we examine the dynamic interplay between love, sex and power, we learn that people in power have an incredible responsibility to protect those under their authority from the manifold temptations to abuse and manipulate that power. Jesus stated that, "From everyone who has been given much, much will be demanded" (Luke 12:48). Christian counselors and pastors certainly have been given much. They have been given the privilege of bringing the good news to the oppressed, of binding up the brokenhearted, of proclaiming the year of the Lord's favor (see Is. 61:1–7; Luke 4:18). They have been given authority and power to rule and lead. With this call comes the powerful temptation to abuse the authority so given.

In the balance of this text we will examine how men and women abuse authority and will outline how victims, coincident victims, and offenders can make progress toward restoration. Forbidden sexual relationships center on the misuse of power in order to obtain personal sexual pleasure and gratification. Because of this misuse of power, it is violence both with (sometimes) and without the use of force. It would be far better for the church and the world if such abuses of power never occurred.

NOTES

1. Cloé Madanes, *Sex, Love, and Violence* (New York: Norton, 1990), 5.

2. John Lennon and Paul McCartney, "All You Need is Love," Maclen Music, Inc., BMI, copyright 1967.

3. Andrew Comiskey, *Pursuing Sexual Wholeness* (Lake Mary, Fl.: Creation House, 1989), 37.

4. Ibid., 40.

5. John White, *Eros Redeemed: Breaking the Stranglehold of Sexual Sin* (Downers Grove: InterVarsity, 1993), 103.

6. Harry Schaumburg, *False Intimacy: Understanding the Struggle of Sexual Addiction* (Colorado Springs, Colo.: NavPress, 1992), 21–22.

7. White, *Eros Redeemed*, 109–10.

8. Nearly 40 percent of conservative, evangelical pastors considered that sexual fantasy about women other than their spouse was acceptable in "Special Report: How Common Is Pastoral Indiscretion? Results of a Leadership Survey," *Leadership* 9, no. 1 (1988): 12–18.

9. C. H. Spurgeon, *The Metropolitan Tabernacle Pulpit*, vol. 32 (Pasadena, Tex.: Pilgrim Publications, 1974), 398.

10. Citizen magazine reported how homosexual men gather at a New York sex club to meet homosexual men who are HIV positive so that they can become infected and not worry any longer about needing to practice safe sex. "Gays Look for Mr. HIV," *Citizen* 7, no. 9 (September 1993): 8.

11. Robert Hicks, *The Masculine Journey: Understanding the Six Stages of Manhood* (Colorado Springs, Colo.: NavPress, 1993).

12. According to one article, " 44 percent of American women have been raped or faced an attempted rape; 43 percent of girls under eighteen have been sexually abused; 85 percent of working women report being sexually harassed during their working lives; between 60 and 70 percent of murdered women were killed by a husband, lover or ex-lover." Carole Pateman, "Sex and Power," *Ethics* 100, no. 2 (1990): 404.

13. Madanes, *Sex, Love, and Power.*

14. Ibid., 6–7.

15. Ibid., 8.

16. Nicholas Groth, *Men Who Rape* (New York: Plenum, 1979).

17. Ilsa Lottes, "Sexual Socialization and Attitudes Toward Rape," in *Rape and Sexual Assault*, vol. 2, ed. Ann Wolbert Burgess (New York: Garland, 1988), 195.

18. David Lisak, "Sexual Aggression, Masculinity, and Fathers," *Signs: Journal of Women in Culture and Society* 16, no. 2 (1991): 238–62.

19. Ibid.

20. Margaret Rinck, *Christian Men Who Hate Women: Healing Hurting Relationships* (Grand Rapids: Zondervan, 1990).

21. Hicks, *Masculine Journey*.

22. Madanes, *Sex, Love, and Violence*, 8.

23. Hicks, *Masculine Journey*, 114.

24. Marie Fortune, *Is Nothing Sacred? When Sex Invades the Pastoral Relationship* (San Francisco: HarperCollins, 1989), 102.

25. Ibid., 3.

Chapter Three

Theological Issues in Preventing Forbidden Sex

Satan fears virtue. He is terrified of humility; he hates it. He sees a humble person and it sends chills down his back. His hair stands up when Christians kneel down, for humility is the surrender of the soul to God. The devil trembles before the meek, because in the very areas where he once had access, there stands the Lord, and Satan is terrified of Jesus Christ.[1]

GOD CALLS US TO REALIZE THE FULLNESS OF OUR HUMANNESS by responding to the call of His Son and walking in obedience to His commands. As we walk in this way we will fulfill God's healing mission, but when we compromise this call we bring harm to ourselves and to others. This is especially true for those who, like pastors and counselors, are in positions of power and influence. We are able to comprehend when evil people profoundly harm children and vulnerable adults, but it is extremely difficult to believe that so many good men (and women) harm children and vulnerable adults through forbidden sex.

In order to frame a biblical theology for preventing forbidden sex, we need to identify the theological issues of sexual misconduct. This theological basis is crucial because nontheological perspectives deny our sinful humanity. Christ crucified directs our attention to our need for God's redemption and gives genuine hope to our potential. When we do not examine God's revelation about the human person, we can only fashion solutions that are incomplete or, worse, distorted and deceived.

Humanistic anthropology, in its effort to understand the nature and origins of man, skates from myth to philosophy to science, but theological anthropology begins with God as Creator. All meaning and interpretation begins with this reality: God has created man with purpose and design, including the role of sexuality—which is so close to the heart of man that much corruption occurs when this image is distorted. A theological anthropology also casts into the forefront the depravity (inhumanity) of human nature and points to reconciliation with God in Christ as essential to the healing process. "For what we recognize to be human nature is nothing other than the disgrace which covers his nature. His inhumanity, perversion, and corruption. . . ."[2] We must uncover this perversion, expose it to the light, and discover what must be done to prevent the corruption of the Christian soul—a corruption that allows forbidden sex to occur.

THE PROBLEM AS HUMAN DILEMMA

THE TWO SELVES

Human beings are divided within themselves: they have the capacity to do good and the capacity to do evil, but, tragically, they know evil far too well. Human beings are also divided into male and female. Ray Anderson asserts that, "God cannot make a solitary being in His image."[3] God declared *male* and *female* to be very good, but because of the Fall, there is division and animosity between the sexes, and more deeply, between the two natures of the self.

This division, which results from the Fall, fragments the person into two selves. First, there is *the broken self*, which exists because of sin (see Rom. 6:12–14 and 7:18). Second, there is the *God-intended self*—created by God to exist as a vital part of His Kingdom (see 1 Cor. 12:18, 22–25; Rom. 7:22). We come into the world broken, lacking what we need most: the God-intended endowment of significance and security. When left untreated (unconverted and without sanctification), this broken self always moves toward alienation, fear, lust, and violence (see Rom. 3:9–18; Gal. 5:19–21).

In the sinful nature, the fallacy is perpetuated that we can meet our deepest needs outside of relatedness to God, a relationship that covers our sin, cleanses our painful wounds, and gives knowledge of the truth. Ray Anderson points out that, "To know my incapacity is to be willing to come out of the garden, and have that meeting with God. To come out of the character armor . . . that I have thrown around myself, to be willing to be stripped and vulnerable and have that meeting; to know my incapacity. To know it is not good to be alone."[4] If a person does not continually come back to God, then he or she is doomed to believe the lie that one's deepest needs are met through mating. By not coming back to God, men and women settle for less than God's best. Due to sin's impartation into the human soul at conception, people are totally incapable of bringing themselves to a state of righteousness.[5]

We must learn to esteem highly the self that God created and to devalue the broken self that is created and molded by sin. In fact, Jesus calls us to die to the broken self. On the other hand, the *God-intended self* conforms to his standards and is willing to suffer harm in order to be shaped into God's purpose. For this life is not lived primarily to gratify self but to learn to deny the broken self and to glorify God. Paul, in Romans 7:14–25, outlines this struggle with clarity and points to the "inner man" as the self that delights in God's law.

This new self admits a need for help; it longs to become the *God-intended self*, choosing to live according to God's purpose. As we yield to God's design, then and only then, do we know deep and genuine satisfaction. As Jesus stated, "I tell you the truth, unless a kernel of wheat falls to the ground and dies, it remains only a single seed. But if it dies, it produces many seeds. The man who loves his life will lose it, while the man who hates his life in this world will keep it for eternal life" (John 12:24–25).

LESSONS FROM THE GENESIS STORY

We read in Genesis 2 that God created male and female, and it was good. They were naked and not ashamed. Prior to the Fall, there was differentiation and *unity*. However, once these two individuals partook of the lie (see Gen. 3), they experienced differentiation and *division*, not only from one another but also from God. They moved from nakedness without shame to knowledge that inflamed them with shame. By rebelling against God, they became *naked and ashamed*. So they covered themselves with a covering that fostered the denial of death and the reality of their fall.

Humans cannot live with the knowledge of good and evil independent of God's redemption. Sin brought awareness of the destructive capability of human nature. Having become aware of their evil capacity, Adam and Eve hid their bodies from each other in fear. This fear also motivated them to hide from God, for they were fearful and ashamed to be in the presence of the One who is only good. When God summoned them from hiding, He first removed their coverings and replaced them with coverings of animals sacrificed for their nakedness. The furs bore the smell of death to remind them of death. God's covering challenged their independence (their reliance on their own methods for recovery from sin) and called them to depend on Him alone.

Consequences to Adam. When Adam was exposed for his failure to adhere to God's command (3:3), he blamed Eve for this failure (3:12), implying that God had failed him in giving him an inferior creature for a companion. Adam was caught between his aloneness and his nakedness in the fear of intimacy, which resulted from knowing good and evil. This tension of the broken self resulted in two universal and harmful male characteristics: (1) the tendency to take women—or one's spouse—for granted (escaping the fear of intimacy), and (2) the tendency to be polygamous, in heart and mind if not in behavior (the false solution for the fear of aloneness).

A fundamental consequence of the Fall was the alienation of male from female. God's order was disrupted and His creatures turned against one another, rather than exulting in their God-intended unity. This spiritual dynamic set the stage for the competitive relationship between the sexes and the distorted attempts of man to rule over woman, especially in sexual conquest. The wounded male, distorting true manhood, descends to what is exclusively male, using his sexual energy to assert his power over women and children.

Fallen men have become polygamous in their hearts with a corrupted desire to rule over women. Once a man conquers a woman and subdues her, the satisfaction of the eros quest quickly fades, and his desire to encounter another woman increases. Robert Hicks states that this conquering element stems in part from man's warrior side[6] (Hebrew *gibbor*). If the dissatisfaction remains for long, then the man will be tempted to look to another conquest as the fulfillment of his corrupted desires. Even in the realm of fantasy, Warren Farrell states that, "Men's primary fantasy is having access to as many beautiful women as desired without *risk or rejection*."[7]

Man's polygamous nature enhances his ability to divide the physiological and erotic from his personhood. Polygamy is harmful to both man and woman because the mystery of sexuality is encompassed within the *wholeness* of one man relating to one woman. The fear of rejection by a woman, however, hinders male attempts at intimacy and perpetuates the fantasy that some woman somewhere will better meet his needs. This fantasy must be controlled, or the man will eventually succumb to its power. This polygamous tendency is also related to the male need to conquer and reach objectives of quantity, rather than to have relationships of depth and reach objectives of quality.

Consequences to Eve. God pinpoints Eve's role in the Fall and curses her with a desire for her husband, a man who will *rule* over her (Gen. 3:16). Because of the broken (female) self, women have a corrupted, codependent desire to please men—a miserable curse when a man is angry at a woman and blames her. This desire to please is one factor that influences a woman to let down her guard in relationships of trust with men. Many women who fall into sexual sin naively trust the helper and misinterpret the sexual deception because of a longing to please a respected male.

A second consequence of the Fall is that women need security; they need to be loved deeply and intimately and to be protected from harm. This leads to the risk of emotional entanglements with men or women of significance, including ministers and helpers. A woman's need for security and protection intersects powerfully with a helper's care since an important function of counseling is the protection and affirmation of those the helper is called to serve.

Finally, the loss of the sense of wonder and uniqueness of women contributes to an increasing abuse of the personhood of women through sexual abuse. A woman is profoundly marked by her first sexual encounter; she gives herself and participates with her whole person. As a result, she is, in a sense, spiritually and emotionally engraved by the first sexual encounter. Thus, if she is abused sexually in the first encounters, often she will become frozen in her sexuality as a means to protect herself from further harm.

DIVIDED AND DISORDERED SEXUALITY

Both man and beast were created on the sixth day. Beyond that commonality, however, the biblical challenge is for humans to separate from the beasts as moral beings reflecting the nature of God. When we do not differentiate, our sexuality deteriorates to the level of the beasts—sex is performed without regard for personhood, like dogs in heat, without regard for the humanity of the other. This is the context of a culture increasingly bereft of godly

anchors. Men and women are afraid to connect with the humanness in the other. So sex is substituted for love, with violence
following hard in the footsteps of these inhumane encounters.

Western culture divides the body from the person—a process of
partialization and objectification that eventually leads to chaos.
Disordered sexuality is sex without meaning: autonomous and
anonymous sexuality. It is not consistent with God's plan of differentiation within unity; it has divided, not rightly differentiated,
the self.

In sin, there is a universal denial of creatureliness. Satan came
to Eve and said, "You will not surely die. . . . For God knows
that when you eat of it your eyes will be opened, and you will be
like God, knowing good and evil" (Gen. 3:4). A self-directed autonomy enters in and we assert, "I can be the author of my own
existence, I can determine the limits of my own life." Sin pushes
us to deny the limitations of our creatureliness. Only when we
submit ourselves to the Word of God and acknowledge our limitations (powerlessness) do we experience the freedom of true
humanity.

As humans we must always keep in mind the reality of our limitations. We are powerless (2 Cor. 1:9–11), and our strength is made
perfect in being weak (2 Cor. 12:9–10). We have to accept our limitations and learn to live with them. Not admitting our limitations
affects any and every area of life: gluttony, sexual sin, rage, impu-
rity, idolatry, discord, jealousy, selfish ambition, envy,
drunkenness, orgies, intolerance, slander, stealing, and murder
(see Gal. 5:19–21; Matt. 15:17–20). Romans 1 reveals the consequences of persons failing to differentiate self from the Creator.
Those who become sexually reprobate are those who "worship the
creature rather than the Creator." "There could be said to be a confusion and frustration at the deepest level of our being when we
are eliminating the modality of differentiation."[8] The failure to differentiate persons from God results in confusion about sexual
identity and personhood.

THE MYSTERY OF SEXUALITY

Like any mystery, sexuality is both fascinating and formidable.
It is formidable because it brings with it a sense of shame; it is fascinating because it is mysterious. This fascination of sex draws us
into discovery—our broken self fueling our desire to experience
the mystery with more than one person. Since the sexual mystery

involves the whole person, it is only fulfilled when a man and a woman live together in the fullness of marriage—spiritually, physically, emotionally, intellectually, and volitionally. A man and a woman are made whole only to the extent that they rightly relate to each other according to God's design and understand and have compassion for each other (see 1 Pet. 3:7). Particularly when one lives in a society with great freedom of choice, this fulfillment of the whole person by lifelong, monogamous sexual intimacy becomes more difficult to achieve.

Ultimately, forbidden sex is sinful betrayal. One cannot truly love another and then betray him or her. When we love, we do not betray. Pastors and counselors, have incredible power, and this power must never be used to harm another. To do so is to deny love and to disobey God—it is also to betray the image of God to another person.

Sexual Behavior and Being. To separate being and behavior in the realm of sexuality leads to moral, ethical, and functional failure of human potential before God. Erotic sex without the involvement of the inner person leads to social and personal breakdown. When we observe the results of our experimentation with sexual promiscuity since the 1960s, we can see the horribly detrimental results of performance without involvement of the person. Godly sexuality requires the interconnection of being and behavior.

For example, when we approach marriage only for its functional value, we lose being in the marriage at the deeper levels that are necessary for wholeness. Our brokenness pulls us away from commitment to marriage and divorce becomes common. In such circumstances people will remain married only "if it feels good," or if it is practical and the expected thing to do, or because it is the only proper outlet for sexual drives. But marriage is not meant only to have function and exclude being. "If sexuality were merely a matter of physiological function (and thus a glandular problem) or of the business of reproduction (and thus again of a function), it would be difficult to see why the partners should not be just as interchangeable as the bearers of any other biological or mechanical functions, such as draft animals, for example, or machines."[9]

By separating sexuality from personhood, people try to manage the anxiety of knowing deeply and being known by another person. In marriage, when people say, "I can't face who you are," they begin to look elsewhere to find what they believe will meet their needs. Divorce becomes a common outcome of such self-centered, utilitarian marriages. Our capacity to love is so fragile because of our bent toward escape and blame (cf Gen. 3:12), but God would rather have us take courage to face our pain, our limitations, and our own humanity. God did not allow Hosea to take this escape option. He called him out to be an empathic prophet, to feel God's pain over Israel's infidelity.

Our culture swells with an ever growing population of people with weak and seared consciences who ignore the pain they cause others in false sexual liaisons. This lust for the flesh appears to satisfy something for the moment, but it does not grip the person and fill the soul. As humans we are not limited so much by what we can do, as we need to be limited by what we ought to do. It is possible for me to do many things, but not all these things are good to do, either for myself or for others. God calls us to choose to do His will, acting in integrity consistent with His wishes.

SEX, POWER, AND BIBLICAL AUTHORITY

Forbidden sex is so harmful because a profound betrayal of trust occurs in the lives of those who are victimized by persons in authority. It is a betrayal of Christ's call to rule in love and grace, to serve rather than use and abuse another. From Genesis to Revelation, the use of power and the desire for control shapes the way that people handle interpersonal interactions. Furthermore, in relationships of trust with helpers in positions of authority, control becomes a vital issue of ethical practice. It is no wonder that the issues of power and authority are central biblical themes.

USES AND MISUSES OF BIBLICAL AUTHORITY

Anyone who has been involved in church life for very long is likely to have experienced the unjust and abusive use of power—abuse of leadership authority based on gender, race, religious beliefs, and social status. Those abused most often include women, children, the elderly, the poor, and the vulnerable. Women, in particular, are subjected to abuse of authority by leaders who insist on their subordinate role in church and by husbands who rule in a parental manner over their wives. Several passages of Scripture, when considered without the balance of other passages, seem to give men license to such absolute authority. Some men misinterpret these passages to justify authoritarian rule in the church in the guise of helping or of proper leadership.

In the old order, prior to the coming of Christ, men were to rule over women, and a woman became trapped in her longing for her husband as a consequence of the Fall (see Gen. 3:16). Today, various New Testament passages are used to support the continuation of this pattern. For example, men see themselves as having absolute authority at home (Eph. 5:22–24; 6:1–3; 1 Pet. 3:1–6); over women in the church (1 Tim. 2:11–12; 1 Cor. 11:1–10); as elders in the church (Titus 3:1–2); and as political rulers (Rom. 13:1–5). The root belief calls for submission to all authority because it is placed by God, and the male is presumed to be the exclusive holder of God's authority.

One of the effects of this view of authority is to disempower women and children from confronting abuse; any questioning is seen either as rebellion or as usurping authority. This oppression also makes a woman fearful to let others know of the misuse of power because she believes she will be blamed for causing problems. This unholy view of authority—a manipulation of the truth—gives men biblical sanction to abuse women, especially those who are easily manipulated and are vulnerable. Stanley Milgram's[10] famous experiment demonstrated that people will blindly trust abusive authority, discounting their own perceptions of reality, even to the extent of allowing tremendous harm to occur to themselves or others.

Jesus on Authority. In contrast to this corrupt view of authority, Jesus established a new order based on the commandment to love one another (see Matt. 22:32–40). Jesus describes this new way of ruling to His disciples in Mark 10:35–45, when James and John seek seats of favor (authority) in the new Kingdom. Jesus responds that His Kingdom is different: "[R]ulers of the Gentiles lord it over them . . . not so with you. Instead, whoever wants to become great among you must be your servant."[11] He refutes the privileges of rank and status, challenging Christians to wash one another's feet instead.

In word and in practice, Jesus modeled this new authority. It is an authority that respects, cherishes, delights in, and serves another. It understands that power is not to be owned by the person but is borrowed from the source (God) for temporary use, especially in servant-leadership in the church and to edify the poor, broken-hearted, and outcast members of society. The symbols of this proper use of power and authority are a basin of water, a towel, and a gentle touch.

Jesus also declares, in Luke 12:35–48, that our use (and misuse) of power will be judged at the final accounting. When the Lord returns He will reward the faithful and wise manager whom He appoints and will punish the foolish manager. The faithful and wise manager is one who lovingly and properly provides for those under his or her care. The foolish manager beats (from the Greek: *tupto*, to pummel with repeated blows, to offend another's conscience and wound) those under his or her charge. God will punish this manager according to the intention and degree of harm caused to others. Jesus concludes by declaring, "From everyone who has been given much, much will be demanded; and from the one who has been entrusted with much, much more will be asked" (verse 48b). The word *entrusted* here (*paratithemi*) literally means "placed alongside" and indicates a deposit made with the ruler for trust and protection.

Paul on Authority. Paul clarifies and models the use of biblical authority in his epistles[12] and in his practice. He emphasizes the importance of recognizing and properly submitting to authority, whether as citizen, man, woman, or child. When Paul writes about the marital relationship, for example, he emphasizes that each one in the marital dyad is to submit to the needs of the other "out of reverence for Christ" (Eph. 5:21). This submission to one another follows the example of Christ, who came to meet our real needs on the cross. Each of these examples has an important context that helps determine its meaning; otherwise these passages are used to maintain the old order.

In his letter to Ephesus, Paul writes, "[All of us] formerly followed the ways of this world and of the kingdom of the air . . . gratifying the cravings of our sinful nature and following its desires and thoughts" (Eph. 2:1–3). He asserts that the authority of the Christian does not give permission to gratify the sinful nature but instead calls us to a new way of using power. Later, in the second letter to Thessalonica, Paul proclaims that believers are free to yield their claim to power and to serve instead as servant-models to others (see 2 Thess. 3:6–9). Further, though he had every right to assert his apostolic power and position, Paul emphasized that his mission was to work with the believers for their joy, not to lord his position over their faith (see 2 Cor. 1:24).

The believer's practice of authority must also be tempered by the knowledge that in the end Jesus will abolish all dominion, authority, and power when he hands the Kingdom over to God (see 1 Cor. 15:25). Paul stresses the temporary nature of our authority and power on earth, a stewardship for which we will give account and for which we will be rewarded or judged. Paul's authority was derived from a visitation by Jesus Himself and reinforced by tremendous suffering, pain, and hardship. In 2 Corinthians, Paul describes his hardships and highlights the fact that his power in Christ is made perfect in *weakness*.[13]

Taking these ideas together, Paul instructs leaders how to function in the church. He tells Timothy that a ruler "must be temperate, self-controlled, . . . not given to drunkenness, not violent but gentle, not quarrelsome, . . . must manage his own family well . . ." (1 Tim. 3:2–4). These words create a picture of a person who is not focused on power and dominion but upon management that is gracious and considerate of the needs of others. Paul proclaims that God gives authority to build others up in the faith in order to be able to serve others.[14] In fact, it is the working of the power of God that enables His *grace* to flow through the one who has yielded to His power (see Eph. 3:7). This godly grace then becomes the means by which others are healed and sanctified; they are no longer subjected to oppression (see Matt. 10:1).

The Goal of Biblical Authority. In the Kingdom where Jesus is Lord, those subjects who serve Him well rule with meekness (power under control). The man or woman who functions in positions of power and has truly yielded his or her brokenness to God becomes a channel of grace and mercy. This model of power follows Paul's example in 2 Corinthians 1, where his wounding becomes the means by which he yields his power and control completely to God. Through our wounds we become aware of our limitations. If we ignore, repress, or drug those wounds rather than yield to God, then we cannot move on toward wholeness. When those wounds are embraced, felt, grieved, and resolved, then we can accept our need to rely on God and not on ourselves.

CHANGED BEHAVIOR AND EXCHANGED HEARTS

Paul challenges us in Romans 12:2, "Do not conform any longer to the pattern of this world, but be transformed by the renewing of your mind. Then you will be able to test and approve what God's will is—his good, pleasing, and perfect will." We often understand the first admonition ("do not conform any longer to the pattern of this world") to mean to stop cheating, raging, swearing, and engaging in promiscuity and drug use. It does mean this but also something far deeper—it means forsaking any element of life that does not adhere to God's intent, including any cultural and familial conditioning that opposes God's plans for our lives.

We are also called to become transformed by the renewal of our minds. This metamorphosis—the exchange of sinful lives for hearts made new in Jesus Christ—changes our whole way of viewing and experiencing reality. It is an awesome and dynamic task that does not end until we see Christ face to face. One of the most detrimental things pastors and counselors can do is to settle in a stage of transformation and believe they have arrived. In the process of living, we are called to press on toward the high calling of Christ (see Phil. 3:14). We must live authentic and honest lives, or we run the risk of seeking other sources of illusory fulfillment besides the very presence of God himself.

To prevent and overcome sexual sin, transformation and conformation must both occur. It is not enough to conform to correct rules of living, we must also experience an inner transformation. A person's conscience must change so he or she can assent to and live by moral principles, not solely by means of a resocialization process. The healing of offenders and consequent prevention of further harm must include a determination to change conduct based on the redemptive experience of an inner transformation.

> The solution to sin, however, is not as simple as some Christians make it sound. Often, Christians tend to dismiss complicated problems easily with an exhortation to trust in God. . . . Sexual [trouble] is a complex problem with multiple causes and far-reaching consequences. It results when persons become dependent on sexual experiences to achieve a sense of personal fulfillment. . . . The force of the allure goes far beyond sex to the depths of the heart, where the deceitfulness is beyond most people's comprehension. Few of us have the courage to enter this subterranean world of the human heart. Several tiers below the surface is a pervasive, integral force that demands the right to avoid pain and experience self-fulfillment. This self-centered energy is the very essence of what the Bible calls "sin."[15]

Some critics have asserted that Christian psychotherapy is not Christian enough, pointing to the lack of a cohesive psychology and treatment theory based on the Bible. There is some merit in this charge. However, many of these critics advocate platitudes—"nothing but the Bible," for example—without providing effective biblical solutions, particularly in the realm of forbidden sex. If platitudes worked, then many of the men who have advocated a "nothing but" position would not have fallen to the plague of forbidden sex. We agree with those critics though who promote a greater reliance on the Word of God as the source of healing and as the foundation for a Christian psychology. A truly biblical approach to forbidden sex prevention will deal with the roots of sin and will challenge the vision of a whole and sanctified and wholly satisfying future.

CONFORMATION

Both Old and New Testaments stress the importance of living in conformity to God's will for both the individual and the community. In the sermon on the mount (Matt. 5–7) Jesus describes the people of God as being meek (5:5) and as salt and light (5:13–16); He says they love their enemies (5:44–48), give generously to the needy (6:2–4), do not judge others (7:1–5), and are known by their good fruit (7:17–20). The Apostle Paul reiterates the importance of conforming to God's standards by saying, "And whatever you do, whether in word or deed, do it all in the name of the Lord Jesus . . ." (Col. 3:17).

Outer Control Is Not Enough. Conformity to an outward law only reaches "the outside of the plate and cup" (see Matt. 23:26ff), and many times not even this in an adequate way. Changed behavior and scrubbed up appearances are insufficient foundations for Christian living. Unfortunately, good behavior, right doctrine, and image management have become the focus of too many Christians in the Western church. The Pharisees perfected image management and all Christians, to some degree, struggle with conformity as an outward standard. No matter how deep our love for God or our motives for the gospel, a constant temptation is to defocus the central things of God—love, faithfulness, justice, and mercy—and move legalistically toward image management and the pretend self. Too many Christians begin their relationship with God by the Spirit but eventually shift to attainment of godly goals by human effort alone (see Gal. 3:1–5).

TRANSFORMATION

Change from the inside out is central to the effective restoration of male and female sexuality. It is never enough to simply conform with outward structures: the change must come from the inside. Indeed, the change can only come from the inside because the struggle to change our flesh to conform with the truth is fruitless; Scripture clearly tells us that the flesh is dead—that God has given up on changing the flesh. "I have been crucified with Christ and I no longer live, but Christ lives in me" (Gal. 2:20).

In the realm of sexuality, it is vital to see that the "desired body belongs to the 'being' of a human being who himself belongs to another; a human being, that is who has been bought with a price (1 Cor. 6:20; 7:23), and has a temporal and eternal destiny, a destiny in which one who claims this other person in his totality responsibly participates."[16] This perspective of seeing a person as a whole being belonging to God not only prevents sexual violation, it liberates the viewer to discover sexual fulfillment as God intended.

A New Way of Seeing. The effect of the Fall on personhood was to change differentiation into alienating division. We are painfully and radically separated from God. The only way for interpersonal restoration to occur, to achieve normal human relatedness, is to come into right relatedness with God. "Our true identity in relation can only be experienced by passing through self-interest. That is, by experiencing grace and forgiveness in the relation."[17]

In men who violate sexual boundaries, this internal healing of the sexual self has not occurred adequately to protect them from mating with those whom they ought not to mate. As Presbyterian minister Don Moomaw said, "With my recent facing of issues dating from childhood, years of denial and faulty coping techniques, it's become clear I have inappropriately tried in my own strength to work through my own problems. Now I am getting honest with myself and others, maybe for the first time."[18]

One of the most difficult boundary issues to face in life is that between possibility and limitation. What do I do if I cannot do as much as I want, or I cannot have as much as I can imagine? Some people deny the inherent limitations of their creatureliness, believing the only limits are those we foolishly place on ourselves. Others deal with this struggle by partializing—focusing only on that which is attainable. Because the demand to love all equally is overwhelming, this individual may make only one person a love project. This narrow, manageable focus helps the person control his or her fear, but it can also be the basis for obsessive legalism, increasing neurosis, and eventual psychopathology.

Partializing appears to give a person freedom from his or her anxiety, but, in fact, it only creates more limitations of freedom, eventually leading to bondage. It becomes more attractive to encounter a stranger or an imaginary lover rather than encountering the known. The one who partializes says, "I know how the one I am married to will respond to me and I don't like it, so why waste time to pursue it any further?" For a person in this place, he or she then finds it easier to believe that the admirer can become a lover, thus feeling good even as he or she deceptively believes this love also heals the other.

To accept our creatureliness—to acknowledge our limits—draws us to accept God's healing grace. We are motivated to yield to God for help because we cannot carry everything by ourselves. The broken, arrogant self wants to consume all possibilities, to conquer all challenges. Though we may do well to stretch our boundaries (for the sake of growth and maturity), to accept limits is good because it leads us to accept God as the one who is able to do what we cannot. By God's grace, true boundaries become known and accepted. We are empowered to let God carry what He is to carry and to carry ourselves what we must without being crushed.

Following the Way of Christ. Consider the way Jesus treated women: not according to their gender or by their sexual attractiveness, but by the character and desires of their heart. Jesus loved and dignified women; He exalted in their love and dedication to Him as God come-in-the-flesh. It is important to understand how radical this was in the context of His culture. The Hebrew, Roman, and Greek worlds were extremely sexist—men viewed women as sexual objects, necessary for procreation, but generally despised them. (Some readers may say, "So what's changed?") But Jesus' concept of women was totally different. He interacted with them in ways that bestowed dignity on them as persons. He loved them as the Father loves them (cf. John 14:9–11a), as the Father beckons all men to relate to them.

So then, to prevent sexual violation there must be an inner transformation that causes us to see other people as individuals who belong not just to themselves, and certainly not to us, but who are bought with an incalculable price—who belong to God. Inasmuch as we fail to see this relatedness to God when we look upon a person, we fail to value that person and lose our protection from sexual temptation. Our potential for failure stems from an unwillingness to see the person with dignity, as belonging to God. If relatedness with another person depends upon what we hope to receive, then when this function weakens or disappears we will abandon that person. When agape is involved, however, then we are able to relate to the person as one who is a being before God, not simply as a person who functions for us.

CAUGHT BETWEEN EROS AND AGAPE

Eros focuses on the intensity of sexuality and human sensual emotions. Eros is both pleasure and ecstasy: wonderful but fleeting emotions. One is not able to remain in those states for long without exhausting the emotions. That is why once fulfilled, eros rapidly dies down—then it grows again with a renewed desire for fulfillment. It is never fully satisfied; there is never enough for eros.

Eros is also subject to the law of attraction and revulsion. Since eros focuses on temporary fulfillment, once it is released and its energy spent, the person can become repulsed by the very object that was the source of desire. "The more erotic behavior is merely a matter of releasing an instinctive impulse, the more it is subject to the law."[19] The purely instinctive nature of the sex urge shows that something other than trust, love, or sympathy is expressing itself.

The erotic urge, because of sin, can quickly reveal its dark and dangerous side. It does not require that love or sympathy become involved in order for it to be expressed. This base character of eros reflects its fallen nature, its divorce from agape because of the Fall. Eros is in serious need of redemption within the soul of each man and woman as part of the total inner transformation. Without God's help, eros is simply hormonal and instinctual.

Humans are not subject to being in heat as are animals—eros is constantly present and so we must guard continually against misdirected sexual arousal. While the strength of the impulse may be subject to fluctuation (whether hormonal, cyclical, or seasonal), this ever-present sexual potential is subject to great risk (cf. 1 Cor. 7:5). Indeed, sexual violence stems from eros gone astray, because eros without grace always aims to take, to give to oneself. Thus, violence lies at the end of the desperate, exclusive pursuit of erotic fulfillment—when eros becomes idolatrous and can never satisfy. It is this yielding to the idol of eros that blinds otherwise good men to the truth, men who eventually digress to a multi-faceted violence in sexual abuse: violence against a person needing help, against the rules of professional behavior, and against the gospel of Jesus Christ.

Agape Love. The love of God calls us to be like Jesus, to see beyond surface beauty or ugliness and look for the *imago dei* (God image) in each person. Then we can celebrate the eternal worth of a person rather than the superficial and fading values. Yet how contrary this is to unredeemed human nature, and how difficult it is to do. Actually, it is impossible to do—impossible unless we are transformed from the inside.

We must recognize and accept that agape is not inherent in human nature. It is given to men and women who seek it from God. And He gives it, not to be held but to be given away. Agape can only be expressed for good (that which builds up another), because it does not seek its own way (see 1 Cor. 13:5). Love is more than simple instinct, a truth reflected in that "gratitude and fulfillment survive the moment of ecstasy and that these moments are only the expression, culmination, and concentration of a continuing relationship which outlasts all changes of mood and feeling."[20]

Eros with Agape. Though it may be overstated, we have heard it said that eros cannot wait to get, while agape cannot wait to give. The tension between these loves is great, and it is easy for Christians to denigrate eros (and the body) and exalt agape. But this is not God's design, for He created both the body and the erotic pleasures that are part of its joys. C. S. Lewis, in *The Four Loves*, challenges this false dichotomy by asserting about the loves that "the highest does not stand without the lowest."[21]

These loves must be integrated in relationships between sexes, which is only possible through the redemption of Christ. Eros unredeemed stresses the utilitarian value of the person—what you can do for me. Agape, on the other hand, is concerned about what I can do for you, how I can serve your very best interests with delight. In agape we come to recognize that

> the value of a person lies in a totally different level from that of his utility value. Hence there can never be any question of a "life worth being allowed to live" . . . a community like that of marriage cannot simply cease to exist when the importance of the person for me (say his importance in fulfilling myself in the eros sense) diminishes or disappears and he fails functionally. Agape discerns in him other, abiding elements.[22]

John White paints a beautiful picture of eros redeemed by its union with agape.

[S]exual love [is not] mere orgasmic ecstasy. When a man feels tiny baby fingers curling around his own little finger, the sensation of wonder and affection as well as the urge to care for and protect arise out of sexual love. It is no longer erotic arousal . . . it is that which erotic arousal has led to: the joy of what is happening to him in that moment, the experience of a tiny replica of his own hand grasping his finger. Flesh that came from him now clings to him. . . . We must not narrow sexual love down to what happens in bed or in a hayloft.[23]

CONCLUSION

Sexual misconduct in counseling and ministry reflects the debasement of agape and the triumph of erotic idolatry. Its pursuit is the practice of a dark and ultimately deadly religion. Wrongful sex can never be sanctified, as God intends to redeem sexual love by the union of agape and eros in marriage. In spite of the impassioned and delusional rhetoric of lovers ensnared in its intoxicating embrace, illicit sex is nothing more than the deceitful use of another person for desperate and selfish purposes. It can create nothing of true love or eternal value; neither can it reap lasting rewards. It can do nothing more than eventually yield a trail of anguish and brokenness spreading tragically over many lives and families, over many communities of faith, across multiple professions, staining the entire society.

In facing the truth about forbidden sex in counseling and ministry, all too often the church has either denied it or focused simply on outward change. Conformity to biblical standards is crucial, but if we accept only conformation we become vulnerable to attack and to gross sin. We believe that true change and lasting renewal in the church, especially in the area of sexual brokenness, must come from inner transformation. Without this change from the inside out—without a regenerate heart that is constantly yielded to God to shape into the fullness of the promise—there is no reliable way for good men and women to avoid falling into immorality, especially sexual sin. By the cross and the empty tomb, God has shown us the way out of sin: the redemptive, curative way of Jesus that leads to abundant life.

NOTES

1. Frances Frangipane, *The Three Battlegrounds* (Cedar Rapids, Iowa: Advancing Church Publications, 1989), 9.

2. Karl Barth, *Church Dogmatics*, vol. III: 2 (Edinburgh: T and T Clark, 1958), 27.

3. Ray Anderson, "A Theological Perspective on Human Personhood," (syllabus for the course on Theology of Personhood, Fuller Theological Seminary, 1977).

4. Ibid., 57.

5. See, for example, Isaiah 64:6 and Jeremiah 17:9.

6. Robert Hicks, *The Masculine Journey: Understanding the Six Stages of Manhood* (Colorado Springs, Colo.: NavPress, 1993), 114.

7. Quoted in Hicks, *Masculine Journey*, 65.

8. Anderson, "Human Personhood," 55.

9. Helmut Thielicke, *The Ethics of Sex*, trans. John W. Doberstein (Grand Rapids: Baker, 1964), 22.

10. Janice T. Gibson and Mika Haritos-Fatouros, "The Education of a Torturer," *Psychology Today* 20, no. 11 (1986): 50–58.

11. Verses 42–43. Also see similar passages in Luke 22:24–30 and Matthew 20:24–28.

12. Notably, Rom. 13:1–5; Eph. 5:22–24; 1 Tim. 2:12; Titus 3:1–2.

13. See chapters 6:3–10; 12:1–10; 13:1–4.

14. See 2 Cor. 10:8; 13:10; and 2 Thess. 3:6–10, especially verse 9.

15. Harry Schaumburg, *False Intimacy: Understanding the Struggle of Sexual Addiction* (Colorado Springs, Colo.: NavPress, 1992), 21–22.

16. Thielicke, *Ethics of Sex*, 24–25.

17. Anderson, "Human Personhood," 56.

18. Editorial, "Reagan's Pastor Stepped Over the Line," *Times-Standard* (Eureka, Calif.), 22 February 1993.

19. Thielicke, *Ethics of Sex*, 37.

20. Ibid.

21. C. S. Lewis, *The Four Loves* (San Diego: Harcourt Brace, 1971), 14.

22. Thielicke, *Ethics of Sex*, 32.

23. John White, *Eros Redeemed: Breaking the Stranglehold of Sexual Sin* (Downers Grove: InterVarsity, 1993), 108.

PART II

Forbidden Sex
Between Adults

Chapter Four

The Dynamics of Adult Sexual Misconduct

Facing the issues distilling around the tragedies of fallen spiritual lead-
ers, I see us at a very crucial point. The handling of these issues may well
become THE issue of our times. If a surrender to slackness in the require-
ments of spiritual leadership is conceded now, and if a creeping humanism
governs the resolution of this problem, the authority of Christ and His
Word will have been supplanted. Unless an honest confrontation with all
the Word of God is made now, the result will be nothing less than a re-
duced view of Christ's Lordship—His rule and His will in His Church.[1]

EVERY CHRISTIAN HELPER IS AT RISK for sexual misconduct with
counselees. Permit us to be redundant: **Every helper is at risk and
ANY helper can fall into sexual sin**. This is not to say that all helpers, especially male helpers, are guilty of misconduct. Rather, we
want to punch holes in the myths and lies that hinder our recognition of the truth that *everyone* is vulnerable, especially men. For the
male counselor and pastor in midlife, relationships with younger
female clients, congregants, staff, or students are particularly risky.

In this chapter we will focus on sexual misconduct by men
against women since these involve the greatest number of violators and victims. We will highlight some of the key factors that
contribute to crossing sexual boundaries. We will address issues related to homosexual misconduct in chapter 6 and issues
related to sexual misconduct with children in chapters 7, 8, and 10.
Later, in Part V, we will return to some of the issues that underlie
sexual misconduct and examine how to treat offenders and prevent further abuse.

WHO ARE THE VICTIMS?

It is a conservative estimate that over one million women have been sexually exploited by a helping professional. Approximately 90 percent of all sexual misconduct is perpetrated by men. Adult women make up about 85 percent of the victims, and children and teens are victims in about 5 percent of the cases. About 10 percent of the violations involve women sexually abusing other women. About 70 percent of therapists report having a counselee who was exploited by another therapist. Women from every socioeconomic level, age, race, denomination, and mental health status have been victims of sexual molestation by professional counselors and clergy.[2]

The typical victim's profile for women largely conforms to histrionic personality traits: attractive, feminine in dress and role, dramatic in expression, insecure about personal worth, naive and dependent in relationships, and often nonorgasmic and sexually insecure. The woman most likely to be molested is white, single or divorced, lonely, depressed, emotionally vulnerable, and generally ten to twenty years younger than her helper. At least 30 percent of these victims, and likely more, are child sexual abuse survivors. Often, the vulnerable woman is in awe of her therapist; she views her helper as a father figure who will be her advocate and helper in the struggle to attain her identity as a woman. Frequently, she struggles with her image of God, and the helper is sought out to help her deal with unresolved spiritual issues.

Most women acknowledge that the helping relationship develops a heightened sense of importance nonsexually before it becomes sexual. In fact, by the time it becomes sexual, it is difficult to resist because the *relationship itself* has become too important to lose. Usually, the victim becomes confused about her status in relationship to the helper. She is uncertain if she is really in love with the helper and wonders whether she is being used by the helper for his own needs.

Most women who yield sexually to a helper do so because they have been trained to comply with men in authority. They are trapped in the lie that submission is all-important and that to resist is to self-destruct. Typical of victimization in any situation, silence and secrecy are mandated for every victim. In part, this silence is maintained by shaming the victim into thinking she caused the moral failure—that she, not the violative male, is at fault. (We will discuss victims and their treatment and recovery in the next chapter.)

Who Are the Violators

Helpers who violate sexual boundaries in counseling do so for various and complex reasons. In our book *Law for the Christian Counselor*,[3] we define a broad range of violators but distill three typologies on a continuum of risk: the predatory violator, the mixed violator (revealing traits and dynamics of those at both ends), and the vulnerable violator. The most dangerous type—the sexual predator—intends to violate sexually and maintains civility primarily to cover the compelling drive of his lust. The vulnerable and mixed violators are less dangerous than predators and are more likely to repudiate and control sexual abuse. Some of these can even be restored to moral living and ministry.

The personal and sexual violations themselves span a wide continuum of exploitation: rape, statutory rape (sex with a minor), apparently consensual relations, violations arising from the use of drugs or hypnotic techniques, and various forms of therapeutic deception used to justify sexual contact. More covert styles of violation include sexual contact by fraud, including disguising sexual activity as treatment or touching sexually while hugging. Sexual harassment includes sexual and voyeuristic comments, pressuring for dates, unwanted touch, and intensely sexual interactions either verbally or by fantasy.

Some helpers develop romantic type relationships within the helping context, and the activity never leaves the office. This may or may not include claims of love or a promise of a future together. Some helpers become romantically involved with counselees outside the office, believing their actions are justified if they take place outside the sphere of counseling. This may occur during the counseling relationship, following a real or bogus termination, or in pursuit of marriage or a long-term romantic relationship. (The issue of sexual or romantic relations following termination of counseling, including the motives for them, is controversial. We will address this issue more fully in chapter 12 when we consider the ethical issues surrounding sexual misconduct.)

The closeness experienced when counseling an attractive and needy counselee can be intoxicating and can easily lead a person into decisions that are destructive for both helper and counselee.

One way to prevent sexual misconduct is to understand the dynamics of increased vulnerability and presume that one is susceptible to their allure. Misconduct usually results from a failure to realistically evaluate one's own vulnerability, becoming intoxicated with the sense of sensual adventure and minimizing one's own potential for misconduct. As we argued earlier, succumbing to sexual sin occurs because of our tendency (1) to assume our invincible goodness, (2) to assert our right to love and be loved, and (3) to deny the power of the flesh to pull us into sinful behavior.

A blurring of professional and private roles also makes any sexual liaison more susceptible to legal action—sexual exploitation suits are already the most successful for victim recovery. Recently, at a conference on professional and clergy sexual misconduct, we heard of a suit brought against a priest for sexual relations out of his official role. Apparently, the priest was taking an evening class and became sexually involved with a woman he met there. Later she sued him for sexual misconduct in violation of his priestly role, *even though he was not functioning in his clerical role at the time.* Legal trends increasingly give weight to the perceptions of victims—if they know you as a priest, pastor, or counselor, you are one. Clergy (especially) and counselors should view themselves as on the job continually; the potential for sexual misconduct is ever-present, whether officially on the job or not.

THE VULNERABLE HELPER

Lee Earnest married Sue Willow shortly before graduating from Bible college. In a short time they were active in their first church as youth pastors with a hundred and one jobs and little of the senior pastor's attention, time, or energy. Anxious to please and always ready to help out, Lee and Sue quickly became two extremely busy people. When the first baby arrived, they had even less time for one another.

Lee became more successful in Christian ministry, yet found it increasingly difficult to get along with his wife. Sue was frustrated about the lack of time with her husband but had difficulty criticizing Lee because he was doing the Lord's work. In spite of prayer and requests for attention, she felt increasingly estranged from her husband and, as a result, became increasingly unavailable to him both emotionally and physically.

In time, second and third children arrived and Lee progressed upward in ministry as an assistant pastor in another church. In his new role as assistant pastor, Lee discovered that people were attracted to him because of his gifts in counseling. He began to spend a great deal of time helping the many people referred to him for pastoral counseling. The demands of ministry steadily increased; Lee spent more and more time helping congregants and had less time and energy for his wife, his family, or his own needs. He was well-liked, proficient, respected, and caring at church, but at home his relationship with his wife was cool, distant, critical, and frequently tense.

Eventually, an attractive and needy woman came to Lee for counseling about her dysfunctional marriage. Pam, a devout Christian, was married to a workaholic and alcoholic husband who was cold, cruel, and emotionally abusive. She was lonely and frightened while at the same time alluring, intelligent, and open in her interaction with Lee.

Lee gradually found himself looking forward to his appointments with Pam, often thinking about her and how he could best help her. In contrast to his wife, Lee found Pam to be charming and appreciative of his help. Lee became aware of his attraction to Pam and began to justify finding time to see her outside of the formal office setting. Pam felt honored to have his time in such a special way and was drawn closer to him. She found him so caring—such an affirming and affectionate contrast to her own husband.

At the end of a particularly emotional appointment, in which Pam had experienced a key breakthrough, she spontaneously embraced Lee in a warm hug, grateful for his gracious help. Lee was surprised and pleased. He found her embrace intoxicating, which made it difficult for him not to dwell on his desire for her. It seemed clear to Lee that Pam felt special about him. These thoughts and feelings quickly became more powerful than the voice of conscience that tugged and urged, "Watch out!"

Several weeks later, as Pam again embraced Lee in a thankful hug at the end of a session, Lee kissed her briefly. At first, Lee struggled with this and felt guilty; he was afraid to talk to anyone about it. Lee and Pam did not discuss it in their next session, and when he kissed her again Pam did not move away from him. This apparent lack of resistance on her part encouraged Lee that he was not doing anything all that wrong.

Lee's thoughts were preoccupied with his desire for Pam—his heart raced when he saw her or heard her voice on the phone. Lee began to convince himself how close he and Pam were—in harsh contrast to his wife—and how compatible they were as a couple. As a result, Lee and Pam's appointments focused less and less on counseling issues and became progressively frequent and intimate. They began a sexual dance that eventually led to an obsessive sexual and emotional relationship.

Profile of the Vulnerable Violator. The vulnerable violator falls sexually because he does not take good care of his personal life and does not respect ethical boundaries in counseling. Avoiding sexual harm in therapy and helping ministry requires that clear boundaries against sexual behavior be set and kept. It is critical to contemplate and practice Paul's warning: "If you think you are standing firm, be careful that you don't fall. No temptation has seized you but such as is common to man; and God is faithful, who will not allow you to be tempted beyond what you are able, but with the temptation will provide the way of escape also, that you may be able to endure it" (1 Cor. 12:10–11).

In assessing persons with high vulnerability for sexual misconduct, the following risk factors usually show up in clusters for the vulnerable violator:

- excessive privacy
- aloofness
- rigid, pietistic moral attitudes
- habitual association with persons other than spouse
- inattention to spouse and family
- poor marital intimacy
- one-track life-style (has no apparent interests outside of helping role)
- workaholic tendencies
- willingness to participate in house calls and other meetings that ignore sexual risks
- disregard for peer accountability

Vulnerable violators—men not intending sexual relations but likely to become involved in sexual misconduct—are especially tragic in ministry because such sin can be prevented so easily.[4] The sin is not deliberate and deceptive, at least not initially, as is the case with the predator. Rather, as Virkler distinguished,[5] these are sins of ignorance, confusion, and lack of understanding (biblically—*agnosia* and *parakon*—see Eph. 4:18 and Acts 17:30) of the power and complexity of emotional and sexual forces.

Whether a licensed clinician or member of the clergy, these men "are accomplished professionals, admired community leaders, and respectable family men whose integrity we tend to take for granted."[6] They are usually middle-aged and are often involved in an unsatisfactory marriage—a small percent are going through a divorce. They have practiced counseling over a decade and have a caseload that is primarily female. While often *appearing* successful, these are likely to be lonely men who are isolated from family and peers. They usually have a good professional reputation and frequently only take cases on referral. They are not necessarily physically attractive, but have charisma—they exude a sense of power and have an attractive and engaging personality.

Vulnerable helpers usually become sexually involved with physically attractive women ten to twenty years younger. Crossing the boundary of sexual trouble is often very subtle—it is usually not even sexual initially. Personal issues are often confided to sexual victims, and a victim's help is accepted or solicited to resolve personal struggles. The roles of counselor and counselee become confused and mixed with personal issues, both his and hers, that she may not have intended to address in counseling. In many cases the sexual violations do not include sexual intercourse, but even when less physical the misconduct is intensely emotional and just as damaging.

The mixed violator, showing some characteristics of the predator, may reveal involvement with pornography, sexual fantasy and story-telling, careless management of money and inappropriate spending, and denial of personal responsibility in problems. If these "early warning signals are taken seriously and reliable intervention, treatment, and furlough or career exit counseling are provided,"[7] then the risks of misconduct are greatly minimized. As might be expected, these issues are more difficult for pastors in independent churches or counselors in solo practices.

THE PREDATORY HELPER

Consider the predatory sexploitation of Billy Looselife. Billy became a Christian in his mid-twenties after a long stint with alcohol abuse. He immediately felt the call of God to enter the ministry. Since he was never a successful student, he gravitated to a church that did not require formal education but focused instead on evidence of the Lord's anointing in a person's life. Billy was a dynamic preacher and forceful evangelist; he appeared more mature than he really was and was given many opportunities for ministry and testimony. In many significant ways, Billy's active public ministry masked his private and weakly-held moral convictions.

In a short time he attracted the attention of Lisa Dependent, a lovely young Christian woman who fell deeply in love with him as he did with her. Shortly after they were married, however, Lisa began to notice things were not well with Billy's private life. Yet her church taught strict submission to a husband's authority so she did not openly question his occasional bouts of drunkenness nor his taste for pornographic magazines. From time to time, Lisa caught her husband appropriating funds from the offerings; he said he was just borrowing the money temporarily. He would spend many late nights in "ministry," yet would refuse to tell Lisa the details of his work or his whereabouts. He became verbally abusive with Lisa, demanding submission and accusing her of rebellion the few times she questioned or challenged his behavior.

Billy had truly experienced an encounter with the Lord, but was a man with many compulsive and addictive habits he was unwilling to submit to God's authority. He experienced both guilt and pleasure when he used pornography, or had a few drinks on occasion, or when he eyeballed and fantasized about attractive women. Though he knew these things were wrong, he did not seek God's help or apply biblical principles to overcome these habits, so he tried to hide them. He could not keep these problems hidden or maintain his denial before his wife, however, and their relationship seriously deteriorated.

Billy planted a small church within a few years of getting saved and, because of his dynamic ministry, it grew rapidly to nearly one hundred adults. Billy encouraged single women to help him in ministry and frequently arranged to have time alone with various ones in the guise of discipleship or counseling. Some of the young women were flattered to have these opportunities and were anxious to please him. He showered them with attention and worked to gain their complete trust. Once he felt he had a woman's total confidence and devotion he would begin to broach sexual topics with her.

Billy was a master at subtle, progressive exploitation. He would intimately hug a vulnerable woman and shame her gently if she felt embarrassed or expressed surprise, telling her that this was how true, loving believers acted toward each other. His touching and hugging became constant, desensitizing the women to his unyielding boundary violations. Eventually, he would initiate kissing and sensuous caressing, always talking in gentle ways and referring to the Lord. All the while, Billy acted in public as zealous and righteous as ever, which only further served to confuse his proteges and reinforce their unwillingness to question publicly his private behavior .

Billy assured each of these young ladies that she was the apple of his eye. If any of them dared to question his behavior he used his power over her to convince her she was wrong for even considering it to be so. In time he convinced each counselee to allow him to undress her, touch her sexually, and finally submit to all manner of sexual interaction. He would always assert that his sexual behavior was the glorious height of spirituality—that sexual pleasure and spiritual ecstasy were one and the same.

Billy's shaky house of sin tumbled down after three of his victims began comparing notes, became outraged at his duplicity, and exposed him. They first confronted him directly, but he denied any wrongdoing and became enraged and verbally abusive. He threatened to hurt all three of them if they did not back down and keep this secret. The women went to the elders of the church, and even though other victimized women then came forward *to expose this sin, the elders disbelieved the seriousness of the charges. Instead, they affirmed their support for Billy's ministry and encouraged the women to forgive Billy for any indiscretions he may have done.*

The women were dumbfounded and enraged. One of them worked for a lawyer who directed them to an experienced malpractice attorney. Later, in trial court, many of these women remembered Billy telling them, "Sin is not the action, but what's in the heart; it's only dirty if you think it so." Before the whole thing blew open publicly with lawsuits, extensive press coverage, and a broken church, Billy had sexually violated or attempted sex with thirteen women. The sexual pleasure and excitement of his compulsion was so fulfilling that he never seriously considered the incredible harm he was doing to his victims.

Profile of the Predatory Violator. The existence of sexual predators in Christian ministry and the mental health professions is one of the more serious moral, professional, and social problems in America today. Predators represent a very small minority of all counselors and clergy, yet they have created the highest number of victims and usually the most severe and long lasting harm. Numerous studies have demonstrated that the largest number of women (40 to 80 percent) who are sexually exploited are hurt by helpers who victimize more than one woman.[8] If the church and the helping professions do not get control of such predatory harm, this will truly become the classic case where the few bad apples will destroy the whole barrel.

Most of the same problems in a vulnerable helper exist in the sexual predator, except that they stem from a more pathological base. Predators frequently struggle with drug and sexual abuse patterns and are often victims of abuse or long-standing parental neglect. They reveal long-term personality disorders, with sociopathy and narcissistic disorders most prominent. Their lust is uncontrolled—evincing many affairs with a variety of women—and they show pornography addictions, excessive power demands, sexual addictions, and tend to be fully corrupted by sin (cf. Rom. 1:21; 2 Tim. 3). Virkler's distinction about sins of defiance and rebellion against God (biblical references to *apeitheia, asebeo,* and *hamartano*) fit the predator.[9]

The predator is a man with a seared conscience, often morally and emotionally numb, caught in the terrible paradox of being unable to experience either guilt and remorse or joy and pleasure. As helpers, predators are usually poorly trained, marginally competent, with ethical-legal trouble in other areas beyond sex. A growing number of predatory abusers are being exposed publicly, but many still maintain a veneer of control to keep their abuse hidden. In fact, many predators are fairly competent and charming socially but are obsessed with interpersonal power and authoritarian control, including control of every aspect of church life. The predatory helper differs from the vulnerable helper in that he has an erotic focus and rarely becomes emotionally involved with his counselee-victim in a positive sense.

Unlike the vulnerable helper, the predatory helper is a man who craves power and sexual conquest, a dangerous individual who fundamentally denies that anything is wrong with these desires and behaviors. Due to this, and also unlike the vulnerable violator, the predator is unlikely to repent and engage in sexual recovery at any meaningful level of change. The predator will continue abusing women until he is stopped—some predators have abuse histories decades long with dozens, even hundreds of victims. In fact, *the simplest test defining the predator is one who has violated sexually many times.* A vulnerable violator is training himself to become a predator if he violates more than once.

While great tragedy has been visited on the church due to the commission of predatory sins, possibly the church's greatest failure in response to this epidemic is a sin of omission. It has simply failed to acknowledge the depth of harm done by its predators and, until recently, has refused to take incisive action to stop this repeated abuse. Marie Fortune's poignant and tragic story[10] of a church's confused and sometimes bumbling response to a textbook predator is so common it should cause us to weep in travail.

Restoration to independent ministry by a predator is unlikely and very risky (an important consideration discussed more fully in chapter 14). We have no doubt that the litigation crisis of the church in response to this trouble and the growing legislative intrusion of the church by the state (discussed in chapter 13) is a direct result of this failure to act against predators. When victims and families who are shattered by this abuse are given the cold shoulder by the church, why are we amazed when they turn to the courts for justice?

CROSSING THE FORBIDDEN BOUNDARY

Psychotherapy and pastoral ministry can foster a closeness between a man and a woman with moments that can be intoxicating.

In these moments, it is imperative that the helper be prepared to deal with the sexual and emotional temptation, for all too easily "[t]he ordinary man, with an inclination to cross over forbidden boundaries, emerges from beneath the professional role."[11] Theologian Robert Hicks, in discussing man as the "noble savage," notes that "[e]ven when the resources of grace are applied to his life in Christ, the struggle with the savage remains. The flesh still rages against the movement of the Spirit within even the renewed male and female (Gal. 5:16–17)."[12]

Anyone involved in a helping ministry is likely to be emotionally drawn to the one helped. This is normal and positively facilitates the helping endeavor. However, this commitment to caring and the resultant emotional bond between the giver and the recipient of that care are also the roots of sexual vulnerability. Danger lurks when these feelings of genuine care get mixed, sometimes without distinction, with attraction and sexual allure. Those who reason with their emotions can easily begin to justify crossing moral and ethical boundaries.

Rutter makes the following observation about the dynamics of the therapeutic process often encountered by a male helper working with a female counselee:

> If we have been working together for some time, a familiarity and trust develops between us that starts to erode the boundaries of seemingly impersonal professional relationships. Whether they say so openly or not, these women often convey their feeling that we are treating them far better that they ever dreamed a man could. As a result, we may find ourselves experiencing a closeness, a comfort, a sense of *completeness* with these women that we have long sought but rarely found; many of them clearly begin to feel the same way about being with us.[13]

WHY FORBIDDEN BOUNDARIES ARE CROSSED

Yielding to temptation is a progressive process—from attraction to fantasy, to touch, to erotic touch, to sexual foreplay, genital stimulation, and intercourse. Though many opportunities exist in the process to halt and stand, as with all sex the deeper you go the less inclined you are to want to stop. Crossing the line of forbidden sex may also involve these things:

It Happens to Good Helpers and Ministers. A common misconception is that only bad helpers fall. The church reels from this plague because too many men of good character, without previous trouble, have also fallen. Allan Petersen stated it so well, "No one, however chosen, blessed, or used of God, is immune to an extra-marital affair. Anyone, regardless of how many victories he (or she) has won, can fall disastrously."[14] Thus it is critically important for church boards, colleagues, and peers in helping to presume vulnerability and hold the helper accountable to do what is right. Boards, supervisors, colleagues, friends, and the helper's wife must challenge moral purity and enforce rest times for the helper, especially after major projects are completed.

Denial of Vulnerability. Some helpers fail to realistically evaluate their own vulnerability. One helper who succumbed to the seduction admitted that he always thought it was impossible for him to fall. The helper often begins with an emotional involvement, then becomes intoxicated with the sense of sexual adventure and tends to minimize the potential for misconduct. When coupled with the repression or denial of sexual urges and lustful thoughts—which increases rather than reduces the risk of acting out the sexual allure—the risk equation can be dramatically inflamed.

A basic distortion about Christian identity is often deceptively present here. Denial and repression are frequent struggles of perfectionist, legalistic Christians who desperately labor to deny the reality of their sin nature. In order to maintain God's grace or favor (and to avoid the terror of His wrath), these Christians embrace a subtle lie that projects to themselves and (usually poorly) to others the constant illusion of being perfect and complete, without sin. Thank God for His promise never to leave us and the encouragement to confess our sins and struggles honestly to ourselves, to him, and to one another!

Attractive "Partners" and Frustrating Spouses. Temptation to cross forbidden boundaries can be especially strong for the man who counsels or works closely with an attractive woman who idolizes or idealizes him. She can easily become intoxicating, especially if she is an appealing and appreciative contrast to a wife the helper perceives as frustrating, critical, and demanding. Even a marriage without overt problems and frustrations, but which may not evidence the intimacy and support that constant marital work demands and yields, can look gray and unattractive in contrast to the colorful attraction of the new person.

> Over a period of time, a friendship develops. The "couple"
> spends more time together, perhaps repressing their awareness

of romantic feelings and rationalizing the growing intimacy by spiritualizing it. Many Christians at this stage pray together, without realizing that the prayers hide an awareness that their relationship is growing too intimate. An "emotional affair" commences, where both allow needs to be met by the affair partner instead of by one's spouse. As they continue to yield to sinful temptation, they become progressively blinded to the psychological realities and the spiritual implications of their behavior (John 3:19–21, 2 Cor. 4:4), and feel increasingly powerless to change it (John 8:34–35, Rom. 6:15–18, 7:14–23).[15]

Professional Justification and Denial of Harm. A significant number of professionals continue to deny and minimize the problem of sexual misconduct. Worse yet, some of these professionals still defend sex between counselor and client as beneficial. In a recent national study on sexual misconduct by psychiatrists, Gartrell and her colleagues found that three-fourths of the violators were motivated by "love" and "pleasure." Over half believed their patients left the sexual involvement with good feelings, and 20 percent intended to improve patient "self-esteem" as a direct result of sexual contact.[16] Contrast this with the wry and classic statement by Judd Marmor, who observed that most encounters were between male therapists and "women who are physically attractive, almost never with the aged, the infirm or the ugly; thus giving the lie to the oft-heard rationalization on the part of such therapists that they were acting in the best interests of their patients!"[17]

Ignorance and Misjudgment about Transference and Countertransference.[18] Much sexual misconduct in therapy and ministry flows from ignorance or denial of transference and countertransference dynamics. Psychiatrist Peter Rutter described a near-seduction experience that alerted him to the subtle but powerful potential for forbidden sex. Some women will act-out seductively toward male counselors—transferring to therapy the behavior and beliefs that trouble them in life. Rutter asserts that seductive women are doing exactly "what patients are supposed to do when they see their doctors . . . bringing her illness, her self-destructive pattern, in the only way she [knows] how—by repeating it with me. . . .[19]

The vulnerable helper often confuses positive client transference—trust, respect, and affection—as genuine love and legitimate sexual attraction. This helper is not consciously exploitive but becomes involved because of the misperception that what is happening is true love, which can get even more confused with the counselee's desire for *nonerotic* physical contact. The helper may argue that matters "just got out of hand," though often the rules about therapy in the office and outside of the appointment time are increasingly ignored.

Many helpers are poorly trained to recognize and deal with countertransference issues. As we noted earlier, some helpers who are vulnerable have unsatisfactory and conflicted marriages. Because of the marital tension, the professional usually doubles efforts in those areas of possible success and loses sight of personal vulnerability. For others, countertransference issues have little to do with the quality of one's marriage, but have deeper roots in childhood traumas that remain hidden and denied by the helper. Predatory abuse often masks a repressed hostility and vindictiveness toward women—unresolved anger, bitterness, and rage over past hurts.

Anger Problems. Some helpers—not just predators with high levels of repressed anger and hostility—have problems with unresolved anger and anger management. They often express their frustrations (sometimes a destructive rage) at home rather than deal with them in godly ways as they occur with staff, counselees, and others. As a result, they end up isolating themselves even further from their spouse and others who might otherwise help them and hold them accountable. This increases vulnerability to someone whom they come to believe will listen to them and accept them unconditionally, someone from whom they usually control and hide their anger early in the illicit courtship process.

The Trust Factor. Trust is central to effective helping, and the Christian professional must safeguard against misinterpreting its meaning. As Rutter states about the trusting woman, "If this man is important to her—as her mentor, her boss, her therapist, her pastor, even her friend or coworker—she may try to overlook the sexual element *or even begin to cater to it,* for fear of losing a relationship of value."[20] Tragically, too many men have yielded to sexual relations based on this misinterpretation of trust, either by exploiting it directly or wrongly viewing it as the woman's quest for sexual intimacy.

Pope states, with respect to the clinician's stature as an object of trust, that "the forceful transference phenomenon, the power differential between therapist and patient, the deep trust necessary to an effective therapeutic relationship, and similar factors significantly diminish the patient's ability to resist sexual advances."[21] Counselees respond to the helper's sensitivity and care with growing admiration and affection, opening up and trusting the helper. Consequently, the helper always has the responsibility to safeguard his moral relationship with counselees. This is particularly true with women because they seem to know that they are the moral policeman in relationships with men—*except in relationships of trust where they let down their guard.*

The Fantasy of Fulfilled Intimacy. The vulnerable Christian mentor, similar to his non-Christian counterpart, can believe something special will happen as the fantasy to be with the counselee is completed. The helper may allow sexual fantasies to develop and expand about this forbidden sexual "object," gradually crossing the boundary between helping and hurting rather than practicing self-control. While to some degree the intoxication is erotic, it is primarily an emotional intoxication as the helper hopes to have unmet inner needs met in this new relationship. Rutter acknowledges that "[j]ust as the woman in a relationship of trust may look to the man in power for an answer to what has been injured or unfulfilled in her, the man may begin to look to the woman as a source of healing for himself."[22]

The sexual encounter holds the illusory promise to heal the wounds of the past and the hope for a real connection with another person in the present. For men these wounds are primarily expressed sexually, while for women they are usually expressed by receiving care, understanding, and emotional support from a male. Both have in common the *expectation of intimacy.* Every person comes out of his or her family of origin with unmet needs and wants. No matter how damaged or not that family of origin, every person emerges with a *hope* to be loved and to be secure. The helping relationship is powerful because it holds out the hope that the person will experience love, understanding, and help. In counseling, the counselee hopes to transcend the limitations of the family of origin, even if it is not understood as originating from those losses.

Isolation. A common element among fallen professionals is isolation in marriage and from friends. This is usually a gradual process and is not readily recognized. It is easy to put off tensions and conflicts in marriage in order to keep the peace, to make the marriage look good, or to meet the demands of one's profession or ministry. The busyness of an active profession or ministry and

the status of the role work together to hinder the formation of intimate friendships where the helper can maintain accountability.
Others deliberately isolate themselves, because they prefer to
maintain exclusive control and do not want the inherent accountability of relatedness.

This isolation from others contributes to loneliness and eventually depression. It creates a vulnerability that can lead one to seek
solace in the comfort of a forbidden relationship. A clinical psychologist stated, "I was in my mid-forties then, and to the outside
world I had everything: a good marriage, healthy children, a
prominent teaching position at the university, and a thriving private practice. But underneath it all I was completely depressed,
although I never told this to anyone."[23] The sexual misconduct crisis trumpets a clear counter-message: *there is no longer any room for
the Lone Ranger role in ministry or the helping professions.*

Pride Goes Before a Fall. Pride—in one's accomplishments, one's
work, even one's relationship with God—opens the heart to temptation. One fallen pastor stated, "I guess I thought I was so special
to God that he wouldn't let anything happen to me."[24] This leads
to resistance to accountability and results in an excessive, vulnerable independence. To protect against the harm of inordinate pride,
every helper needs sure accountability to peers with whom he (or
she) will be genuine.

The press for success and the drive to fulfill goals often leads to
compulsive work and reinforced pride. Deceptively, the helper often remains publicly effective long past the point where work
ceases to be inwardly fulfilling. This workaholic syndrome—the
idolatrous worship of work— creates an inner vacuum that may
lead the helper to seek fulfillment in an affair. For this reason, married helpers must be accountable to their spouse, committed to
resolving marital disputes, and committed to discovering the
deeper intimacies and joys of marriage.

Fame and Fortune: The Star Factor. A unique variant of pride that
contributes to the fall of the counselor, perhaps particularly the
clergy member, is the "star factor."[25] Clergy play a key role in leading people into relationship with God. This is pretty heady stuff
and can open a person to the vulnerabilities of stardom: pride in
this role—including its sexual appeal—and adulation by
congregants. Rediger sees the "consistent connection between the
stimulation of the role and the attraction and satisfaction derived
from role performance."[26]

The clergy's overidentification with the role as worship leader and teacher often leads to euphoria during worship and exhaustion afterward. The star factor requires a performer and an appreciative audience (an alien dynamic in light of the biblical model of corporate worship). When the star factor is operative in its negative sense, "the audience does not really care for the performer, and the performer loses real contact with the audience."[27] Danger then lurks when controls are relaxed, sexual stimulation is substituted for genuine spiritual satisfaction, and the pastoral helper's opportunities for privacy and intimate contact with counselees are increased.

Other cultural influences combine with the star role of the clergy to break down the barriers that used to help prevent sexual involvement. These include the glamorization of religious celebrities, constant sexual stimulation by advertising and the media, clergy divorces, the loss of family controls, and the breakdown of denominational structures of discipline. Because of the dynamics of the star factor, clergy may come to believe that they can break the rules because of the call of God. This in turn can lead them to believe they do not have normal limits; thus they can become much more susceptible to burnout and sexual temptation.

Money to Burn. Excess money can contribute to the downfall of a vulnerable helper. In our professional counseling ministry, we have seen a consistent correlation between discretionary wealth and people (Christian or not) who yield to infidelity. More money comes with increased fame or vocational success, which can make discretionary spending on gifts and trips to be with a lover so much easier. Money can also foster the delusion that one can weather the loss of public disclosure and that family victims will at least be materially cared for in the event of divorce. One may see in this thinking the subtle corruption of values that denigrates the spiritual, relational, and emotional sides of life in favor of the material lie so loved by our consumeristic culture.

STEPS INTO THE FORBIDDEN ZONE

Peter Rutter outlines three major steps men take that lead them to violate the sexual barrier.[28] These are

1. testing the sexual barrier,
2. attempting to redefine the sexual barrier,
3. dispensing with the sexual barrier altogether.

Testing the Sexual Barrier. A subtle change begins to take place in the man's violative attitude that is often imperceptible to the counselee. His fantasy world involving her begins to be tested in the relationship to see if she will accept his advances. With each step taken to test the barrier, the man deceives himself and tries to induce the woman to believe with him that it is acceptable to change the rules. Every step we note here does not always occur, nor in this order, but this progression is common as the man moves toward breaking the sexual barrier.

Usually, the helper begins his invasion visually—by looking over her body—a basic male instinct that can be innocent, or it can develop into suggestive moves toward a woman. The helper may begin to wonder if the counselee is interested in him. At this point, the therapeutic objective weakens and can even take on secondary importance, especially if this erotic interest grows.

The helper may then begin to wonder what it would be like to touch the counselee sexually. As long as this remains in the realm of fantasy and the man is willing to be accountable to a peer about his fantasy, the counselee is likely to be safe. If the man dwells on this fantasy to touch with sexual *intention,* then the relationship has become risky. If he begins to act on this fantasy, helping ceases and trouble begins. While fantasy is common for the natural man, the Christian helper is called to yield that natural desire to the Lordship of Jesus Christ—to maintain purity in thought and attitude as well as in behavior.

If helpers do not get their thought life under control, they may not be able to stop fantasizing about the counselee even when they are away from her. Disclosing the sexual struggle to a trusted colleague—becoming accountable and working through this fantasy process—can be vital for the counselor's growth and learning. It is best that a supervisor or colleague help discover what "her image represents to him,"[29] what steps are necessary to control acting-out, and how to resolve the inner dynamics of the struggle.

If the helper does not take this action toward prevention and professional growth, it is very likely that he will only intensify the fantasy and the need to act upon it. This may move the invasion from the visual to the verbal—asking the counselee about her sex life, asking if she has fantasies about the helper, or telling her the fantasies the helper is having about her. As Rutter points out, "When a man inquires about a woman's sex life because it serves his fantasy about her, he is already beginning to exploit her [and this] . . . represents a proposition in disguise."[30]

The helper will move further and deeper if not checked, acting to close the physical space between himself and the counselee and monitoring the counselee's reaction. This becomes a clear physical step of invasiveness, as the helper tests the fantasy in a concrete way, hoping the counselee will not resist and will find him irresistible. Beginning forms of touch, including affectionate hugs, may also be used as a test of responsiveness to physical violation.

Attempting to Redefine the Sexual Barrier. The next steps in succumbing to forbidden sex are the helper's attempts to redefine his relationships in order to justify crossing wrongful barriers. By becoming overtly suggestive, the helper hopes for a welcome response. If there is none, this is still safe enough to argue that the counselee misunderstood his actions. These actions can be verbal and/or nonverbal, yet they are arguably nonsexual and more easily denied if sexual intent is confronted. Rutter points out that an "erotic intoxication" takes place in this process that blurs the helper's clear thinking. This intoxication fosters an ability to cross from the professional role to the personal, thus sustaining the denial process and shielding the natural yearnings with the lies of the helper's need to be ethical.

If the helper harbors an illicit fantasy life about the counselee—having a sexual encounter with an attractive woman other than one's spouse—restraint will become even more difficult. A man may deceive himself here and lie by denying his own seduction. He may claim he became sexually involved because of the woman's need and further assert that refusal would have injured her self-esteem. On the other hand, he may claim that to have denied the woman would only have provoked her, producing some other disastrous results (to which we encourage consideration of Joseph in Genesis 39). As this seduction process continues, the man must deal with conflict within his internal values. Since most men who violate are not sociopathic but are men of some morality and integrity, the moral struggle to violate revolves around three quandaries:

1. Practical considerations: Can I get away with it? What will it cost me? At this point most men may minimize cost, arguing that the likelihood of being caught is minimal. A helper in an empty marriage may justify the actions, judging the

cost of his marriage (even the cost of divorce) to be worth paying.

2. Emotional considerations: The great deception of emotional reasoning asks, "How can something that feels so strong and good be wrong?" The intoxication of illicit sex can be so powerful that it is easy to believe it is right. This reinforces the fallacy of being untouchable by the outside world or that this relationship is so important it is worth any risk. It is also easy to deceive oneself into believing that a sexual relationship will be good for the woman.

3. Moral considerations—the last hurdle: The voice of conscience is hard to still. The final barrier for a man close to violation is the moral sense that to go ahead would violate what is right. The vulnerable violator must deny, distort, or drown out the moral voice that asserts, "SEXUAL PURSUIT HERE IS WRONG!"

Dispensing with the Barrier Altogether. Once the helper dispenses with the barriers to illicit sex, the only obstacle remaining is how to get the woman to go along with his agenda. The helper who waives all restraint and decides to move ahead becomes intoxicated by the apparent freedom to fulfill the fantasy and by the excitement of the danger involved. Counseling is lost as the helper becomes charged by the unrestrained fantasy and the challenge of the conquest.

Following revelation of the personal/sexual interest, numerous kinds of violative action may be revealed. Some helpers may even talk to the counselee about the suspect morality of sexual involvement but still proceed to become sexually involved. There may be ongoing struggles with conscience or little struggle at all. Some mixed vulnerable-predatory violators may even keep coming back and discussing the moral issues over and over again, even as they are repeatedly sexual. These men have lost concern for the immoral and destructive impact of their wrongdoing as they engage in an absurd drama over the paradox and conflicts of the divided self.

There may be attempts to establish a separate personal relationship outside of the professional one, for example by asking for dates or arranging a meeting outside the office. Others will terminate a professional relationship in order to become intimate. The wrongfulness is recognized, so they attempt to cover by terminating counseling in order exploit the sexual dimension of the relationship. This is done without genuine consideration of the impact upon the woman. In this state of intoxication the helper may even promise to divorce his present spouse and marry the counselee. It is almost impossible for a vulnerable woman who longs to feel special to resist this kind of promise from one who is perceived as powerful and attractive.

CONCLUSION

Helpers who violate others sexually and those who are violated should not be simplistically categorized because a wide spectrum of individuals and dynamics are involved. We have recognized, however, that there are identifiable patterns in both victim and offenders that must be more clearly understood. And understanding must lead to effective action against this plague. We must address the ethical, preventative, and remedial issues carefully and expeditiously if we are going to be able to hinder the advance of evil perpetrated within the context of counseling ministries.

NOTES

1. Tim LaHaye, *If Ministers Fall, Can They Be Restored?* (Grand Rapids: Zondervan, 1990), 139, quoting from Jack Hayford's book *Restoring Fallen Leaders* (Ventura, Calif.: Regal Books, 1988).

2. See Kenneth S. Pope, "Sexual Involvement Between Therapists and Patients," *The Harvard Mental Health Letter* 11, no. 8 (1994): 5–6; and Laura Markowitz, "Crossing the Line: Who Protects Clients from Their Protectors," *The Family Therapy Networker* (November-December 1992): 25–31.

3. George Ohlschlager and Peter Mosgofian, *Law for the Christian Counselor: A Guidebook for Clinicians and Pastors* (Dallas: Word, 1992), 61–63.

4. See Janet Sonne and Kenneth S. Pope, "Treating Victims of Therapist-Patient Sexual Involvement," *Psychotherapy* 28, no. 1 (1991): table 2, at 183. Our profile is not meant to convey that there is but one type of abuser. Pope reveals ten abuse orientations around the themes of power, anger, and sadism.

5. Henry Virkler, "When Temptation Knocks: Reducing Your Vulnerability," *Christian Counseling Today* 2 (Summer 1994): 41; also Henry Virkler, *Broken Promises* (Dallas: Word, 1992).

6. Peter Rutter, *Sex in the Forbidden Zone* (Los Angeles: Jeremy P. Tarcher, Inc., 1989), 2.

7. G. Lloyd Rediger, *Ministry and Sexuality: Cases, Counseling and Care* (Minneapolis: Fortress, 1990), 122.

8. See Pope, "Sexual Involvement," 5–6; and Gary Schoener et al., *Psychotherapists' Sexual Involvement with Clients: Intervention and Prevention* (Minneapolis: Walk-In Counseling Center, 1989).

9. Virkler, "When Temptation Knocks," 39.

10. Marie Fortune, *Is Nothing Sacred?* (New York: HarperCollins, 1989).

11. Rutter, *Forbidden Zone*, 22.

12. Robert Hicks, *The Masculine Journey: Understanding the Six Stages of Manhood* (Colorado Springs, Colo.: NavPress, 1993), 41.

13. Rutter, *Forbidden Zone*, 7.

14. J. Allan Petersen, *The Myth of the Greener Grass* (Wheaton: Tyndale, 1983), 32.

15. Virkler, "When Temptation Knocks," 41.

16. See N. Gartrell, et al., "Psychiatrist-Patient Sexual Contact: Results of a National Survey, I: Prevalence," *American Journal of Psychiatry* 143, no. 9 (1986): 1126–31; N. Gartrell, et al., "Reporting Practices of Psychiatrists Who Knew of Sexual Misconduct of Colleagues," *American Journal of Orthopsychiatry* 57 (1987): 287–95.

17. Judd Marmor, "Some Psychodynamic Aspects of the Seduction of Patients in Psychotherapy," *The American Journal of Psychoanalysis* 36 (1976): 319–23.

18. Simply stated, transference is the process of placing hope, intense feelings, and unresolved needs regarding significant people onto the helper. These people can include parents, parent figures, and possibly one's current spouse and/or lover. Countertransference is the response one makes back to the counselee as an expression of one's own unmet needs and hopes. Much of this process is unconscious on the part of the persons involved. However, it is critical that the helper accepts the reality of transference and countertransference, makes it part of his or her conscious awareness, and acts ethically to protect the valid expression of transference in the helping process.

19. Rutter, *Forbidden Zone*, 5.

20. Ibid., 20, italics added.

21. Pope, "Sexual Involvement." 14.

22. Rutter, *Forbidden Zone*, 6.

23. Ibid., 94.

24. LaHaye, *If Ministers Fall*, 42.

25. Rediger, *Ministry and Sexuality*, provides an excellent discussion of this factor, outlining in more detail the issues involved.

26. Ibid., 16.

27. Ibid., 18.

28. Rutter, *Forbidden Zone*.

29. Ibid., 140.

30. Ibid.

Chapter Five

Helping Adult Victims of Sexual Misconduct

I don't know why I am writing this down. I'll die if anyone ever sees this, but I have no one to talk to. I just can't bring myself to tell anyone. I would be out of ministry in a flash if anyone ever knew. I keep trying to change this drive to be with women, to make love with them—as many as possible. I am never really satisfied. But even when I restrain myself, there is always someone who entices me and draws me into her net. There are so many women who just want to be close to me, who don't even resist my touching. It is incredible. I don't understand why they don't resist if they are supposed to know it is not okay.

Very few men care for women the way I do. They tell me how their husbands are so insensitive and cruel. It amazes me how these men could be so thoughtless with their wives. They are so insensitive and hard with sex (they call it lovemaking); no wonder the women come to me for help. I take such good care of them, and I am kind when I make love. It is making love. But sometimes, like today, I wonder if God wants me to stop. I still can't believe how hurt and enraged my client was today when she found out she was not the only one. Oh God, I hope she doesn't report me. . . .

EVERY WOMAN WHO SEEKS COUNSELING from a male helper is vulnerable to sexual misconduct. Again, we do not imply that all men are abusers or that women cannot trust male therapists—we make this assertion in view of the universality of our fallen natures and the inherent risks of male-female relations. The female counselee is challenged to open her deep secrets and deal with those areas of life that are normally not open to others. Sexual thoughts, feelings, fantasies, fear, shame, and guilt about sexual impulses and memories are things that are talked about in psychotherapy. These things pull at the hearts of vulnerable helpers and can tempt the arousal of male counselors who hear them.

The inherent power imbalance of counseling relationships—exaggerated when the counselor is a man and the client a woman—creates special duties to protect the client's dignity. As one writer aptly noted, "The dynamics of the [sexual] forbidden zone can render a woman unable to *withhold* consent."[1] Another writer, in recalling her experience of sexual violation, stated, "I remember walking into Dr. X's office feeling absolutely humiliated that I needed psychological help and, at the same time, feeling out of control emotionally."[2] This vulnerable emotional state can be easily manipulated by therapists who try to seduce or play upon the needs of clients.

We respect the evidence that sexual contact in counseling is almost exclusively a problem of male violators and female victims—about 85 percent of all cases. We emphasize this pattern here to explain our woman-centered treatment outline. We do not mean to imply that women do not abuse or that men and children are not victims. These things are more fully addressed in chapters 6–8.

VICTIMS AT RISK

Diane was twenty-nine years old when she was molested by a well-known Christian therapist. A Christian since high school, Diane was intelligent, sensitive, attractive, and more shy and codependent than assertive in relationships. She had been struggling with depression for several months following the break-up of her second engagement.

Eventually, Diane decided to seek professional help with a respected Christian counselor. Dr. Warm was an ordained pastor and a licensed professional counselor. Diane remembers walking into his office with strong feelings of ambivalence—feeling humiliated because she needed counseling but also fascinated by the prospect of therapy, wondering what it would be like, if it would help.

Dr. Warm was a gentle and kindly man in his late forties who accepted Diane and affirmed her decision to enter counseling. Since her sleep and appetite were disrupted, he referred her to her family physician for a mild antidepressant. Dr. Warm encouraged Diane to talk honestly and fully about her struggles, fears, griefs, and hopes. Although he probed her views and challenged some beliefs, he never seemed to condemn or shame her for her misbehavior, bad feelings, or wrong thinking. Diane assumed without question that his interest would be in helping her to get well. She felt like a child around Dr. Warm, struggling to survive emotionally, searching for answers.

Diane was delighted to be able to talk honestly about her failures and struggles to an authoritative Christian without feeling guilty or condemned. She trusted

Dr. Warm and worked with him, making genuine strides toward recovery. Soon after beginning the medication, her sleep and appetite improved and within several months her depression started to lift. Her hope for the future was renewed, and she became more engaged with life. Diane began to feel like a good Christian and a decent human being. This success served to deepen her trust and dependence on Dr. Warm's help.

One day Diane came to therapy with a disturbing dream. She was quite upset and believed that Dr. Warm would dismiss her and end the counseling relationship. With much trepidation she told him her dream reminded her that she had been sexually molested numerous times by a neighborhood teenager when she was eleven and twelve years old. She was extremely ashamed and even tried to leave the session early to escape the pain she felt. At that crucial point, Dr. Warm stood up and walked over to Diane, asked her to stand, and proceeded to hug her and let her sob into his shoulder. Diane was so relieved. She yielded and cried deeply into his shoulder as if he were the father she could never tell about her painful and shameful experiences.

After this, Dr. Warm suggested that they shift the focus of their therapy to help her recall these molest experiences so that God might heal her of the trauma and its effect on her current relationships. Diane remembers feeling afraid to do this. She feared what she might discover about her past, expecting to be overwhelmed by it. Dr. Warm reassured her that her fears were common, and although inner healing work is sometimes painful, he would not allow her to be hurt.

At their next session, Dr. Warm had Diane lay on his couch, close her eyes, and pray for God's protection and healing. He guided her through some exercises to help her relax and then began to touch various nonsexual parts of her body, explaining that this was necessary to help her recall and release the abuse pain associated with those parts. Diane stiffened and told Dr. Warm that she was afraid—that this was very difficult for her. Dr. Warm immediately stopped and reassured her that this difficulty was normal and that she would eventually get over it. He ended the session by challenging Diane to think and pray about whether they should move to this deeper level of therapy.

Diane recalls that the time between these sessions was maddening for her. She was convinced she had offended Dr. Warm and was again afraid that he would terminate therapy. She was angry with herself for worrying about Dr. Warm's intentions. She convinced herself that she was the one who had evil thoughts about his sexual intentions and that she needed to learn to trust and overcome her hang-ups. Dr. Warm had always been so kind and helpful, had never done her any wrong, and was so respectful of her fears and moral boundaries. Besides, he was a Christian, a married man with three children—surely he was not interested in her sexually!

Diane was eager to see Dr. Warm and apologize to him, to reaffirm her commitment to go forward with their work. She was pleased and relieved that Dr. Warm responded so positively to her assertions. He praised her for her courage and reassured her that most women had such fears and resistance. He made her feel special, like she was a pioneer, an empowered woman who no longer allowed her fears to paralyze her growth and maturity. Many weeks went by as Diane complied with this therapeutic process, learned to relax, deepened her trust in Dr. Warm, and began to derive further benefit from the process.

Then, six months after her therapy began, everything started to fall apart in the space of one fifty-minute session, which Dr. Warm had scheduled last in his day. After he had Diane lay back and relax in this session, his body-touching process moved to her breasts. Diane was stunned and immobilized. She did not speak a word or utter a sound. He began to kiss her gently, first on the forehead and cheeks, then on her mouth. He spoke to her gently, soothingly, telling her that this was all part of the deeper therapeutic process.

As Dr. Warm continued to soothingly but very carefully massage past her sexual boundaries, she fiercely tried to concentrate on the therapeutic goal—an impossible task. She remembers her mind screaming, "Stop, STOP, STOP IT!!" but she was silent and frozen. She felt as if she weighed tons and was pinned to the couch by some super heavy force. She finally began to make some whimpering noises that caused Dr. Warm to stop. He seemed distressed but tried to reassure her that he had her best intentions at heart and that this would help. Diane does not remember exactly how she fled his office, but she does remember him telling her to return to therapy and not to tell anyone what had happened.

The week after this incident Diane lived in a surreal fog. Her thoughts raced, her sleep was erratic and her dreams disturbed, her work and concentration were constantly distracted, and her emotions were going crazy. She still vividly recalls her intense moral and emotional conflict. She was amazed at the experience of utter fear and revulsion mingled with the excitement of her vulnerability and the intense clinging trust that she refused to give up.

Diane told no one what happened, uncertain whether she was motivated by Dr. Warm's plea or by the impossible thought that no one would believe such an absurd story anyway. She fiercely denied attributing any sexual intent to Dr. Warm and again assumed that something was wrong with her. He had always, ALWAYS been so kind, gracious, caring, and respectful. The thought intruded constantly, but she refused to believe that he would use her sexually. Her heart and mind could not stand the terrible thought.

She returned to Dr. Warm, yielding to the therapy process in the desperate hope that he would prove her worst thoughts about him wrong. She wanted to conclude her therapy and desperately wanted to believe that Dr. Warm really was concerned for her and was not out for his own pleasure. She recalls now that it was strange they never discussed what had happened in the previous session; they just moved right to the procedure. Diane now believes that she was too afraid to talk and have him prove her worst thoughts about him. She also believes he thought that her lack of protest meant that she consented to his sexual advances. This was the second hidden and dishonest interaction in their counseling sessions. Combined with the sexual wrong, this signalled the demise of their therapeutic relationship.

Instead, their relationship descended into an evil sexual deception—a progressive spiritual, psychological, and criminal abuse. During that next session, Dr. Warm moved from touching her breasts to squeezing and fondling them, from kissing her on the mouth to forcing his tongue inside it, and to stroking her thighs, pubic mound, and buttocks. Again, she screamed in her mind for him to stop. She said nothing, however, and he did not stop for the entire session.

Diane went completely numb that day—the "black day," as she recalls. She was not just stunned and silent nor immobilized physically, but regressing into a state of dissociation. She had begun to shut down emotionally and to feel the strange surreal terror of her mind and emotions cut off from her body.

Diane continued to meet with Dr. Warm for several more months as he became progressively more sexually involved with her. She recalls about a dozen sexual encounters. Robot-like she complied with his requests to wear tight dresses and sexy underwear, yielding to degrading and often painful sexual acts. They never again talked about her therapy or about God, or anything other than sexual instructions, comments, and praises. Their entire time together for "therapy" became consumed by sex—and he continued to charge her, and she continued to pay her full fee.

From the first day that he had touched her sexually, Diane began to deteriorate into the deep depression she had only so recently begun to escape. She suffered this and far more—a progressively numbing and confusing dissociation, identity disturbance, guilt and shame, and a self-loathing that shouted a terrible inner condemnation like she had never known. She was convinced she was going crazy, abandoned by God, and that her life and most trusted values were completely upside-down. Yet she could tell no one what she was experiencing, and she would not risk letting Dr. Warm know her true feelings, convinced he would abandon her.

Diane withdrew into herself and wallowed deeper and deeper into a pit of despair. She was contemplating suicide when Dr. Warm abruptly terminated her counseling. She desperately tried to call him to beg to continue or at least have an explanation for his behavior, but he never returned her calls. Her sense of hopelessness and worthlessness were acute. For two weeks, Diane hovered on the edge of suicide, overwhelmed by her loss and blaming herself for it. Finally one night, she mechanically swallowed nearly twenty sleeping pills and awoke dangerously sick and confused in an acute psychiatric emergency center.

While in the hospital her pastor came to see her and, racking with guilty sobs, she poured out the whole sordid story to him. She was stunned when he told her another client of Dr. Warm had filed suit against him for similar practices and that he was under investigation by the state licensing board. Diane's pastor helped her get immediate support and take constructive action to overcome her crisis. She renewed therapy with an experienced woman who worked professionally with sexual abuse victims. Both her pastor and therapist helped her take legal action against her abuser and, once again, she commenced the long process of healing and reconstructing her life.

THE HARM SUFFERED

Significant personal, marital, social, and financial harm is suffered by most people who are involved sexually through a helping relationship. This is true for both victim and abuser, though the frequency and degree of victim's harm is usually much greater. One writer reviewed the empirical research and concluded that "serious harm result[ed] to almost all patients sexually involved with their therapists."[3] A study of California psychologists[4] who worked with clients who had been involved sexually with former therapists reported that 90 percent of these victims had suffered adverse effects. Eleven percent required hospitalization, and 1 percent had committed suicide. Suicidal ideation is common, as is loss of spouse or support networks (often because of divorce, shame, self-blame, or even the suicide of a spouse).

Other studies reinforce the evidence of significant harm. This includes depression, emotional disturbance, sexual dysfunction, guilt, shame, impaired social adjustment, increased drug and alcohol abuse, major weight gain or loss, marital conflict, divorce, and the inability to use subsequent therapy.[5] In addition, some of these victims suffer from post-traumatic stress disorder (PTSD) and various forms of dissociation, including some with multiple personality disorder (MPD). Abuse victims experience great difficulty in talking about the trauma because they are afraid of being blamed or they fear that their self-blaming judgments will be validated. It has been suggested that, "Nearly all victims of sexual abuse by professionals report experiences of shock, suppression of the memory, guilt about their own falsely presumed responsibility, and worry that no one would believe their report of abuse."[6] Women who are sexually abused in therapy have significantly more mistrust and anger toward men, including problems of mistrust and aversion toward their husbands.

We agree that "most women who have had exploitive sexual relationships experience a deep wound to their most inner, sacred sense of self. This psychological injury—often felt as the death of hope itself—remains the greatest casualty of sex in the forbidden zone."[7] This betrayal of hope lies at the heart of the crushing impact of sexual misconduct with a Christian helper. The woman, who already felt so needy, has her worst fears confirmed by a pastor or professional Christian helper: she is only valued as a sexual object. Because of the sexual violation, the women concludes in her heart that she is worthless to God and to others. Her "good" Christian helper confirms for her the worst lies: that she is good for nothing. She believes she can only expect to be used and abused, that she is beyond all hope of healing.

Marie Fortune recognized that even more is at stake in these corrupting relationships.

> Spiritually, victimization by a [Christian helper] has a profound effect. . . . Not only is the victimization experienced as a betrayal of what should have been a trust relationship, but . . . it is experienced as a betrayal by God. . . . The pastor/pastoral counselor . . . has access to the spiritual core of a person's being, perhaps a person's truest self. This access carries with it a dimension of power exceeding that of the secular therapist as well as an even greater potential for abuse. . . . If a woman feels . . . betrayed by God, the foundation of her relationship with God is shaken. If, in addition, the church does little or nothing in response to her call for help, then she may readily conclude that neither God nor the church body is available in her suffering. Then when her anger and rage do surface, not surprisingly they are frequently directed toward God and the church. This emotional crisis is also a crisis of faith that may lead to complete abandonment of a faith life and of anything to do with the institutional church. The way to reconcile the relationship with God or the church is not easy and must be grounded in an experience of justice for the person betrayed.[8]

Far too many people minimize the impact of sexual abuse on women, including sexual misconduct in the professional arena. For most women the impact of this harm is deep and debilitating, validating Rediger's assertion that "it is almost impossible for anyone who has not been victimized sexually to comprehend the enormity of the experience."[9]

CLINICAL ASSESSMENT PRINCIPLES

The identification and treatment of sexual exploitation is a complex endeavor, a problem usually enmeshed with many other issues in the victim's life. Although abuse issues are a key reason many people seek counseling, clients abused by a previous counselor often do not disclose this abuse to subsequent counselors. Some sexual abuse victims, due to the great shame and confusion related to the exploitation, are unable to ask for help or even to admit the truth about the abuse.

Commonly, abuse victims will come into therapy grieving a loss or expressing confusion and difficulty in making sense out of things. They are usually acutely aware of strong feelings of shame, rage, guilt, fear, or depression. They may talk about deep distrust of themselves and of others, their ambivalent thoughts and feelings about the offending therapist, and sometimes about suicide. It is important for counselors to deliberately question, explore, and assess this area to ensure that the issue of prior abuse will be fully and competently addressed.

STRUCTURED EVALUATION

Leupker advocates a structured assessment interview with known and suspected sexual misconduct victims. The therapist should move the client backward in time from immediate needs, to the therapy abuse, and finally to earlier life experiences and how they may be related to the therapy abuse itself. . . . The assessment interview should explore the following:

- current problems, needs, suicide risk;
- specific history of counseling abuse (who did what to whom, when, and how);
- meaning of the counseling abuse to the client;
- neglect/exacerbation of original problems by the counseling abuse;
- previous functioning and earlier life history;
- relation of earlier life themes to counseling abuse as perceived by the client;
- identification of intervention needs and resources.[10]

To this excellent outline we would add exploration of the impact of the abuse on one's relationship to God and to the church. Also, it would be important to explore spiritual needs and to consider what practical resources are available through the network of Christian counselors and church relationships. Adapting Leupker's model further, we encourage structured use of the following queries when seeking information about the sexual exploitation.

Stage 1: From the beginning of counseling to the initiation of sexual exploitation. What led you to seek counseling? How did you choose this counselor? How did counseling proceed initially? What worked and what did not work? How did you feel about the counselor and his work initially?

Stage 2: From the beginning of the sexual exploitation to the end of the relationship. When did the sexual involvement begin? What happened, exactly? How did it start? How did you feel about it initially? How far did the sexual behavior proceed? What happened to your view of yourself, of God, your marriage, the counselor? Was there any true counseling work after sexual relations began? Have sexual relations ended? If not, what is still going on sexually and relationally? If sexually relations ended, how did they end? How did/do you feel about terminating sexual relations?

Stage 3: From the termination of relations to the present. Has counseling been terminated? If not, what is the nature of continued relations? If so, how was it ended? Was it terminated to continue the relationship? How do you feel about the relationship ending? Do you sometimes wish the relationship were still going on? Were there any other ways in which you felt abused or taken advantage of? What has happened to the main problem you brought to counseling? What is your view now of the counselor and of this whole experience?

Assessing Serious Disorders

Some victims experience severe distress, requiring assessment of post-traumatic stress disorder (PTSD), severe mood disorders, demonization, and various states of dissociation, including multiple personality disorder (MPD). While it is beyond the scope of this work to detail the etiology and treatment of these disorders, we do want to outline characteristic symptoms so that counselors can recognize evidence of these disorders and, if necessary, *refer counselees or congregants to professionals skilled in the treatment of these more severe disorders.*

In his excellent work on MPD,[11] psychiatrist Frank Putnam outlines the continuum of dissociation (events as mild as daydreaming to states as pathological as MPD) as being largely traumatically induced. He believes these disorders are adaptive coping mechanisms. They serve to protect the traumatized individual from the worst suffering, allowing ongoing management of the trauma and daily-life stressors. He suggests that post-traumatic stress is closely related to these disorders; we recognize PTSD as part of a number of related disturbances we will call trauma response disorders (TRDs). Besides PTSD and MPD, other TRDs include psychogenic amnesia, depersonalization disorders, derealization, demonization, out-of-body experiences, and trance-like states of confusion and disorientation, whether mild or severe.

Dissociation is a disturbance of identity ("I don't know who I am") or memory ("I can't remember anything about that"). Depersonalization, derealization, and out-of-body experiences reflect identity dissociation. The familiar perception of one's self is distorted, strange, unreal, disconnected from the body, often causing the person marked distress. The sexploitation victim might report, for example, "It was so bizarre to be in that situation that I felt I was outside myself watching us have sex." Memory dissociation is exemplified by psychogenic amnesia—the controversial repressed memory experience of sexual abuse victims (addressed more fully in chapter 6). Loss of memory may be localized and selective, or more generalized, covering a long period of time in the person's life.

Post-traumatic stress is characterized by reliving—not just simple recalling—the traumatic event in a way that produces intense distress, strong avoidance behavior, emotional numbing, and a hypervigilant arousal that keeps one on guard and on edge. Phenomenologically, it seems the opposite experience of the amnesic: intense reliving of the abuse versus profound forgetting. It is commonly reported in the mental health community that many amnesics experience PTSD when lost memories of the abuse return abruptly to one's consciousness. PTSD symptoms include the following:

- flashbacks
- disturbing dreams
- re-experiences of trauma that are recurrent and intensive
- strong avoidance behavior
- amnesic reactions to stimuli associated with the trauma
- difficulty with sleep and concentration
- irritability
- problems with relationships
- hypervigilence
- an exaggerated startle response

Multiple personality disorder is the extreme dissociative response to trauma. In nearly all cases, and in other severe TRDs, there is likely a history of childhood sexual or physical abuse. Simply, MPD is the existence of two or more distinct personalities in the same person (known as alters), wherein at least two of these alters recurrently take full control of the person's behavior. Putnam refers to MPD as "one of the most amazing and unusual mental conditions known. The existence of apparently separate and autonomous alter personalities, exchanging control over an individual's behavior, elicits intense fascination in some and protests of disbelief in others."[12]

Dissociation vs. Demonization. Christian counselors must also acknowledge and treat the reality of demonization in some severe cases. Some types of sexual abuse, especially ritualistic abuse, are doorways to demonic influence. Much controversy exists about these dynamics, including questions of their very existence and the difficulty of distinguishing spiritual and psychiatric processes. Our view is that demonization and MPD are separate realities with "differential diagnoses and treatments," although they sometimes happen concurrently and must be jointly treated.

Diagnostically, it can be extremely difficult to distinguish demons from alter personalities, a task we believe calls for Spirit-empowered gifts of discernment and wisdom.[13] We also believe that MPD is rarer than the popular resurgence of interest is indicating; MPD labels are being wrongly attached to more common and less severe forms of dissociation. Treatment problems are further complicated by the need to refer and interact with other service and ministry providers. It can be quite a challenge to work with unbelievers—mental health professionals who reject the reality of demonic forces. On the other hand, pastors and Christians can tend to spiritualize all disorders, rejecting the reality of severe psychiatric conditions. We are concerned about counselors who inaccurately diagnose either by denying MPD and falsely demonizing the presence of alters or by denying demons altogether, deceived when they present themselves in the guise of an alter.

CLINICAL TREATMENT PRINCIPLES

A woman's sexual victimization is a serious matter and likely the most important issue in her treatment plan. Schoener reports that victims most frequently cite two things that are helpful in treatment: (1) talking with other victims about the experience and (2) taking some sort of professional/ethical/legal action against the abuser.[14]

As with all Christian therapy, integrity is the road and love is the fuel that begets the miracle of recovery and renewal in Christ. Certainly a key part of the Gospel message is that Jesus came "to preach good news to the poor . . . to proclaim freedom for prisoners . . . to release the oppressed" (Luke 4:18–19). Sexual abuse victims must also hear and finally receive the good news of liberty from oppression. It is crucial that Christian counselors be highly skilled or willing to refer to skilled counselors who can genuinely help women recover from such violations.

EMPOWERING WOMEN TO GUARD SEXUAL BOUNDARIES

Counselors should help women learn to define and guard sexual boundaries in all ministerial and professional relationships. This includes recognizing ethical boundaries, learning to effectively monitor these boundaries, and defending the boundaries through personal actions that challenge any breach, including making legal or ethical complaints. Sharing vital legal and ethical information, combined with personal support, can help a woman believe that her abusing helper was at fault and that feelings of violation are valid. Tragically, less than 5 percent of all sexually abused women report these violations, and as many as 50 percent do not know that it is unethical and illegal for a professional man to be sexually involved with his client.[15]

Therefore, the first and constant rule of counseling sexually abused women is to help them understand that "it is always the therapist's responsibility to ensure that sexual contact with the patient never occurs."[16] No matter how seductive the client is with her counselor, no matter what consent she may give or what desire for sex she might express, it is always the counselor's responsibility to avoid sexual misconduct. Furthermore, the constant, overarching objective of treatment is to help empower women to guard and ultimately to be in charge of their own sexual lives—to enable them to challenge men and institutions to respect their sexual boundaries in all situations.

CHOOSING THE BEST TREATMENT MODALITY

There are six types of interventions for victims of sexual misconduct:

1. crisis intervention
2. psychiatric consultation
3. supportive advocacy
4. individual therapy
5. group therapy (and lay support groups)
6. marriage/family therapy

These treatment modes are often used in combination, either concurrently or as needed at different stages throughout the healing process. In our agency, we emphasize an integrated individual/group model with the other modalities used as they may be needed.

Individual therapy is indicated for victims who want one-on-one work and are fearful of the group process. For those in groups concurrently, individual work is helpful to address more directly issues that are stirred up in the group process. Individual therapy may also be best (or individual/group) for those with more severe disorders or with multiple diagnoses (showing other mood, dissociation, sexual, identity, substance abuse, or personality disorders).

Groups are indicated for those who tend to isolate socially and would benefit from others who have suffered in similar ways. Groups may also feel safer to those who have generalized their trauma so that they mistrust any type of individual therapy or find it too intense. For those who are emotionally paralyzed by the trauma and have great difficulty finding the words to express their experience, groups that model proper disclosure and allow time to come out can be very beneficial. Groups are usually not indicated for severe personality disorders, especially borderline disorders, nor for those with severe childhood abuse histories or strong impulse control and interpersonal boundary problems.

Crisis intervention and psychiatric consultation for medication and hospitalization assistance are sometimes necessary for those overwhelmed by the abuse, especially if they suffer any trauma response disorder. Advocacy, in a sense, is like crisis intervention in that it gives close assistance and support to those filing complaints and taking public action against perpetrators. The disclosure of sexploitation can often throw marriage and family relations into turmoil and may require intensive intervention due to the stresses placed on the relationship system.

COMMON PROBLEMS AND SUGGESTED RESPONSES

First Things First. As always in counseling, it is important to focus on crisis issues first and not to fixate on the abuse. Other problems in the victim's life may be more pressing, and the victim may be better able to address them initially rather than the abuse. Marriage and family relations can be chaotic following disclosure of the misconduct (especially public media exposure) and may demand initial stabilizing intervention. It might be helpful to conduct or arrange for a comprehensive psychological evaluation. It is also helpful to encourage the victim to read appropriate literature and to become involved with victim support groups.

Relaxing and Being Clear. It is vital that the counselor demonstrate ease with the problem—giving clear, matter-of-fact, noncoercive permission to address the abuse. An appropriate and clearly written treatment plan should be developed with the client. This plan serves as a reference to check progress with the counselee, helping her gain renewed confidence while demystifying the counseling endeavor. We have found it helpful to encourage the victim to journal her recovery, sometimes even to artistically draw it out. The victim can also write letters challenging the abuser and complaining to agencies of church, profession, or state. (The process of writing and acting out how to challenge the abuse is helpful whether such letters are delivered or not.)

Controlling Biases. Assumptions and biases are common in counseling, but when working with abuse victims these must be left outside the consulting room. The counselor must avoid presuming the horror of the abuse, or the terrible effect on the victim, or who did what to whom. The behavior and experience of sexual misconduct is extremely varied, and your client will surprise you if you let your presumptions about abuse control your approach to intervention. Schoener suggests that this counseling can be "the ultimate countertransference trap"—with helpers tripped up by the need to be perfect, by a strong compassion to help, by assuming the "rage" of the victim, and by an excessive desire to undo the harm of sexual abuse.[17]

Blaming the Victim and Self-blame. Frequently, women victims are blamed (and often blame themselves) for wanting or not preventing the sexual misconduct. (We discuss the systemic and patriarchal roots of this in other chapters.) A victim's state of mind—a belief that her sexual struggle or seduction *caused* the counselor to become sexual—is reinforced by this victim-blaming attack. Worse yet, some therapists tend to approach women as helpless victims in need of a cure—a condescending and parental approach that is more harmful than helpful. The victim needs to understand why she became a victim and must learn that seductiveness, apparent consent, and sexual arousal are *not* valid reasons to believe the victimization was justified or inevitable.

Safety and Vulnerability. Discussion of the abuse and of more general sexual issues is fraught with emotional difficulty, so the counselor must be clear about its presentation and limits. The client must feel free to disclose the abuse and describe what happened; the helper must listen carefully and not crowd the victim since feeling safe is essential for her. When a client opens up to a therapist about sexual betrayal by a previous counselor, it is a moment of extreme vulnerability; the fear of further betrayal is acute. Bates writes in this regard, "Though I wanted to trust others, I could not overcome my fear of being emotionally maligned again."[18] This willingness to become vulnerable again must be affirmed and fostered. Disclosures that trigger powerful feelings of shame, guilt, and avoidance must be praised as courageous and encouraged to come forth.

Renewing Trust. Understandably, many sexual abuse victims find it difficult to trust in male counselors. There are often feelings of hopelessness, despair, and a deep distrust of one's own and other's perceptions and judgments. Rutter comments that "the expectations about therapy and the ability to form a trusting relationship have been altered, often drastically, by the trauma of the sexualized relationship with the former therapist. Thus, for example, the transference that forms in the subsequent therapy is often extremely intense, ambivalent, and confusing."[19]

This raises a valid question about the selection of a woman therapist. We believe that a male counselor can be valuable for a violated woman, helping her work through the intense transference of male violation. However, we recognize that most victims request and need a female counselor following victimization by a male helper. Whether male or female, the counselor is challenged to be slow to judge and careful to avoid expressly challenging the victim into a relationship of trust. Instead, the counselor must be quick to extend patience and give permission to the victim to talk openly about her therapeutic trust issues. The new helper must reassure the victim, frequently and in different ways, that none of the destructive behaviors of the harmful mentor will recur. This process of building trust is a difficult and time-consuming process that must develop naturally without coercion.

Respecting Sexual and Physical Boundaries. Since broken trust is a central issue in these cases, the helper must be especially careful about crossing boundaries of sexual discussion, touching, and hugging. Backing away from the interaction as an immediate response to troubled sexual exchanges is essential in these counseling situations. It gives the client room to retreat to safety and to discuss the rules for discussion of emotionally charged material. Male counselors, especially, should adhere to a policy of no touching, no hugging, and no intrusive talks. Even female counselors need to be careful about the boundaries of touch with female victims and should not assume they can act safely here because of their gender.[20]

CLINICAL TREATMENT PROCESS

Pope and Bouhoutsos suggest seven issues that need to be resolved in the process of counseling a sexual abuse victim: (1) ambivalence, (2) anger, (3) guilt, (4) depression and suicide risk, (5) isolation, (6) sexual confusion, and (7) cognitive dysfunction.[21] To their list we have added a number of issues for Christian counselors to address.

Accepting Ambivalence. A key challenge to treatment is understanding the client's ambivalence toward her former helper. Pope notes that, "In most instances it seems to take a long time and great effort and tenacity for patients to work through their extremely deep contradictory feelings."[22] Like a child who has been sexually violated by a father, the adult victim often struggles to believe that this helper really did harm *on purpose* and that she is not to blame.

For many women the process of sexual violation is intertwined with strong loving emotions. The intense mixed-up experience of "love" with the abuser conflicts with the toxic truth of manipulation and betrayal. As a result, admission of harm may waiver as the victim progresses in counseling. The power of this ambivalence demands the utmost respect as the counselor helps the victim to break away emotionally and to see the violation truthfully.

A counselee's loving or romantic feelings for the abusive helper may not make logical sense to the observer but are a common paradox that must be handled sensitively. Schoener wisely cautions against the false assumption that an abused counselee must always be angry about the abuse.[23] Some victims, in fact, may be hurt again by constant pressure in counseling to find and "get in touch with your rage." In reality, the rage problem may be much more true for the new helper than for the victim.

Helping the Victim to Resolve Anger, Depression, and Suicide Risk. Many victims of abuse are understandably angry at the offending helper. The counseling environment must be a safe place to express anger, even to vent rage. The offending helper has taught the counselee, by verbal and modeled behavior, to suppress and redirect her anger; she has been taught to redefine feelings in ways that benefit the abuser. As a woman risks seeking help from others, she may fear that her anger will destroy her or cause the current helper to abandon her.

Deep depression is common in victims as a result of self-directed anger and the loss of the abusing helper. Frequently, depression is the reason that the person originally sought counseling help. The effect of the violation is to push the victim back into a deeper depression with the added baggage of the sexual violation. This often inflames hopelessness and shame, confirming the victim's worst fear that all men see her as a sexual object. The victim loses her sense of worth as a person—she struggles against the false but powerful belief that she has no value apart from sexual function and role.

Suicidal thoughts and plans are also common in this process, so the new helper must plan to assess this risk and deliver appropriate intervention. Denying these feelings or reacting fearfully to them will sabotage the victim's recovery. The skilled counselor can offer support by validating that suicidal thoughts are common, by fostering hope of recovery, and by promoting a safe environment for a healthy expression and resolution of these feelings.

Helping the Victim to Manage Guilt. One of the devastating impacts of sexual violation is the victim's awesome sense of guilt and shame. In the abuse situation, guilt is multiplied as the offending helper places the blame for the abuse on the counselee—so the offender always looks good while the counselee seems bad. In effect, the helper blames the victim for the sexual behavior, maintaining coercive power over her. Additionally, many offenders further induce guilt by portraying terrible consequences if they are ever found out. In this way the helper attempts to control the secret by making the woman an accomplice in keeping the misconduct for their eyes only.

A woman who reports abuse will tend to feel guilty for reporting. She may blame herself for breaking her promise to the
offender not to tell anyone their shared secret. This paradox is a
real and complex moral bind and can be extremely difficult to resolve. The helper must acknowledge this dilemma but firmly
challenge and reinterpret these lies against the systematic deceit
of the offender and the professional system that may reinforce
them. This can validate the victim's need to resolve the moral bind
and increase her motivation for counseling.

Helping the Victim to Overcome Isolation and Loneliness. A common
companion to depression is the struggle with loneliness. The offending
helper exploits this factor by reasoning that he can risk misconduct,
because the isolated woman will be unlikely to report his misbehavior to anyone. Some exploitive helpers purposely isolate the
counselee in order to minimize exposure and foster dependency.
The sexual misconduct further isolates the victim and reinforces
dependency through the inflammation of shameful guilt.

When the abuse is revealed and the relationship ended, the victim may feel terribly alone. She has lost her special relationship
with the man she trusted to share her deepest and most vulnerable self. Furthermore, she does not expect anyone to understand
the loss she is experiencing, nor does she believe that real help is
possible. In fact, she expects to be blamed and shamed, and to experience further loss in counseling and in family and support
relations. Effective treatment of isolation includes education and
advocacy by the helper, guidance in finding a support group of
other women who have experienced sexual abuse, and assistance
in marriage and family counseling.

Anticipating Sexual Confusion. Sexual violation by a helper often
distorts the victim's understanding of her sexuality and appropriate sexual behavior. Some victims began counseling because of
sexual dysfunction, which worsens due to the sexual exploitation.
Others may develop compulsive sexual behavior, often accompanied by depression, shame, guilt, and feelings of suicide. In
addition, the counselee may have sexualized most of her feelings
so that any emotion is susceptible to being experienced and interpreted sexually.

In treating problems of a sexual nature it is necessary for the
helper to create a safe therapeutic environment. It is wise to ask
the victim what can be done to help her feel as safe as possible in
the counseling process. Frequently reassure her that you will not

be sexual with her and will work with her to define and redefine sexual boundaries. Stress how important it is that she not censor thoughts, feeling, fantasies, or impulses that might be relevant for understanding her current psychological and spiritual state. Only as the helper avoids critical judgment and supports the counselee will she be able to take the incredible risk of making herself vulnerable once again.

The helper must also be careful not to act like the controlling parent toward the wounded child. The goal is to help the counselee conform to biblical sexuality, but this will not be the starting point. The helper must be able to manage personal reactions to strange sexual expression by the counselee, who must be reassured that she will not be judged or forced to speak about difficult issues prematurely. Although it may be pertinent to discuss how a lack of openness can be detrimental, it is important to allow the victim to develop trust and engage in honest disclosure as she feels comfortable with it over a period of time.

Repairing Cognitive Dysfunction. Sexual deceit and betrayal, combined with mood disorders of various kinds, impair a number of mental or cognitive functions. These include increased attention and concentration problems, rumination about worthlessness and hopelessness, memory dysfunction, anxious anticipation, and obsession regarding out-of-control thoughts (nightmares, flashbacks, unbidden thoughts, and intrusive images). Sexual abuse victims routinely experience disturbed thinking. Their inner world is "painful, threatening, and unpredictable."[24]

Cognitive therapy should include numerous prayer, planning, and thought-changing elements. First, agree to an overall framework and plan for counseling. The demands of constructing a rational, step-by-step program will challenge mental disorganization and focus helpful direction. Second, the counselee must learn to control morbid self-talk and disturbed images through thought-stopping and substitution of prayer, constructive self-talk, and safe, healthy imagery. Third, post-traumatic stress disorder must be evaluated and discussed, giving the victim room to recover slowly from the trauma. Finally, those aspects of the trauma that have been hidden via repressed memories, nightmares, and flashbacks must gradually be examined, worked through, and resolved.

Assisting the Holy Spirit in the Spiritual War. Research has shown that dissociation and post-traumatic stress are generally more severe and long-lasting if the stressor is of human origin.[25] The victim of sexual abuse by a pastor or Christian counselor often enters a profound struggle with God, the church, and his/her view of self in relationship to God. Quite often, victims blame God or themselves for the misconduct. They see themselves as people who are inherently evil in God's sight, persons to be despised, who are unable to be saved.

One terrible result of sexual abuse (especially when perpetrated by a man who is known as a Christian) is that victims are pushed to reject God by a profound sense of guilt, self-loathing, and worthlessness. Some abandon Christian beliefs and morals, succumbing to actions consistent with the belief in their wickedness. Research shows that a significant number of women who were sexually abused as children grew up in conservative Christian homes.[26] These women were least likely to be religious practitioners as adults. Victims struggle to believe in a God who would allow such things to happen to them within the context of a Christian church or home.

Challenging Denial in the Guise of Quick Forgiveness. Some victims of sexual misconduct express a simplistic notion and a premature desire to forgive the violator. This is easily exploited by some counselors because forgiveness is a proper goal and is so biblically rooted. Victims are strongly motivated to resolve the uneasy experience of strong feelings of compassion and continuing desire for the violative counselor mixed with a acute awareness of betrayal and disgust at the violation.

Rutter wisely advises that such victims should "not attempt premature forgiveness or reconciliation."[27] Sometimes a woman is too eager to forgive because she believes she is at fault and the forgiveness will relieve her guilt. She reasons that if she forgives and lets go, everything will be fine. But this is often a form of denial in the guise of godly action, which serves the misbelief that the counselor was overcome by her seduction. Wise counselors will promote the process of forgiveness while maintaining caution against its distorted use as a form of denial.

Providing Hope in Christ and Help from Others. Based on a proven relationship of therapeutic trust, we recommend that the helper gently reintroduce the victim to the gracious, merciful God revealed in the Suffering Servant of Christ. He knows her suffering beyond human understanding and took her grief and shame to the Cross. Challenging relations and worship of God the Father may be too traumatic for some, especially early in counseling, due to the association with a violative father-figure. The counselor must trust that since Christ is the mediator between the Father and the victim, He knows the perfect time to reconcile the Fatherly dimension of godly relations.

Finally, help facilitate a viable Christian support system for the injured woman. One suggestion is to find or create a church-based support group for women who have been sexually abused. Another is to build a personal support network to include the pastor, lay ministers, and friends who will make a special commitment to the woman for a period of time. This support network must validate the counselee's feelings by respecting and empathizing with the shame and ambivalence of the experience. This group should also lift up, without judgment or coercion, the healing and forgiving power of Christ.

TAKING ACTION AGAINST SEXUAL VIOLATORS

A critical issue is helping the victim decide whether to complain and pursue legal or other action against the offending helper. Helpers in a growing number of states are now mandated to report such abuse or to assist the victim in a structured decision-making process. If you are a licensed therapist, it is imperative to know whether your state has adopted mandatory reporting in this area. You must be careful of your own biases here—either for or against action—and avoid taking responsibility for the victim's decision. Rather, we will state again the importance of empowering the victim so that *she* can take the steps necessary to deal with the offense.

Discuss the reporting options or mandatory reporting procedures with the victim prior to action by either of you. Respect the victim's right to take or not to take action against the offending helper. If your counselee chooses legal action, help her retain an attorney with whom you will work closely. The counselee must understand her own and her new helper's legal responsibilities; the helper must keep accurate and appropriate records regarding reports of the abuse. It is wise for the helper to enter an agreement with the victim's lawyer to route all requests and demands for information through the attorney.

Since most victims have been lied to by the violator, it is critical that the helper provide accurate information about legal rights and consequences regarding disclosures in counseling. Affirm a commitment to confidentiality and clarify that notes made in counseling sessions will likely be subpoenaed in the event of legal action. (Privilege that guards the secrecy about the former abusive counseling is generally waived if a suit is filed.) Remind the victim, however, that she holds confidentiality and privilege,[28] and that you will not disclose sexual abuse information without her complete consent or foreknowledge.

Weighing the Costs of Public Action. Counselors need to keep in mind that filing a legal or ethical complaint often revictimizes the woman. She will have to deal with this difficult private matter in public and will have to defend herself in front of those who may suspect her motives and challenge her morality. This is stressful, to say the least, and can be a reason for not pursuing action against the abuser. However, we recognize that the law is changing and increasingly is responsive to victim's concerns. We hope that victims and those who support them will continue to advocate for better treatment from the law as we vigorously challenge these issues.

Clinically, assertive action against the violator strengthens and heals most victims. It helps to clarify the confusing moral ambiguity of these cases and challenges the tendency toward learned helplessness and a mentality of victimization. Also, each complaint serves to positively confront the prevailing social and legal structure. Each woman must be made aware that her complaint may not result in her vindication, yet as each case is presented, the volume of cases will begin to influence those who decide to deliver justice to oppressed victims. Ultimately, this kind of personal empowerment and systemic challenge could reap enormous clinical rewards in the victim's life.

CONCLUSION

The sexual revolution in the West has not produced an enlightened culture free of the puritanical sexual mores that the revolution condemned. It has fostered a new class of sexual slaves and left a multitude of victims whose lives are injured and broken. In our clinical practice, we are in a unique position to witness the fruit of this sexual revolution. Though we maintain a diverse, generalist Christian counseling practice with thousands of different clients and a myriad of problem issues across the spectrum of Christian denominations, approximately one-half of our entire agency caseload is touched by some form of sexual abuse.

The victims of sexual abuse by counselors (both licensed and pastoral) is a small slice of a massive societal epidemic. We pray the church will marshal all of its power to confront this epidemic with the good news of deliverance in Christ Jesus. Healing therapy and spiritual and social support are essential ministry to abuse victims. We urge the whole church, which has the ability in Christ, to find the will to deliver this kind of ministry in order to create a *redemptive* revolution.

NOTES

1. Rutter, *Forbidden Zone*, 7.

2. Carolyn Bates and Annette Brodsky, *Sex in the Therapy Hour: A Case of Professional Incest* (New York: Guilford Press, 1989), 21.

3. Kenneth S. Pope and Jacqueline C. Bouhoutsos, *Sexual Intimacy Between Therapists and Patients* (New York: Praeger, 1986), 63.

4. J. C. Bouhoutsos et al., "Sexual Intimacy Between Psychotherapists and Patients," *Professional Psychology: Research and Practice*, 14, no. 2 (1983): 185–96.

5. S. Feldman-Summers and G. Jones, "Psychological Impact of Sexual Contact Between Therapists or Other Health Care Practitioners and Their Clients," *Journal of Consulting and Clinical Psychology* 52, no. 6 (1984): 1054; see also Chesler, *Women and Madness* 136–57.

6. Rediger, *Ministry and Sexuality*, 24.

7. Rutter, *Forbidden Zone*, 44.

8. Marie Fortune, "Betrayal of the Pastoral Relationship: Sexual Contact by Pastors and Pastoral Counselors," in *Psychotherapists' Sexual Involvement with Clients: Intervention and Prevention*, ed. G. R. Schoener, et al. (Minneapolis: Walk-in Counseling Center, 1989), 87–88.

9. Rediger, *Ministry and Sexuality*, 23.

10. Ellen Leupker, "Clinical Assessment of Clients Who Have Been Sexually Exploited by Their Therapists and Development of Differential Treatment Plans," in *Psychotherapists' Sexual Involvement with Clients: Intervention and Prevention*, ed. G. R. Schoener, et al. (Minneapolis: Walk-in Counseling Center, 1989), 162.

11. Frank Putnam, *Diagnosis and Treatment of Multiple Personality Disorder* (New York: The Guilford Press, 1989).

12. Ibid., 26.

13. For a fuller treatment of these difficult issues, see James Friesen, *Uncovering the Mystery of MPD: Its Shocking Origins . . . Its Surprising Cure* (San Bernardino, Calif.: Here's Life Publishers, 1991); and the special issue on satanic ritual abuse and MPD in the *Journal of Psychology and Theology*, (Fall 1992).

14. Gary Schoener, "Common Errors in Treatment of Victims/Survivors of Sexual Misconduct by Professionals," paper presented at the seminar, Intervention with Victim/Survivors of Sexual Misconduct by Professionals, Minneapolis, Minnesota, February 18, 1994.

15. Rutter, *Forbidden Zone*,.

16. Pope and Bouhoutsos, *Sexual Intimacy*, 70.

17. Schoener, "Common Errors."

18. Bates and Brodsky, *Sex in the Therapy Hour*, 41.

19. Rutter, *Sex Zone*, 91.

20. See Mindy Benowitz, "Comparing the Experiences of Women Clients Sexually Exploited by Female versus Male Psychotherapists," *Women and Therapy* 15, no. 1 (1994): special issue.

21. Pope and Bouhoutsos, *Sexual Intimacy*; see also Kenneth S. Pope, *Sexual Involvement with Therapists: Patient Assessment, Subsequent Therapy, Forensics* (Washington D.C.: American Psychological Associaton Press, 1994).

22. Ibid., 93.

23. Schoener, "Common Errors."

24. Pope and Bouhoutsos, *Sexual Intimacy*, 106.

25. American Psychiatric Association, *Diagnostic and Statistical Manual of Mental Disorders*, 4th ed., DSM-IV (Washington, D.C.: American Psychiatric Association, 1994).

26. Diana M. Eliot, "The Impact of Conservative Christian Faith on the Prevalence and Sequelae of Sexual Abuse," paper presented at Christian Association for Psychological Studies, 1991. Reprint requests may be sent to the author at Rosemead Graduate School of Psychology, 13800 Biola Avenue, La Mirada, CA 90639-0001.

27. Rutter, *Sex Zone*, 186.

28. For a fuller understanding of confidentiality and privilege, see chapter 7 in Ohlschlager and Mosgofian, *Law for the Christian Counselor*.

Chapter Six

Problem Cases in Sexual Misconduct

Boundary crossings may be benign or harmful, may take many forms, and may pose problems related to both treatment and potential liability. The differences in impact may depend on whether clinical judgment has been used to make the decision, whether adequate discussion and exploration have taken place, and whether documentation adequately records the details.[1]

IN THIS CHAPTER WE EXPLORE FIVE PROBLEMS in counseling that involve boundary violations related to sexual misconduct. These issues are controversial and represent the treacherous waters that helpers and counselees must navigate in order to arrive safely at the counseling destination—the healing shore. If the lighthouse, the crew, and the ship are not in sound condition, there will be shipwreck. When these five problem areas are understood, respected, and deftly and ethically navigated, then the result is progress toward the healing shoreline. Ultimately, the successful navigation of these waters leads to healing and renewal, a strong blow against the wiles of the enemy.

HOMOSEXUAL MISCONDUCT

Juanita had finally been able to begin to break away from her abusive husband through the intervention of a women's shelter. While spending time in the shelter, she was encouraged to begin counseling to help her decide what direction to take with her marriage. Juanita was referred to

Karen, a licensed psychologist, and began weekly therapy. Juanita knew that Karen was married and was a well-respected professional. Karen was caring and comforting, so Juanita did not hesitate to share her darkest secrets, including details of confusion about her sexuality. Karen was warm, supportive, and even spent extra time on the phone with Juanita between sessions. Juanita made gradual progress in this counseling situation and decided to divorce her husband and begin a new life. During this time, Karen encouraged her to come to counseling twice weekly.

Karen had often embraced Juanita before, during, or after an appointment, and was regularly touching her as a means to offer support at difficult points in the counseling sessions. About five months into therapy, as Karen sat with Juanita and embraced her, she began kissing Juanita. Juanita was frozen as this occurred but gave no indication to Karen of her inner confusion. Juanita continued coming to counseling, as she had become quite dependent on Karen, but counseling became gradually more sexual in nature. Juanita had never been sexual with a woman and was feeling highly confused about the relationship with Karen. She was unable to tell anyone, fearing charges of homosexuality, and fearing harm to Karen if her actions were exposed. She began to deteriorate and eventually needed hospitalization for acute panic disorder.

As indicated previously, the greatest number of forbidden sexual contacts is with adult males violating women and children (over 85 percent of all violations). Among adults, the next highest group of abusers involves women abusing women (around 10 percent), with men violating other men at about 5 percent.[2] Since the largest group of homosexual violators is comprised of women abusing women, we will focus on that pattern in this section. At this time, little reliable information exists that addresses men violating men since male victims are unlikely to report sexual incidents, especially when it involves same sex relationships.

The information on homosexual misconduct is minimal, so it is somewhat difficult to generalize based on the scant data. However, the following concepts are indicators of possible trends.[3] It does appear that female offenders are more likely to initiate the sexual relationship than male offenders and are more likely to initiate sexual activity sooner than most male counterparts. Women offenders do not necessarily have long-term exclusive relationships with other females in counseling. More than half are likely to offend with more than one counselee.

In addition, the sexual orientation of the helper does not necessarily correlate with the likelihood of exploitation. About one third of the offenders are married, one third are bisexual, and one third are homosexual in orientation. Lastly, the data suggests that people who are victims of homosexual misconduct suffer the same consequences as those who are abused in a heterosexual relationship. These effects include post-traumatic stress disorder, shame, depression, panic attacks and anxiety, suicidal thoughts, relationship problems, and identity disorders.

HOMOSEXUAL EXPLOITATION

There are several pertinent issues regarding exploitation by same-sex helpers. A number of these helpers are themselves struggling with sexual identity, and they act out their struggles in the protected privacy of the counseling relationship, though not necessarily in overtly destructive ways. Nevertheless, this sexual identity conflict is thus projected onto the counselee, compounding the counselee's confusion and complicating his or her guilt and shame. Since homosexuality is particularly problematic for many Christians, those who struggle with homosexual feelings and behavior may seek out prohomosexual or practicing homosexual counselors for assistance in resolving these sexual identity issues. This may lead to extreme complications with Christian beliefs and practices, particularly when exploitation occurs.

Also, since passage of the sexual exploitation law in Texas (January, 1994), professional counselors in Texas (and all Christian counselors) must reflect on how the law is being twisted to conform to a radical gay rights agenda. In Texas, it is now illegal "sexual exploitation/abuse" to "create a hostile environment" in counseling by "making sexually demeaning comments to or about an individual's sexual orientation."[4] We agree that counselors who do this should be sanctioned (the hate and homophobia of some in the church is a great offense to Christ). However, it is easy to imagine how this law may be used to attack Christian counselors for any biblically-based challenge to homosexual behavior and offer of reparative therapy. (Those who counsel homosexuals will want to review this issue further in chapter 13 and will want to consider utilizing our homosexual disclosure/consent form in appendix C.)

True Exploitation. One of the most damaging and exploitive circumstances occurs when helpers who are deeply conflicted about their own same-sex feelings, and are internally homophobic, act out sexually with same-sex counselees. Often they project their intense conflict onto the counselee and overtly or covertly blame them for the sick and perverted behavior, or deny the reality that the behavior was homosexual. The helper's psychopathology creates intense pain, conflict, and isolation for the counselee-victim because of the exploitive dynamics combined with the internalized homophobia. In many instances, these helpers are Christian counselors and clergy, which only serves to further complicate the counselee's struggles with God and faith in Christ.

Reporting Problems. When it comes to reporting homosexual misconduct, the victim struggles with all the troubles that affect other victims, with several additional factors. It is usually even more difficult to admit to homosexual abuse due to sexual identity issues, especially the fear of being labeled lesbian or gay. This may be true if the person already is homosexual but wants to keep that information private. Another hindrance to reporting is the realistic fear, based on loyalty to the helper, that the same-sex violator will suffer harsher consequences in the legal system than the heterosexual violator. By and large these fears are confirmed by fact, which reinforces their power. Finally, these victims are concerned that people are less likely to believe a report of homosexual exploitation, especially if the offender appears to be heterosexual.

Treatment Issues. In addition to the issues discussed in chapter 5, treatment should be sensitive to the following issues. The counselor must not assume to know the impact of the homosexual contact on the counselee, but must let that person explain his or her feelings, thoughts, and beliefs. Clarification of sexual orientation is often a critical issue, which requires empathic listening and a clear understanding of the options available in Christ.[5] Since many of the victims are unlikely to have had any sexual contact with a person of the same sex prior to this abuse, this issue is a major factor to understand and resolve in treatment. As in any exploitive relationship, it is important to address the fact that exploitation is not primarily sexual but stems from a host of boundary violations. Therapy needs to help the victim understand the exploitation and the power differences; these are critical factors.

THE SEDUCTIVE CLIENT

Over a period of eleven years, Sandra had seen seven different counselors—six men and one woman, including two pastoral counselors. Sandra was bright, beautiful, and seductive. In five of those counseling relationships, Sandra was able to successfully persuade the male helpers to have some level of inappropriate sensual or sexual involvement with her during the course of treatment. Though occasionally in conflict within herself over her success, she wore these conquests as a sign of her power over those in authority, especially male authority. Secretly, she felt driven to seduce as many counselors as possible.

Andre Bustanoby tells another kind of story—one that accurately describes the tension that can exist for a counselor when a seductive female begins a counseling relationship.

> She was a very attractive woman, by my estimate about thirty-five years old. (She turned out to be a well-preserved forty-five.) I introduced myself in the waiting room and told her I would be her counselor. "I'm Colleen," she said. Then, lowering her head slightly, she looked me intently in the eye. It was one of those looks that needed no words. I got the message, even though I don't normally attract the instant attention of women. Colleen then fluffed her hair, pulled her sweater tightly over her well-endowed figure, and looked back at me coquettishly as if to say, "Do you like what you see?" I knew at that moment that Colleen's sexuality and my reaction to it would be a primary dynamic in the counseling to follow.[6]

Over the years, many helpers have claimed they had no intention of being sexually involved with counselees, admitting instead to having been sexually seduced. Often, the excuse—the wrongful permission—to cross the forbidden boundary stems from the belief that because the counselee wanted sex, it was in the best interests of the counselee to comply with those wishes. With the increased awareness of harm to counselees and the ensuing legal calamity, it is imperative that the male counselor understand a seductive woman and be prepared to prevent crossing forbidden boundaries. As Comiskey warns, "From that day forward I held no illusion about my absolute safety from seducing or being seduced. Satan, the enemy, knew my vulnerability and was waging a war against me. I needed to be aware of his devices. . . ."[7]

STYLES OF SEDUCTIVE BEHAVIOR

A person who attempts to seduce his or her counselor is acting out a destructive life pattern in the therapeutic environment. That person is doing what has been compulsively learned as the way to influence and attract other people. We observe three types of counselees who attempt to seduce helpers.

The Naive Seductress. These individuals have little or no awareness of their seductive behavior but instinctively project their
sexuality as a way to get attention and create interest. They have little
to no awareness of what they are doing to attract attention because
it has gone on for so long in their lives. They act it out in this manner as a reflection of unresolved relational and sexual issues.

The Deliberate Coquette. Coquettes think of themselves as sexual
persons—ones who consciously use their sexual power, regardless
whether they enjoy it or do it compulsively without pleasure. They
find fulfillment in seducing other persons, especially those in authority. Schaumburg states that sexual addicts "are compelled to
use sexual behaviors to meet their needs on demand. Refusing to
face relational emptiness . . . they seek relief and satisfaction
through sexual acts."[8]

The Hostile or Sly Entrapper. These individuals act out their pathology as a ploy to entrap a helper and turn that person over to
the authorities. Some have barely concealed hostility toward therapists, or Christians, or those in authority, and are determined to
bring them down. Others are people who become aware of the
power of the law, especially in its potential for earning an income
through lawsuit settlements.

SEDUCTION AS PSYCHOSPIRITUAL PATHOLOGY

As indicated above, some women purposely set out to seduce
their counselor, while others are less aware of their motives. As
Serban argues, however, these women are almost always devastated and enraged because of their failed expectations of "finding
either a sexual and emotional partner or otherwise to make a hand-
some financial profit by defrauding the therapist's insurance, if not
to victimize him as a revenge against men."[9] Those who seduce
are ultimately not seeking sexual behavior, they simply do not
know how to ask for help other than through sexual activity.

Seductive women are most apt to be those who have been violated sexually as children, or who are suffering from serious
pathology or chronic personality disorders. These women see
themselves as having value only as sexual objects. For the helper
to become sexual with these women, no matter how justifiable it
may seem, serves only to betray the small core of hope that could
have been revived and healed through counseling.

Guarding Boundaries and Protecting the Seductive Client. It is grievous how many Christian helpers—naive, immature, vulnerable,

poorly-trained, and marginally ethical pastors and counselors—are brought down by seductive counselees. Most Christian helpers know better, however, and we are appalled to hear how some counselors still defend and justify their sexual misconduct. Based on the false assumption of being a victim of seduction or, worse yet, that women who act out seductively deserve to be violated, these defenders of sexual violation must be challenged for their deluded judgment and distorted morality.

Seduction by a counselee never justifies sexual misconduct. The counselor must see beyond the seduction to identify the deep needs revealed in the seductive behavior. The mature counselor will respond to seductive behavior with therapy that challenges change and offers help to accomplish it. If this cannot be done, and it is likely that the seduction will be consummated sexually, termination and referral are essential. A counselor who becomes seduced by a woman's sexual, sensual, or emotional power must take steps to protect himself and the counselee from harm (see chapter 14).

TOUCHING AND THERAPEUTIC TOUCH

Touch is one of the major forms of communication between persons. However, due to the sexual misconduct crisis, touch has become a controversial subject in counseling relationships. In the history of psychotherapy, when the Freudian model was ascendant, the analytic rule was to avoid touch because of theoretical issues dealing with transference or because of the dangers related to sexual misconduct. Predictably, during the period of liberation from the "repressed moral thinkers" (the 1960s), many counselors began to advocate the healing benefits of touch.

However, by the mid 1980s more and more counselees began to reveal the harm in touch, particularly when it led to sexual involvement. The counter-tendency, especially by many Christians, has been to take an all-or-nothing approach, eliminating all touch with counselees. However, touch is not so much about rules as it is about the intent of the heart. Therefore, it is important to review how touch can communicate well-being or harm so that the helper can determine whether or not touch is appropriate.[10]

THE THERAPEUTIC POWER OF TOUCH

Touch can powerfully communicate interest in others. For some people, the absence of touch may be perceived as rejection or

disgust. Kertay and Reviere report, after an extensive review of
the available literature, that "the general trend in the research con-
ducted thus far suggests that the use of touch in psychotherapy
can lead to positive outcomes at best, and at worst does not appear to cause harm to patients when used appropriately."[11] Many
types of touch are fine without fantasy, but touch that fulfills sexual
interest or acts out fantasy must be prohibited at all times, no matter how safe it might seem.

Most of us understand the power of touch to encourage, heal,
and comfort those we care about. In nonprofessional relations, as
well as in some professional and ministerial bonds, touch comes
naturally: to console those who grieve, to express delight in those
who find answers and see great change, to greet others, or to say
good-bye. With right intent and without contact of sexual body
parts, touch can have a healing, bonding, and beneficial effect. Many
ministers, both pastoral and lay, also take seriously the call to anoint
with oil and lay hands on the sick, the infirm, and the oppressed.
A rigid rule against touch would ultimately violate a practice
Scripture surely affirms.

The Hazards of Touch. It is important to explore the kinds of behavior that can lead a helper to cross the line from beneficial touch
to misconduct—a line that may vary from person to person. Touching the shoulder, arm, or hand is probably the least controversial
touch for a helper. Touching a counselee's leg, knee, face, neck, or
hair is more invasive to the person, and sexual intent is more easily confused. Likewise, holding hands is generally not a safe form
of touch, although holding hands for prayer can be safe and normative for some Christian helpers. Other forms of precarious touch
that are likely to be too dangerous to practice include sitting next
to a counselee body-to-body, holding a counselee on the lap, suggestive looks or remarks, and any type of kissing, even on the
forehead or hand.

Hugging is controversial; it can be therapeutic or quite hazard-
ous because it can draw out deep feelings, including sexual
feelings. Consequently, it is important to differentiate between safe
and harmful hugs, friendly as opposed to seductive hugs. Hugs
that go on too long, that are too tight, that caress any part of the
body, or linger by touch in a sensuous way should obviously be
avoided. Friendly hugs do not arouse sexual feelings, while seductive hugs serve the purpose of arousing sensual feeling and
eventually igniting sexual interest.

Know the Danger Signs. Counselors need to be aware of their personal attitudes toward touch and be sensitive to the counselee's receptivity to touch and its impact on the therapeutic process. While touch may be used to help promote healing, it should be strictly avoided when it promotes negative feelings in the counselee. In fact, it is best never to touch counselees without their permission. Touch of any kind is likely not indicated if the counselee is a sexual abuse survivor, shows severe dissociation or multiple personality, suffers psychotic disorders (especially of the paranoid variety), or suffers certain personality disorders (especially borderline personality). Obviously, a counselor should also avoid touch or any invasive behavior when the counselee has made it clear that he or she is angry with the counselor. Whether this is communicated directly or nonverbally, the counselor must keep an appropriate distance until the anger is resolved.

In conclusion, counselors who observe three important signposts will protect themselves from crossing the sometimes elusive boundary between beneficial and harmful touch. First, helpers who have a tendency to touch counselees based on gender, age, and sexual attractiveness are at a higher risk to offend. Second, touch that leads to sexual arousal on the part of the helper or the counselee should be discontinued and discussed with a colleague or supervisor. Third, any touch that is subtly coercive must be discontinued.

REPRESSED AND RECOVERED MEMORIES

The last two topics in this chapter deal with related issues: recovered memories and false allegations. During the early 1990s, the battle over recovered memories grew increasingly fierce. The controversial False Memory Syndrome Foundation held its first conference in April 1993. Early in 1994, one of America's most well-known and beloved Catholic Cardinals was first sued and then exonerated of child sexual abuse charges based on false recovered memories. As those accused of sexual abuse fight back, there is a growing backlash against the concept and the abuse of recovered memories. As one author stated, "Sexual abuse as an expression of power over children or vulnerable adults is finally receiving greatly needed public exposure. But the act of uncovering abuse can itself be abused."[12]

CONTROVERSIES ABOUND

Uncovering repressed memories has been the source of contro-versy almost since its inception as a therapeutic tool. The question is not whether people repress memories or not, as even leading advocates who strive to protect the accused from false accusations acknowledge that repressed memories exist.[13] And the process of restoring these memories has helped numbers of people recall sources of trauma that influence current problems, especially mood disorders like depression, anxiety, phobias, and panic. But this process has also been criticized as being misused, or even de-rided as a bogus technique—one in which unethical or incompetent helpers induce false memories in vulnerable and pli-able clients.

In working with counselees who have lost a loved one to death, it is remarkable how consistently the survivors struggle to remem-ber details about the deceased person. Within only a few years, however, many memories and especially the ability to recall the person in detail, become progressively selective and fuzzy. "When the record of some past experience is dissociated or separated off from ongoing awareness—because of pain, fear, shock, stress, or an altered state of consciousness—then it may be possible to re-cover the memories."[14]

The work of recovering repressed memories primarily applies to adults whose therapy involves recalling memories of abuse as children. It may also apply to adults who suffered severe sexual exploitation—rape, for example. It is rare for the professionally exploited client who has suffered no other form of abuse to suffer this malady. However, it could appear in instances such as those being claimed against the Catholic Church—in recovered memo-ries by adult males who were abused by church personnel as children or adolescents.

Repressed Memories or Implanted Suggestion? One controversy fo-cuses on the persuasive power of helpers and lawyers to lead counselees to believe that the cause of their psychological and so-cial harm is located in repressed memories of sexual, physical, or emotional abuse. This controversy was undoubtedly fueled by Steven Cook's initial admission that his recovered memories of abuse by Cardinal Bernadin were true, then his subsequent admission that they were, in fact, false. Perception, imagination, emotions, cognition, and environmental factors—the impact of disease or the abuse of drugs, for example—intertwine to shape the highly selective process we call human memory.

While there can be clear, focused memories of events, it is also true that memory is shaped by other forces. Human imagination and defense mechanisms reinterpret experiences and produce "memory" that is influenced, even distorted by the bio-medical status, socio-cultural conditions, and psychological needs and quirks of the individual. Human memory is certainly not like a computer diskette, repeating accurately and verbatim all that was seen or experienced. We agree with the assertion that, "Some repressed memories are real, some memories are incorrectly remembered, and some are imagined."[15]

The fact that memory is shaped by many factors contributes to the power of suggestion to influence what is remembered. This does not mean that people are lying, it simply reflects the power of the mind to create or to shape memories that best serve the person's needs and view of self. In this context, it is best to wait an extensive period of time before pursuing lawsuit activity. "Suggestibility . . . enables individuals to suspend disbelief and accept as valid the exhortations of persuasive leaders. When one combines human suggestibility, magical thinking, and the desire for a powerful leader, the ground is set for mass hysteria."[16] In other words, vulnerable persons are especially likely to believe powerful leaders and to follow their advise.

Does Hypnosis Help or Hurt? Properly and ethically used, hypnotic techniques can be useful for memory recall and healing therapy. While clinicians may be concerned primarily whether hypnotherapists are well trained and practice hypnosis ehtically, some Christians are troubled by the belief that hypnosis is immoral, or even Satanic. The Bernardin case will not help the cause of competent hypnosis in Christian counseling. In this case, the accuser had seen a poorly trained hypnotist to help deal with the physical symptoms of AIDS. In the course of their work, Steven Cook uncovered "memories" indicating he had been abused by two priests, including Bernardin. The hypnotist did not follow protocol, documenting the memory recovery process to guard against the charge that the memories were suggested or tainted. Later facts bore out the truth that the memories were not real.

Proper Litigation or Salem Witch Hunts Reborn? The standards for utilizing hypnotic or other techniques to uncover repressed memories in counseling and the use of data derived from those techniques as evidence in a court of law are two very different matters. One of the greatest problems here involves helpers who strongly encourage, even push, counselees to sue alleged offenders or encourage counselees to seek legal assistance who then promote suit. While it is important to help sexual abuse victims to understand the options for justice, it is neither ethical nor wise to push them to sue. Helpers should encourage counselees to examine the underlying goals in pursuing lawsuits and question the validity of this method for resolving anger.

The hazards of presenting charges to the public before they can be reasonably verified can lead to great harm to those accused. Counselors who do not handle the matter properly are now at risk legally. In a recent case in California, *Ramona v. Isabella, et al.*, an accused father (Mr. Romona) alleged that his college-age daughter's therapists implanted false memories of childhood sexual abuse into her mind.[17] When she (Holly) confronted her father about past incestuous abuse, it was done poorly and led to great personal and financial harm to Mr. Ramona. He won a $500,000 judgment at trial for loss of earnings due to the therapist's negligence.

While this case sets no formal legal precedent, it does signal the need for great caution on the part of those who treat sexual abuse survivors. Sadly, this case never did answer the deepest questions of the alleged victim: Did the abuse really happen, and how do I resolve the trauma surrounding it? Systemically, this case may chill further research and efforts to advance our understanding and proper practice of this controversial form of therapy.

As a result of the real and potential harm to the person accused in these situations, a number of authors compare the current hysteria over child sexual abuse with the hysteria generated during the Salem witch trials. In those trials, a great number of innocent victims died based on false accusations stemming from bizarre forms of evidence. Essentially, testimony from children was used against adults without any factual corroboration. Consequently, one author suggests that these types of cases should be protected from public view until there is reasonable verification, in order to protect the innocent accused offender while respecting the alleged victim(s).[18]

ENSURE CAREFUL AND ETHICAL PRACTICE

In conclusion, helpers must ensure that their counseling practices do not excessively encourage counselees to recover false memories of abuse. Caution must be exercised when using any special technique to assist counselees in recalling events that may have been forgotten or repressed. If special techniques (hypnosis, visualization, medications, etc.) are used, "therapists must be prepared to demonstrate that they have had sufficient education, training and experience in the use of such techniques" including proof that the technique was "clinically appropriate under the circumstances."[19]

Failure to follow careful procedures and to faithfully document the recovery of repressed traumas will expose counselors to legal and ethical risk. Also, the counselee faces losing a case if he or she decides to take action against an abuser, and the helper may face liability for negligent action. As much as possible, helpers should encourage counselees to withhold any legal action against an accused offender based solely on the restoration of lost memories. More importantly, the costs to the helper's clinical objectives must be considered against the benefits of any legal action. Counseling can be lost in the overpowering attention a lawsuit can attract. For many counselors, considering deferral of what may be premature legal or abuser challenge action may benefit the client's interest to first gain more ground in the healing quest.

FALSE ALLEGATIONS OF ABUSE

The Ramona case, noted above, brought national media attention to the issue of false allegations of past abuse. Even more dramatic was the shock of the Chicago Archdiocese of the Roman Catholic Church and the nation in November 1993 when a civil suit was filed against the popular and highly respected Cardinal Joseph Bernardin. The suit asserted that he had committed sexual acts with a teenage boy some seventeen years earlier when Bernardin was archbishop of Cincinatti. This accusation seemed even more contradictory because the Cardinal had been well known as an outspoken advocate for protecting others from victimization.

Less than four months after the accusations were filed, the alleged victim withdrew his suit because he found that the "memories" discovered while under hypnosis could not be substantiated; in fact, they clearly violated the known circumstances of the case. Chicago attorney Cathy Pilkington saw in Cardinal Bernadin's experience a parallel to the Salem witch trials of 1692–93, where spectral evidence was used against people accused of witchcraft.

Fortunately for Bernardin, the evidence presented was not legally substantial. Naturally, Bernardin was greatly relieved by the withdrawal of the suit. He also received praise for the way he handled himself with integrity in this case, defending himself against false accusations without impugning most victims as false accusers.

ALLEGATIONS—TRUE OR FALSE?

Because of the increase in people who have come forward in the last decade to reveal abuse memories, a growing number of adults who have been accused of such behavior have claimed that no abuse ever occurred. Increasingly, many of those who have been accused of abuse have formed associations to defend themselves against these supposed false allegations with an additional goal being to educate the public that this type of harm can occur. Some of those accused have begun to fight back by using the legal system to sue counselors who have helped uncover these alleged memories. While suppressing fake allegations is critically important, we are also concerned about real abuse being denied and cloaked under the countercharge of false allegations.

The Christian helper must be particularly careful to assess the veracity of any reports of abuse before encouraging or taking action on those complaints. This may place the counselor in an awkward situation (because of the difficulty for a genuine victim to come forth and share his or her story). However, it is necessary, not only because of the potential legal harm that can occur to helpers who work with sexual abuse survivors but because of the need to provide professional excellence and ethical practice.

False allegations can occur for a number of reasons. These include counselees who misinterpret touch, words, or looks, and counselees who mistake the identity of an actual offender. Sometimes there is an exaggeration or distortion of the facts; at other times people report sexual misconduct although they were never actually the helper's counselee. Finally, some people fabricate misconduct stories because of anger with the helper, because of psychopatholgy, or because of a desire for financial gain.

It is difficult to determine the frequency of false allegations. While the general consensus is that they are relatively rare, they do occur, so it is necessary to develop methods for evaluating the veracity of complaints. In addition, the number of false allegations may be increasing because of the large sums of money being awarded to victims, particularly victims of clergy misconduct. Consequently, it behooves helpers to develop practices that will safeguard them against the problems associated with false allegations.

DETERMINING THE TRUTHFULNESS OF COMPLAINTS

Confirmation. Though it can be difficult to assess the truthfulness of a complaint, the following factors are indicative, especially when several confirm one another.

1. The accused helper admits to the allegations in whole or in part.

2. Several counselees who do not know one another or have not spoken to one another come forth with similar details in their complaints. If they have spoken together, they report shock at learning of the same abuse going on, a revelation that motivated them to come forward.

3. Alleged complaints are verified by facts such as testimony from witnesses, pictures, gifts, and photos of the two together. Evidence can also include notes or a diary kept by the helper or counselee that confirms the allegations.

4. The counselee has intimate knowledge of the helper's body, home, or personal life—information that would not normally come through the helping process.

Disconfirmation. It may be difficult to prove false allegations, but the following factors can help.

1. The counselee admits to a fabrication and/or an exaggeration.

2. Witnesses provide accurate information that contradicts all or part of the complaint or provides evidence of a past history of this behavior by the complainant.

3. The helper has evidence that demonstrates falsehood of the allegations. This may include case notes, letters, or tapes. Naturally, case notes can be doctored to change evidence, so these must be examined carefully.

4. The helper who practices in a dangerous zone (especially when working with borderline or seductive counselees) can provide evidence of routinely seeking consultation and accountability with others, who can vouch for the veracity of efforts to remain ethical.

5. The helper did not use controversial techniques and procedures. If unusual methods are used, the helper must perform
competently and be fully able to defend the methods—this
should include familiarity with the relevant literature.

We agree with Bustanoby's comments about false allegations.
"There is no fail-safe way to protect yourself completely from allegations of impropriety, no matter how professional and careful you
might be."[20] However, by leading a personal and professional life
that exemplifies humility, by treating others with respect and purity (especially women for the male helper), and by carefully
guarding the helping boundaries, Christian helpers can go a long
way to protect themselves against the harm of false allegations.
Ethical helpers are careful about making exceptions to healthy and
ethical boundaries, and are careful to use consultants and supervisors when handling difficult cases.

CONCLUSION

Counseling consistently deals with the issues of boundaries and
power. The helper who wants to remain pure in heart will faithfully guard the boundaries, particularly in these five precarious
areas. By so doing, helpers use their power to promote healing and
restoration; they avoid harming counselees and protect themselves
from excessive risk of lawsuit harm.

NOTES

1. Thomas Gutheil and Glen Gabbard, "The Concept of Boundaries in Clinical Practice: Theoretical and Risk-Management Dimensions," *American Journal of
Psychiatry* 150, no. 2 (1993): 195.

2. Laura Markowitz, "Crossing the Line: Who Protects Clients from Their Protectors," *The Family Therapy Networker* (November/December 1992): 25–31. Also
see J. C. Gonsiorek, "Sexual Exploitation by Psychotherapists: Some Observations on Male Victims and Sexual Orientation Issues," in *Psychotherapists' Sexual
Involvement with Clients: Intervention and Prevention*, ed. G. R. Schoener, et al.
(Minneapolis: Walk-in Counseling Center, 1989), 113–119; and Mindy
Benowitz, "Comparing the Experiences of Women Clients Sexually Exploited
by Female versus Male Psychotherapists," *Women and Therapy*, 15, no. 1 (1994):
special issue.

3. Based primarily on data from Benowitz, "Comparing the Experiences."

4. Texas State Board of Examiners of Professional Counselors, *Rules* (Austin,
Tex.: 1994) from section 681.33 (g)(A)(4), 6–7.

5. See chapter 13, for an explanation of the options available for persons with homosexual behavior or feelings. For further reading we recommend Andrew Comiskey, *Pursuing Sexual Wholeness* (Lake Mary, Fl.: Creation House, 1989); Leanne Payne, *The Broken Image: Restoring Personal Wholeness Through Healing Prayer* (Westchester: Crossway, 1981); and Elizabeth Moberly, *Homosexuality: A New Christian Ethic* (Greenwood: Attic Press, 1983).

6. Andre Bustanoby, "Counseling the Seductive Female," *Leadership* 9, no. 1 (1988): 48.

7. Comisky, *Pursuing Sexual Wholeness*, 90.

8. Schaumburg, *False Intimacy*, 61.

9. G. Serban, "Sexual Activity in Therapy," *American Journal of Psychotherapy* 35 (1981): 81.

10. See the excellent study by Jayne E. Stake and Joan Oliver, "Sexual Contact and Touching Between Therapist and Client: A Survey of Psychologists' Attitudes and Behavior," *Professional Psychology: Research and Practice* 22, no. 2 (1991): 297–307.

11. Les Kertay and Susan L. Reviere, "The Use of Touch in Psychotherapy: Theoretical and Ethical Considerations," *Psychotherapy* 30, no. 1 (1993): 32–40.

12. James M. Wall, "The Bernardin Factor," *Christian Century* 110, no. 34 (1993): 1195.

13. See Richard Gardner's comments on page 2 in Mike Kinsley and John Sununu, "Memories, Real or Not?" *CNN Crossfire*, transcript #1039 (Denver, Colo.: Journal Graphics, Inc., March 1, 1994). In addition, see the article by Elizabeth F. Loftus, "The Reality of Repressed Memories," *The American Psychologist* 48, no. 5 (1993): 518–37.

14. Sidney Callahan, "Memory Can Play Tricks and So Can Therapists," *Commonweal* 120, no. 22 (1993): 6–7.

15. Richard S. Leslie, "Child and Sexual Abuse Repressed Memories: Real or Imagined? Staying Clear of Unethical Behavior," *The California Therapist*, 6, no. 1 (1994): 22.

16. Gardner, *Sex Abuse Hysteria*, 41.

17. See Kathleen McKee, "The Napa Repressed Memory Case," *The California Therapist* 6, no.4 (1994): 24–26; and Jill Smolowe, "Dubious Memories: A Father Accused of Sexual Abuse Wins a Malpractice Judgment Against His Daughter's Therapists," *Time* 23 May 1994, 51.

18. Wall, "The Bernardin Factor," 1196.

19. McKee, "The Napa Repressed Memory Case," 26.

20. Bustanoby, "Counseling the Seductive Female," 54.

PART III

Forbidden Sex Against Children

Chapter Seven

Child Sexual Abuse in Society and the Church[1]

Children know, instinctive taught, the friend or foe.

Sir Walter Scott

Fourteen-year-old Sally had been the victim of incest by her stepfather for three years. The man groomed her for over a year, progressively forcing himself on her sexually, eventually penetrating her vaginally and anally, and forcing her to fellate him. She was threatened and sometimes beaten when she did not comply wholeheartedly. Sally told her mother about the abuse but was ignored. She sought help from a friendly teacher and a minister who led a youth group she attended occasionally, but they did not believe her. She ran away to a large city where she was raped, and forced to become a drug addict and prostitute. She worked desperately for six months until she was beaten to death by an enraged client out-of-his-mind on alcohol and cocaine. Her unclaimed body was cremated by the city and it was over a year before her family learned of her horrible end.

SEXUAL ABUSE AGAINST CHILDREN IS *epidemic* in the world and in the church. It is an epidemic that touches multiple types of people in all walks of life. Hundreds of thousands of abusers and millions of victims are our neighbors through all strata of society. Child sexual abuse cases are flooding our courts, state agencies, media channels and, due to abuse by ministers and members, church leadership councils. Because the church has largely failed to find effective ways to control this epidemic, the state is beginning to subject the church to its law, its prejudice, and its severe punishment.

Though epidemic in our modern age, sexual abuse is not new. Child sexual abuse along with homosexuality was common in ancient Sodom (see Gen.19:5–8). Child sacrifice and sexual abuse through incestuous relations, common among the pagan religions of ancient Palestine, were strictly forbidden by God (Lev. 18:6–16; 20:1–5). In Leviticus 19:29, a father is instructed: "Do not degrade your daughter by making her a prostitute. . . ." The gravity of sexual abuse against children is also implied in Jesus Christ's sober warning in Matthew 18:6, "If anyone causes one of these little ones who believe in me to sin, it would be better for him to have a large millstone hung around his neck and to be drowned in the depths of the sea."

This chapter presents the horror of sexual abuse against children in Western society and the church. We will define abuse and its prevalence in society, review the dynamics and harm done to victims, profile child sexual abusers, and discuss the abuse of children in the context of church ministry. Treatment and healing strategies for child victims will be presented in chapter 8.

WHAT IS CHILD SEXUAL ABUSE?

Child sexual abuse is the immoral and criminal use of a child as a sexual object by an adult or older minor child. David Finkelhor's seminal research[2] on this problem shows the difficulty of shaping agreed standards that define and evaluate child abuse—an increasing problem in social science analysis that reflects our post-Christian culture adrift from biblical anchors. We have synthesized biblical revelation, current law, and Finkelhor's clinical research to offer a simple, cross-cultural standard of child sexual abuse behavior. This standard outlines a four-level gradation of abuse based on abuse behavior by the perpetrator, the age of the victim, the relationship of the victim to the abuser, and the severity of the abuse and consequent criminal penalties.

CLASS A: THE WORST ABUSE

This is the most harm-causing abuse by adults against (especially younger) children. It involves oral, vaginal, or anal penetration of the child by any body part (especially the penis) or instrument used by the abuser. This behavior includes sexual abuse combined with physical assault, ritualistic abuse, and the use of terror and threats/acts of murder against children.

CLASS B: VERY SERIOUS ABUSE

This abuse typically involves direct genital fondling, kissing/ fondling bare breasts, or simulated intercourse by an adult against a child. It can also be Class A behavior by a minor teen against a younger teen or preteen, or by an adult with an older consenting teenage victim. (Legally, a minor cannot consent to illicit sex, though it may mitigate criminal consequences.)

CLASS C: SERIOUS ABUSE

This involves kissing or fondling a child's buttocks, thighs, or other body parts, or fondling breasts or genitals through clothing. As above, it can also involve more serious Class B behavior with less serious relationships (other than adult to young child).

CLASS D: LESS SERIOUS ABUSE

This is noncontact (no physical contact), exhibitionistic abuse— exposure of genitals by an adult to a child, or Class C contact in a less serious relationship.

SEXUAL ABUSE IS PERVASIVE AND HARMFUL

Controversy abounds regarding the prevalence of child sexual abuse: Is abuse and the number of victims increasing? Or is child abuse being reported more? The short answer to both questions is *yes*. Though definitional and methodological questions abound and will continue to generate controversy in seeking clear answers, there is a persistent increase in the absolute numbers of abuse victims and in abuse reporting figures in the United States.[3] Recent and extensive studies of sexual abuse in Canada and England have also shown high and increasing rates of sexual abuse.[4]

The 1985 *Los Angeles Times* randomly surveyed over 2600 men and women from all fifty states.[5] This poll indicated that 27 percent of American women and 16 percent of American men were sexual abuse victims—a staggering thirty-eight million people nationwide. The Canadian study revealed that 28 percent of Canadian women and 10 percent of Canadian men experienced some form of sexual abuse as children. Sexual abuse was prevalent across all societal boundaries—rich, poor, and middle class; white and minority; educated or noneducated; and religious or nonreligious.

Studies of special populations show the terrible linkage of child sexual abuse to numerous human and social problems.[6] A study of prostitutes showed that 60 percent were sexually abused as children, with two-thirds of these abused by their father or father-figure. A Canadian study of juvenile runaways revealed that 73 percent of the females and 38 percent of the males had been sexually abused or exposed to pornographic materials. Many others studies reveal the data that experienced therapists see constantly in their practices—there are significantly higher rates of child sexual abuse victimization among (1) general psychiatric populations and (2) those who abuse their own children as adults.

Numerous studies have catalogued and evaluated the impact of sexual abuse on children.[7] The physical harm shows vaginal infections, difficulty walking or sitting, unusual and offensive body odors, and loss of sphincter control with anal abuse. Harmful behavioral effects include refusal to be left with offenders, fear or repulsion when touched by adults, regression to infantile behavior (bed-wetting, thumb sucking, etc.), suicidal thoughts and actions, obsessive-compulsive behaviors, self-mutilation, problems in school, running away, abrupt personality changes, nightmares and sleep disturbances, and delinquency.

The emotional harm involves guilt, anger, depression, anxiety and phobias, panic disorders, preoccupation with death and dying, and grief/loss experiences. Sexual harm involves increased sex with adults and/or other children, increased peer homosexual play, precocious or provocative sexual behavior, and excessive masturbation. Harm to interpersonal relations show isolation and withdrawal, difficulty relating to and trusting others, and tragically—in a perpetuating cycle of evil—sexual abuse and violence against younger children.

THE DYNAMICS OF CHILD SEXUAL ABUSE

Most child sexual abuse is incestuous—perpetrated primarily by fathers, stepfathers, grandfathers, uncles, and father-figures against their daughters and sons, nephews and nieces, and grandchildren. Incest is the least reported and least discussed form of abuse. Its pervasive secrecy, wrapped within the sacred boundary of family—a boundary too often defended by the church to the harm of victims—helps maintain the abuse. In fact, many churches in which higher abuse rates exist also reveal the dynamics of incestuous families. Experienced counselors and ministers will recognize here the patterns that foster other kinds of abuse: legalism, spousal abuse, emotional and verbal abuse, and the abuse and manipulation of power seen in toxic faith communities.

The sexually incestuous family or church is a closed, pathological, legalistic, and secret system. Tremendous energy is invested in hiding evil while maintaining a righteous and religious appearance. The outside world—the world beyond the rigid and narrow bounds of the immediate family—is portrayed as threatening, hostile, anti-Christian, and completely untrustworthy. Attempts by family or church members to individuate—to leave the system and establish their own life—are challenged with predictions of chaotic consequences and punished by hostile rejection. Power, once again, is all important and is exercised coercively and capriciously through threats, intimidation, guilt promotion, silent withdrawal, even physical force.

The Unholy Triad. The three unholy rules of dysfunctional families—don't think, don't feel, don't talk—govern the incestuous family or church. Proper role and moral boundaries in the sexually incestuous family are confused, even nonexistent. Parents may talk more openly about sex, may walk around in their underwear, walk into children's bedrooms without knocking, and display little respect for the privacy of others. In the worst cases, parents and children alike may roam the house nude, walk in on anyone in the bathroom, in any state of undress, and inquire about, even coach the sexual behavior of their children.

Denial and lying are normative in the abusive family. Abuse is usually justified as a form of discipline, or sex education, or family love. Abusers reward their children for having sex with them and lying to keep it secret by giving them money, attention, affection, and avoiding physical abuse. Child victims sometimes have no sense of the harm done to them; they simply know nothing but a life of abuse and will report they were "learning about life" or "helping dad relax."

Similarly, under the guise of godly authority, incestuous churches will presume to control the marital, sexual, financial, vocational, and other decisions of its members. Abuse by the church or its members is denied and justified as right discipline or just consequences. Church, male, and parental authority and child (and usually adult female) submissiveness is defended at all cost.

Anyone who challenges these abusive church dynamics is considered deceived, reprobate, or under Satan's spell and is rebuked and shunned.

Even in healthier churches, children can be at some risk in relationships of trust with teachers and helpers who are in unique positions to molest children. Christian children, especially, are taught to "obey your parents [and any Christian adult in authority] . . . that it may go well with you . . ." (Eph. 6:1–3). This correct teaching, when corrupted by a sex offender, can make a child an easy target for sexual abuse.[8]

Sexual Abuse for Profit. Child sex-for-profit is a worldwide multibillion dollar human slave-trade that routinely brutalizes children through prostitution, beatings, torture, drug abuse, and murder. The hard-porn magazine *Nymph Lover* recently displayed a heavily drugged seven-year-old girl being raped and sodomized by a man and a woman. Children enter this deadly system by abduction, following abandonment by families, by sale from parents, and through international child-slavery rings posing as adoption and relief agencies.

Pedophile organizations are increasingly international, well funded, tightly run, highly sophisticated in their savvy and secrecy, and ruthless in their pursuit of child victims. Groups such as the Rene Guyon Society ("Sex by year eight or else it's too late") and NAMBLA (North American Man-Boy Love Association) push their perverted agendas under the guise of children's rights and political action. In a widely circulated booklet, *How to Have Sex with Kids,* the author states:

> It is best when beginning sex with a kid to do it as part of a game. . . . Curiosity is a big factor; exploring somebody and having them explore you. . . . Just about everything that adults can do together an adult and a kid can do. . . . Sometimes starting out sex is better if other kids are there doing it too. Group sex is a good way to experiment and experience all kinds of sex with all sorts of different partners. What better way to learn![9]

Divorce and family instability are key contributors to sexual abuse vulnerability. In one study, stepfathers were six times more likely to abuse stepdaughters compared to biological fathers.[10] A pedophile who had abused some 130 boys revealed, "For me, the magic words are 'My folks are divorced.' [Most] of the boys I've had sex with came from single-parent families. The others had family troubles."[11]

CHILD SEX ABUSERS IN THE MINISTRY

The tragic story of the Schultz family from New Jersey is all too typical across America.[12] In the fall of 1978, after a summer camp experience sponsored by a Newark parish, the eleven- and thirteen-year-old Schultz sons reported that they had been sexually abused while at camp. Brother Edmund, who had a history of sexual abuse prior to this job, was hired as an instructor in the parish school and as camp scoutmaster. He swam nude with the boys, exposed them to pornography, had them pose for pornographic pictures, masturbated in their presence, and forced the boys to manually masturbate himself. He threatened the boys not to tell their parents, but the boys returned home disturbed by all this and the truth finally came spilling out. The youngest boy was especially hurt by this abuse; he received extensive medical and psychiatric help but committed suicide in May 1979.

PROFILE OF PEDOPHILES AND EPHEBOPHILES

A pedophile is an adult who is sexually aroused by and/or acts out sexually on prepubescent children; the ebephophile is oriented to the pubescent preteen or teenager. The baseline profile of these child sexual offenders both fulfills and violates some common myths about them.[13] They are primarily men whose average age is thirty-five years and who have some relationship with the victim and the victim's family (one-half are relatives or caretakers of some sort).

The primary sexual activity of these abusers is exposure to pornography, genital fondling, and masturbation (intercourse is rarer). Sexual contact tends to happen without overt force but follows the grooming behavior of the pedophile that desensitizes the child to wrongful sex. This often makes the child compliant and appear to be cooperative, giving the pedophile the illusion of child consent and justification for the crime. Pedophilic grooming is a systematic seduction that wins the vulnerable and needy child's trusting openness by loving attention, physical affection, praise, sympathy, money, and material rewards.

Violence and forced sex are less common, even rare with these offenders. The harm to victims is often more subtle, more moral-spiritual and psychopathological than physical. Many pedophiles, as may be easily inferred from the many violators among church leadership, are intelligent and have some moral sensitivity. Their deviant sexual troubles are usually well hidden and maintained with enough control to continue abusing over many years without exposure.

Though many male pedophiles act-out sexually with boys, they should not be seen as pedohomosexuals. Though some pedophiles are homosexual or bisexual, the pure pedophile shows no sexual interest in or arousal by adults, whether heterosexual or homosexual. Pedophilia at its root is a unique sexual deviation.

A consistent finding in the research is that pedophiles and ebephophiles were often sexually abused as minors, frequently at the age that corresponds to their primary sexual interest. Flowing from this is the psychodynamic/developmental theory that the deviant behavior is motivated by the unconscious urge to return to the original abuse trauma. The abuser is thought to recreate his or her own abuse experience as a means to resolve deep inner turmoil.

Recent research, such as that in the area of homosexual development, points to biological influences—genetic, hormonal, and neurochemical bases for sexual pathologies. The renowned Sexual Disorders Clinic at Johns Hopkins University Hospitals, among others, reports that more severe pedophiles show sexual involvement with an adult as a child, or strong biological abnormalities, or both.[14] This is also consistent with the inhibiting impact of certain drugs that, outside the United States, are more regularly used in the treatment of this disorder.[15]

Fixated vs. Regressed Pedophiles. Nicholas Groth's research suggests classification of pedophiles as either fixated or regressed.[16] The fixated offender, who displays a deep-seated arrest or retardation of psychosexual development, is oriented to abuse children sexually due to an identification with children and a global motivation to live as a child. These offenders target boys more than girls, are extremely immature, have poor social and coping skills, and tend not to be remorseful about abusing children.

Regressed offenders display more mature levels of psychosexual development and tend not to be predisposed to sexual activity with children. They are more oriented to their peers, have better relationship skills, and often have adult sexual relations. The motivation to offend operates more as a stress-relief function than a fixated orientation—child sexual activity serves as a stress-release or conflict-reduction mechanism. Regressed pedophiles tend to act-out sexually with girls, victims usually known or related to the offender.

One Strike and You're Out. A constellation of factors are converging at the close of the twentieth century that raise the legitimate question whether the minister or counselor who sexually violates children should ever continue in professional ministry. First of all, apart from castration (a treatment that will not likely take hold in the United States), recidivism rates for all other forms of intervention are unacceptably high.[16] Second, legal trends—the growing liability for abuse, canceled insurance when pedophile restoration is attempted, and the crushing costs of legal defense and damages for some churches[17]—are making it nearly impossible to restore abusers to ministry. Finally, the resistance of church parents is fatal to restoration. As one parent of young children told us emphatically, "Whether or not a pedophile can be restored, I am not going to allow my children to be the guinea pigs that prove the success of the church's restoration experiment."

CONCLUSION: A TIME FOR ACTION

The wages of sexual sin and abuse against children in Christian counseling, the church, and in society is terrible—it is corrupting millions of lives and costing hundreds of millions of dollars in legal damages and treatment costs. If we are to urge abusers to come forth, confess their sins, and know Christ's forgiveness and redeeming power, we must be willing to pay for the resources to bring healing to fruition.

The church should make enormous investments in remedial recovery and move beyond that to emphasize prevention practices in every way possible. This includes training and education for sexual understanding and control, early assessment and intervention with at-risk counselors and ministers, development and maintenance of professional support systems, and genuine accountability. This work should become an integral core to ministry training in colleges, Bible schools, and seminaries and must be carried on in denominations, dioceses, and local churches and parishes. We must also, as the Body of Christ, be prepared to deal with the moral and legal ramifications and the lengthy time it may take to quell this epidemic. It is imperative that professional associations and church leadership take charge of this great challenge.

NOTES

1. This chapter is an expanded revision of the authors' article "Suffer the Little Children: Child Sexual Abuse in Society and the Church," *Christian Counseling Today* 1, no. 2 (April 1993), 14–18 and is used by permission.

2. See David Finkelhor, *Sexually Victimized Children* (New York: Free Press, 1979); *Child Sexual Abuse: New Theory and Research* (New York: Free Press, 1984).

3. See Finkelhor above; Douglas Besharov, "Doing Something about Child Abuse," *Harvard Journal of Law and Public Policy* 8 (1985): 539–89; Diana Russell, "The Incidence and Prevalence of Intrafamilial and Extrafamilial Sexual Abuse of Female Children," *International Journal of Child Abuse and Neglect* 7 (1983): 133–39.

4. Canadian National Population Survey. *Sexual Offenses Against Children: Report of the Committee on Sexual Offenses Against Children and Youth* (Ottawa: Canadian Government Publishing Centre, 1984); Anthony Baker and Sylvia Duncan, "Child Sexual Abuse: A Study of Prevalence in Great Britain," *International Journal of Child Abuse and Neglect* 9 (1985): 457–67.

5. See the *Los Angeles Times*, 25 August 1985; the national sexual abuse poll was summarized on page 1 on both days.

6. M. Silbert and A. Pines, "Sexual Abuse as an Antecedent to Prostitution," *International Journal of Child Abuse and Neglect* 5 (1981): 407–11; A. MacCormack, M. Janus, and A. Burgess, "Runaway Youths and Sexual Victimization: Gender Differences in an Adolescent Runaway Population," *International Journal of Child Abuse and Neglect* 10 (1986): 387–95; B. Bess and Y. Janssen, "Incest: A Pilot Study," *Hillside Journal of Clinical Psychiatry* 4 (1982): 39–52; J. Goodwin, T. McCarthy, and P. DiVasto, "Prior Incest in Mothers of Abused Children," *International Journal of Child Abuse and Neglect* 5 (1981): 87–96.

7. Jeffrey J. Haugaard and N. Dickon Reppucci, *The Sexual Abuse of Children* (San Francisco: Jossey-Bass, 1988); Grant L. Martin, *Critical Problems in Children and Youth* (Dallas: Word, 1992); and William Friedrich, "Sexual Victimization and Sexual Behavior in Children: A Review of Recent Literature," *International Journal of Child Abuse and Neglect* 17 (1993): 59–66.

8. See Roland C. Summit, "The Child Sexual Abuse Accommodation Syndrome," *International Journal of Child Abuse and Neglect*, 7 (1983): 177–93.

9. David Sonenschein, *How to Have Sex with Kids*, Austin Pedophile Study Group II. Pamplet presented by the San Bernardino Sheriff's Crimes Against Children Detail, 655 East Third Street, San Bernardino, California 92415.

10. See Haugaard and Reppucci, *The Sexual Abuse of Children*.

11. Sonenschein, *How to Have Sex*.

12. Reported in the case of *Schultz v. Roman Catholic Archdiocese of Newark*, 95 N. J. 530, 472 A. 2d 531 (1984).

13. See Fred Berlin and E. W. Krout, "Pedophilia: Diagnostic Concepts, Treatment, and Ethical Considerations," *American Journal of Forensic Psychiatry* 7 (1983): 13–30; and Kenneth Plummer, "Pedophilia: Constructing a Sociological Baseline," in *Adult Sexual Interest in Children: Personality and Psychopathy*, ed. Mark Cook and Kevin Howells (London: Academic Press, 1981), 221.

14. Reported in Raymond C. O'Brien, "Pedophilia: The Legal Predicament of Clergy," *Journal of Contemporary Health Law and Policy* 4, (1988): 91–154.

15. See Berlin and Krout, "Pedophilia," 13–30.

16. A. Nicholas Groth, *Men Who Rape* (New York: Plenum, 1979); and A. N. Groth and R. C. Birnbaum, "Adult Sexual Orientation and Attraction to Underage Persons," *Archives of Sexual Behavior* 7 (1978): 175–81.

17. Studies of castrated men in Sweden, Holland, and Switzerland show recidivism rates of 1 to 3 percent, while recidivism for other forms of treatment fall in the 40 to 80 percent range. Reported in Berlin and Krout, "Pedophilia," 13–30.

18. The Catholic Archdiocese of New Mexico is currently facing fifty million dollars in legal costs and damage awards, a sum widely considered capable of bankrupting the Archdiocese. Reported in *The National Catholic Reporter* 30, no. 14 (February 1994): 5.

Chapter Eight

Who Will Heal the Little Ones? Helping Child Victims

by Carol Carrell, MA, MFCC[1]

PHOEBE: *I love you, Wabbit. Will you be my friend?*
WABBIT: *I'd love to be your friend, but I don't know how. What must I do?*
PHOEBE: *Just play with me.*
WABBIT: *OK, I can do that. And friends take care of each other. What must I do to take care of you?* (Wabbit touches her hand)
PHOEBE: *I'll take care of you, Wabbit.*
WABBIT: *Of course you will. And I need to know how to take of you, too.*
PHOEBE: *Well, when I get scared . . . When I have nightmares . . . Well, if the house catches on fire, you will help me jump into a bathtub filled with water, so we won't get burned—or maybe into a lake. Or maybe we'll need more water—so maybe into the ocean . . .*
WABBIT: *Well, I can help you and me into a bathtub and maybe a lake—but I'll need your help with an ocean, 'cause I can't swim.*
PHOEBE: *There'll be a big island, Wabbit* (petting it and head very close). *I won't let you drown.*
WABBIT: *Good. You know, I used to get scared at night, too.*
PHOEBE: *You got scared? Oh Wabbit, what did you get scared of?*
WABBIT: *I once dreamed a nightmare about being all alone. It scared me a lot then. But then I woke up and told Rocky Raccoon about it, and she held me and I wasn't alone anymore. Now I'm older and I can be your friend and protect you.*
PHOEBE: (Moving very close) *I have scary dreams, too.* (She pets Wabbit, looking at the puppet's face . . .) [2]

Child therapist using the puppet Wabbit to build trust, elicit information, and help five-year-old Phoebe.

First THEY TELL ME THAT THERE IS no tooth fairy, no Easter bunny, and no Santa Claus—when are they going to tell me there is no Jesus?" A little, blond, blue-eyed girl sits in front of the therapist with her chin held high, lips tight, and a look in her eyes that goes way beyond her six years. Why should she trust this person? She trusted before and was betrayed by a person that was called by God.

Considering the manifest horror of child sexual abuse, it is no wonder that Jesus would be incensed with this kind of evil—especially when done under God's name. "Woe to you, Pharisees, and you religious leaders! You are like beautiful mausoleums—full of dead men's bones, and of foulness, and corruption. You try to look like saintly men, but underneath those pious robes of yours are hearts besmirched with every sort of hypocrisy and sin. Snakes! Sons of vipers! How shall you escape the judgment of hell?"[3]

Working with children who are victims of sexual abuse by counselors and clergy involves some special skills because of the dynamic of betrayed trust by a highly placed person in authority. There is an added burden in helping children who suffer abuse from clergy because the whole question of God's involvement becomes critical.[4] There are countless wounded, bleeding children (many in adult bodies) in congregations and communities. Not only do we need to be aware of the warning signs of sexual abuse and exploitation, we need to learn to heal and prevent the ever-expanding epidemic from destroying our future.

CHILD SEXUAL ABUSE SEDUCTION

In light of the variety of sexual harm that is perpetrated on children, Sue Bloom suggested a new definition for incest. She proposes that *incest* can be seen as *the imposition of sexually inappropriate acts, or acts with sexual overtones, by—or any use of a minor child to meet the sexual or sexual/emotional needs of—one or more persons who derive authority through ongoing emotional bonding with that child.*[5]

The dynamics of child sexual abuse are illustrated by five interrelated stages of abusive interaction: grooming, sexual activity, secrets, disclosure, and suppression.[6]

GROOMING

Grooming means to prepare another, to desensitize a child to participate in sexual activity with an adult. The grooming behavior begins with the offender treating the child as special. Often the intended victim is the first child in a group of children to be acknowledged and the recipient of the last word of contact. Special gifts, trips, and one-on-one time help to single out the intended victim from family or friends. There may be exaggerated promises of gifts, presents, or special times together. Unfortunately, parents and guardians tend to blindly trust professional caregivers, who may also be abusive—clergy, psychotherapists, health providers, and teachers.

In addition to the special bonding, the offender will start to occasionally add pleasant physical sensations. These may include tickling, brushing hair, back or body rubs, or hugs that last longer than hugs from others. The child begins to associate the pleasant physical sensations with the offender in addition to the gifts, trips, and the feeling of being a special person (above everyone else) in the offender's life.

He said I was special to God and to him. Being special was a secret that we couldn't tell mommy or daddy.

SEXUAL ACTIVITY

The process of engaging a child in sexual activity starts with the grooming process and gradually expands with the addition of pleasant physical sensations. Up to this point, it is unlikely that any sexual abuse has occurred. Nudity is often introduced by providing opportunities for the child to observe the offender nude, after a bath or shower, or while changing clothes. The genitals may be exposed with or without comment. The offender may observe the child while they bathe or be vigilant while they play unattended.

Pornography, whether video, audio, or printed, may be shared in a way that emphasizes the special bond and further promotes the secret aspect of the abuse process. The physical aspect of the abuse progresses from longer and longer hugs to kissing, fondling, masturbation, and eventually sexual intercourse. The perversely skilled molester will take the time to desensitize and make the child feel comfortable at each progressive stage.

The first time I saw him with no clothes was at family camp. He helped me change my bathing suit. He changed his too. That's when I first saw his private parts.

KEEPING SECRETS

The offender will attempt to isolate the child by bribery, threats, blame, intimidation, and to the extreme—torture and violence.

Bribery may include promises to buy treasured items if the child does not talk. Threats may include statements like, "They'll send me to jail if you tell," or "You'll never see me again if anyone finds out." Statements of blame include, "You didn't say no," and "You wanted to do it." The adult may intimidate by saying something like, "I'm an adult and no one believes kids anyway. After all, I am a Sunday School teacher!"

Torture may include injuring the child physically during the sexual act, injuring or hurting the child separate from the sexual act, and imprisoning the child for a short time. It can also include killing or harming a pet or animal while the child observes and/or threatening to harm the child's siblings or parents. These terrorist acts will help ensure that the child keeps the secret.

He said if I told he wouldn't be my Sunday School teacher anymore, and the other kids would be upset with me 'cause I made him go away.

DISCLOSURE

Sexual abuse is usually not reported. Because of the special relationship with the offender or the fear of reprisals to family members, the victim will often seek to protect the offender. Also, children frequently do not have the verbal or cognitive skills to understand and clearly report what has happened to them. When abuse has occurred over a period of time, children become confused and think the abuse was their fault; they feel partially responsible because they did not disclose at the start. One child stated, "Pastor said because I didn't tell at first it was my fault, because I kept staying after youth group when everyone else went home."

When the child does disclose the abuse it is important to validate the disclosure—"Thank you for telling me." The child may be uncomfortable with the words used to tell and the subject matter itself. Children usually do not lie regarding sexual abuse issues.[7] It is important to let the child know that you believe the disclosure, not only to build therapeutic trust but to validate the child's struggle.

It is not necessary to have all the details and exact chronological order of events. (However, you may need to put them into chronological order later if you are going to testify in court.) Children remember by reference to holidays, school being in or out of session, and by their birthdays rather than by months, days, or weeks.

A child may not be able to give all the details at the first mention of the abuse.

It is important not to put words into the child's mouth who is relating information about the abuse. This is not the time to correct misconceptions or discuss proper names for body parts. This type of digression often confuses the child and reaffirms that adults do not believe children.

Children may be embarrassed, scared, and confused during disclosure. It is important to remember that the child may have been bribed, threatened, blamed, intimidated, physically harmed, or tortured. Affirm that the abuse was NOT the child's fault. Inform the child what may happen next, that a report will be filed (if it has not been filed already), and that others (policemen or child protection workers) may talk to him or her about the abuse. Do not promise what may or may not happen to the abuser.

Disclosure may occur at inappropriate times and/or places. For example, the child may share at the dinner table, while driving to the store, in a classroom, or even while parents and family members are watching television. One mother shared her experience: "We had friends over for dinner. After dinner we were all sitting around the fireplace drinking coffee when Kattie calmly said John had been putting his hands in her underpants. I just couldn't believe what I was hearing."

SUPPRESSION

Often, after the emotional and physically trying disclosure, the child may attempt to return to the precrime state by suppressing, denying, and/or rationalizing the abuse. "It's no big deal in my life. I'm fine." The child may even articulate the desire of wishing that he or she had not disclosed. "I wish I never had told. My life has been a constant up and down ever since! Nothing would have happened if I hadn't told." These are examples of the burden of guilt for all the ramifications that often occur to family, friends, and community.

It will be important to acknowledge the need for times of respite and to provide physical and emotional safety for the child. The therapeutic environment should foster these things, and the therapist should become one to whom the child retreats for affirmation, support, and encouragement. Understanding the ambivalence and emotional distress of the disclosure/suppression process is crucial for the therapist working with child victims.

THE IMPACT ON THE CHILD

In addition to the feelings and reactions that we listed in chapter 7, probably the most significant feeling for many children is one of shame. A child feels shame due to the sexual behavior—taking responsibility for the actions of significant adults. Because the offender is a person associated with God, the child is robbed of the one place he or she should know constant safety and healing. God may become identified as a coconspirator with the offender to bring harm instead of hope to the child.

One child stated, "He would touch me in church, you know when no one else was around. That is God's House. God knows all. I guess God didn't stop him 'cause it was all my fault. You know he really is the good person 'cause God chose him. I guess God doesn't choose kids." The child in this situation may readily identify with the Psalmist's words: "My God, my God; why have you forsaken me? Why are you so far from helping me, from the words of my groaning? O my God, I cry by day, but you do not answer: and by night, but find no rest" (Ps. 22: 1–2).

Webster's New World Dictionary defines shame as "a painful feeling of having lost the respect of others because of the improper behavior, incompetence, etc. of oneself or another; a tendency to have feelings of this kind or a capacity of such feeling; dishonor or disgrace; a person or thing that brings shame, dishonor, or disgrace; something regrettable, unfortunate, or outrageous."[8]

Numerous studies have indicated that children hold on to guilt and shame and use it to mold into place crude foundational blocks that shape their very beings as adults. Listen to the following words as children tell their stories.

— *I grew up knowing that God loved me. I just thought it was because he had to, not because I was worthy, deserved love, or was valuable. I was just another obligation.*

— *Jesus loves me when I am a good girl. Larry hurt me and I didn't like it. He said I was a bad girl. Jesus doesn't love me anymore.*

— *All you have to do is call on Jesus to save you and He will. Well He didn't! And you want me to come to church and hear a bunch of false promises again? No thanks!*

— *I can't get close to Heavenly Father. My biological father was a preacher who would preach hellfire and brimstone on Sundays and touch us girls in ways no father should. God is my father's God—*

not mine! I would rather have nothing than endure the hypocrisy of
the church. Every time I look at a preacher I want to scream liar,
thief. If there is indeed a God, I hope He will condemn you to the
hellfire and brimstone my father was so fond of.

— *Everyone knew what happened to our family after everything (in-*
cestuous abuse) became public. We were treated as if we had leprosy.
On Sundays ladies would smile, nod, or pat my hand yet scurry off
quickly to avoid any possible conversation of my family's plight. If
we don't talk about it, it really doesn't exist, especially in our church.

— *Where do I take my anger with God? If I say I am mad at God, I*
get people shoving Scripture down my throat. Where is all that good
Christian love? It's there only when life is pretty and pink, never
when it is filled with shame, guilt, despair, and dirt.

These abuse experiences become the building blocks of pain, despair, and depression that can last a lifetime. As stewards of these children, we need to heed the warning signs, listen to the children, and feel and acknowledge the pain that has left them with long-lasting scars. Our children look to us for truth in words and actions that is consistent with God's Word.

THE COUNSELING ENVIRONMENT

ROOM SETTING

The area of the room is not as important as the atmosphere. Too many toys may suggest a play time, while no toys may suggest "adults only" to the child. During the interview there should be no interruptions: no one should enter the room, and the phone should be placed on hold. Ideally, a child-size table and chairs or large pillows will help the child acclimate to the interview process.

PARENTS IN THE ROOM

It is usually recommended that parents wait in another room while the clinical interview takes place. Otherwise, a child will look to the parents for cues, assessing their reaction to what is being said before proceeding. Sometimes the child will not proceed at all due to parental tension. It is recommended that the child be shown exactly where the parent(s) will be while the child is in the interview room. If the child is not able to tolerate the parents' absence, instruct the parents to sit behind the child out of direct sight.

Supplies

Basic supplies for an interview include a set of anatomical dolls, crayons, markers and paper or a white board, hand puppets, stuffed animals, play house with figures, and a sand tray with figures. Crayons should be nontoxic and washable. Colored pencils and pens can be added according to space and budget. The paper can be any size or color.

Hand puppets represent themes of security (soft and cuddly), authority, and fear (dangerous and scary). Soft and cuddly puppets can be kittens, puppies, bears, and bunnies. Authority puppets are larger animals such as a dog compared to a puppy, or puppets of a mom, dad, doctor, nurse, policeman, teacher, or pastor represent authority figures. Scary puppets might include lions, tigers, dinosaurs, or something with large teeth and/or claws.

Stuffed animals in similar categories are useful for children who are not comfortable with puppets or do not possess the mechanical skills to operate a hand puppet. Preference for hand puppets or stuffed animals may develop with the interviewer over a period of time, but the ultimate decision must be based on the child's ability and preferences.

A playhouse needs to be sturdy and accessible to a child. It should include a kitchen, living room, bedroom, and bathroom. The playhouse figures should be nonbreakable and include adults and children.

Sand trays vary from twenty to thirty inches long and should be at least four to eight inches deep. It is best to have one tray for dry sand and one tray for wet sand. In the sand tray area provide water, towels, tissues, and a rug or tarp to protect the floor. Objects used in sand play therapy include, people, animals, aliens, cartoon characters, vehicles, artificial plants, and natural objects such as wood, rocks, and shells.[9]

Anatomical Dolls

The use of anatomical dolls can be helpful and also risky. In order to minimize the risk of false attributions by children when using these dolls and to increase the validity of the helper's interpretations for courtroom testimony, I make the following recommendations.

First of all, the helper should be well trained in the use of anatomical dolls before attempting to use them. Second, when a court battle clearly looms, it is wise to videotape the session or to have the session with a trained observer (behind a one-way mirror) who can monitor the behavior of the child and the helper. These precautionary measures are critical in order to avoid false accusations by the child, or suggestions that the helper produced false memories. .

The set of anatomical dolls should include both sexes with adult and child dolls of distinct sizes for easy differentiation by the child. It is preferable for the dolls to be of the same ethnic origin as the child, although this is not vital. The dolls should be large enough to handle easily—usually about eighteen to twenty-four inches. Smaller dolls are difficult for young children to manipulate due to their limited motor skills.

The female dolls should have oral, vaginal, and anal openings, and the male dolls should have oral and anal openings, penis, and scrotum. The hands need to be detailed, with thumbs and fingers, in order to be able to assess digital penetration and fondling topics. (Dolls with mitt type hands can be confusing when a child is trying to demonstrate what happened.) Adult dolls should have all the parts appropriate to male or female, and the pubic hair should be depicted by cloth, string, fur, or drawings on the doll's body.

The clothing on the dolls should be easy for children to remove. Velcro is an ideal closure for pants, shirts, and dresses as buttons and button holes can be frustrating for young children. Basic clothing consists of pants, shirt, and underwear for male dolls; female dolls should have a dress and underpants with a bra for the adult female doll. If both child dolls are dressed in pants and shirts, the child should be able to identify the boy from the girl easily, either by differences in hair styles or by gender-specific objects such as barrettes or ribbons.

The anatomical dolls are used first to assess the child's knowledge of body parts and body functions. The dolls are introduced as *tools*. For example, the counselor may say to the child, "Tools like hammers and nails help you to build a house. Tools like forks and spoons help you to eat your dinner. These dolls are tools that help us talk about people's bodies." Referring to them simply as dolls may encourage the child to indulge in fantasy play activity. As a result, "what a child does with these dolls may have nothing to do at all with what has taken place in reality."[10]

It is important to substantiate abuse by independent, corroborative means. The helper should not depend on the dolls alone. If part A fits into part B, this does not necessarily indicate that a child has been sexually abused. A child may do this because he or she is curious, inquisitive, or bored with the interview process. To substantiate abuse, the child's actions with the dolls need to be clarified as an event that happened to the child, not simply as a function of fantasy play.

CHILD TREATMENT

Jesus commanded, "Let the little children come to me, and do not hinder them, for the kingdom of God belongs to such as these" (Mark 10:14).

The treatment process must respect the five seduction elements outlined above. Treatment is designed to challenge the lies inherent in the seduction process, to give the child experiences that demonstrate respect for boundaries, and to provide therapy that encourages healing for the deep feelings of betrayal, anxiety, fear, anger, and shame. In addition, effective healing includes equipping children to be able to effectively challenge inappropriate uses of authority in their lives.

Abused children often grow up with only happy, mad, glad, or sad as their emotional expressions. With their suppressed feelings held behind a barrier of anger, they do not have the ability to express and experience feelings of joy, adulation, love, caring, wonderment, assurance, and power. Passion in the mental, physical, and spiritual dimensions is lost. The offender has robbed the child of the ability to experience true passion—and giggles.

When a child's trust and innocence is broken, the child may not appear angry. In fact, the child may deny any emotional response at all. Yet as he or she grows and develops, emotional, physical, and spiritual scars become evident. During the healing process, whether as a child or an adult, anger will often surface—it is generally one of the first emotions that surfaces. It has served as a reliable barrier to hold back rage, disgust, hate, loathing, fear, loneliness, isolation, desperation, suicide, emptiness, shame, guilt, and depression.

Numerous models exist for child sexual abuse treatment with the processes divided into two phases: (1) crisis intervention and (2) treatment. Crisis intervention often requires complete life support help for the victim and family. Central tasks involve reporting, providing protection, investigating, and planning and coordinating the range of social, legal, medical, and mental health services needed. The treatment phase is outlined below.

THE EVALUATION INTERVIEW

The interview process will proceed in three stages according to the child's age and development: (1) the first component assesses the child's language development and cognitive ability; (2) the second component focuses on the sexual issue—whether sexual trauma, knowledge, experience, or play; (3) the third component is closure. Closure may occur during the first or second component if the child becomes markedly distraught by the material, becomes inattentive (due to age and energy level), or if required by time parameters. If the child becomes distraught during the interview, the counselor will need to end the session or change the modality—move from anatomical dolls to puppets or the sand tray. The interview process is not intended to retraumatize the child.

First Stage. The first stage of the interview addresses the safety issues for the child and puts the parent or primary caregiver at ease. In the interview room, give the child permission to check in with parents as reassurance that he or she is not being captured or abandoned. The interviewer should introduce herself or himself to the child and ask the child's name. The focus of the interview is determined by previous disclosure from the parents or caregivers and the intent is clarification. If there has been no disclosure but there is suspicion of abuse, then the interview will focus on disclosure and clarification.

When working with very young children it is wise to restrict sentences to a minimal vocabulary and to ask only one question at a time. Sometimes it may be necessary to ask the same question in different ways. For example, "Was his penis *on* your bottom?" or "Was his penis *in* your bottom?" or "Was his penis *next to* your bottom?" or "Was his penis *below* your bottom?" Asking simple questions in various ways, after disclosure has been indicated, can help the child to identify precisely what occurred. However, the counselor must be careful not to lead the child to an answer, especially if the information is likely to be required in court testimony.

In addition to asking simple questions, the counselor must constantly assess the child's ability to understand and respond with correct information. The interviewer must always be aware that the child may give an incorrect answer or a misleading answer to protect the abuser, to protect parents, or to please the interviewer. Helping the child distinguish between the truth and a lie will establish an appropriate atmosphere for the interview. Affirming that it is always better to tell the truth often helps the child to understand the seriousness of the process. Children may want to please the interviewer by responding "yes" or "no" to a question if they perceive a positive response from the interviewer, which can lead to false accusations and confusion. Thus, it is important for the counselor to be somewhat tentative and to reinforce the importance of telling the truth.

Sometimes children who are distracted by toys they have not seen or played with in the past may look on the interview as just another playtime. Since playtime can include fantasy and make believe, it is important to stress the need to talk about what really happened. Remember that when children become stressed during the interview, they may divert into fantasy play.

Second Stage. This stage focuses on gathering accurate information regarding the sexual abuse experience. The counselor must try to determine what happened from the child's perspective and how the abuse is affecting him or her at this point. The child may say, "Daddy hurt my private parts." It is important to find out who daddy is—a biological father, stepfather, foster father, or someone else's daddy. Ask the child who Daddy is and what is his name.

The names that the child uses for body parts should also be used by the counselor during the interview. The interview is not an educational time and new names can confuse children and cause them to feel inferior for not knowing the right words. If the child should use the term *wiener*, it is important not to correct the child's use of the word and suggest the term *penis*. In addition, correcting the child in this way can be interpreted by the judicial system as leading the child and would, therefore, be inadmissable as evidence. The couselor must be able to say (without any perceptual reaction) the child's words for body parts, bodily functions, and sexual vernacular. During the session, the counselor must also be aware of body posture, tone of voice, and facial expression. If the child detects any unease, distaste, or revulsion on the part of the counselor, the child may stop the interview or edit the information.

Last Stage—Closure. It is helpful to leave time at the end of the session for the child to transition out of the topic of sexual abuse. This can be accomplished by drawing pictures of lighthearted topics, such as flowers or a favorite animal, or by another activity that is emotionally neutral. This enables the child to regain composure and focus before returning to the parents or primary caregiver.

Treatment Options

Group Therapy for Children. One of the benefits of working in a group is that children realize they are not the only child who has been abused. They can relate to other children who have endured "special" relationships and have been told "not to tell or else." As children spend time together in therapy they learn to trust themselves, their peers, and the adult leader(s). The leaders must carefully monitor the group process so that a child is not pressured to admit to something that did not happen, nor repress something that did occur.

As group trust develops, the children learn appropriate social skills and sexual boundaries. They learn how to handle differences within the group structure and how to resolve conflict without threats, intimidation, or violence. Self-esteem that has been damaged and changed by the abuse can be healed, encouraged, and strengthened in an atmosphere where the child is respected, valued, and cared for.

Ideally, group size for an individual counselor will range from four to seven members. If a cofacilitator is available, the group size may increase up to as many as twelve to fourteen members. Factors that determine the direction of group therapy include (1) the intensity of the topic, (2) the age of the group, and (3) the modality used. For example, play therapy is particularly useful for young children, who generally become bored after ten minutes of discussion.

Group Therapy for Adolescents. Group therapy is a good choice for adolescents because of the power of peer influence, if that peer pressure is harnessed by the counselor for therapeutic benefit. Peers who have experienced similar trauma can be highly effective sources of support, care, challenge, and persuasion for teens who are dealing with the fear, rage, and confusion of abuse and family upheaval. They can also model inappropriate rage, avoidance, and annoying distractions.

The most effective groups are open: experienced members help new members; members are free to discuss and explore any issue; and members can ask questions and know they will receive clear answers. The most effective counselors are those who model godly values and appropriate behavior, who guide the discussion without controlling it, and who facilitate peer influence for the best interest of victims.

Family Therapy. The goal of family therapy is to restore families to an open and nurturing system with the understanding that protecting the child from further abuse must be a priority before family reunification. Families need to be assessed for both the incestuous behavior pattern and the family's contribution to the abuse—how members colluded with the abuser and denied the molest experience.

Families in therapy for sexual abuse are usually in disarray, are divided, and frequently are battling the criminal justice and social service systems. They are angry, frightened, resentful, and often in treatment involuntarily. The family therapist must firmly and compassionately maintain an abuse focus or the family will deny and defocus this central issue.

Themes common to family therapy for sexual abuse include the following:

- abuse of power and authority
- failure to respect privacy
- failure to protect the abused
- poor communication patterns
- blurred role boundaries
- inadequate or abusive child discipline
- emotional abuse and deprivation
- denial and lying
- magical expectations about change

Family therapy with offending family systems is usually very intense and demands from the counselor a high level of skill, energy, dedication, self-awareness, and ethical focus. Novice and inexperienced counselors should avoid this clinical and moral minefield!

Individual Therapy. Child sexual abuse treatment for younger children centers around expressive therapies: art, music, dolls, puppets, dance, and play therapy. These modes of therapy are also helpful for older, even adolescent children who are withdrawn into depression or hostility. Traumatized children who are unable to verbalize their abuse experience respond well to the arts. These active, expressive therapies provide an effective forum for the communication and resolution of the abuse.

Art therapy includes several mediums such as drawing, painting, paste and paper, finger painting, and collage. The visual image enables victims to express and communicate what they are not able to express verbally. With art therapy, children can change and alter the circumstances of the abuse, learn safety measures, and practice those measures. For example, by using a puppet they can learn to say "No, I don't want to. I am going to tell my Mom now." Fear can be acted out with the puppets, anger can be expressed by smashing an offender made of clay, and isolation can be shown in a drawing.

TREATMENT PROCESS

Therapy with children is a distinctive process. It requires a special skill grounded upon a fundamental notion of child development theory. That is to view the child as a child, a unique being in his or her own right and not a miniature adult. Children cannot be helped by a mere adaptation of adult treatment principles.

A number of factors affect the nature, length, and depth of the treatment process. As Grant Martin states, "The smaller the base of support for the child, the more dysfunctional the family system, and the more significant the offender, the longer the expected treatment period."[11] The length of time for the therapy sessions will depend upon the child's ability, age, and development. It may be useful to schedule one to two hours for an initial interview. However, it is not unusual for the initial interview process to require more than one session since the clinical interview is a new process for the child. In addition, the child must focus on subjects that can be disturbing, confusing, and painful to relate.

Very young children have unique developmental needs. They should not be scheduled during their normal nap or meal time as they can be tired, irritated, and hungry, which can all interfere with the counseling process. If additional sessions are needed, it is advisable to schedule them at the same time of day. During the disclosure period, sessions may need to be scheduled close together due to the shorter memory spans of young children.

Issues in Treating Children Abused by Christian Ministers. As can be expected, when a child is abused by a clergyperson or Christian counselor, the significance of that role in the life of the child contributes a great deal to his or her harm. As a result, the following treatment issues become critical in the healing process. These issues will need to be addressed with the child as well as with her or his parents or primary caregivers.

- **feelings of ambivalence toward the offender**—Help the child resolve these feelings by accepting the necessary experience of a range of feelings and encouraging the child to express the full range. It is also important to help the child differentiate between genuine love and physical touch.

- **struggles with the image of God** — The child often has feelings of ambivalence toward God and may present difficult questions. The counselor needs to distinguish the evil behavior and the offender's refusal to do God's will from God's grace. The child needs to understand that Christ suffered and can help heal. Gently affirm God's care, but give the child lots of room to work through the pain of felt abandonment and betrayal.

- **fear and anxiety** — Children will need assurance of protection from reprisal by offender, parents, siblings, church members, and others. They will need help to express fears and to sort out realistic fears from unrealistic ones. It is vital that the counselor affirm the child's decision to disclose.

- **guilt and low self-esteem** — These two reactions are often related as the child deals with a sense of blame for sexual involvement. Help the child vent feelings of guilt and encourage the child to receive God's unconditional love. Frequently reinforce the message that the child did not cause the abuse, nor is the child responsible for the chaos that follows disclosure. Identify and affirm the child's good qualities in a consistent way.

- **trust and role confusion** — Acknowledge the real harm that occurs when an important person betrays a child. Give the child lots of room to learn to trust you as another person in authority—but do not push the child to rely on your good qualities. Be careful to respect boundaries such as touch, and respect the child's wishes.

- **anger and depression** — Often, children are outwardly depressed and inwardly hostile. They feel powerless because of the type of harm and may tend toward self-destructive or suicidal behavior. Gently lead the child to release pent-up feelings of anger and aim to support them unconditionally. Group therapy may be a good place to model constructive anger release.

- **difficulty in talking about the abuse** — The child may lack the language skills necessary to talk clearly about the abuse. In such cases the counselor can emphasize the importance of alternative ways to express feelings and thoughts. The child may not

identify what happened as abuse and will need to be gently educated to understand the harm and the importance of stopping.
Encourage the child to talk openly and to break the pattern of
keeping secrets enforced by the offender.

- **preoccupation with sexual issues** — Due to evil violations, the
sexual innocence of children is lost. They are prematurely conditioned by sexual feelings and often become preoccupied with sex
in inappropriate ways. The counselor will need to educate the
child regarding sexual feelings and inappropriate sexual behavior and relating. This is done by modeling, discussing, and
allowing for open sharing about sexual matters without ever
crossing inappropriate boundaries.

CONCLUSION

One of the harshest judgments against sin is Jesus' declaration
against those who harm children, "And whoever welcomes a little
child like this in my name welcomes me. But if anyone causes one
of these little ones who believe in me to sin, it would be better for
him to have a large millstone hung around his neck and to be
drowned in the depths of the sea" (Matt. 18:5–6). One can scarcely
imagine the horrific end of those who will face God one day with
lives blackened with this unrepentant evil. May God have mercy!

Naturally, the best thing would be for men and women to heed the
warning and avoid harming children. When this does not happen,
counselors must be prepared to help the little ones afflicted with harm.
The wise counselor will be at least adequately prepared to treat children who are victims of sexual abuse and will continue to learn the
most efficacious ways to provide that treatment. Our children's future
rests on our willingness to help them heal.

NOTES

1. Carol A. Carrell, is licensed in California as a marriage, family, and child
counselor. She is Associate Clinical Director of The Redwood Family Institute in
Eureka, California, where she maintains an active clinical and consulting practice specializing in the treatment of children, adults molested as children, and
family therapy.

2. Bunny Duhl and Frederick Duhl, "Integrative Family Therapy," in *Handbook of Family Therapy*, vol. 1, ed. A. Gurman and D. Kniskern (New York: Bruner/
Mazel, 1981), 490–91.

3. Matthew 23: 27–28, 33; *The Living Bible*, paraphrased.

4. As indicated in chapter 4, there are no reliable statistics available on the numbers of children molested by professional counselors. We do know, however, that a significant number of children have been victims of clergy sexual misconduct. This chapter focuses on issues that emphasize the impact of clergy abuse. Many of these dynamics do not differ significantly from child sexual abuse in general. For another excellent study of the topic of child sexual abuse, see Grant Martin's chapters in *Critical Problems in Children and Youth* (Dallas: Word, 1992).

5. E. Sue Blume, *Secret Survivors: Uncovering Incest and its After Effects* (New York: Wiley, 1990), 4 (italics in original).

6. See Roland Summit, "The Child Abuse Accommodation Syndrome," *International Journal of Child Abuse and Neglect* 7 (1983): 177–93.

7. But, as Grant Martin (*Critical Problems*) so cogently states, "children do lie" (107); see exhibit 4.1 and 4.2 on evaluating the veracity of abuse allegations (112–20).

8. *Webster's New World Dictionary, Second College Edition* (Cleveland: Prentice Hall, 1986), 1308.

9. Gisela S. DeDomenico, "Sand Tray, World Play: A Psychotherapeutic Technique for Individuals, Couples, and Families," *The California Therapist* 5, no. 1 (1993): 57.

10. Richard Gardner, *Sex Abuse Hysteria: Salem Witch Trials Revisited* (Cresskill, N.J.: Creative Therapeutics, 1991), 53.

11. Martin, *Critical Problems*, 129. I am grateful to Grant Martin for his efforts to distinguish the treatment issues and acknowledge my debt to his work in this area. See chapter 4 of his text.

PART IV

Policy and Practice in the Church

Chapter Nine

Misconduct Policy and Practice in the Protestant Church

The church has within it the resources to name and confront sexual abuse. In fact, Scripture mandates the church to stand with those who are objects of harm and exploitation, to protect the little ones, to offer hospitality to the vulnerable, to set free those imprisoned by social convention. Jesus' ministry with women and children provides an unequivocal model of justice-making as the appropriate response to the injustices heaped on the oppressed.[1]

THE PROTESTANT CHURCH HAS DONE BOTH well and poorly in fulfilling the mandate that Marie Fortune outlines in the paragraph above. (We consider the Catholic church in regard to this crisis in the next chapter.) She argues, and argues well, that the church's response to sexual abuse "has been a prime example of *religion in service to patriarchy.*"[2] We agree with her in other writings, however, that elements of the Protestant church have begun to take assertive action against sexual abuse within its leadership. Yet the response has been slow in coming, and there are parts of the church that still effectively deny the harm of sexual misconduct and refuse to take appropriate action. Even in those parts of the church where misconduct response policy has developed well, prevention and justice practices have often fallen far behind policy.

CHURCH POLICY REGARDING SEXUAL MISCONDUCT

Every church, at both local and corporate levels, should have an effective sexual misconduct response policy in place. Not to have such a policy by the last half of the 1990s is negligent and fool-ish—groups that do not, court institutional and legal disaster. The failure to have policies that guide the investigation and resolution of complaints often leaves victims feeling revictimized and more wounded and angry. In this chapter we will outline the most im-portant elements for consideration in a misconduct policy. (Examples of functioning church policy are provided in appendix A.) We also analyze the policy and behavior of the Protestant church to date, calling on the church to rise to the demands of the policy crisis.

Policies should begin with the call of Christ to sexual sanctifica-tion and integrity. (See 1 Thess. 4:1–8.) The policy should include

- a clear definition of sexual misconduct;
- a definition of a misconduct response team (committee) and its specific duties;
- procedures for investigation and adjudication of complaints (in-cluding discovery);
- assistance and intervention to help victims (including profes-sional consultation);
- procedures to challenge, suspend, investigate, get help for, and if necessary, take action against offenders.

We suggest churches include a code of client and congregant rights that promotes the priority of protection against sexual abuse and healing and justice for victims. There must be a clearly de-fined and dedicated group within the church who will maintain a commitment to the victims of abuse. Otherwise, churches too of-ten get pulled into a vortex of charges and countercharges that paralyzes the church and focuses too much concern on the rights and prerogatives of offenders; this results in neither healing nor justice. As we have noted previously, this chaotic experience is the impetus to suit for many victims.

Policies regarding the at-risk or offending minister should cover several critical points. These include the priority of choosing the right man for counseling or ministry by screening for and inter-vening with the sexually at-risk professional candidate.[3] It must also address how to redeem the weak-but-restorable offender, in-cluding steps for recovery and restoration of vulnerable violators. Finally, effective policy must deal with the necessity to stop and bind the power of the evil person—taking assertive action against sexual predators in ministry.[4]

The goal of these policies is to deal truthfully, compassionately, and actively with sexual misconduct problems. Protecting and vindicating the victims will be balanced with holding offenders accountable with negative consequences—including restitution to the victims. Any church policy must be adhered to rigorously for the sake of integrity in witness to the world, to honor Christ, and to be the vehicle of healing to a broken world. There must be a dedicated commitment to honor policy with faithful practice, no matter how painful and difficult such practice is perceived.

LIFE IN AN ADULTEROUS CHURCH: A CASE OF FAILED POLICY

Summer 1975. My name is Jane. My life was miserable. I was confused, upset, and depressed. I slept in a separate room from my husband as we fought often, both verbally and physically. I sought God's help and spent hours praying. I was active in several Bible studies and genuinely tried to do God's will. Mostly, I failed.

Fall 1975. My husband, Bill, and I began counseling with pastor Gus. Gus saw me with my husband one time, then decided to see only me. He related like a friend and shared with me quite a bit about his own marital struggles. He felt more like a dad to me than anyone ever had—we became quite close in a short time.

Summer 1976. Shortly after Gus referred me to a women's Bible study, one of the leaders, Hanna, befriended me, and I felt safe for the first time in a long time. She actually wanted to be my friend—even though I was a total wreck. By the summer, Hanna and her husband invited me to move in with them. She and I got very close, spending lots of time sharing deeply. But then she began to caress and kiss me. This contact made me extremely sick—emotionally, physically, spiritually, and mentally. I stopped it, yet it is painful to remember how much I loved Hanna.

Winter 1977 and after. Instead of getting better, I began to deteriorate again, but I did not know where to turn or what to do. I had become totally dependent on Hanna and the women's group. Different members of the group were sexually involved with one another, and I found out that Hanna's husband was also having an affair. At one point he actually gave Hanna permission to have a physical relationship with another woman in the group. All of this was terribly confusing to me, especially since many of these people were in significant leadership roles in the church.

Summer 1985. The news I discovered was shocking and needed to be told so that steps could be taken to bring pastor Gus to full restoration and to redeem our church. It happened on the day I stopped by to see Helen (Gus's personal secretary) at her home because she had been extremely depressed. She told me that she and Gus had been having an affair for six years—often making love in his office at church. Although others had noticed that his relationship with Helen was too close, he denied it, and no one knew just how close they had become.

I became a member of a secret triangle, a confidant to their innermost secrets and struggles. I felt good about being their friend and included so closely, but I was confused about how all this could be happening—they were both married and respected members of the church community. When I met alone with them at the church office, they would kiss and hug openly in front of me. They shared with me intimate details about how they were able to hide their relationship from others—they knew no one suspected. I even went on a retreat to a small cabin with them, sleeping in the living room while they slept together in the bedroom.

Fall 1985. Helen and Gus made plans to secretly divorce their spouses, marry one another, and move away. They were both tormented about this decision, but they decided that they could no longer hide their true desires. They wanted out of the old relationships. So they left town to pursue their dream. As it turned out, Gus was so tormented and fearful of following through that Helen returned home. Shortly thereafter, Helen broke off the relationship since he would not confess to his wife or anyone else that he wanted Helen.

Gus became severely depressed after Helen left him. He moved out of the area, telling the church that he needed to get away and rest because he had worked so hard and given so much to the church. Essentially, he blamed the church for his problems, saying the church had demanded too much of him and had let him down. He did not confess to his adulterous relationship, but resigned solely under the pretense that the church had worn him out. He stayed in touch with me after he left, trying to get me to bring Helen back, but she no longer trusted him.

I visited Gus a couple of years later. He held a new position as an associate pastor in another church. At first he was guarded about talking, but eventually he became quite open about how he was doing. He stated that he was continuing to minister and that he felt fully forgiven for what he had done. However, he told me that he was still unable to make love with his wife and that he expected their relationship would never improve. He also told me that he had not discussed his sexual relationship with Helen with the senior pastor of the church or any other church official.

CHALLENGING ADULTEROUS CHURCH PRACTICE

At the request of the interim pastor and with the support of the church board, Jane wrote a letter to the church's regional director in order to expose Gus's lies. She wanted to bring healing to Gus and to the church. She also wanted to protect other women from harm by Gus. She had ample evidence (including cards, letters, and receipts) of the long-standing deceit and abuse. However, *the denominational leaders chose not to look at the evidence,* but to believe that Gus was telling them the truth. They were more concerned about the harm exposure would cause the denomination and Gus's family than about the harm he inflicted on the church he had pastored and the potential for harm in his subsequent pastorate.

Jane talked with her pastor about writing again to the denomination's regional leadership, and he encouraged her to write directly to the national headquarters. This second letter was difficult for her to write, especially because the regional director had tried to persuade her that she was wrong about her information. We agreed to write a cover letter as a means of verifying her credibility and to challenge the church to take action to rectify matters. This is the essence of that letter:

> The matters which are covered in these materials are of the most serious nature, and I find it difficult to believe that these sins have apparently not been handled in an open, courageous, and decisive manner by the leadership immediately superior to [pastor Gus]. I am convinced that, as a result of what appears to be a "cover-up" of some kind, the body of believers at [First Church] have been and are suffering painful consequences.
>
> These consequences include, but are not limited to, (1) the damaging effects on the women directly involved, (2) the effect on women [Gus] counseled and hurt through poor counsel, (3) the impact on the church and local community because of his and the [denomination's] cover-up. I know [about this pain] because I have had the opportunity to counsel a significant number of these people over the last couple of years. I am also concerned about this apparent "cover-up" because of the impact [Gus's] "ministry" will continue to have as he serves [the church] without having been honest with those he has greatly wounded.
>
> Essentially, it appears that [the regional director] ignored the evidence and chose to protect his associate . . . I have listened to the . . . tapes of [Gus's] supposed confession to the body . . . and he never was clear about what he did. He either passed it off . . . [or] tried blameshifting and overwork as the reasons for his malaise. As far as I know, since that time, he still has not been open and clear about these matters.
>
> Morally and ethically, it seems that you must deal with this matter. . . . I want this letter to be a restorative vehicle so that [Gus] and [the church] can heal. I am also concerned about protecting other women from this type of predatory action in the ministry. In that regard, this letter is also a warning to your organization that, if this matter is not dealt with and

[Gus] does anything along these lines again, [there will be] much greater negative consequences precisely because it appears that you apparently have not dealt with these issues at hand.

These are serious times in the Body of Christ when God is calling us to strict accountability for our sins. The world has watched as we have permitted sin to continue among the leaders as if there were no consequences. We are mocked and Christ is mocked because of this supposed type of love. I would appreciate a response to this letter as soon as possible. I am praying that restoration will occur.

In her letter, Jane pointed out that many members of the church were still hurting years later because the truth was still unknown. (As we will discuss later in chapter 11, when a church is not told the truth, confusion reigns and great harm ensues.)[5] The church body had long been divided between those who believed the pastor was wrongfully accused and abused, and those who believed he lied. Jane wrote that she was concerned that Gus might put other women at risk if his behavior patterns were not healed and changed. In addition, Jane felt victimized as she was constrained to maintain the secrets she knew about the whole affair. Finally, she told about evidence she still had available and how the regional director had responded in denial.

FAILURE AT THE HIGHEST LEVEL

About six weeks after these letters were sent, we received a written response from the national headquarters—we were shocked. The writer declared there was no cover-up and that the "problem [had been] openly dealt with." Three lies were glaringly present. First, the writer asserted that Gus, in moving to another local church, had submitted to and counseled with the senior pastor. It was asserted that the senior pastor had attested that Gus "shows all the evidence of complete recovery," including an "intact" marriage. Yet Gus had admitted to Jane that he had not ever been honest about the nature of his misconduct with the pastor. To simply trust that the senior pastor knew about this betrayal and had assessed and adequately treated the matter was not only foolish but directly contradicted what Gus had told Jane earlier about his marriage.

The second lie was the assertion that Jane's pastor "did not indicate any lingering problem concerning the matter within the faithful body of the church." We had talked with the current pastor prior to writing the letter to headquarters, and he agreed that significant harm still existed. We also discussed the letter we received from headquarters with the pastor, who was annoyed because he had not told the leadership that there were no lingering problems. He felt misrepresented, yet caught in a dilemma about challenging their perception.

The third falsehood was that headquarters held Gus harmless because they believed there was no lingering harm in the church Gus left. Yet this was directly contradicted by one of the victims who told us that she knew of at least twenty people who were still hurting because this matter was mishandled in the first place. A large number of those she identified were still active in the church.

The truth is that Gus practiced a wide variety of boundary violations with women—he was guilty of much more than sexual misconduct. He crossed the boundaries of godly helping when he shared his marital burdens and infidelity with women who came to him for help. Jane still bears the burden of keeping the secrets of wrong conduct. He also violated the Gospel of Christ when he made promises to women about how they could trust him to guarantee their salvation—then left town without a word of apology, abandoning those whom he had encouraged to rely fully on him.

Sober Lessons

In sum, significant harm still exists more than *eight years* after Gus left town. Knowledge of this harm is represented by many people who have come to us for help. We can only guess how many more people were wounded by the terrible mishandling of this matter. We do not know how many people left the church, left Christ, or suffered some other grievous harm.

This case illustrates well that there is still too much denial and deceit in far too many churches and ministries about sexual misconduct and the harm it does. Churches not only need written sexual misconduct policy and procedures, but must use them properly and with courageous integrity. As Deborah House, an attorney for abuse victims declares, "For all the great procedures on the books, many local churches still haven't 'gotten it.'"[6]

Good Policy Versus Poor Practice

"From the least to the greatest, all are greedy for gain; prophets and priests alike, all practice deceit. They dress the wound of my people as

though it were not serious. 'Peace, peace,' they say, when there is no peace.
Are they ashamed of their loathsome conduct? No, they have no shame at
all; they do not even know how to blush. So they will fall among the fallen;
they will be brought down when I punish them," says the Lord.

Jeremiah 6:13–15

There are two trends in the Protestant church today that hinder effective control of sexual misconduct in ministry, permitting leaders to continue to fall and victims to be abused. One is that while some churches are doing reasonably well in developing policy, they are doing poorly in implementation. The other is that certain churches have been slow in making policy or are avoiding it altogether.

Mainline churches—and increasingly the evangelical church—have done a good job of establishing policy and educating their clergy in the last few years. However, the record of policy action is decidedly mixed as many of these churches still behave as if they had no policy. Furthermore, as Jeremiah so dreadfully proclaims, there are far too many churches—concentrated more among fundamentalist and some charismatic/pentecostal groups—who have not taken "loathsome conduct" seriously and acted to establish effective misconduct response policy.

GOOD POLICY, FAULTY PRACTICE

Many churches that have sexual misconduct policy do poorly in implementing that policy—a practice that fits Jeremiah's words: "Prophets and priests alike, all practice deceit. They dress the wound of my people as though it were not serious." This is surely the embittered perception of many victims in this situation. They feel (and to some degree they are) deceived by churches with policies that are not honored, that are a woefully deficient dressing of serious wounds. There seem to be several reasons why this is true.

Church Government. The type of church government influences how policy will be implemented. Since many churches in America are governed by congregational polity, each congregation has a great deal of autonomy regarding policy development, acceptance, and adoption. In these churches, denominational governments ask, urge, plead, suggest, advise, or recommend adoption of misconduct policy but cannot require action on policy. As a result, many local churches have not yet implemented their denominational recommendations. This contributes to continued denial of the problem and revictimizes women and children.

This may be why policy implementation seems to be moving more quickly in churches with episcopal and presbyterian forms of government. Local congregations, bound to the authority of the denomination, move to implement denominational directives. This form of government may also be the reason why these churches can be the most troubled with systemic harm of sexual misconduct: it is easier to move offending ministers out of victimized churches and into new ones in the hope the problem has been resolved. When the problem is not resolved and the abuse continues in a new church, the denomination is an easy target for legal action, especially when it has pooled financial resources to pay higher damage awards. This is a vexing paradox that demands policy review and revision of practice from top to bottom.

Resistance to Change Based on Naive Notions of Human Nature. Many people in local church leadership are not convinced that change is needed, so they resist implementing recommendations from the denomination. Many also fail to understand or maintain a naive denial of the deceptive power of sin and the ease of falling to sexual temptation. Since there is still a lot of controversy about false memories and false allegations, many assume that real abuse would not occur in their setting. Also, since the vast majority of pastors appear to be good men, it is difficult for most parishioners to understand the urgency for adopting sexual misconduct policy.

Even when some church members or the denomination leadership stresses the value of such policy and warns against the probable harm if policy is not implemented, there is still a tendency to resist the assertion that this harm would occur in "our church." Again, especially if there has been no trouble of this kind in the local church, it is inconceivable to many that it could happen—a denial shaped around the common notion that "our good church" is too mature for such trouble. Like the sociology of natural disasters, preventive action and preparation for disaster usually happen after the fact—after the flood or earthquake or sexual disaster has already devastated the community.

DEFICIENT OR NO POLICY

Some churches have been slow to make policy or have avoided it altogether. Many of these churches—and many of their highest leaders—still deny the incidence of sexual abuse among clergy.

There is a steadfast tendency to believe that other denominations are beset by the problem, but "we are exempt" because of our righteous standing, our right doctrine, and our zealous practice of the faith. These churches fit Jeremiah's declaration, "'Peace, peace,' they say, when there is no peace. Are they ashamed of their loathsome conduct? No, they have no shame at all; they do not even know how to blush." There is a great deal of hiding and minimizing that, in effect, covers the shame with deceit.

The Threat of Worldly Culture and Secular State. A large number of churches live in the high-risk zone without any policy due to basic separatist ideals. These churches advocate for complete separation of church and state, steadfastly refusing to cooperate with secular governments when its laws are imposed in areas that the church deems as strictly religious. These churches declare that the moral standards and moral sanctions against its clergy are strictly church matters, issues to be resolved in-house.

This is a difficult dilemma; in principle we agree with some level of church resistance as the state is too intrusive in church affairs in many areas. However, the refusal to face the misconduct caused by not adhering to godly principles and the failure to promote healing and justice in the church is leading to harm for many victims. It is also harming the church, as the state takes an increasingly invasive role against all churches to stop harmful practices. The new professional sexual misconduct law enacted recently in Texas (see chapter 13 and Appendix B), which explicitly incorporates pastors and churches, was influenced in part by the church attitude that refuses to cooperate with the state to stop this plague.

Sex and Sexual Ethics: Continued Taboos in the Church. Fear, shame, and confusion over sexuality and sexual ethics have long been the hallmarks of many churches and many people in the church, including its leaders. Sexual discussion has been forbidden for the most part, kept in the closet. Rather than admit to the shame, fear, and unease that are triggered when the subject arises, many deny honest discussion of sex with biblical references and compelling but faulty moral reasoning. ("Christians shouldn't be doing that anyway." "Talking about it will only lead us into trouble.") This serves, not the good of the church, but the maintenance of secrecy and denial, which allows sexual problems to remain hidden and powerful.

Marie Fortune was also queried about progress and problems in this arena.[7] She asserted that clarification about sexuality and sexual ethics will go a long way to help churches accept that the problem is real and there is a need for an effective policy dealing with sexual exploitation. This is an accurate observation, and we must find ways to facilitate the honest and honorable discussion of sexual problems in the church. It will take more than a willingness to talk and pursue intellectual clarity, however, to heal the brokenness of sin and the bent toward corruption that lies at the root of this struggle.

Church Resistance Based on Suspicion of Worldliness. A troubling dilemma, perhaps mostly for conservative and fundamentalist churches, are hyper-suspicions of perceived external and heretical forces: the women's movement, "liberal" churches, state legal pressures, Christian counseling, or the recovery movement. This is largely unstated but is reflected in threatened postures and resistant attitudes toward women's equality in Christ—reflected in hierarchical marital relationships and ministry roles in the church. This suspicion often creates extreme black-or-white perceptions of events and resistance to effective policy-making and just action based on these strong judgments.

Applied to the sexual misconduct crisis, a distorted and divergent picture appears that has all the capabilities of serious trouble. On the one hand, since women may be viewed as inherently weak or sinful, all women are viewed as victims or as potential seducers. At the opposite extreme, out of disgust with the growing cult of victimization in our culture, people can become suspicious of women who truly are victims—especially if, as women, they are already low on the ladder of respect and power.

If allegations are made against a strong and beloved church leader, the victim's charges can be denied and easily labeled as lies. In this dynamic, all women may be painted as seducers, with a call for strong action against them to "save" the church from conspiratorial disaster. Because the topic of sex is so uncomfortable, so often a moral taboo, it is likely to be ignored as a subject of honest and serious discussion. When these dynamics are inflamed in an abuse crisis, especially if the wrongdoing involves a leader, churches are often split between warring camps; and victims are treated in ways that eventually result in lawsuits. Breaking through the bondage of this dilemma is a major challenge for the conservative church at the end of the twentieth century.

THE PERSISTENCE OF PATRIARCHY

Kenneth Pope tells this penetrating story, revealing the tragicomedy of patriarchy so well.

It might be useful to consider Israel's approach to the problem of rape, which was reaching epidemic proportions in Tel Aviv. The Prime Minister's cabinet (mostly male) spent considerable time discussing ways in which women were putting themselves at risk (e.g., in venturing out alone, in staying out after dark). The cabinet concluded that, in light of women's seeming contribution to the epidemic, a legally enforced curfew for women in the city should be enacted. The Prime Minister, Golda Meier, changed the focus of the deliberations by remarking, "Why not a curfew for the men? They are the ones doing the raping."[8]

Tragically, the same godless patriarchal structures that empower, promote, and protect the inherently polygamous heart of man are far too conspicuous in the church. In 1990, three years after her ground-breaking book on sexual misconduct (*Is Nothing Sacred*), Marie Fortune was queried on the success of her antimisconduct mission.[9] She stated that all was not well, especially in churches that had taken initial and effective misconduct response action. Her frustration was palpable, and we were struck by how she seemed to have underestimated the strength of her own incisive analysis—how she misjudged the persistent power of patriarchy.

We must recognize and humbly confess in our midst the subtle (and sometimes clear) evidence of evil patriarchal systems, patterns, and policies that protect sinful, polygamous desire. We must challenge the denial of that desire and the blaming of victims that is often presumed to disappear simply because we are Christians. This is not a challenge to God's regenerate power in us nor to legitimate male leadership in church or family. Instead, we challenge the corrupted possession of power, the perverse rule over others that imposes control by threat and force and degrades those oppressed by such rule. This is a war of light versus darkness, of sacrificial servanthood in Christ versus coercive and abusive control of others in the guise of Christian ministry and godly family life.

Patriarchy in the Mental Health Professions. Pope reviewed the scope of this problem in the mental health field in a powerful article in 1990. He demonstrated that while some progress has been made toward resolving the problem of professional sexual misconduct, resistance to dealing with the magnitude of this problem remains quite strong.[10] Further, he suggests this occurs because "the male professional's sense of identification with the male perpetrator . . . elicits the [male] professional's collusion in exonerating the perpetrator's accountability for his acts and/or enabling the perpetrator to continue the abuse."[11] In other words, patriarchy is alive and well in the helping professions—professions that, at least rhetorically, are dedicated to its eradication. Pope gave numerous evidences of this stubborn patriarchy in mental health:

- Early research evidence on the pervasive scope of the sexual misconduct problem was suppressed by leading psychiatric, psychological, and social work organizations.

- Even recently, the American Psychiatric Association (APA) resisted a national study on sexual misconduct by psychiatrists. The chair of the ethics committee of the APA explained that the group did not believe in querying members on "sensitive information about themselves." Psychiatrist Nanette Gartrell, former Harvard professor and leading investigator of the primary national study of sexual abuse by psychiatrists, quit the APA in protest for its pervasive failure to act to protect patients and hold perpetrators accountable.

- Exclusion of sexual misconduct claims and severe caps on insurance payments to sexual victims points to collusion between the insurance industry and the major mental health professional associations—keeping malpractice premiums as low as possible seems to be a priority over protecting patients and clients.

- Akin to the tobacco industry's specious challenge of the mass of research on the health effects of smoking, some mental health professionals challenge, even deny, the pervasive evidence of sexual misconduct harm. They decry the lack of empirical rigor and zero in on the methodological errors of some of the research on the harmful effects of sexual abuse on victims.

- That so many violators are found to be prominent members and even leaders of the major professional associations (and, as we have found, in the high councils of the church) suggests that the powerful apply different rules to themselves—an elitist mentality fosters the fallacy of being above the law and beyond accountability for abusive behavior.

- One of mental health's dirty little secrets is consistently suppressed: the pervasive failure of rehabilitation programs and the high rate of sexual offender recidivism.

- Finally, as shown in the paragraph above on the Israeli rape crisis, blaming the victim remains rampant—men use the structures of patriarchy to blame women for male sex crimes. Not only in psychotherapy but also in the law, women and even children are considered to invite, seduce, manipulate, provocate, coerce, secretly enjoy, or take revenge against hapless and harmless men who are victimized by the intoxicating wiles of womanhood.

Patriarchy Protecting Polygamy. This collusion of patriarchy and polygamy is based on aggressive self-exaltation rather than on respect for the moral ethic that professionals will protect and foster the best interests of their clients and parishioners. This perverted selfishness stems from the natural and carnal natures (biblically speaking) and the resulting effort to maintain the power of the male over the female in the old order. Jesus Christ, in spite of protestations to the contrary by church leaders who are deluded and trapped in this web, does not live in this house.

We describe this evil dynamic as *patriarchy protecting polygamy.* This perverse interest, as ancient as the Fall and so pervasive in the world, is incredibly strong. It will not easily be broken. Again, this reveals our deep need for redemption from sin and for the defeat of evil structures that foster and support this sin. This is a much larger task than will be accomplished in a few years time, but we must join forces under God's redemptive banner and proclaim the truth against this evil (see chapter 16).

CONCLUSION

A clarion call has gone forth from the heart of God: a call to the church to adhere fully to the healing ministry of Jesus without hesitation, falter, or denial. The longer the church plays around with serious sin and injustice, and the more it allows brothers to protect brothers in unjust ways, the more invasive the state will become in holding the church accountable.[12] (See appendix B on a proposal to divert sexual misconduct cases and other church disputes into a national religious court and alternative dispute resolution center.)

At this time, very few women pursue civil and criminal actions against their sexual violators, but the number of suits is rising dramatically. Also, some states have made it mandatory to report professional counselors who are involved in sexual misconduct, and the net is spreading to include the church.[13] It is time to be zealous in the house of God, to become morally pure before the state and the culture. Otherwise, as with Israel, God will allow the ham-fisted power of the secular state to punish wayward believers, especially the leaders of the church.[14]

NOTES

1. Marie Fortune, forward to *Sexual Abuse in Christian Homes and Churches*, by Carolyn Holderread Heggen (Scottsdale, Penn.: Herald Press, 1993).

2. Ibid.

3. This is discussed in chapter 15.

4. These latter two topics are discussed in chapter 14.

5. For an excellent example of this in a detailed case, see Marie Fortune, *Is Nothing Sacred?* (New York: HarperCollins, 1989).

6. Quoted in Thomas Giles, "Coping with Sexual Misconduct in the Church," *Christianity Today* 37, no. 1 (1993): 48.

7. Lewis Rambo, "Interview with Reverend Marie Fortune, August 8, 1990," *Pastoral Psychology* 39, no. 5 (1991): 305–19.

8. Kenneth S. Pope, "Therapist-Patient Sex as Sex Abuse: Six Scientific, Professional, and Practical Dilemmas in Addressing Victimization and Rehabilitation," *Professional Psychology: Research and Practice* 21, no. 4 (1990): 236.

9. Rambo, "Interview with Reverend Marie Fortune," 305–19.

10. Pope, "Therapist-Patient Sex," 227–39.

11. Ibid., 229.

12. We predicted just such action in our book *Law for the Christian Counselor*, 63–64. The state increasingly has been setting boundaries and taking punitive action against the church, especially because of the continuing harm to sexual abuse victims due to the church's failure to deal forthrightly with violators.

13. Notably, Texas enacted such a law, which went into effect on January 1, 1994. Minnesota has a similar law, although one that is not as tough. See chapter 13 for further information.

14. For example, see Isaiah 9:8–13; Jeremiah 25 (especially verses 8–9); and Ezekiel 5:5–17.

Chapter Ten

Priestly Misconduct and the Catholic Church Crisis

by Canice Connors, OFM, Conv., PhD[1]

It is some comfort for the church that nearly all these cases involve old-school priests and years-old crimes. The wounds to the victims are deep, the stain on the vestments indelible. Fair or not, the sins of the Fathers will continue to be visited upon a new generation of clergy and congregants.[2]

WHAT FOUNDATION EXECUTIVE WOULD FUND a project to research the policy of the Roman Catholic Church concerning sexual abuse by its clergy? Likely none, for the Roman Catholic Church's policy position has been public and codified in canon law for centuries, with punitive sanctions for clergy offenders. Yet this issue surfaces repeatedly in the media: does the Church have a national policy on clergy sexual abuse of minors? Stammering respondents, along with ambiguous positive and conditioned negative responses, have generated doubt and distrust toward a church that proclaims strict moral standards on every aspect of sexual behavior.

The sexual misconduct crisis over the past decade, involving two to four percent of the 66,000 Catholic clergy in North America and costing over 400 million dollars in settlements, has revealed significant policy gaps and implementation failures. What is at the base of these policy and practice issues—especially the painful gap between policy and practice? What is the Church doing at this moment to correct the variety of policy situations concerning sexual abuse?

In addressing these questions, this presentation accepts the approach of this volume that the abuse situation involves value interactions between love, sexuality, and power. The perspective of this analysis is that the clergy abuse crisis has revealed significant policy and practice blind spots articulating these three values. A sound policy development process demands adequate intelligence gathering, open agitation for and against a variety of policy alternatives, and a prescriptive procedure for making the policy legitimate and public. Then in application, policy requires a consistent implementation phase, an ongoing analysis of its effectiveness, and a termination of any competing or contradictory policy positions.[3] This exposition will suggest that there existed, and continues to exist, serious deficits in one or several of these policy processes.

PARADOXICAL ROOTS TO THE CRISIS

Ironically, public agitation concerning the sexual abuse of minors by Catholic clergy began in two Roman Catholic strongholds: the archdiocese of St. John in Newfoundland and the diocese of Lafayette in Louisiana. In both locales the media, the justice system, and the popular culture were decidedly pro-Catholic. Both Archbishop Alphonse Penny in Newfoundland and Bishop Gerard Frey in Louisiana were viewed as benign autocrats who only slowly and reluctantly installed the reforms of Vatican Council II. James Hickey in Newfoundland and Gilbert Gauthe in Louisiana were the priest abusers whose crimes agitated public fury. Both had been trusted, effective leaders (Hickey was the chancellor of the diocese) whom their bishops defended in the face of significant evidence of their guilt.[4]

These bastions of denial were breached by an investigative team of RCMP officers in Newfoundland and by an investigative reporter (Jason Berry) in Louisiana. Local Catholic reaction was stunned disbelief that evolved into rage toward the Church. The victims in both locales suffered intense scrutiny and criticism. Eventually, they had recourse to attorneys and litigation—a major signal of the Church's failure of a compassionate, pastoral policy response.

In both locales the institutional Church slowly altered its pattern of denial and defensiveness into effective action against the abusers and for the victims. In Newfoundland, Archbishop Penny requested a Royal Commission of Enquiry, which published its findings in June 1990. The archbishop resigned shortly after its publication. In Louisiana a new bishop was appointed, Harry Flynn, who initiated what many consider a model of healing and reconciliation. He met regularly with the families of the victims, offered the victims counseling, and convened his clergy in small groups to process their anger and hurt.

In an uncanny way, these originating flash points became templates of recurring patterns as the crisis erupted across North America. An analysis of this template may be instructive in designing an alternative future. This crisis, though complex, can be reduced to abuses of love, sex, and power. The response pattern might be summarized in the sequence of disbelief, denial, and recovery. This commentary will be limited to systemic observations, but the pain, suffering, and healing was experienced by namable individuals.

THE VALUE AND SITUATION OF LOVE

Clearly, every Christian church exists to mediate the love of Jesus Christ, to proclaim his moral teachings, and to give witness through servant leadership. Throughout the sexual misconduct crisis, the Roman Catholic Church has often been abusive. It has become publicly discredited when it failed in being this type of church. In Newfoundland and Louisiana the institutional church initially chose to use its considerable power, wealth, and political connections to protect its public image at the price of intensifying the suffering of the victims and their families. Church leaders responded defensively to allegations with the language and manner of lawyers rather than as pastors.

THE AUSTRALIAN MODEL

In contrast, the Christian Brothers of Melbourne, Australia, when faced with similar allegations, chose to reflect on gospel values before reacting. They engaged a woman consultant who was an expert in communications and policy development and was not intimidated by ecclesial power. Over extended work days she assisted the Brothers' leadership in clarifying their basic values and in articulating their position on celibacy. She sensitized them to the dynamics of sexual abuse and developed a coherent, loving, pastoral response to their various publics.

When the Brothers were prepared, they spoke clearly and precisely in a manner and tone that identified them as a church institution honoring to Christ. Their policy and procedures were clearly rooted in Christian values—especially love and humility. A full-time, independent psychologist was hired and given sufficient resources to empower each victim to select options salutary to his or her healing. The media reported behavior accurately, and the public responded with respect. No lawsuits have been instituted against the Brothers.

When the Church responds as a church it loses nothing and gains respect for responding honestly toward a shame-filled human problem. Too often during this crisis the Church's initial reaction has been self-serving, with disastrous consequences to the victims as well as to the Church itself. For example, in one recent situation a bishop who is highly respected for his pastoral skills met with a woman who was abused by a priest during her adolescence. She was seeking understanding and healing. The bishop proved compassionate and understanding, and the session concluded warmly with a promise that the diocese would provide financial assistance for her counseling. A week later, however, the woman received a letter from the bishop requesting a waiver of future action against the Church and offering a sum of money out of charity. Obviously, the bishop had consulted with his lawyer after the pastoral session. The woman felt betrayed; she is angry and is considering litigation.

To speak the truth in love and to die unto self are biblical policy positions respected even in the secular realm. When the Church behaves this way, its victims are healed and redeemed. When the Church avoids the truth to protect its image, it becomes unloving toward its children and colludes in the secrecy and silence that constitute the infrastructure of sexual abuse. The victims of this pattern become fixed in their anger and woundedness and, all too frequently, end up suing the Church.

THE VALUE AND SITUATION OF POWER

The clergy sexual abuse crisis has revealed the ineffective use of power within the Roman Catholic Church system in the United States. Contrary to popular opinion, the Catholic Church is not an efficiently organized institution. There are 188 distinct dioceses in the United States. The bishop of each diocese travels to Rome once in a five year period to render an account of his stewardship. In this sense the Catholic Church is highly centralized; all roads lead to Rome and to a single papal power figure. However, the power distribution at a national level is diffuse, even murky. The National Conference of Catholic Bishops (NCCB) in the United States has a central office in Washington, D. C. The Conference meets twice annually, and while it promulgates instructional documents, it has no direct policy jurisdiction over individual dioceses.

On February 9, 1988, two-and-a-half years after the initial public disclosure of extensive clergy child abuse, the NCCB issued its first public statement: a document drafted by Mark Chopko, the general counsel of the conference.[5] The 750-word statement was appropriate to the office of general counsel (legal damage control) but had none of the pastoral tone that might be expected from a conference of bishops.

The statement never once referred to priests but only to "persons who are leaders of the community and others who have been placed in positions of great trust." On November 5, 1989 the administrative committee of the NCCB explained how cases of abuse were mishandled in the past when psychology was less sophisticated and reiterated that this abuse "was viewed as simply a moral failing for which one should be repentant, rather than a psychological addiction for which treatment was mandatory—today things are different."[6]

It was not until 1992 that Archbishop Pilarczyk, president of the Conference for that year, made clear how different things actually are.[7] The archbishop apologized for the lack of understanding and for mistakes that had added to the suffering of victims and their families. He pointed out that on five occasions at national meetings the NCCB had discussed how to treat and prevent the problem. He stated that for the previous five years the NCCB had strongly recommended to all dioceses the following course of action:

1. respond promptly to any allegation that has a reasonable foundation;

2. if the allegation is supported by sufficient evidence, relieve the alleged perpetrator of his ministerial duties immediately and refer him to medical evaluation;

3. comply with civil laws in reporting incidents, and cooperate with investigations;

4. reach out to victims with care for their spiritual and emotional well-being;

5. deal as openly as possible with members of the community within the limits for protecting an individual's privacy.

DISCREPANT MESSAGES

Over this same time period, the media had consistently asked about the existence of a national policy. Regretfully, they were not told the strong policy recommendations noted above but were told that each diocese had to come up with its own position. The public was dismayed by such moral impotency. In fact, 180 of the 188 dioceses do have policy positions in complete conformity with the NCCB's guidelines. Many dioceses such as Chicago and Minneapolis-St. Paul (see appendix A) mounted exemplary and effective policy processes. But each effort appeared isolated from the other while the consciousness of the crisis was aggregated as a national phenomenon.

Adhering to legal advise aimed at limiting exposure to additional litigation against the NCCB, the Church forfeited an opportunity to promulgate an effective national pastoral document. Many wondered how the Church could be so clear and declarative on policy issues touching on abortion and birth control but so ineffective in responding to a crisis involving its priests. In contrast, the Roman Catholic Church in Canada did issue a common document called *From Pain to Hope* (Ottawa: CCCB, 1992). The response of the public has been one of respect and gratitude.

Acting through a subcommittee of the Priestly Life and Ministry Committee, in February of 1992 the NCCB sponsored a think tank on the crisis, which included clergy, bishops, victims, abusers, and professionals. The spirit of the working document is suggested in the preamble and the conclusion:

> We are concerned that the hierarchy's authority and credibility in the United States is eroding because of a perceived inability to deal more effectively with the problem of child sexual abuse. We have developed our recommendations with a sense of urgency for action. The allegations of sexual misconduct against Catholic priests and the perceived inability of some church authorities to respond with decisive pastoral leadership has resulted in a sustained crisis in the Church.[8]

The full report was submitted to the 1993 meeting of the bishops in Washington. Instead of urgent action, the NCCB chose to appoint a committee of bishops under the leadership of Bishop Kinney.

After months of labor with limited outcomes, the committee obtained the services of Everett O'Neil, a canon lawyer who was instrumental in producing the Canadian document, *From Pain to Hope*. He has focused the committee's work on five objectives, including an analysis of policies currently in place and the establishment of a statistical data base on the magnitude of the problem. As of the publication of this book, the committee does not have a final report prepared for approval and action at the bishops' meeting. Meanwhile, as the crisis continues unabated, more victims are added to the swelling ranks, more priests fall to this plague, many more lawsuits are filed, and the media howls ever more loudly.

THE SITUATION AND VALUE OF SEXUALITY

The two Vatican Sacred Congregations responsible for processing petitions [for leaving the religious life] admitted in 1986 they had received almost 250,000 submissions since 1980 from nuns and priests. Nine out of ten applicants gave as their reason . . . an inability to cope with the Church's treatment of their sexuality.[9]

A question persistently appearing throughout the crisis has concerned any causal connection between the discipline of celibacy and sexual abuse. One can easily shrug off the question by directing attention to the national estimate that 85 percent of child sexual abuse occurs within family settings. While no thoughtful person believes that celibacy or priesthood causes sexual abuse, much less pedophilia, there are questions about seminary life, mandatory celibacy, and an all-male priesthood in relation to the sexual abuse of minors by priests.

It is important to distinguish, both in numbers and psychosexual dynamics, pedophiles and ephebophiles from other types of offenders. Out of 571 priests evaluated for sexual dysfunctions at the Saint Luke Institute, only 44 have been identified as pedophiles (those sexually aroused by prepubescent children). The sexual abuse of adolescent males (ephebophilia) is the more extensive problem.

Psychologist Judith Becker asks several pertinent questions in this regard.

Does the ephebophilic character of the problem indicate
that it is related to priest's earlier seminary life, when male

bonding took place in an all-male environment? How much of the problem might involve "repressed" homosexuality—men involved with teenage boys while preferring adult males? What kind of ephebophilia is involved in a given case: (1) a preferential ephebophile, (2) an ephebophile who is also an adult homosexual, or (3) an ephebophile who is also an adult heterosexual?[10]

THE CELIBACY QUESTION

One may assume, along with Robert Coles,[11] that celibacy is itself an aspect of sexuality and a mode of coming to terms with ones sexual energies. In this light, then, the policy and practice questions can be focused into three areas: (1) recruitment, (2) seminary education, and (3) the manner of supporting healthy celibate living.

Recruitment. The critical policy question in this situation is whether the Church exercises due diligence in screening applicants for the priesthood. The majority of clergy currently in treatment are there for abusive activity that occurred twenty and more years ago. The allegations are being brought forward by persons in their middle years who are discovering the impact of earlier abuse during the course of counseling. While there are current abuse cases, the crisis focuses largely on priests who entered the system under policies and practices predating the reforms of Vatican Council II.

During the 1950s and into the late 1960s, the screening of candidates was limited to academic criteria, evidence of moral rectitude, and declaration of motivation. Most candidates came from stable Catholic families, were products of parochial education, and were well known by their parish priests, who provided recommendations concerning conduct and moral readiness. Significant numbers entered after the eighth grade and the remainder during the course of high school or shortly thereafter. In 1955 a psychiatrist addressing bishops and religious superiors noted, "The Church takes our best young men from thirteen to seventeen years of age, carefully educates them, feeds them well, nurtures their physical development, and seven to twelve years later, turns out well-fed, well-educated emotional thirteen-year-olds."[12] It is likely that emotional thirteen-year-olds will be sexually attracted to thirteen-year-olds.

Today, candidates for the priesthood are more likely to be college graduates. It is now both policy and practice to demand psychological screening of candidates for the priesthood. Screening protocols are diverse, some relying exclusively on the MMPI, others employing batteries of tests including projective techniques. Unfortunately, little effort has been made to define national norms. It is possible and probable for a candidate rejected by one Church jurisdiction to apply elsewhere and be accepted without reference to the first process. While there is intense interest in finding the test that will screen out potential abusers, many practitioners believe that the significant missing piece is compiling an adequate sexual history.

The policy assumptions underlying evaluation procedures and the climate of the testing need to be examined. Here, too, the Church must act as church—mirroring the pastoral love of Christ. If the process is designed only to finger the unworthy, then it is one-sided and potentially abusive. Each diocese and religious order has limited resources for helping candidates to resolve developmental and critical issues. The discovery of any developmental deficit should be matched with the capacity of the jurisdiction to provide supportive counseling and a safe environment to resolve those personal issues.

A complicating issue on the implementation of sound screening policy and practice is the pressure created by the shrinking pool of applicants to the priesthood. The population of Catholics in North America continues to increase while ordinations decrease. The Church is replacing only six priests for each ten it loses. This creates pressures to tolerate high-risk candidates or to import candidates from other cultures with the compounding difficulty of cultural adaptation. Though it should be amply clear that the Church can no longer afford to ordain sexually-at-risk priests, this can only exacerbate the systemic crisis of an inadequate priestly population.

Seminary Education and Issues with Celibacy. Nowhere in the North American Roman Catholic Church has more reform taken place than in seminary education. Faculties have higher academic standing, curriculum reforms have incorporated significant offerings on human development, and specialists in spiritual formation have been hired. However, the majority of priest abusers now in treatment would have entered the seminary prior to these reforms. Many entered as freshmen in high school having had little if any opportunity to achieve psychosexual maturity.

The sexual ethic of this earlier period emphasized avoidance of women. In preparation for summer vacations, adolescent seminarians were advised that the sighting of an approaching attractive girl should be handled by crossing the street. Such prescriptions generated fuzzy moral thinking: "It's wrong to get sexually involved with women but no one said anything about boys." While some high school seminaries survive, they are becoming harder to find.

The average age of seminarians has moved steadily upward with an unprecedented inclusion of older, second-career candidates with diverse life experience. Schools of theology have instituted programs on human sexuality that focus on healthy ways of living a celibate commitment. Advanced reform efforts are creating safe environments within which candidates can identify their sexual issues and process them without fear of being ejected. Past practice would have rewarded silence and secrecy.

Supporting Healthy Celibate Life in the Ministry. The policy reforms and practices required for sound professional education are well in place. The psycho-sexual histories accumulated at Saint Luke Institute indicate that the significant period for effective intervention is during the first five years after ordination. Many priest-patients were able to conceal or cope with their sexual issues while in the structured environment of a seminary. However, the early years of ministry provided the critical moments when stresses and pressures collapsed thin defenses and evoked inappropriate sexual activity.

New programs are being created for a nonthreatening environment where young priests can review the manner in which they are handling stress. Applied vigorously to young priests in the early years of ministry, such stress-management prevention programs will be crucial to turn the sexual misconduct tide in the future.

POLICY AND PRACTICE ISSUES

Jesuit scholar Norbert J. Rigali recently reviewed the evidence of the NCCB's activity regarding priestly misconduct over the past decade. He concluded,

> Many questions will have to be answered before the Church can finally name its complex problem and trace its sources. Reflection on the Church's conversation thus far about the problem, however suggests certain rules for the rest of the discussion.
>
> 1. Free-floating, undefined terms and vague generalities—especially with regard to key concepts such as child,

sexual abuse, disorder, addiction—must be replaced with language responsibly backed up by precise definitions.

2. A priori declarations (whether medicalization, moralization, or anything else) about the nature of the problem and its sources must become a thing of the past.

3. The entire conversation must be based, as in the Chicago report, on the facts of the problem, facts brought into the open rather than on vague concepts and generalities in place of facts. If the conversation can become a search for the meaning of the facts, the Church will have come far toward becoming a home of openness and truth.[13]

APPLICATION AT THE PARISH LEVEL

A review of policy and practice issues at the parish level and with regard to treatment of victims and priest offenders illustrates some of the successes and pitfalls in this process.

The parents of children abused by clergy have been parishioners who, by and large, invested unconditional confidence in their parish priests and teaching Brothers. Many abusers gained access to their victims by becoming included in the inner sanctum of family life with privileges of a blood member. Little wonder, then, that it is within the system of parish life that the impact of the abuse crisis has been most keenly and chaotically experienced.

Steve Rossetti has given both statistical evidence and human characterization to the loss of trust and the erosion of confidence in ecclesial leadership.[14] Paul Wilkes has vividly described the thicket and tangle of feelings as parishioners moved through (1) initial resentment toward the accuser, (2) defense of the pastor, (3) realization of the truth of the allegations, and (4) resentment at being left in ignorance by Church officials.

The Clash of Parish Values with Diocesan Policy. The sexual misconduct crisis has given full dimension to the policy and practice vacuum at the parish level in the way the institutional Church shares power and truth with its members. During the 1970s parish renewal programs were initiated throughout North America. Laity were invited to participate in parish councils, systems of financial accountability were introduced, and efforts were made to involve parishioners in selecting pastors.

However, these efforts to share power and introduce accountability fell short of expectations. Power was advisory, accountability became an annual report, and the patriarchal system of "bishop knows best" remained in place. Catholics became informed about the abuse crisis through the secular media because bishops and priests wanted to protect their flock from scandal. Since the pulpit was not the source of accurate information and interpretation of the crisis, fear stimulated strong reactions at the parish level.

The Need for Flexible Policy Application. Eighteen years ago a newly ordained Afro-American priest became intensely involved in youth ministry in a midwestern diocese. Emotionally, the priest was at the level of the youth he was leading. He had also been a victim of sexual abuse. He soon became sexually involved with one of the youths under his pastoral care. Later, he came to his senses and terminated the sexual activity. He entered counseling, worked through his childhood abuse issues, and saw to it that the young man received counseling. He moved on in his life and became an effective, well-known and loved leader in the black community. Not long ago the abuse came to the attention of the diocese, and it acted swiftly and determinately to remove this priest from his parish and send him for evaluation.

The parishioners reacted to what they perceived as harsh treatment of a beloved leader. They had all the information on the abuse incident and still wanted their pastor back. Since they are a faith community that frequently relates with members who are in recovery from a variety of addictions and abuses, they understand and accept that people can change and move on. Paradoxically, the new policy and practices of this diocese—though well-intentioned and designed to protect victims and the church—are so rigid they do not allow for special circumstances, nor for the forgiveness and reconciliation that had already taken place.

POLICY AND PRACTICE TOWARD VICTIMS

The new Church policy statements on sexual misconduct by priests begin with a mandate for immediate response to victim complaints and a swift pastoral response to victim suffering. Most victims would testify that their experience of Church practice up to this point has constituted re-abuse. Too often, the Church has not believed the victims, has suspected them of wanting nothing more than cash settlements, and has accused them of ruining the reputation of the Church. The multitude of victim stories cataloguing the betrayal, confusion, despair, loss of faith, lack of justice, and unremitting rage at being twice-abused by both priest and Church are mind-boggling both in scope and intensity.

In reaction to these experiences, several victim networks have developed to provide mutual support and information. Efforts have been made by the Bishops' Committee on Child Abuse to make active and collaborative contact with these groups. Early efforts stumbled when the victim leadership wanted a signed agreement that bishops would not countersue victims. They also believed that the decisions concerning meeting place and agenda development were under the control of the bishops.

Bishops have confessed their confusion in trying to respond to the just claims of victims and simultaneously trying to limit the exposure of Church assets. Their sentiments were partially reflected in an article in *Commonweal*:

> I question the huge sums of money the church is being asked to pay to victims for the crimes. If some victims hate the church, I can understand their feelings of vindictiveness and their desire for retribution. But if the goal is to recover health and wholeness, is pandering to desires for revenge and ratifying resentment real healing? Financial settlements seem like a simplistic and illusory response to a complex and emotional issue.[16]

Leadership and membership that have been able to get beyond a purely adversarial relationship and perception (such as that shown by our brethren in the Australian Church noted above) are blazing the trail toward healing, confession, forgiveness, reconciliation, and restoration. The Church that lives this mission enables the love of Christ to come alive and redeem actions that otherwise seem impossible to change. Not only victims, but the Church and the watching world is transformed when it participates in this kind of life.

TREATMENT PRACTICE AND POLICY

In the last decade the Roman Catholic Church in North America has invested heavily in long-term treatment of clergy sex abusers. Church-related residential treatment centers in New Mexico, Maryland (Saint Luke Institute), Pennsylvania, and Ontario have developed comprehensive evaluative and treatment programs. On average, these programs have cost the dioceses and religious orders $70,000 per priest for the treatment regimen.

It is common practice to send a priest against whom an allegation has been lodged for a week-long evaluation. Treatment protocols involve intensive individual and group therapies with special sensitivity to spiritual and vocational issues. Most programs demand a continuing-care contract incorporating regular assessment visits, involvement in recovery groups, and supervision for a five year period after treatment. Priests who have maintained this rigorous aftercare regimen—which for most has been crucial to their reassignment to active ministry—have shown a near-zero sexual offense relapse rate.

Documented Hope on Restoration to Ministry. Can priests-in-recovery be placed back in ministry without endangering children? The documented history of ten years of follow-up research on priests who have gone through the Saint Luke program would indicate a solid yes. A psychologist with many years of experience at the Institute of Living has developed criteria for making the decision to restore a priest to active ministry.

In assessing a priest's capacity for treatment and his prognosis the following issues need to be explored:

1. the capacity for empathy with the victim;

2. the level of aggression employed in the sexual act;

3. the level of emotional maturity;

4. evidence of appropriate social skills;

5. capacity to involve himself in age-appropriate relationships;

6. ability to control alcohol and drug use;

7. psychological mindedness;

8. level of cognitive distortions, especially as related to the celibacy vow;

9. evidence of acute cognitive disorganization;

10. capacity for frustration tolerance, anxiety tolerance, and delay of gratification.[17]

Restoration Is Possible but Increasingly Unlikely. Paradoxically, as the staffs of these treatment centers have become more confident in their treatment protocols and more proficient in continuing-care recommendations, bishops have become more reluctant to reassign to ministry after treatment. This practice is being driven by the fear of further litigation and the unchallenged public perception that these priests are predatory pedophiles—unredeemable and beyond hope of recovery to ministry. Yet, will any policy reform ever meet the standards of the Gospels unless it incorporates forgiveness as the ultimate healing value for both victim and abuser?

I join with my author-colleagues in asserting that it would be a terribly unjust outcome for the Church—both Catholic and Protestant alike—to bow to fear and litigious pressures and not create the means or allow the restoration to ministry of nonpredatory priests, pastors, and counselors. Yes, predators must be stopped and never allowed access to vulnerable parishioners. But it is also necessary for the Church to stop allowing lawyers and insurance executives to dictate church policy that falsely assumes all abusers are unredeemable predators. No matter how well-intentioned and seemingly safe, such action disavows the Church's pastoral mission to both victims and abusers.

This also touches another policy and program issue: what to do with unassignable clergy. The current trend involves placing them in group homes usually in rural settings with a variety of supportive services but no active ministry. This may be, along with de-ordination and alternate vocational training, the best and safest path for the predatory abuser. To become the widespread policy for all misconduct cases, however, dishonors the way of Christ and demeans the precious call to ministry that is so central to the pastoral vocation.

CONCLUSION

The NCCB has demonstrated its capacity to generate sound, significant policy documents on such complex issues as peace, economics, and family life. In these cases, the conference gathered excellent intelligence, sponsored national meetings to elicit responses to policy recommendations, and eventually spoke to the nation as a single episcopal voice. The failure to do so on the question of clergy sexual abuse was a serious mistake and has resulted in a significant loss of respect. The attempt at damage control by concealing facts, intimidating victims, and hoping that it would all go away was at the service of preserving a false image of the Church.

The antidote for this disease of institutional denial was clearly set forth by the Canadian bishops:

> The path of truth becomes immediately evident. All our
> considerations convinced us that child sexual abuse occurs
> and will continue in a climate of deception, hypocrisy, and

lies. This is why our suggestions and recommendations are clearly oriented toward the search for truth: The truthfulness of statements made to the media. Personal truthfulness and honesty in the preparation of candidates for the priesthood. Insistence on the truth throughout the therapy of the abusers. Truthfulness with those few parishes asked to accept a priest who is being reintegrated into the ministry.

The path of humility is no less important. Even if a tiny fraction of Canada's 11,000 priests in active ministry have been implicated in cases of abuse, the Church must humbly admit that some of its ministers are in flagrant contradiction to the message they have been commissioned to preach. In this spirit of humility, we suggest that more energy be put into correcting wrongs, than into safeguarding appearances, into humble care of the wounded, than into attempts to justify; into effective forms of education and careful research into ways of improving services for children, the poor, and the most vulnerable in our society.[18]

The Church must boldly continue the war on institutional denial by gathering the facts and then trusting the people of God with the truth. Perhaps the most serious policy/practice deficit is at the parish level. The Church has not yet terminated the old paternalistic system of viewing parishioners as children who need to be protected from harsh realities. Significant reform steps have been taken. The call for independent review boards and for more lay participation in evaluating seminary interns, along with the effective sharing of power, are steps in the right direction.

For the past twenty-five years a variety of leaders among the Catholic clergy have called for a statement of professional standards for clergy behavior. Bishops are searching for more effective methods to dismiss problem priests from active ministry. Priests are questioning long-standing dependency patterns on bishops, reinforced by low wages. Significant institutional and leadership reforms are under consideration, including perhaps the most difficult question: Can the Church, in light of the decreasing applicants, continue to demand celibacy of all its priests? Regardless how these and other important questions are answered, this crisis must hasten the realization of this movement.

NOTES

1. Dr. Canice Connors is president and CEO of the Saint Luke Institute in Suitland, Maryland. Saint Luke is a psychiatric and residential treatment facility on the cutting edge of helping priests with sexual misconduct problems. A Catholic priest and clinical psychologist, Dr. Connors holds an MA in philosophy from the Catholic University of America, an MA in psychology from the University of Ottawa, and a PhD in psychology from the University of Pittsburgh.

2. Aric Press and Carolyn Friday, "Priests and Abuse," *Newsweek*, 16 August 1993, 44.

3. Harold Laswell, *A Preview of the Policy Sciences* (New York: Elsevier, 1971), chapters 1 and 17.

4. Jason Berry, *Lead Us Not Into Temptation* (New York: Doubleday, 1992), part 1.

5. Editorial, "USCC Pedophilia Statement," *Origins* 17 (1988): 624.

6. Editorial, "Statement on Priests and Child Abuse," *Origins* 19 (1989): 395.

7. Editorial, "Painful Pastoral Question: Sexual Abuse of Minors," *Origins* 22 (1992): 177–78.

8. National Conference of Catholic Bishops, "Recommendations of the Think Tank on Child Sexual Abuse," (Washington, D.C.: NCCB, 1992), 1, 17.

9. Gordon Thomas, *Desire and Denial: Celibacy and the Church* (Boston: Little, Brown and Co., 1986), 6.

10. Issues raised by Dr. Judith Becker, professor of psychiatry at the University of Arizona, presented in the Chicago Report, NCCB, "Recommendations of the Think Tank on Child Sexual Abuse," appendices 6–10 at 67.

11. A. W. Richard Sipe, *A Secret World* (New York: Brunner-Mazel, 1990), iv.

12. Leo H. Bartemejer MD, as quoted by A. W. Richard Sipe in "Sexual Abuse of Clergy: Who and Why," as testimony at the Governor's Conference on Child Abuse and Neglect, Baltimore, Maryland, 1993.

13. Norbert J. Rigali, "Note on Pedophilia," *Theological Studies* 55 (1994): 139.

14. Stephen Rossetti, "Parishes as Victims of Abuse," *Human Development* Winter 1993: 15–17.

15. Paul Wilkes, "Unholy Acts," *New Yorker*, 7 June 1993, 62–79.

16. John J. Driese, "A Priest Looks at Priest Pedophilia," *Commonweal* 121 (April 1994): 13.

17. L. M. Lothstein, "Can a Sexually Addicted Priest Return to Ministry After Treatment? Psychological Issues and Possible Forensic Solutions," *Catholic Lawyer* 1 (1991): 107.

18. Canadian Council of Catholic Bishops, *From Pain to Hope* (Ottawa: CCCB, 1992): 64.

Chapter Eleven

Coincident Abuse and Congregational Healing

The body is a unit, though it is made up of many parts; and though all its parts are many, they form one body. So it is with Christ. For we were all baptized by one Spirit into one body—whether Jews or Greeks, slave or free—and we were all given the one Spirit to drink. Now the body is not made up of one part but of many. . . . If one part suffers, every part suffers with it. . . .

1 Corinthians 12:12–14, 26

THE APOSTLE PAUL, UNDER THE REVELATORY POWER of the Holy Spirit, was one of history's great systems thinkers. He revealed core truths, not only about the church as the Body of Christ but also about the universal intricacies of organizational relationships—dynamics being validated today by social science research. One of the cardinal principles of social systems theory is that whatever happens to part of the system affects the entire organism. A child's school or athletic achievement draws the entire family to celebration; a bad earnings year affects all the company employees. Likewise, the sexual abuse of a congregant by a ministerial leader impacts an entire church and calls forth the challenge of congregational healing.

The healing of congregations may be the most neglected aspect of the effects of sexual misconduct. So much attention and energy is rightly expended on the victims and the violators, including their immediate families, that the coincident effects on the congregation are easily overlooked. While this harm may not be as intense as the harm to those directly involved, the impact is nonetheless serious because of the numbers of people involved. When further multiplied by the adverse reputation a church or counseling ministry may develop in the community due to the stained association with moral failure, the total cost of the misconduct increases exponentially beyond that of the victims and perpetrators.

The Varieties of Abuse Response

Churches respond to revelations of sexual abuse by their leaders in varied and characteristic ways. Sexual misconduct is an event that precipitates a systemic, churchwide reaction by an affected congregation. It is safe to say that some churches will never be the same after such an experience. But because of the Holy Spirit's redeeming and transforming power, it is not safe to predict that a church will be irrevocably harmed. Though the road will be treacherous and the journey filled with pain, it is possible for the church body to be transformed into something better through the resolution of a sexual crisis. (Unfortunately, this seems to be the exception rather than the general rule regarding sexual misconduct cases in the church.)

The Minnesota Interfaith Committee on Sexual Exploitation by Clergy[1] has noted some common responses of churches and families to sexual abuse within the church. These include the following:

- attempts to maintain normalcy at all costs
- attempts to avoid confrontation of the behavior
- efforts to maintain a good family image by not talking to outsiders about the family or congregational needs and inadequacies, including sexual exploitation
- fear of disintegration of family or congregation
- feelings of helplessness, inadequacy, or unacceptability
- shocked disbelief, anger, and rage
- inability to deal with the conflict and anger in helpful ways
- feelings of betrayal and abandonment
- denial
- blame directed toward the victim
- faith and spiritual crisis

ASSESSMENT OF SYSTEMIC ABUSE

Sexual misconduct impacts a church community in many ways. Consistent with trauma theory and the denial/shock response, most church organisms are thrown into immediate disarray and act to protect the rest of the body, or parts of it, from further harm. One important systems process is to recognize how subgroups form and react to the event in different ways. Sometimes these actions result in more harm: denying obvious wrongdoing or tainting others with suspicion and false accusations. Latent and otherwise manageable cracks in the church system such as differences, mutual dislikes, etc., may be inflamed and stressed to breaking points.

Walter Bera has presented an excellent outline for understanding and working with an entire church following sexual misconduct by one of its leaders.[2] We have adapted and developed his work to profile seven response groups that impact the direction and success of the congregational healing endeavor.

1. *"Not My Pastor!"* These are the perpetrator's best friends and allies in crisis. They are loyalists whose emotional closeness and commitment to the abuser causes them to refuse to believe their pastor-hero did any wrong. They are usually blind to the possibility of wrongdoing; they see only the leader's righteousness and good works in ministry and, therefore, engage in powerful forms of denial. They tend to blame the victim, or rationalize the victim's charges as being motivated by jealousy, mental illness, or the devil. If there are multiple victims, they are judged as a group that is conspiring to destroy the pastor. In this situation battle lines are easily drawn, especially if a violative leader decides to cover his wrong and hide behind the protective cloak of these people.

2. *Dazed and Confused.* This group is less devoted to the pastor but is committed at some level to the church and its ministry and wants the minister to get a fair hearing in the matter. Tending toward a simple faith and a black-and-white view of morality, these individuals are mystified—revealing ignorance and expressing confusion—by the contradictions and paradox of the misconduct. They are often stunned at the revelations of wrongdoing and repeatedly ask how someone so good and anointed of the Lord could have committed such heinous crimes. Their faith and understanding of life is sometimes shaken deeply.

3. *The Cautious Believers.* This groups accepts the fact that wrongdoing occurred and that it was serious. Though somewhat

confused by the moral contradictions, this group understands the struggle between light and darkness—the conflict of the two selves (see chapter 3) that continues throughout the Christian life. They wonder how the abuse could have gone on for so long, how the congregation could have overlooked it, and how it was kept a secret for so long. Cautious believers tend to be more spiritually and psychologically mature. They are grounded in reality yet moved by the challenge of faith and healing. This group struggles to gather the facts and to understand the complex dynamics of sexual misconduct cases.

4. *Peace-at-Any-Price.* This group is characterized by a forgive-and-forget approach to the crisis. They engage in a different form of denial compared to a violator's supporters. They will concede that wrongdoing was perpetrated but tend to minimize its seriousness and seek a quick and easy resolution. Their approach is to acknowledge, even feel sorry that something inappropriate happened. However, since we are all sinners in need of redeeming grace, in the crisis they call on the church to forgive the wrongdoer and get on with the life of ministry. While affirming and consistently reminding a church of its obligations to forgive and heal, this message is often communicated simplistically, as a form of grace or peace without justice. These people are uncomfortable with crises and conflict and tend to assume the distorted role of peacemaker—a role susceptible to the allure of peace at any price.

5. *The Angry Victims.* The direct victims (the victims themselves, their families, and closest friends) tend to be an angry and active group. They feel betrayed and are angry at the abuser, at the church, and at those who are denying or minimizing the seriousness of the crisis. These are the individuals who will not let the crisis be resolved without justice, who keep pressing the issue when others are tired of it, and as a result, tend to be targets of some of the other groups' frustrations. This group or various individuals in it—the parents of a victim, for example—often investigates and uncovers the fullness of the wrong, finding other victims or uncovering the seamy side of the abuser's life. This group can easily be shunned and forced out of the church's life and attention—action that is repeatedly noted by plaintiffs as a key motivator to legal action.

6. *The Enraged Dividers.* This group, if it exists, can be a wild card in the equation for resolution. It is a small but extremely vocal and often divisive group that uses the crisis to express personal rage,

even hatred, at the abuser, the church, or at God. Individuals in the group may include past victims of the offender, those who have been abused by others, and those with mental disorders and spiritual oppressions who otherwise maintain some control of these problems in church life.

Crises of any significance in the church can bring out the passions and poison of this group. It can be an explosive group, demanding extreme solutions and easily consuming a church's attention and energy because of the lack of crisis experience at this level and comparative timidity of other groups and positions. Sometimes, at their worst, some of these people will threaten suicide or homicidal harm against the offender.

7. *The Healing Remnant.* This group must come forth or be created from the best members of other groups as it is vital for the healing and renewed direction of the church. Made up of wise leaders who are committed to a just and redemptive resolution of the crisis, these people must be empowered to guide the church through the crisis to God's healing. If this group is not empowered to control the process, then by default such control will be assumed by other individuals who are more angry and enraged—a chaotic and dangerous dynamic for a church.

When best empowered, this group tends to be made up of angry victims and cautious believers, with a minority of individuals from the other groups as well. This group should be recognized by as many leaders and members as possible and should quickly assume active control of meetings, agendas, and other processes of the church that address the crisis. Anyone working and consulting with an objective of congregational healing must ally with or even create this group to bring about a just and redemptive resolution to the matter.

SYSTEMIC INTERVENTION WITH CHURCHES

He has showed you, O man, what is good. And what does the LORD require of you? To act justly and to love mercy and to walk humbly with your God.

Micah 6:8

Systemic intervention—working to bring healing and justice to an entire congregation—is best done soon after the disclosure of abuse and any suspension or removal of the offender. This is when the crisis is at its peak for the church, a time when the fluidity of the situation renders the body most amenable to constructive direction. The more time that passes, the more likely personal opinions will become rigid, and contending groups will escalate their potential conflict.

THE TWIN MISSIONS

The congregational healer must strike a balance between pastoral and prophetic missions, the twin objectives of church intervention. Forging an alliance with the healing remnant group described earlier, the healer must assist this group to proceed with both of these missions. As Marie Fortune sees it, the pastoral mission is a work of mercy, while the prophetic mission is a work of justice.[3]

The Pastoral Mission. Intervention for pastoral purposes is a healing-consoling work for the wounded body of believers. The healer's leadership during this time is nondirective, subtle, facilitative, and interactive. The healer facilitates a subtly directed time of discussing and expressing feelings by the entire church body. During this time, permission is given to grieve, to cry, to be angry, to express confusion, to question, to pray, and to come forward with new revelations. It is a time for the body to corporately express shock and grief, to support one another in this difficult and emotional experience, and to invite the Holy Spirit to be present as the Comforter of God. Creating opportunity and time for this ministry often yields a powerful bond and reconciliation between otherwise divided members.

The Prophetic Mission. The prophetic mission is an active work of intervention that has two objectives: (1) justice for the victims and redemption for the abuser, and (2) leadership facilitation and support for the ongoing ministry of the church. The more directive work of this mission includes a psychospiritual-educational process of informing the congregation about sexual abuse. The dynamics and seriousness of sexual abuse is shared in general principles and as it applies in the more specific context of the actual abuse situation. The facts and allegations of the situation as they are currently known are shared with the group. Rumors, speculations, and exaggerations are tagged as such, and the congregation is challenged to adhere to what is known—to avoid speculating and creating rumors about what is not known. The prophetic mission challenges the church to maintain its mission and focus as a church apart from the crisis itself.

THE HEALING PROCESS

Marie Fortune has outlined an excellent process of congregational healing.[4] We have adapted her challenge to "Do Justice and Mercy" in the outline below.

Truth-Telling. The power of secrecy and mass denial of violation must be broken in a church caught up in the aftermath of sexual misconduct. This is done by creating an environment where victims can tell the truth of what happened either to the whole church or to a small group representing the entire body (representatives who will convey the story accurately to the church). Helping the victim overcome the fear of telling the truth (a fear often induced by the threats or guilt-laden manipulations of the abuser) is a significant step in the healing process.

Acknowledging the Violation. The congregation must not only be willing to hear the truth of the misconduct but must also be willing to acknowledge the violation and thus break its power to continue to harm. Even when some may question the misconduct charges or blame the victim for the wrong, these attitudes must be suppressed in this phase so that the rest of the church can hear and acknowledge the sin.

Marie Fortune cogently argues that, "The absence of acknowledging the cruelty of injustice serves to justify the maltreatment. Thus we should never underestimate the power of the explicit acknowledgment of violation in the process of healing for victims."[5] The church must follow up on this hearing with assertive and effective action.

Compassion for Victims and All Harmed in the Church. Some in the church need to be able to "suffer with" the victims, to grieve with, cry with, and express genuine compassion for those who are hurt. Others who have been hurt by the sexual betrayal, including those indirectly harmed, also need to be validated. The church membership must be challenged to bear one another's burdens as a corporate experience of suffering.

This call to compassion must be deliberate and sustained, as the divisive energy can be strong and too many in the church do not care to suffer with others or are uncomfortable with the reality of pain and suffering. Those who show compassion are the mercy-givers, who themselves shall receive mercy in their hour of need. Care-giving gifts are revealed and mercy-based ministry is encouraged to come forth during this step. New dimensions of the Holy Spirit's power are sought and experienced in new ways. The fruit of this work can extend far beyond this crisis and infuse a church with new purpose and vitality once the crisis has passed.

Accountability by the Violator. The violator, in most cases, should come before the church (or before the victims and key representatives of the church) and give a full account of his wrongdoing. This can include apologies to those harmed and disclosure of any commitments to restitution and plans for offender healing and restoration. In churches where this has not happened, or happens only partially, the fuller promise of healing is often thwarted or denied.

Biblical accountability is premised on Jesus' instruction in Luke 17:3, "If your brother sins, rebuke him, and if he repents, forgive him." The fullness of congregational healing is inhibited if the wrongdoer is not confronted with his sin. When the abuser is not given a chance to repent to the church, this devalues him and hinders his full recovery. This type of accountability is not punitive, even though it is confrontational and painful. Rather, such accountability is an exercise of godly justice—a justice without which true mercy and eventual healing cannot be complete.

Restitution Made to Victims. Restitution might be called "accountability with bite." It is a tangible act of repayment by the offender that attempts to cover the costs of harm to the victims and restore them to a place of healing. It usually involves some form of financial remuneration or payment by the offender to cover the cost of restoration for victims. The offender who sacrifices his resources to pay for a victim's counseling and other direct damages also expresses his repentance in ways that give power to the witness for Christ.

A failure to make restitution is a key motivator to lawsuit—if justice and award for damages are not freely given by the offender or the church, they will be gained through the courts. The illusion that insurance will cover litigation costs and damages only serves a denial of the terrible costs—to finances, reputations, spiritual well-being, testimonies, and organizations—that are attached to a public lawsuit.

Vindication from the Wrong and Its Legacy of Shame. The classic definition of vindication is "to set free." True vindication denotes deliverance from the spiritual and emotional shackles of past abuse and freedom to look forward to the best that God and life have to offer. Our modern culture, however, divorced from genuine justice by its denial of biblical morality, has corrupted the meaning to a sense of vengeance or retribution.

In instances of sexual misconduct, vindication means exoneration of victims from the associated guilt and shame; it means justification for taking truth-telling action, especially when done in the face of great resistance and counterattack. The vindicated victim is set free to rejoin the life of the community as an accepted and unstained member.

To the degree a church is able to accomplish this healing-justice work, it vindicates not only the victims but also the entire church body. The victims and the church can shed the legacy of shame and confusion, free to live out the miracle of new life in Christ with invigorated power. God is truly able to crate beauty from ashes, to resurrect to life all who are deadened by this sin.

CONCLUSION

Marie Fortune reminds us that complete or perfect justice is unattainable—we live in an imperfect and fallen world, even in the church. However, we can attain an approximation of justice, and we can give genuine mercy to the abused and the fallen. Sexual misconduct can be the kind of systemic crisis that leads an entire church into the deeper life of Christ. To those victimized, it can lead to deeper grace, healed wounds, and a willingness to forgive. To those who would deny or minimize the wrong, it can lead to a deeper understanding of sin, pain, suffering, and true justice.

To those charged with subsequent leadership, it can lead to a deeper reliance on the Holy Spirit and to wellsprings of wisdom and trust. To the church universal, it can lead to a deeper walk with our Creator God, to severing the world's corrupting influences, and to discovering new dimensions of joy and peace. Jesus gives his life—his crucified, empowering, purifying, and redeeming life—to those who ask for it. A sexual misconduct crisis can motivate an entire church body to seek his life with a new fervor.

NOTES

1. Minnesota Interfaith Committee on Sexual Exploitation by Clergy, *Sexual Exploitation by Clergy: Reflections and Guidelines for Religious Leaders.* (Minneapolis: Minnesota Interfaith Committee on Sexual Exploitation by Clergy, 1989).

2. Walter Bera, "Betrayal: Clergy Sexual Abuse and Male Survivors," *Dulwich Centre Newsletter* 3, no. 4 (1993): 62–75.

3. Marie Fortune, *Is Nothing Sacred? When Sex Invades the Pastoral Relationship* (San Francisco: HarperCollins, 1989): 114–18.

4. Ibid.

5. Ibid., 115.

PART V

Law and Ethics in Sexual Misconduct

Chapter Twelve

Ethical Issues in Forbidden Sex Prevention

Ethics and theology have provided little guidance in understanding the difference between sexual activity and sexual violence for a society faced daily with experiences that reflect the confusion between the two. . . . Christian ethics have failed to confront the problem of sexual violence itself, thus there has been no mandate for Christians to address this widespread problem.

Too often the teachings of the traditional Church confuse sexual activity with sexual violence. In doing so, they focus on the sexual rather than on the violent aspect and they blame the victim and fail to hold the offender accountable.[1]

Possibly nowhere else in our culture—in our church—does confusion reign more than in the area of sexual ethics. The perverse sexual values of our sex-sated culture have infected Western society with epidemic levels of sexual violence, sexual disease, sexual fear, and deep sexual confusion. Significant parts of the church are infected with this spiritual-moral-cultural disease. Numerous major denominations, especially mainline and liberal churches, are locked in battle over the ethics and propriety of homosexuality, premarital sex, abortion, and the importance of sexuality as a marker of identity.

In reaction to this cultural and church excess, an anti-sexual counterculture that purports to be Christian has arisen. This counterculture has also found deep roots in parts of the church, especially in the conservative and fundamentalist camps of Christianity. Honest and open discussion of sexuality and sexual troubles occurs with great difficulty in this culture. Sexual pleasure is denigrated as procreation becomes a paramount value. Sexual ethics are often enforced through fear, guilt, shame, and manipulation.

In a recently published article entitled, "Sex Therapy in the Body: A Roadmap to Christian Sexual Treatment,"[2] we argued for a third way as an alternative approach to human sexuality and sexual treatment. We refuse to accept either of the polarized extremes—the sex-sated or antisexual cultures—that currently contend for moral and political power in Western society. The church need not succumb either to the false allure of a cultural ethic that has forsaken biblical values or to a counterethic that is more a reaction to moral-cultural excess than a reasoned biblical ethic. Instead, we have outlined ten principles we believe are a better ethical foundation for Christian sexual treatment. Summarized below is a comprehensive ethical framework grounded on Scripture, professional ethics, and the best clinical treatment principles.

1. *Sex is good, not bad.* God created sex and declared his creation to be "very good." Understanding human sexuality must begin by understanding it as God's good and wonderful gift.

2. *Sex is for procreation and pleasure.* When either of these dual objectives is stressed at the expense of the other, godly sexual values become imbalanced, and trouble eventually follows.

3. *Sex is flawed by the fall.* Sin inevitably mars human sexuality and experience. Denying the reality of sin-promoting sexual liberation without regard to biblical boundaries has resulted in the multiple sexual epidemics harming both church and culture today.

4. *Sexuality is redeemed in Christ.* Christ sets us free to be the people we are created to be—identified in Him rather than in our gender, or by our politics, or sexual orientation. The Spirit of Christ allows us to enjoy and respect the power of our sexual nature.

5. *Sex is a heterosexual marriage behavior.* God confined the fullness of sexual activity to consensual heterosexual marriage. Sex outside this boundary eventually bears troubled fruit for individuals, families, churches, communities, and society.

6. *Sexual treatment demands mature helpers.* Sex therapy is not for novices. A maturity of therapeutic experience, professional judgment, and personal self-control is essential to successfully navigate the complex channels and dangerous shoals of sexual practice.

7. *Sexual treatment demands competence.* Sex therapy is not for the incompetent. Competence usually requires specialized training, experience, and in some cases certification in the area of treatment. The competent helper knows the limits of his or her expertise and uses consultation and referral when faced with issues beyond skill or scope of practice.

8. *Sexual treatment demands informed consent.* Those seeking sexual counseling have a right to be fully informed of treatment, its risks, and its alternatives so that they can make a truly voluntary choice to engage in the work. Such consent also protects the helper from the surprises and problems that can lead to suit.

9. *Sexual treatment must involve confidentiality.* Since sex and attendant feelings of guilt and shame are the treatment focus, strict confidentiality is vital. Since courts and other authorities may be involved, the limits to confidence must be clearly spelled out and consent given.

10. *Sexual misconduct demands both prevention and remediation.* This has been the subject matter of this entire book. We deal with prevention and remediation directly in chapters 14 and 15. We continue in this chapter to address more specific ethical problems and dilemmas.

PROFESSIONAL ETHICAL LIABILITY

By 1990, the decades-long ethical war about sex in psychotherapy was over. The agents promoting sex in psychotherapy were forced into unconditional surrender. Though the war still rages among lawyers[3] and in some other professions, every major mental health professional group, including those that regulate pastoral and Christian counseling, now condemns sexual activities with clients as unethical.[4]

MENTAL HEALTH ETHICS STATEMENTS

Psychiatry, the preeminent mental health profession, reinforces both its relationship to medicine and a psychodynamic view of treatment in its ethical code statement against sex in the professional sphere.

> 1. The patient may place his/her trust in his/her psychiatrist knowing that the psychiatrist's ethics and professional responsibilities preclude him/her from gratifying his/her own needs by exploiting the patient. This becomes particularly important

because of the essentially private, highly personal, and sometimes intensely emotional nature of the relationship
established with the psychiatrist.

2. The requirement that the physician "conduct himself
with propriety in his professional and in all actions of his life"
is especially important in the case of the psychiatrist because
the patient tends to model his/her behavior after that of his/
her therapist by identification. Further, the necessary intensity of the therapeutic relationship may tend to activate sexual
and other needs and fantasies on the part of both patient and
therapist, while weakening the objectivity necessary for control. Sexual activity with a patient is unethical.[5]

The latest "Ethical Principles of Psychologists" of the American
Psychological Association (APA) retains its rather cryptic but
all-inclusive statement, "Psychologists do not engage in sexual
intimacies with current patients or clients."[6] The newly revised
"National Association of Social Workers (NASW) Code of Ethics"
also condemns any form of client exploitation and asserts that,
"The social worker should under no circumstances engage in
sexual activities with clients."[7] Commenting on the language used
in this prohibition, the NASW Task Force on Ethics stated that it
"deliberately used the strongest language of absolute prohibition,
'under no circumstances' found any place in the code" in view of
the "great damage" done to sexually exploited clients.[8]

Christian Ethical Code Prohibitions. The newly published (1992)
"Ethical Guidelines for the Christian Association for Psychological
Studies" (CAPS) states that "sexual contact or sexual exploitation—both covert and overt—with any client will be scrupulously
avoided."[9] The recently revised (1991) "Code of the American Association of Pastoral Counselors" (AAPC) states:

> All forms of sexual behavior or harassment with clients are
> unethical, even when a client invites or consents to such be-
> havior or involvement. Sexual behavior is defined as, but not
> limited to, all forms of overt and covert seductive sexual
> speech, gestures and behavior as well as physical contact of a
> sexual nature; harassment is defined as, but not limited to, re-
> peated comments, gestures, or physical contacts of a sexual
> nature.
> We recognize that the therapist/client relationship involves a
> power imbalance, the residual effects of which are operative
> following the termination of the therapy relationship. Therefore,

all sexual behavior or harassment as defined . . . [above] with former clients is unethical."[10]

The draft statement of the developing "Christian Counseling Code of Ethics"[11] of the American Association of Christian Counselors (AACC) outlines a comprehensive, law-tuned, and behaviorally detailed ethical prohibition regarding sexual misconduct:

Avoidance of Client Harm and Exploitation. Aware of our social and spiritual influence and the inherent power imbalance of helping and mentoring relationships, Christian counselors avoid all harm and exploitation in relations with clients, congregants, supervisees, students, trainees, employees, and colleagues. Christian counselors also humbly and accurately expose harm and exploitation where it is found, and work to bring redemptive healing and justice to victims and perpetrators alike.

Sexual Misconduct Forbidden. All forms of sexual misconduct, abuse, or harassment in any professional or lay relationships are unethical. This includes relations where the sexual involvement is invited or informed consent presumably exists—such apparent consent is illusory due to the unique helping nature, lack of equality, and power imbalance in the relationship.

Forbidden sexual activities include, but are not limited to, direct sexual touch or contact, seductive sexual speech or nonverbal behavior, solicitation of sexual relations, sexual harassment by comments, touch, or promises/threats of special favor or action, and sexual misconduct as defined by all applicable laws, ethics, and church, organizational, or practice policies.

Sexual Relations with Former Clients Forbidden. Due to the biblical prohibition of sexual relations outside consensual heterosexual marriage, the continuing influence of the counselor-client relationship following termination, and the possibility that clients may engage in or return to counseling in the future, all sexual relations as defined [in the section] above with former clients are unethical, except for the restricted marital situation defined below.

This prohibition may be excepted in the event of marriage between counselor and a former client, if the marriage takes place after two years following termination of counseling relations. This exception is legitimate only if (1) counseling relations were legitimately terminated—not with the intended or possible future relationship in view, (2) no contact between counselor and former client was made during the two-year period, (3) the renewed relationship was begun for reasons other than to restart counseling relations, and (4) no other factors about the relationship exist to suggest that the counselor is exploiting or acting in ways that could harm the former client.

Counseling with Sexual/Marital Partners. Christian counselors do not counsel, but make appropriate referral, with current or former sexual and/or marital partners.

TAKING PROFESSIONAL ETHICS ACTION

Professional associations exist to advance the profession, to set standards for membership and professional behavior, to investigate complaints, and to discipline erring members. Many, but not all, therapists and counselors belong to them for these reasons. A victim can file a complaint with the association, which (based on evidence of violation against its ethical code) may take various disciplinary actions, including removal of the offending member from the association. This is not the same as license revocation; the erring therapist might still practice even if removed from professional association. Furthermore, there is still considerable debate about the effectiveness of these organizations in disciplining their members. Compared to the various kinds of legal action that can be taken (detailed in the next chapter), this option is recognized as the weakest in terms of punishment and protection of the public from further harm.

SEX WITH FORMER CLIENTS?

Though the moral and ethical battle about sex with current clients is over, a skirmish still rages over the issue of sex with former clients: Is it permissible or not? Some groups, like the AAPC (pastoral counselors) and various state and local counseling organizations have come down against any sex with former clients. The proposed code for the AACC states that it is unethical, except for a narrowly proscribed marriage exception (noted above). We present an expanded biblical-ethical analysis of this controversial issue to suggest a way of analysis and argument that will help Christians who will be engaged in moral discourse and ethical debate around these issues within the church, with counseling professionals and government personnel, and with society-at-large.

POSITIONS FOR AND AGAINST

The two associations of psychiatrists and psychologists have stated publicly that sex with former clients is possible, though only in rare and exceptional circumstances. The revised code of the American Psychological Association, influenced strongly by its Committee on Women in Psychology,[12] makes the most detailed statement of all ethics codes on this issue. It asserts that its members are not to engage in sex with former clients "even after [its required] 2 year interval following termination except in the most unusual circumstances."[13] It then details seven factors that a psychologist must prove to show the avoidance of any client exploitation. These issues take into account the (1) circumstances of and (2) time passed since termination, (3) duration and nature of therapy, the (4) client's history and (5) current mental status, the (6) likelihood of any adverse impact on the client due to sexual contact, and (7) any evidence that relations were terminated with the possibility of a romance in view.

The code of the American Psychiatric Association holds that sex with former patients is "almost always unethical," with the inference of exceptional ethicality creating a firestorm of controversy in that organization. In 1991 in the *American Journal of Psychiatry*, Paul Appelbaum and Linda Jorgenson, two of the fields most respected forensic experts, published an article proposing the possibility of consensual sex under certain conditions after a one-year, no-contact, post-termination period.[14] While cautioning that their position was highly exceptional to the general rule against such sex, they argued that a complete ban was tantamount to moral and legal overkill.

Jeremy Lazarus, in an editorial as chairman of the APA Ethics Committee, opined that, theoretically, there could be some patients who "enter into a sexual relationship with a psychiatrist with true autonomy (without coercion or manipulation). . . ."[15] Since medical ethics are not absolutes and "will be revised from time to time," he was loathe to prescribe a hard rule against sex with former patients or a definitive time period. Wisely, he conclusively retreated to the safer course of asserting that "the current 'almost always' position . . . ought to be so strong that a proscription against sexual contact with current or former patients should presumptively be accepted [by] a psychiatrist. . . ."

Counter-Responses. The APA was inundated with letters in response, with most opposing the view that such sex could be sanctioned. One letter from a group, including such leading mental health clinician/researchers as Annette Brodsky, Nannette Gartrell, Jacqueline Bouhoutsos, Glen Gabbard, and Kenneth Pope, strongly opposed this idea. They argued that the enduring consequences of therapy last for many years beyond termination and that an arbitrary one-year wait could in no way genuinely prove protective against further harm. Rather than protect patients, such a rule would instead communicate an implicit permission to harmful sex.

> When the possibility of a sexual relationship exists in the mind . . . of the therapist, psychotherapy can and too often does become a courtship, a process of grooming in which a vulnerable individual is shaped to meet the sexual and narcissistic needs of the therapist. . . . This grooming . . . is inevitably countertherapeutic.[16]

Other respondents challenged the harm to psychiatry—the reduced public esteem that will likely attach to the profession—by not taking a clear stand against all sexual contact. "In these times when we are working to improve the public image of psychiatry, who would be harmed by our professional society taking an ethical position that, for purposes of our own, stated, 'Once a patient, always a patient'"?[17] Another psychiatrist sarcastically goaded his colleagues, "Given our rather dismal behavior in the past advocating for chronically mentally ill and sexually abused patients, it is perhaps too much to hope that we could take the lead to oppose exploitation, but it would certainly be a step in the right direction for psychiatric organizations not to condone it."[18]

BIBLICAL AND ETHICAL ANALYSIS OF CLIENT SEX

After decades of living with the costly and still-accumulating consequences of the sexual revolution, the helping professions have garnered data that affirms the biblical revelation: sexual immorality is harmful, even deadly to some. The truth of this assertion is now affirmed by both moral and statistical argument. The ethics of these professions—at least those regarding sexual exploitation with current clients—have evolved to reflect these enduring truths as well.

The room allowed for the possibility of sex with former clients still reflects the stubborn truth that God is not honored by these major professional groups (a marital exception is not even considered as part of this debate). Action consistent with God's truths still comes only as a result of hard and undeniable evidence of destructive consequences (and such evidence is usually denied as long as possible until it becomes undeniable to a majority of its leaders). Even then, God is rarely, if ever, acknowledged. Nor is there much ontological learning—an education that leads to the knowledge of God and the acceptance of a priori moral principles.

The counseling professions, however, do concede that the harm of sex with former clients is significant, and this is at least partly reflected in their ethics. As asserted by the group noted above (a veritable Who's Who against sexual misconduct), there is no data that post-termination sex is not harmful and much data that the harm of such sex to victims can last almost interminably.[19] Based on this growing mass of research evidence, these leaders argue that a rule allowing sex with former patient-clients is extremely ill-advised.

The Stubborn Persistence of Sanctioned Sexual Trouble. Why then, in the face of overwhelming evidence to the contrary, do the major helping professions stubbornly leave open the door to further trouble by allowing the ethicality of such sex? Two issues are presented that suggest these professions are increasingly trapped in ideological dogma that overshadows good science and clouds ethical judgment. A complete sexual bar is resisted (1) as a violation of personal autonomy and (2) to avoid sexism, in appearance at least if not in fact.

These stubborn and seductive arguments are based, it seems, on that old sexual revolutionary icon about the per se legitimacy of sex between consenting adults. It is argued that barring sex with a former client devalues both the counselor's and the client's autonomous power—the fundamental right of consenting adults—to choose their own poison. Not only do the detractors argue that such ethical rule-making is too paternalistic, it is also sexist. Since most former clients in this situation are female, ruling against such sex (an externalized form of feminine disempowerment it seems) robs women of the right or opportunity to deal autonomously with men.[20] Also, in the statements by psychiatry ethics chief Lazarus, it is hard to escape the strong inference that he would hate to be branded a rigid, moralizing absolutist.

Counter-Arguments. The excessive support for personal autonomy crosses the boundary of idolatry, paradoxically trapping its adherents in an absolute position for client self-determination. This argument casts the "competent" client-patient—not God, nor the vows of marriage, nor societal laws and customs—as the final judge and determiner of his or her own life. This is the secular-humanist-libertarian foundation for the arguments in support of abortion-on-demand, or the right to assisted suicide, or even the right to take drugs or smoke oneself to death. This pernicious self-exaltation denies the prophetic truth that "we will all stand before God's judgment seat," before Him who "will judge the world in righteousness" (Rom. 14:10, Ps. 9:8).

Though sexist charges are legitimate in neighboring issues,[21] here it cries with a fallacious and whiny whimper. The argument ignores that the sexual prohibition is based, not on sexist paternalism but on the inherent power imbalance of all professional-client relations, a dynamic universally understood. It also turns a legitimate sexist argument on its head by denying the fact that the power equation is further imbalanced because most abusers are men and most victims are women (85 to 90 percent of all cases). Finally, Lazarus seems to bow to the postmodern god of tolerance-at-all-costs. This modern religion's basic commandment is "Thou shalt not let thyself or thy cause be labeled *intolerant*." In the politically-correct morality of this world, it is better to err by allowing some wrongdoing than to break this unholy rule.

Altogether, the argument for an ethical exception to sex with former clients is woefully weak unless it is shaped around the biblical blessing to marriage. Any other justification reveals an illogical, feeble moral force similar to that which labels any challenge to homosexual behavior as homophobic or brands as anti-Christian any criticism of Republican party policy or support for a Democratic candidate. Though such jargon may seize the passions of narrow politically-correct or theologically-correct worlds, whether liberal or conservative, it should move the thoughtful Christian to clear and critical analysis. Some notions, no matter how bankrupt on biblical, moral, legal, public policy, or empirical grounds, do not die the quick and utter death they deserve.

Honoring the Biblical Ethic. Biblical analysis condemns counselor-client sexual contact—whether with current or former clients—on multiple grounds. The principles of sexual treatment described at the beginning of this chapter indicate that such sex (1) violates God's created design for good sex; (2) takes place outside marriage and violates the loving objectives of both procreation and (enduring) pleasure; (3) as such, is sin; (4) exemplifies the worst kind of immaturity and incompetence in clinical practice and helping ministry; (5) makes informed consent impossible to give; and (6) puts client confidentiality greatly at risk—it is necessarily broken for justice to be done.

The three primary Christian codes acknowledge and reflect this revelatory truth from the Holy Scriptures. The AAPC code has blazed the trail for all counseling professions, both Christian and secular, by constructing a complete and behaviorally detailed prohibition of all sexual contact. The AACC proposed code follows the lead of the AAPC in the complete sexual ban regarding current clients. By allowing a biblically defensible marital exception with former clients,[22] contingent on the integrity of counseling termination and the lack of any exploitation, the AACC proposed code diverges from the AAPC rule.

The CAPS code is likewise clear on the prohibition of sex with current clients, but is regrettably silent on the issue of sex with former clients. It is easy to imagine, since this code is so consciously biblical, that they would not allow it. Or they might craft a narrow marital exception akin to the AACC proposed code. It will be interesting to see how this important code evolves as it deals more directly and in-depth with these complex ethical issues into the twenty-first century.

ETHICAL PRINCIPLES FOR SEXUAL MISCONDUCT INTERVENTION

Professional therapists are bound both to the ethical rules of any denomination or professional association to which they belong and to the statutory code of professional misconduct (a legalized code of ethics) that is part of the licensing laws governing mental health practice. To these general rules we offer the following ethical practice suggestions for working with all those harmed by sexual misconduct, whether adult victims, child victims, or sexual violators.

A. GENERAL ETHICAL PRINCIPLES

1. Sexual misconduct treatment, whether with victims or offenders, shall not be done by novice therapists but only by those with the requisite training and experience to understand and adequately manage the complex issues and dynamics involved.

2. Therapist competence shall be a high priority; helpers must be aware of the limits of competence and have a strong commitment to consult and refer when limits are reached. Helpers who have been abused themselves, whether as a child or an adult, should have these issues sufficiently resolved in their own lives before engaging in sexual abuse recovery work.

3. Sexual misconduct treatment demands agreement around specific goals, costs (if any), projected time frame, confidentiality, and relations and duties to courts, churches, or other authoritative bodies concerned with the outcome. The treatment contract should clearly define the limits and consequences of failure to work or make adequate progress toward treatment objectives.

4. To maintain professional objectivity, client empathy, and to avoid loss of perspective of the wider picture of sexual abuse, it is preferred that counselors work with both victim and offender populations rather than with either exclusively.

5. In any conflict of interest between victim, violator, and community safety, priority order shall be with the safety and concerns of victims first (especially when minors), then with the community.

6. Duties and limits to confidentiality shall be given special attention, with discussion and consent from clients about duties and limits mandatory. This is necessary because of the sexual nature of the therapeutic focus and also because some cases are limited in confidential scope due to involvement of the court and other authoritative bodies.

B. ETHICS FOR WORKING WITH ADULT VICTIMS

1. Counselors working with adult victims should have a thorough and respectful understanding of the dynamics and harm of sexual abuse. The counselor will not ignore or minimize this harm, nor exaggerate the harm and assume victim rage by overidentifying with the victim.

2. Helpers should know and respect the limits of their competence, with clear boundaries and liberal use of supervision, consultative help, and referral resources. This requires that helpers have sufficient understanding and commitment to consult or refer when symptoms of depression, suicide, post-traumatic stress, dissociation, or other severe disorders are present.

3. Helpers should be dedicated to an empowering goal in teaching victims to know and guard their sexual boundaries, encouraging proper healing and justice activity, assisting mature decision-making, including review of options and their consequences, and refusing to tell victims what to do or doing things for them.

4. Helpers need to pursue a balance of empathy and challenge in working with sexual abuse victims. The helper should be able to empathize, to deeply understand and feel with the victims, yet

remain free to challenge excessive victimization-irresponsibility, excuse-making, resistance to active change, codependency, and blame projection.

5. Helpers of sexual abuse victims should expect times of trouble and turbulence, even relapses in the healing journey. Things sometimes get worse before they get better as victims face the full consequences of the abuse. Helpers should be prepared to travel with counselees through some dark and slow detours.

C. Ethics for Working with Child Victims

1. Counselors working with child victims should have a thorough understanding of the dynamics and harm of child sexual abuse. This includes a comprehensive understanding of the type of abuse and its impact on the developmental stage of the child or adolescent.

2. Helpers should know and respect the limits of their competence, with clear lines and liberal use of supervision, consultative help, and referral resources. This requires that helpers have sufficient understanding and commitment to consult or refer when appropriate.

3. Helpers should be dedicated to an empowering goal in teaching child victims and parents to know and guard their sexual boundaries, encouraging proper healing activity, assisting mature decision-making, including review of options and their consequences, and providing age-appropriate guidance.

4. Helpers need to pursue a balance of empathy and challenge in working with sexual abuse victims; they need to balance mercy with an ability to challenge excessive victimization.

5. Helpers of sexual abuse victims should expect times of trouble and turbulence, even relapses in the healing journey, especially when dealing with courts and personal issues. Helpers should be prepared to provide appropriate advocacy to protect the interests of the child(ren).

6. Helpers should have a clear understanding of the legal issues related to working with children, particularly in the realm of abuse reporting, privilege/confidentiality, consent for treatment, and documentation for court and other hearings.

D. Ethics for Working with Offenders

1. Counselors who work with offenders should accept a dual-client approach to offender treatment: one that balances client

self-determination with respect and cooperation with the goals of courts, church councils, and other authoritative bodies.

2. Helpers should, when possible, actively involve the courts, the church, correction officers, child protection workers, and victim therapists in case management.

3. Helpers should have a thorough understanding of the dynamics and treatment of sex offenders, being especially vigilant to challenge thinking and behavior that is deceptive and/or harmful to the offender or to others.

4. Helpers should know and respect the limits of their competence, with clear lines and liberal use of supervision, consultative help, and referral resources. This requires that helpers have sufficient understanding and commitment to consult or refer when symptoms of drug abuse, depression, suicide, post-traumatic stress, relationship conflicts, personality disorders, or other severe disorders are present.

5. Helpers need to pursue a balance of empathy and challenge in working with sex offenders. They should be able to empathize with the offender's struggles, while challenging denial, minimization, irresponsibility, excuse-making, resistance to active change, and blame projection.

6. Helpers of sex offenders should expect times of trouble and turbulence, even relapses as offenders face the full implications of their behavior and attitudes. However, when an offender is not making fair progress toward the changes necessary to reduce the risk to the community, helpers have an ethical obligation to refer the offender to a more comprehensive treatment program and/or to the judicial system.

CONCLUSION

The realm of sexual misconduct ethics is both very old and very new. Professionals have been apprised of the wrongfulness of therapist-patient sex for 2500 years, since the earliest forms of the Hippocratic Oath. Professionals are still struggling (and will continue to do so into the twenty-first century) about the boundaries of the prohibition, reflective of the clash and confusion of modern value systems that often have little in common or agreement.

Respect for the Scriptures as the revelatory base upon which to build a modern moral-ethical code needs reaffirmation. The Scriptures are a clear beacon of light to shine into the darkness; they affirm the moral-ethical universals that God revealed to the ancients. For the present struggle, Scripture delineates clear boundaries that, if respected, will engender respect for the church and professions from the society-at-large. All we have to do is agree with God: renounce our self-exalting pride, humble ourselves, and obey His prescriptions. Though it may be too much to expect this from the culture as a whole, we should at least challenge that it be done by those who profess to be the church of Jesus Christ.

NOTES

1. Kathe Stark, "Child Sexual Abuse Within the Catholic Church," in *Psychotherapists' Sexual Involvement with Clients: Intervention and Prevention*, ed. Gary Schoener, et al. (Minneapolis: Walk-in Counseling Center, 1989), 795.

2. George Ohlschlager and Peter Mosgofian, "Sex Therapy in the Body: A Roadmap to Christian Sexual Treatment," *Christian Counseling Today* 2 (Summer 1994): 9–13.

3. See David Wilkins, "Who Should Regulate Lawyers?" *Harvard Law Review* 105 (1992): 799.

4. See American Psychiatric Association, "The Principles of Medical Ethics with Annotations Especially Applicable to Psychiatry," *American Journal of Psychiatry* 130 (1985): 1057; American Psychological Association, "Ethical Principles of Psychologists and Code of Conduct," *American Psychologist* 47, no. 12 (1992): 1597–611; National Association of Social Workers, *NASW Code of Ethics* (Washington, D.C.: National Association of Social Workers, 1993); American Association for Marriage and Family Therapy, *AAMFT Code of Ethical Principles for Marriage and Family Therapists* (Washington, D.C.: American Association for Marriage and Family Therapy, 1988); American Association of Pastoral Counselors, "Ethical Code," in *AAPC Handbook* (Fairfax, Vir.: American Association of Pastoral Counselors, 1991); Christian Association for Psychological Studies, *Ethical Guidelines for CAPS* (Temecula, Calif.: Christian Association for Psychological Studies, 1992).

5. American Psychiatric Association, "The Principles of Medical Ethics," 1057.

6. American Psychological Association, "Ethical Principles of Psychologists," 1597–611, sect. 4.05.

7. National Association of Social Workers, *NASW Code of Ethics*, 5.

8. NASW Task Force on Ethics, "Ethics Analysis—Conduct and Responsibility to Clients," *NASW News* (May 1980): 12.

9. Christian Association for Psychological Studies, *Ethical Guidelines*, sect. 2.6.

10. American Association of Pastoral Counselors, *AAPC Handbook*, principle III, G and H.

11. "The AACC Christian Counseling Code of Ethics" (Law and Ethics Committee draft, 1994). This code, in provisional form, is now being drafted by George Ohlschlager and reviewed/revised by the leadership of the AACC. It will be submitted to the membership of the AACC for review, revision, debate, and, eventually, approval vote. The statement of the code in this book may not be the final code statement once it is enacted, likely sometime in 1996 or 1997.

208   SEXUAL MISCONDUCT IN COUNSELING

12. See, Committee on Women in Psychology of the American Psychological Association, "If Sex Enters Into the Psychotherapy Relationship," *Professional Psychology* 20 (1989): 112–15.

13. American Psychological Association, "Ethical Principles of Psychologists," 1597–1611.

14. Paul Appelbaum and Linda Jorgenson, "Psychotherapist-Patient Sexual Contact After Termination of Treatment: An Analysis and a Proposal," *American Journal of Psychiatry* 148, no. 11 (1991): 1466–73.

15. Jeremy Lazarus, "Sex With Former Patients Almost Always Unethical," *American Journal of Psychiatry* 149, no. 7 (1992): 855–857.

16. Laura Brown et al., "Psychotherapist-Patient Sexual Contact After Termination of Treatment: A Reply," *American Journal of Psychiatry* 149, no. 8 (1992): 979–80.

17. Theodore Anderson, "Psychotherapist-Patient Sexual Contact After Termination of Treatment: A Reply," *American Journal of Psychiatry* 149, no. 8 (1992): 985.

18. Edward Drummond, "Psychotherapist-Patient Sexual Contact After Termination of Treatment: A Reply," *American Journal of Psychiatry* 149, no. 8 (1992): 983.

19. Ibid.

20. See Appelbaum and Jorgenson, "Psychotherapist-Patient Sexual Contact," 987–99; and Paul Appelbaum and Linda Jorgenson, "Dr. Appelbaum and Ms. Jorgenson Reply," *American Journal of Psychiatry* 149, no. 8 (1992): 987–99.

21. Sexism and the patriarchal roots of abuse are legitimate issues when considering the male-female psychodynamic of sexual abuse (see chapter 4) and the systemic failure that protects violators and denies justice to victims (see chapters 9, 14, and 15).

22. It is noteworthy regarding the psychiatric controversy (and observing how far the professions have moved from biblical morality), that only one insightful psychiatrist, among the dozens of respondents to this issue, raised a central question that went begging throughout the debate, "It is an unfortunate reflection of the preoccupation of our society with genital activities that [the Appelbaum/Jorgenson article and debate on sexual contact] should fail to consider the most common setting for sexual contact in our society: marriage." Laura Brown et al., "Psychotherapist-Patient Sexual Contact," 986.

Chapter Thirteen

The Law of Sexual Misconduct

Can a man scoop fire into his lap without his clothes being burned?
Can a man walk on hot coals without his feet being scorched? So is he who
sleeps with another man's wife; no one who touches her will go
unpunished. . . . But a man who commits adultery lacks judgment; who-
ever does so destroys himself. Blows and disgrace are his lot, and his shame
will never be wiped away.

Proverbs 6:27–29, 32–33

THE CRIMINALIZATION OF SEXUAL MISCONDUCT IN COUNSELING and pastoral ministry has begun, and some who are engaged in this wrong will one day be imprisoned for it. The law against professional sexual misconduct is rapidly changing, and we cannot predict when the current fluidity will gel into a tangible body of predictable legal doctrine. It is now clear, however, that the sex-offending counselor will be severely affected by any victim who takes any type of action against this behavior.

This chapter, containing both practical suggestions and policy prescriptions, is a treatise on the status and development of sexual misconduct law to the mid-1990s. In keeping with our primary objectives, we intend to first inform counselors and ministers about the law. However, recognizing that this book will be useful to a much wider audience, this chapter is also written for lawyers, judges, lawmakers, academics, and policy professionals.

It is beyond dispute that the failure of the professions and the church to control their harmful members, especially their sex-abusing members, invites the legal control the church detests.

Remember, *over half the lawsuits and legal actions against all counselors are for some form of sexual misconduct, and over two-thirds of these actions are successful.* We have no doubt that the failure of in-house professional or church action combined with the evidence of serious harm to victims of therapeutic sexual abuse is a key reason for both the incidence and the growing success of legal action.

Contrast this with the evidence that only 1 to 5 percent of therapeutic sexual abuse is reported.[1] If these dismal reporting rates were merely doubled—if just one victim in ten took action against the abuser—the courts and licensing boards would be flooded with suits and disciplinary actions. A sleeping giant of sexually victimized people is awakening from slumber. And when it is fully awake and acts, it will bring just retribution on sexual violators and forever change the social fabric of our church and Western society.

THE GROWTH IN CHURCH LITIGATION

More and more victims are filing and winning lawsuits against sexually abusing counselors, including pastoral counselors and the church. The tragedy of this growing phenomena of suing the church is that such action could so easily be prevented. It might be unavoidable for some to simply charge that Christians have become as suit-happy as the culture at large—an argument that probably has some merit. However, Elizabeth Stellas, of the church-consulting Center for the Prevention of Sexual and Domestic Violence, said she has never talked to a victim "whose first thought is to sue the church."[2]

Victims of sexual misconduct in the church almost always take action within the bounds of the church. Complainants rarely, if ever, think of lawsuit—at least initially. Many, we would guess, recoil and reject this option when it is initially proposed. Most Christians who sue do so only as the last agonizing step in a long chain of denial, victim-blaming, shunning, and continued abusive behavior by churches that respond irresponsibly to a complaint of misconduct. For the great majority of cases, churches get sued because churches behave in the worst ways toward their most needy members—heaping added abuse onto a victim already sexually violated.

Lawsuits are succeeding against pastors and churches because people are more willing to press cases against the church when they are harmed by it. Also, traditional legal barriers to suit success, especially those that have historically protected the church, are increasingly being overcome.[3] The growing frequency and success of these suits against therapists and pastors (over 70 percent now result in plaintiff victory or settlement of some kind) is reflected by the widespread insurance industry's refusal to cover liability for sexual misconduct (an injustice discussed further below). We believe the upward spiral of lawsuits for church-related malpractice will continue for some time, a troubling trend that will not level off and decline until the church becomes honest, finds courage, and assumes control of its sexual misconduct crisis.

CIVIL LIABILITY FOR SEXUAL MISCONDUCT

The varieties of legal liability for individuals held accountable for wrongful sex are rapidly expanding. Respecting the major division of law into civil and criminal realms, we first consider various doctrines and issues under civil liability for sexual misconduct.

CIVIL LAWSUITS UNDER TORT AND RELATED LAW

Probably the most well-known form of legal action against an abusing counselor is the tort-based civil lawsuit. In 1968, in a ground-breaking malpractice case that was nearly lost by the plaintiff,[4] Ada Zipkin won damages of $17,000 (later reduced to just $5,000) against her abusive psychiatrist. This was for behavior in which the psychiatrist induced his patient to leave her husband and move into an apartment above his practice while still in therapy. He then coerced her to file lawsuits against her husband, to burglarize her husband's home, to give the doctor money for speculative business ventures, to engage in nude swimming parties, and to have frequent sex, including when she escorted him to psychiatric and other professional conferences.

The basis for the malpractice—the failure to maintain a minimal standard of psychotherapeutic care—is mishandling of the therapeutic transference. This reflects the influence of psychodynamic theory in both psychotherapy and the law. In *Simmons v. United States*, a federal appeals court stated:

> Transference . . . denote[s] a patient's emotional reaction to a therapist and is "generally applied to the projection of

feelings, thoughts, and wishes onto the analyst, who has come to represent some person from the patient's past." . . . Transference [attributes to the therapist] those feelings which he may have repressed toward his own parents. . . . When the therapist mishandles transference and becomes sexually involved with a patient, medical authorities are nearly unanimous in considering such conduct to be malpractice.[5]

Over the past quarter century hundreds of suits, with about thirty cases at various appellate court levels, have secured the legal relationship between therapist-patient sex and malpractice with abuse of the patient transference. This increasing success reflects how well plaintiffs, by legislation and court rule, are overcoming four problem areas that have traditionally blocked winning civil lawsuits: (1) credibility, (2) consent to sex, (3) statute of limitations, and (4) the difficulties with traditional tort standards.

Credibility Problems for Mental Health Patients. In the well-known case of *Roy v. Hartogs*,[6] the defendant psychiatrist was nearly successful in denying sexual contact and blaming the victim for her own distress. The case was won by the plaintiff-victim only after three former sexual abuse victims of the psychiatrist came forward and testified against him. Until recently, the presumptions for the veracity and integrity of the professional-defendant were usually only overcome by the testimony of multiple victims, and the best litigators posture cases to disallow this testimony.

Traditionally, violators have benefited from the contrasting attributions cast upon professionals versus mental health clients. A presumption of honesty and integrity was given the professional that has been hard to overcome by plaintiffs, especially when plaintiffs also have to overcome the stigmas that have historically attached to mental patient status—mental instability, lack of credibility, and impugned motives cast in the guise of hostile transference.

It is still difficult to overcome these presumptions on the testimony of one victim—and to some degree it should be for the sake of innocent defendants—but it is certainly getting easier to prove. So many sexual abuse cases now exist that, in the minds of jurors, the presumption may even be shifting against the professional toward an attitude that asserts a defendant is guilty if charged. If true, this is a major perceptual shift in the presumption of guilt and is one more reason to avoid becoming a sexual misconduct defendant.

The Consent Barrier. Historically, not only did victims have to prove each element required under malpractice (duty, breach of duty, harm, and causation), they also had to prove they did not consent to sexual relations. Many a successful defense was based on patient consent, especially in cases where the sex continued over time and it was only the therapist's word against the patient's. Because the presumption against consent was not traditionally accepted in the law, client consent to sex has been fairly easy to prove or at least to make it look plausible.

Now, however, growing numbers of courts and legislatures are limiting this defense, based on the acceptance of two theories into the law. The legislatures of Minnesota, Wisconsin, and California,[7] for example, have removed or weakened the consent defense, based in part on the inherent power imbalance of therapist-patient relations. The argument here is that true consent is only possible between adults on equal standing, something that does not exist in professional therapy relations where the therapist holds greater power over the client.

Similarly, courts are beginning to deny that consent is valid when done in the context of therapy. Sex pursued in this manner is seen as a form of therapeutic deception and any patient consent is held invalid. In *Cotton v. Kambly,*[8] a Michigan appellate court ruled that the psychiatrist's sexual actions were "under the guise of psychiatric treatment," and therefore, the patient could not consent to sex related to therapy. The consent defense remains a real though weakening barrier to claimant relief, and we should anticipate more states legislating and courts ruling easier ways for sexual abuse victims to gain relief.

Similar to the ethical debate, sex after termination of therapy has been controversial in the law. Consent to sex is beginning to be allowed after psychotherapy has been terminated if sufficient time has passed and therapy was not terminated for the purpose of another kind of relationship. Both the Minnesota and California statutes noted above require, at minimum, a two-year interim between the end of therapy and the start of new relations. Minnesota further requires that the former patient not be "emotionally dependent" on the therapist and that the sexual relationship not occur by way of "therapeutic deception."[9]

Statute of Limitations. The controversies over apparent consent to sex, the maintenance of sexual relations over a long period of time, and repressed and recovered memories have intersected with statute of limitations rules.[10] Suits brought after the time limit allowed by statute have sought, with growing success, to come under an exception that allows the statute to begin running only after the plaintiff becomes aware of the harm. This has nearly demanded that plaintiffs who file years after an offense present a case of recovered memories that only recently erupted or of some other mental/emotional state that rendered them incapable of knowing the harm of sexual misconduct.

This was exactly the matter in the *Simmons* case noted earlier, as the action was filed after the statute of limitations had tolled. The therapist had engaged in a classic pattern of misconduct by promoting the esteem-building value of sex to a confused and dependent plaintiff, who was consumed by her own sense of worthlessness and guilt. Believing her emotional trauma was purely of her own making after ending therapy, she was then informed by a subsequent therapist that her post-traumatic stress was caused by the sexual abuse and deception of the former therapist. The federal appeals court allowed the case, ruling that the transferent dependence of patients combined with the therapist's assurances that sex is good for them "makes it very difficult for patients to believe the therapist caused their emotional damage; instead they blame themselves."[11]

LAWSUITS BASED ON OTHER LEGAL THEORIES

Finally, courts are beginning to accept liability for sexual misconduct under legal theories other than tort. Proving all four elements of professional malpractice (duty, harm, causation, and damages) is not easy. Legitimate cases of sexual misconduct have failed because one of these element's was not proven. This is now rapidly changing by court acceptance of other legal bases for recovery in sexual misconduct cases.

Infliction of Emotional Distress. Traditionally, tort recovery was not possible without some physical damage—mental and emotional harm was not considered real or tangible enough to justify awarding damages. Recent years have witnessed the acceptance of claims based on mental and emotional harm. Yet as an exception to traditional tort law, something more than mere emotional injury was required—emotional injury with "physical impact," or evidence that the defendant's conduct was "outrageous" and the mental/emotional harm "severe."[12] This standard of evidence was so high that it was hard to prove sexually based harm even though the presumption of such harm is accepted in principle.

In 1986, however, the Supreme Judicial Court of Maine broke new legal ground by allowing a cause of negligent infliction of emotional distress for sexual misconduct without attaching physical impact or tougher tort law requirements.[13] In *Rowe v. Bennett*, a clinical social worker lied to and effectively abandoned her client after she herself became romantically and sexually involved with the client's lesbian lover. The court recognized that psychotherapist-patient relationships were of a unique nature, requiring special rules of protection. In so doing the law recognized the validity of the psychosocial argument—any sexual misconduct is per se wrongful conduct in the context of psychotherapy, even when it involves sex with persons close to the client. The harm suffered by client victims is real and serious, not feigned nor slight of weight.

Breach of Contract. Until recently, actions for breach of contract comprised only 3 percent of all suits against psychotherapists.[14] This figure is rising and will likely continue to rise due to the ease, relative to tort-based actions, of proving contract breach. Furthermore, in a managed care era of short-term, contract-based therapy, therapist-client relations are being increasingly cast in contractual terms. Most contract-based suits revolve around issues of promise of gain or cure, lack of risk, and treatment superiority.[15] Sexual misconduct is a prima facia case of breach of the inherent duties to good faith and fair dealing that undergird all contract relations.

Breach of Fiduciary Duty. The *Rowe* case above, finding an independent cause for infliction of emotional distress, was grounded in fiduciary law. Fiduciary law much more accurately reflects the nature of the therapist's duty to clients. Rapidly evolving from its historic association with financial trust, it is being applied to a broad range of professional services, including those provided by mental health professionals.[16]

Rooted in ancient Roman law, the fiduciary is one who holds a special duty to act always in the best interests of the one served, never taking advantage of that trust nor advancing personal interests.[17] This duty is grounded in the special trust and confidence placed in the professional by the client and the power to abuse that trust with devastating consequence. The application to sexual misconduct is apt.

In *Destefano v. Grabrian*,[18] the plaintiff-husband sued his Catholic priest and archdiocese for a sexual affair between his wife and the priest. The affair, which allegedly led to an eventual divorce between the couple, was initiated while the couple were in marriage counseling with the priest. The Colorado Court of Appeals dismissed the case, holding that the priest's conduct was not actionable under tort law. The Colorado Supreme Court reversed by finding liability under fiduciary trust—the priest "had a duty, given the nature of the counseling relationship, *to engage in conduct designed to improve the Destafanos' marital relationship.*"[19] Breach of fiduciary trust has been argued in other cases against the clergy.[20] It is likely that we will see this cause increasingly argued against the church and its ministers (as well as mental health professionals) into the twenty-first century.

Specious Religious Freedom Defense. The Colorado Supreme Court also reversed *Destafano,* in part, by undercutting a constitutional defense that had been speciously argued by the church in sexual misconduct cases. This is the historic first amendment religious freedom defense: barring suits for actions related to church ministry protected by the first amendment. In rejecting this defense by the priest, the Court asserted that "every Catholic is well aware of the vow of celibacy required of a priest. . . . Sexual activity by a priest is fundamentally antithetical to Catholic doctrine. The conduct . . . is, by definition, not an expression of a sincerely held religious belief."[21] Since priestly sex could not be associated in any manner with legitimate religious behavior, first amendment protection of religion was not allowed to guard the priest and the church from liability.

A GOD-HONORING FIDUCIARY TRUST STANDARD

The fiduciary trust is a superior legal framework for defining the duties and understanding the relationship between Christian helper and counselee. We believe this trust is far more consistent with biblical norms of ministerial practice than is the law of malpractice or contract. Fiduciary duties are grounded in the root commitment to hold the interests of those served above those who are the designated servants. Practically, a fiduciary trust standard demands that the client's or parishioner's interests are held above all others at all times in the helping relationship.

There is no question that pastors, Christian counselors, and church leaders are called to this duty. Jesus asserted that loving God and one's neighbor as one's self is the greatest of the commandments (see Mark 12:28–31; Luke 10:25–37). Furthermore, in His kingdom, the one who would rule or be great is the one who most humbly serves the rest, who gives up his or her life for the good of others (see Matt. 20:25–28; Luke 22:25–30). Paul challenges us to imitate Christ's humility: "Do nothing out of selfish ambition or vain conceit, but in humility consider others better than yourselves. Each of you should look not only to your own interests, but also to the interests of others" (Phil.2:3–4). This core duty of fiduciary law also fulfills fundamental ethical duties that uphold counselee interests as primary and bars exploitation and abuse of the helping relationship.

Fiduciary law is a good standard for both church and state. For the foreseeable future, however, fiduciary law will compete for the court's attention with many legal theories of counseling liability. We believe the courts will be increasingly attracted to this standard because it holds counselee and consumer protection values as primary. If (or when) a fiduciary standard becomes ascendant in law, it will simplify the understanding and application of legal duty to Christian counseling. The fiduciary definition is broad enough conceptually to include the many biblical, ethical, and legal duties that are being attached to Christian counseling. This standard is consistent with the actual moral and ethical standards that guide Christian helpers in their day-to-day ministry. Such a standard would be useful, then, to Christian counselors in assessing their liability by knowing that it is intimately related to their biblical, moral, and ethical boundaries.

Christians—Set the Standards. The litigious pressures on the church and the imposition of legal standards that inaccurately reflect the nature of Christian counseling ministry makes the value of fiduciary trust all the more attractive at the close of the twentieth century. As lawsuits of many kinds increase against pastors and counselors, we call upon informed Christians and the church-at-large to more assertively influence this standard-defining process. Courts, lawyers, and legal theorists are advancing these standards already, and the church may disagree with their premises and values and be quite displeased with the results. Fiduciary trust, as a unifying concept and as law that is friendly to biblical standards, could allow us to forge the lead in establishing right standards. Christians could lead the way in taking action that truly protects and brings justice to those we serve, whether victim or violator.

License Revocation Under Administrative Law

Professional Licensure. Every state regulates its mental health care system to some degree. Licensure of mental health practitioners—

psychiatrists, psychiatric nurses, psychologists, and clinical social workers in all states, and family therapists and licensed professional counselors in nearly half the states—is a primary method of state regulation. The central justification by states for this regulatory scheme is protection of the public from incompetent and unethical clinicians and counselors.[22] Again, as in professional association discipline, there is much question about the effectiveness of state disciplinary action.[23]

California has been a leading regulatory state in the licensure of its mental health professionals, and its model has influenced licensure laws in other states. No one, except those exempted by statute,[24] can provide counseling and mental health services for a fee without being licensed. Psychiatrists are regulated by the Medical Board, psychologists by the Board of Psychology, and clinical social workers and marriage and family therapists by the Board of Behavioral Science Examiners. Each Board defines the title, nature of practice, education and intern preparation, functions and limits, and professional requirements necessary to obtain and maintain licensure. They also define professional misconduct and the procedure by which a license may be suspended or revoked.[25]

The Legalization of Professional Ethics. A developing and controversial issue in America is the degree to which the state incrementally incorporates professional ethics into the statutory code of professional misconduct.[26] The state, then, uses its power to revoke or deny a license to anyone who fails the statutory standard of professional misconduct. The demand that states effectively police their erring licensees is forcing a tense marriage of ethical codes with state statutes. Positively for victims and the general public, such action puts teeth into the enforcement of ethical rules.

Negatively for the professions, this process of legalizing professional ethics codes, in effect, transfers control of the profession from the profession itself to the state. For the many states that are legislating comprehensive and mandatory licensing laws, this is a significant shift of power with major implications regarding professional self-control for all mental health professions. Eventually, the control of Christian counseling itself will be significantly affected by this dynamic. Christian counseling leaders must be apprised of the seriousness of this systemic transformation and act to protect the maturing profession from excessive state control.

Other Issues in Licensure Regulation. As states increasingly license and regulate mental health professionals, the threat of license revocation becomes a more powerful tool for compliance with statutory standards of professional conduct. Courts have uniformly upheld the power of licensure boards to deny or revoke license under administrative law.[27] The problems of proving sexual misconduct are easier in this domain for a victim since there is often no statute of limitation and the standards of proof are less stringent than those required in a courtroom. Proof of sexual misconduct by a licensed professional almost certainly leads to loss of that license and an inability to practice in a growing number of states.

Numerous problems exist in the use of license revocation as a regulatory device for control of sexual misconduct. While states are rapidly filling the gaps, the most significant problem remains the lack of comprehensive mental health licensure. "While psychiatrists, psychologists, and social workers are licensed, other therapists go unregulated. [In some states] virtually any person, qualified or unqualified, can hang out a shingle and put an ad in the yellow pages describing services as that of 'counselor.' . . . While most states license hairdressers, [etc.], a significant portion of this critical industry of therapy providers goes totally unregulated."[28]

Even when licensure boards function, the discrepancy between the high incidence of abuse and the extremely low numbers of disciplinary actions raises serious questions about their effectiveness. The assertion that licensure means competence (a widely disputed assumption) is a problem for both clients and referring professional colleagues. Benetin and Wilder argue:

> Though licensure statutes serve a purpose in protecting patients from illegitimate and incompetent treatment in the medical profession, they do not accomplish the same purpose in the mental health industry. Their success depends on requiring licensing of the entire mental health industry, providing adequate enforcement mechanisms against those who abuse the privilege they have been granted, and educating the public as to the requirements for and meaning of a license. By licensing some but not all of the industry, the state places the burden of selecting a competent, ethical therapist on the patient—often with little information about the ramifications of selecting an unlicensed therapist.[29]

Though licensure statues serve a purpose in protecting patients from illegitimate and incompetent treatment in the medical profession, they do not accomplish the same purpose in the mental health industry. Their success depends on requiring licensing of the entire mental health industry, providing adequate enforcement mechanisms against those who abuse the privilege they have been granted, and educating the public as to the requirements for and meaning of a license. By licensing some but not all of the industry, the state places the burden of selecting a competent, ethical therapist on the patient—often with little information about the ramifications of selecting an unlicensed therapist.[30]

CRIMINAL LIABILITY: THE GRAVE NEW WORLD IS HERE

In 1989, psychologist Phillip French lost his argument with the state of Minnesota that his client was merely a "friend" and that their sexual relationship was consensual and outside therapy. When he finally admitted that his conduct was wrong and pled to one count of criminal sexual conduct in the third degree, he also pled for leniency. Judge Bruce Reuther instead sentenced him to prison for two years, as mandated by law, commenting:

> . . . there should never have been any questions in your mind but that the situation was in your control, and if it wasn't it should have been. . . .The victim was never at fault. . . . You were the one that was and should have remained at all times in control. . . . It was inappropriate to be involved with a patient, a former patient, a prospective patient, whatever, sexually.
>
> To have arrived at that conclusion now is fine, and I don't mean to rub it in, but it's obviously a little late. . . . How you could, with all the publicity that appears in professional magazines, in the common Sunday supplements, in magazines, and everything that everyone reads now, professional, lay, or whatever, how anyone could have concluded that sexual activity between a psychologist and a patient of any degree is appropriate is inexplicable as far as the Court is concerned. . . . You should never have arrived at any other conclusion legally or professionally. . . .[31]

Due to the growing evidence of pervasive harm, and the perception that the current regulatory environment is an insufficient curb, criminal liability is increasingly being attached to sexual misconduct in psychotherapy. By 1993, eleven states had criminalized sexual misconduct between counselors and clients. These include Wisconsin, the first to make this conduct criminal in 1983, Minnesota, Colorado, North Dakota, California, Maine, Florida, Michigan, New Hampshire, Rhode Island, and Wyoming.[32] On New Years Day of 1994, Texas became the twelfth state to criminalize sexual misconduct, wrapping the church and its ministers under its sweeping jurisdiction.[33] Numerous other states are considering passage of similar legislation. It is likely that sexual misconduct will be criminalized throughout most of America early in the new millennium.

California's law makes it a crime for a "psychotherapist, or any person holding himself or herself out to be a psychotherapist, [to] engage in sexual intercourse, sodomy, oral copulation, or sexual contact with a patient or client, or with a former patient or client when the relationship was terminated primarily for the purpose of engaging in those acts."[34] Like the civil code, the California criminal law bars the consent defense (as do most of the other codes) and requires at least a two-year waiting period before therapist-patient sex might be deemed allowable. A first offense in California is punished as a misdemeanor, and second and subsequent offenses may be felonies with fines up to $5,000 and a year in state prison.

The criminal laws and penalties in other states are even more stringent than California's. Colorado law, for example, applies to anyone doing psychotherapy and defines therapy so broadly that pastoral counselors would easily come under this rule.[35] Wisconsin's statute explicitly includes any "physician, psychologist, social worker, nurse, chemical dependency counselor, *member of the clergy* or other person, whether or not licensed by the state who performs or purports to perform psychotherapy"[36] (emphasis added). Minnesota, as we noted briefly earlier, criminalizes sex with current patients and former patients who remain "emotionally dependent" on the counselor. It includes sex by way of "therapeutic deception"—convincing the client that it is a form of valid treatment—and bars any consent to sex given by the client.[37]

All these states regard sexual contact as felonious behavior and have prosecuted offending therapists, some of whom are now imprisoned. Sexual penetration in Colorado is aggravated sexual assault and can lead to an eight year prison sentence.[38] The same act in Minnesota, criminal sexual conduct in the third degree, is punishable by up to ten years in prison with fines up to $20,000.[39]

Sentencing and imprisonment of sexual offenders was brought under the Minnesota Sentencing Guidelines Commission in 1985. This modification of law required *presumptive sentencing*—all first offenders, without any prior criminal history, receive a mandatory prison term of two years.

Alternative Models of Criminal Sexual Exploitation

Some commentators argue that criminalizing sexual misconduct on the basis of the status of the offender (solely for being a physician or psychotherapist) overreaches and abuses the intent of the criminal law.[40] Instead, they prefer to extend rape and statutory rape (for sex with minors) laws to punish therapists who force or manipulate patients into having sex. In fact, many physicians and therapists have been convicted this way for a long time—for raping unconscious or incapacitated patients, for having sex with minors, and for using drugs to reduce resistance or having sex with patients under the influence of drugs.[41]

Wyoming's criminal misconduct law is unique in this regard and may be a preferred alternative for future development of the law. In Wyoming, the basis for the criminal behavior is not the status of the violator but the coercive influence—the abuse of power—applied to manipulate sexual contact. Hence, not just psychotherapists but anyone in a position of power who uses that role to wrongfully coerce sexual contact engages in criminal behavior. The Wyoming law renders criminal sexual contact of vulnerable persons by physicians and psychotherapist and "a parent, guardian, relative, household member, teacher, employer, custodian or any other person who, *by reason of his position, is able to exercise significant influence over a person* . . ."[42] (emphasis added).

The New Texas Sexual Exploitation Statute

The recently legislated sexual exploitation statute in Texas criminalizes sexual misconduct and wraps the church into its jurisdiction like no other statute has done. The Texas law tracks the principles and language of many other states but goes much further in a variety of areas. It requires strong action in the face of abuse allegations and requires that employers do thorough background checks—looking for sexual abuse histories going back at least five years in a prospective employee's work life.

Pastors and churches are required to do the same with all new employees and are subject to the same criminal penalties as nonchurch organizations if they do not. Secondly, as we noted in chapter 6, the law criminalizes "making sexually demeaning comments to or about an individual's sexual orientation," [43] a vague standard that may be easily twisted to prosecute Christian counselors who honorably challenge homosexual lifestyles and behavior. (See appendix C for a suggested disclosure/consent form to work carefully with this risky statute.)

Proper Public Protection or Oppressive State Legalism? The definitional scope of sexual misconduct in the new law is amazing—thirty-eight varieties of sexual wrongdoing with a catch-all clause are described in 139 lines of legal text. The law not only covers every situation one could reasonably imagine, but also hypothetical and rare situations one might never imagine. As in other states, the Texas law prosecutes for "sexual harassment, sexual solicitation" and "verbal and non-verbal conduct that is sexual in nature." The Lone Star State goes much further by criminalizing "any *behavior, gestures, or expressions* which may reasonably *be interpreted* as inappropriately seductive or sexual" [44] (emphasis added). Texas authorities can imprison a counselor for asking a client for a date or for asking for a client's sexual history "when not necessary for counseling of the individual." [45] Counselors in Texas must beware of what they ask for on intake forms.

Does the Texas statute lead us in the right direction toward proper public protection, or is it overreaching? As we note in chapter 6 and earlier in this chapter, leaders in the Christian Counselors of Texas asserted that one motivation for this law was the legislatures' frustration about the high rate of abuse and misconduct going on in churches and the failure of many churches to cooperate with the state and take serious action to protect victims.

The state of Texas is obviously determined that churches be forced to protect their parishioners or face severe consequences: criminal penalties. The new Texas law tracks our prediction that if churches refuse to work voluntarily with states to control problems of sexual misconduct, they will be forced to comply with laws that will be coercive, unwanted, and far more oppressive than if the churches themselves had put effective policies in place.

SEXUAL MISCONDUCT REPORTING

Every state requires its licensed mental health practitioners to report child sexual abuse to state authorities. The criminalization of sexual misconduct has lead to various reporting schemes regarding adult victims. There are three models of sexual misconduct reporting developing in the law, best exemplified by statutes from Minnesota, Wisconsin, and California.

The Minnesota Mandatory Model. Like child abuse reporting laws, Minnesota mandates therapist reporting of sexual misconduct if reported by a client. There are numerous differences and confusions about the boundaries and content of reporting among the various professions in Minnesota,[46] but the core mandatory reporting duty remains. While the therapist who reports is immune from legal action for good-faith reporting, he or she is also liable to the state for failing to report as required to the appropriate state licensing board.

The California Consultative Model. At the opposite end of the spectrum is the California model. Here the therapist acts as a consultant to client decision-making and action. The California legislature has mandated that all licensed mental health professionals in the state have available for review a small booklet for abused clients entitled "Professional Therapy *Never* Includes Sex."[47] As a consumer-oriented response to the sexual misconduct epidemic, the state hopes to educate and embolden victims to overcome the dismal reporting rate of such abuse and get the help they need. The therapist is required to review four action options with the client, but the victim retains control of whatever action he or she takes, including the choice of no action.

The Wisconsin Discretionary Model. The core action of this statute is the therapist seeking client permission (a release of confidential information) to allow the therapist to report sexual misconduct. Reports are made to the state's licensing authority or to the district attorney's office if the violator is unlicensed (such as a pastor). This statute, representing a middle ground between the other models, has elements of both laws. Like Minnesota, it incorporates therapist responsibility to report with the discretionary decision-making by the client of the California law. The key here is if the client does not allow it, the therapist does not report it.

It is hard to tell which model, if any, will become ascendant in twenty-first century law. If Texas is the wave of the future, mandatory reporting will be the norm. We prefer the California or Wisconsin models because they leave the power to decide where it belongs: with the client victim. Wisconsin's may be the best model as it provides for a stronger likelihood of reporting for the devastated and codependent client. This victim is the one who might choose not to report or take any action if all the overwhelming responsibility for legal action were left to him or her.

THE MIXED BLESSING OF CRIMINALIZATION

Criminalizing sexual misconduct is truly a mixed blessing for victim and violator.[48] Positively, it communicates a powerful warning that could deter the vulnerable or mixed violator (see chapter 4) from engaging in wrongful sex. Though deterrence is not likely in the case of the sexual predator, retribution through criminal punishment is certainly just desserts for such intentional exploitation. Theoretically, money through state victim assistance programs will also be available for the therapy of sexual abuse victims.

Negatively, criminalizing this behavior may paradoxically deter desired reporting. Victims and subsequent therapists may be inhibited by the thought that criminal penalties are too severe a response. Rehabilitation of offenders who can genuinely change, but who refuse to come forward for fear of criminal retribution, will also be hampered. Also, deterrence may be more illusory than real; out of 1600 victims reporting to the Walk-in Counseling Center in Minneapolis, the state had prosecuted just nine cases of criminal sexual contact in therapy.[49] The criminal process itself removes effective control of the process from the victim, denying the therapeutic and spiritual need for personal action and empowerment.

Criminalizing sexual misconduct may also hamper the process of license revocation and civil suit, which may have to wait until a criminal trial is ended. Insurance companies are strengthened in their drive to exclude this behavior from coverage, making financial recovery for victims all the harder (see final section below). Some states are making insurers indemnify sexual abuse claims even though the behavior is criminal. A Minnesota appellate court upheld a suit against an insurance company to collect damages by holding that the sexual misconduct was the "incidental outgrowth of the primary malpractice"—the mishandling of client transference.[50]

Better Ways to Enforce the Law. Summarily, we would prefer to see less criminal legislation and better law that strengthens victim's access to civil remedies and enforcement of licensure duties. Criminalizing sexual misconduct fails at three critical points: (1) it is not likely to deter the sexual predator, who must be stopped, but rather will drive predatory behavior into deeper darkness;

(2) it paralyzes constructive victim action (which is crucial to both therapeutic recovery and justice, see chapter 5), making victims the passive assistants to state action; and (3) it tempts states to overreach their just authority and oppressively impinge upon legitimate professional autonomy and church ministry.

Improved licensure enforcement and statutory relief through civil lawsuits against violators is better law and better social policy. At best, criminal action should cover the worst power abuses, as in Wyoming's approach, or prosecution should be made contingent on failed justice in these other areas of victim action. Churches must better assist this healing/justice work, however, or it will become increasingly subject to the legislative overkill of laws like that recently passed in Texas.

CORPORATE AND INSTITUTIONAL LIABILITY

Lawsuits happen not only against individuals but also against churches, clinics, agencies, and partnerships as corporate institutions. In fact, the "deep pockets" doctrine demands that plaintiffs pursue the legal entity (often a corporation over an individual) that has the greater assets to pay damages. Traditional legal barriers that have blocked attaching liability to churches and church superiors for the wrongdoing of its servants are rapidly breaking down. Some of the most pertinent issues are discussed below.

VICARIOUS LIABILITY: RESPONDEAT SUPERIOR AND CANONICAL AGENCY

Historically, the law has held the employing institutions liable for the wrongs of the employee who is acting within the scope of employment. Respondeat superior is the legal doctrine that attaches the same liability upon the superior as that attached to the employee or volunteer worker. In effect, the entire supervisory chain of command is liable for the misconduct of the direct service provider. The law of agency, close sibling to respondeat superior, asserts that the agent acts for or represents the superior. Until recently, sexual misconduct was uniformly considered outside the scope of employment, making claims against an employing institution impossible to prevail.

Again, the *Simmons* case[51] broke new ground legally by upholding a claim for respondeat superior against the federal government, the abuser's employer in this case. By accepting the power of transferent dependence, the *Simmons* court reasoned that any sexual contact was impossible to separate from the therapeutic context. No superficial separation of sex outside the therapy time or the office setting rendered the act outside the scope of employment. In this scheme, separating consensual sex from therapeutic employment is considered a fiction. In effect, *Simmons* acknowledged the psychological and moral truth of these relationships—once a therapist, always a therapist in the eyes of a client. This rule greatly expands the potential liability of the employer as it desecrates the scope of employment rule that has traditionally protected the corporate entity.

Respondeat superior has been even more difficult to apply to the church. The historic but now defunct doctrine of charitable immunity[52] served to shield the church from most liability. That doctrine, combined with the judgment that sexual acts were always outside the scope of employment, made it almost impossible to sue the church. This reasoning, weak as it is, was applied recently in California in a suit against a Baptist church following the sexual abuse of a young boy by the boy's Sunday school teacher.[53] The court simply (and simplistically) reasoned that since the abuser was not employed to molest young boys, the church could not be held responsible for the abuse.

This reasoning, arguing the traditional rule of respondeat superior, has also shielded the Catholic church from much liability.[54] It has not been as successful, though nearly so, under the theory of canonical agency. Here, the church has been held responsible for actions of priests because, under an expansive theory of canonical agency, the priest always represents the church no matter what he is doing.[55] However, other courts still retain a more restrictive view of agency that has operated to limit church liability in a way similar to that of respondeat superior. Yet it is clear that legal trends are developing toward the expansive view that holds the church liable.

The shield against church liability is also eroding in state legislatures, much as it is the realm of case law. Like the new Texas sexual exploitation law, many legislatures are passing laws that make the church directly liable for the actions of its employees and servants—modern statutes are overcoming the traditional barriers of the common law. This trend is rapidly becoming the norm, and the church must not assume that its special status as a religious institution will protect it from legal action as we march into the grave new world of the twenty-first century.

Forms of Direct Corporate Liability

Many churches and agencies are also sued for behavior that directly violates legal canons beyond that of the employer-employee relationship—legal grounds that also avoid much of the problems in attaching liability vicariously. Two of the most common actions here are inadequate hiring practices and deficient and grossly negligent supervision. Organizational failure to review a new worker's employment history for sexual misconduct problems (as is now legislatively mandated in Texas) has become an accepted basis for claimant recovery.

Likewise, poor supervisory practices have become mostly indefensible. Failing to take protective action at the reception of a complaint and, worse, transferring a known abuser to different settings that leave new service recipients exposed to abuse are especially fatal legally. This was the case in *Destafano*. The Catholic church was held liable, not for respondeat superior but for negligent hiring and supervision.[56] It knew that the offending priest had violated other parishioners and did nothing about it. The Roman Catholic Church has been particularly guilty of this habit, but unyielding law and wiser church policy is rapidly altering this harmful practice.

Blaming the Victim. A new form of systemic liability is also looming on the horizon. Churches and clinics that (by design or effect) require victims to prove their allegations by treading a procedural gauntlet of shame and great emotional distress are at increasing legal risk. An Oregon appellate court allowed action against a Lutheran church that had caused a victim "extreme distress by requiring her to confront the church congregation in order to pursue her grievance against the minister who had abused her."[57] Institutions that "blame the victim" by reacting harshly and abusively to charges, forcing the victim to confront an entire congregation, or telling victims to merely forgive the abuser, forget the abuse, and go on for the good of all will find these practices challenged in court.

Judgments Without Justice?

When so much litigation and adversarial conflict exists in any realm of society, justice becomes an increasing and paradoxical victim. We note two issues below where increased attention will likely be focused in the near future.

BACKLASH COMING? COUNTERSUITS BY VIOLATORS

Churches and counseling groups must prepare for an inevitable legal backlash—countersuits by perpetrators whose real or illusory lawsuit victimization will compel legal action. Many of these suits will be specious—pushed by predators who will sue and threaten suit as a manipulative ploy and a continuing posture of denial and self-justification. Some suits, however, will have solid legal justification and will be pursued in spite of biblical admonitions against civil actions among Believers.

A recent issue of the *Christian Century* exposed the growing phenomenon of churches that are firing pastors who are disliked. Small power groups within churches unjustly accuse pastors of wrong and dismiss them, many times without any semblance of due process or respect for labor law rights.[58] The Southern Baptist Convention has reported great ferment in this area—no doubt related to its significant doctrinal war over biblical inerrancy. Over 2,100 of its pastors were dismissed during an eighteen month period in the late 1980s.

Pastors are suing and will increasingly sue churches who fire them without cause or respect for due process, and pastors dismissed for sexual misconduct will inevitably join this litigious movement. Allegations of sexual abuse and misconduct severely disrupt the normal routine of church life and create a near-chaotic situation in many churches. Like the chaotic fog of modern high-tech warfare, where so many casualties are due to confused "friendly fire," churches can easily shoot and abuse both victim and violator without wanting or meaning to do so. We doubt that a church without misconduct response policies in place can realistically avoid this chaos. Churches that have good policies and honor them in practice will greatly reduce the likelihood of suit and will prevent losing one even if suit avoidance is not possible.

JUSTICE FOR SUCCESSFUL PLAINTIFFS?

The victim who prevails in a civil suit is the recipient of a court order for monetary damages to be paid by the defendant. In theory at least, this makes such lawsuits an important restorative vehicle for the sexually abused. In practice, however, an award for damages has become a hollow victory for many. The now standard insurance industry practice of excluding or severely limiting claims for sexual misconduct often renders a judgment for the victim without resources to recover, unless the professional has some personal assets to claim.

If such assets are available, they must come directly out of the defendant's pockets—the offender is often driven to poverty and bankruptcy. This is questionable justice (unless retribution is the sole aim) if the offender has a family to support or might be restored to productive practice or ministry. Furthermore, it reinforces the motivation to sue any institution remotely attached to the case, as the institution's resources become the only "deep pockets" available for a plaintiff.

While this insurance industry exclusion is arguably justified on purely economic grounds, broader analysis shows it works an injustice that disserves victims, hurts those related to offenders by blood or professional affiliation, and violates the already tattered social compact to societal fairplay. Like the compelling case for insurance industry reform in the health care debate, avoidance of gross and multiple injustice here may require further legislative action that mandates some minimal level of insurance coverage (beyond the $25,000 industry standard) for cases of sexual misconduct. The argument that insurance coverage may increase the incentive to misconduct should be considered, but the assertion that the lack of coverage truly deters sexual wrongdoing is very questionable.

We would call upon our colleagues in the church and the mental health professions, the affected industries, and lawmakers to at least consider and debate this issue at a national level. We would also challenge for the inclusion of spiritual, moral, and social values to check and balance the economic and power values that too often dominate and distort these decisions—ultimately hurting the common citizen and reinforcing societal fragmentation. Judgments without justice leach away respect for the law and honor for institutions—the church, mental health professions, legislatures, courts, and the insurance industry—that can ill afford further erosion of trust.

CONCLUSION

Earlier, we discussed the need for outer control and inner transformation in response to the sexual misconduct crisis. Legal and ethical liability are expressions of the outer control necessary to check harmful action at the threshold of wrongdoing. Criminal sanction is, no doubt, the harshest and most serious response possible by the state to the sexual misconduct epidemic. In spite of the many problems with this legislation and the fact that better legal alternatives exist, more and more states will criminalize this behavior as the epidemic and its destructive fruit continue. For the nonpredatory offender and at-risk minister, the criminalization of this behavior may serve as a necessary shower of cold water to deter sexual misconduct. For predators, prison and criminal punishment may be the just dessert for their corrupted actions.

Legal control alone, however, is insufficient for redemptive change. Though God will never abolish the law, he makes it very clear that the law, by itself, cannot save. "Therefore no one will be declared righteous in [God's] sight by observing the law; rather, through the law we become conscious of sin. But now a righteousness from God apart from the law has been made known, to which the Law and the Prophets testify. This righteousness from God comes through faith in Jesus Christ to all who believe" (Rom. 3:20–22a). Inner transformation, which comes through faith in Jesus Christ, is essential to freedom from the plague of sexual misconduct. Even so, the law of the state is rapidly developing to reflect the law of God—sexual misconduct is wrong, and those who cross the line will pay in one way or another.

NOTES

1. A compilation of the data from various studies indicates that victims report the incidence of sexual misconduct by therapists only 1 to 5 percent of the time. Considering that sexual misconduct cases are now the most prevalent and successful legal actions for plaintiffs, it is easy to conclude that even a small increase in the barely existent reporting rate will influence a major increase in legal actions of all types against sexually abusing therapists.

2. Quoted in Thomas Giles, "Coping with Sexual Misconduct in the Church," *Christianity Today* 37, no. 1 (1993): 48–49.

3. See chapters 3 and 4 of our book, *Law for the Christian Counselor* (Dallas: Word, 1992) for a more extensive review of these dynamics; see also H. Newton Malony, Thomas Needham, and Samuel Southard, eds., *Clergy Malpractice* (Philadelphia: Westminster, 1986).

4. See *Zipkin v. Freeman*, 436 S.W.2d 753 (Mo. 1968).

5. *Simmons v. United States*, 805 F.2d 1363 (9th Cir. 1986), 1364–65.

6. *Roy v. Hartogs*, 85 Misc. 2d 891, 381 N.Y.S. 2d 587 (Sup. Ct. 1976).

7. See *Minnesota Statutes Annotated*, sections 148A.01–06 (West 1993); *Wisconsin Statutes Annotated*, section 895.70 (West 1993); *California Civil Code*, section 43.93 (West 1993).

8. *Cotton v. Kambly*, 101 Mich.App. 537, 300 N.W.2d 627 (1980).

232   SEXUAL MISCONDUCT IN COUNSELING

9. *Minnesota Statutes Annotated,* sections 148A.01(1), (2), and (3) (West 1993).

10. By legislation, all states limit the time within which one is able to sue in order that potential defendants do not face a life of perpetual liability, to keep evidence and memory from growing stale by too much passage of time, and so that the courts are not overwhelmed with cases. Traditionally, the statutory time period began at the point when the harmful act was done and injury ensued. Many courts, to overcome the injustice of the rigid application of the rule in numerous kinds of mental disability and emotional damage cases, have carved out a limited exception that allows the statute to begin when the victim learns that the defendant's conduct has been harmful, even if that knowledge comes years after the harmful event.

11. *Simmons v. United States,* 805 F. 2d 1363 (9th Cir. 1986), at 1368; see also *Greenberg v. McCabe,* 453 F. Supp. 765 (E.D. Penn. 1978), affirmed 594 F. 2d 854 (3d Cir. 1979), cert. denied 444 U.S. 840; but see, in contrary rulings on this controversial issue, *Seymour v. Lofgreen,* 209 Kan. 72, 495 p. 2d 969 (1972); and *Decker v. Fink,* 47 Md. App. 202, 422 A. 2d 389 (1980).

12. American Law Institute, *Restatement (Second) of Torts* (American Law Institute, 1965), section 46, comments d-j.

13. See *Rowe v. Bennett,* 514 A. 2d 802 (Me. 1986); and *Horak v. Biris,* 130 Ill. App. 3d 140, 474 N.E. 2d 13 (1985).

14. See Daniel Hogan, *The Regulation of Psychotherapists: A Review of Malpractice Suits in the United States,* vol. 3 (Cambridge, Mass.: Ballinger, 1979).

15. See, for example, *Moxon v. County of Kern,* 233 Cal. App. 2d 393, 43 Cal. Rptr. 481 (1965).

16. See T. Frankel, "Fiduciary Law," *California Law Review* 71 (1983): 795–836; also Herb Kutchins, "The Fiduciary Relationship: The Legal Basis for Social Workers' Responsibilities to Clients," *Social Work* 36, no. 2 (1991): 106–13.

17. See Henry C. Black et al., *Black's Law Dictionary,* 5th ed., M. J. Connolly, eds. (St. Paul, Minn.: West Publishing, 1979), 563–64.

18. *Destefano v. Grabrian,* 763 P. 2d 275 (Colorado 1988).

19. Ibid., 284.

20. See, for example, *Erickson v. Christenson,* 99 Or. App. 104 (1989).

21. *Destefano,* 284. See also *Strock v. Presnell,* 527 N.E. 2d 1235, at 1238 (Ohio 1988); where the Supreme Court of Ohio used essentially the same reasoning in rejecting the First Amendment defense of a Lutheran pastor charged with a sexual affair while involved in marital counseling. The Court assertively held that this behavior was not religiously motivated but was instead a "bizarre deviation from normal spiritual counseling practices of ministers in the Lutheran church."

22. See J. Fischer, "State Regulation of Psychologists," *Washington University Law Quarterly* 58, (1980): 639; and D. A. Hardcastle, "Certification, Licensure and Other Forms of Regulation," in *Handbook of Clinical Social Work,* ed. A. Rosenblatt and D. Waldfogel (San Francisco: Jossey-Bass, 1983).

23. Robert Raven, "Disciplinary Enforcement: Time for Re-examination," *American Bar Association Journal* (May 1989): 8.

24. This includes members of the clergy. "Nothing in this article shall prevent qualified members of other professional groups from doing work of a psychosocial nature consistent with the standards and ethics of their respective professions. . . . These qualified members of other professional groups include,

but are not limited to, the following: . . . (e) A priest, rabbi or minister of the gospel of any religious denomination." *California Business and Professions Code,* ch.14, sect. 4996.13.

25. Some of the many ways a license can be denied or revoked in California include misrepresentation of qualifications or competence, aiding and abetting unlicensed practice, any manner of sexual relations or solicitation with a client, failure to maintain confidentiality, failure to disclose fees, false advertising, intentional infliction of emotional distress, negligent supervision of staff and subordinates, failure to report child or elder abuse, and any act of gross negligence. Ibid., ch. 18, sect. 1881.

26. See, for an example of this problem in California, E. Belser, "BBSE Joint Hearing with the Board of Psychology: Public Input Sought Regarding Dual Relationships," *NASW California News* 17, no. 5 (February 1991): 6.

27. Juanita Benetin and Mary Wilder, "Sexual Exploitation and Psychotherapy," *Women's Rights Law Reporter* 11, no. 2 (1989): 121–35.

28. Ibid., 132.

29. Ibid., 133.

30. Ibid.

31. See *Minnesota v. Phillip Lorenzo French,* reported in *Psychotherapists' Sexual Involvement,* Schoener, et al. eds., 557–58.

32. *Wisconsin Statutes Annotated,* section 940.22 (West Supp. 1992); *Minnesota Statutes Annotated,* section 609.341–45 (West Supp. 1993); *Colorado Revised Statutes,* section 18-3-405.5 (Supp 1992); *North Dakota Revised Statutes Annotated,* section 12.1-20-06.1 (Supp 1991); *California Business and Professions Code,* section 729 (West Supp. 1990); *Maine Revised Statutes Annotated,* title 17-A, section 253(2) (West Supp. 1992); *Florida Statutes Annotated,* section 491.0112 (West 1991); *Michigan Laws Annotated,* sections 750.90, 520b(1)(f) (West 1991); *New Hampshire Revised Statutes Annotated,* section 632-A:2 (Supp 1992); *Rhode Island General Laws,* section 11-37-2(C) (Supp. 1992); *Wyoming Statutes,* section 6-2-303(a) (1988).

33. Reported at the Annual Conference of the Christian Counselors of Texas, at Dallas Texas, February 1994. It was asserted by some CCT leaders that one of the reasons this bill included churches was the widespread failure of many churches to work with the state in the prosecution of sexually abusing church leaders and members.

34. *California Business and Professions Code,* section 729(a) (West Supp. 1990).

35. *Colorado Revised Statutes,* section 18-3-405.5(b) and (c).

36. *Wisconsin Statutes Annotated,* section 940.22(1)(i).

37. *Minnesota Statutes Annotated,* section 609.341–45 (West Supp. 1993).

38. *Colorado Revised Statutes.*

39. *Minnesota Statutes Annotated,* section 609.341–45 (West Supp. 1993).

40. See Jeffrey Barker, "Professional-Client Sex: Is Criminal Liability An Appropriate Means of Enforcing Professional Responsibility?" *UCLA Law Review* 40 (1993): 1275–340.

41. See, for example, *People v. Bernstein,* 340 P. 2d 299 (Cal. Ct. App. 1959); *People v. Middleton,* 350 N.E. 2d 223 (Ill. App. Ct. 1976); *State v. Ely,* 194 P. 988 (Wash. 1921).

42. *Wyoming Statutes,* section 6-2-303(a)(vi) (1988).

43. See section 681.33 (g)(1)(A)(4) of "Rules" of the Texas State Board of Examiners of Professional Counselors, (1994), 6–7.

234

SEXUAL MISCONDUCT IN COUNSELING

44. Ibid., section 681.33 (g)(1)(B)(2), 7.

45. Ibid., section 681.33 (g)(1)(B)(6) and (9), 7.

46. As reported by Gary Schoener, "The New Laws," in *Psychotherapists' Sexual Involvement*, Schoener, et al. eds., 537–65.

47. Available through the California Department of Consumer Affairs, 400 R Street, Suite 3150, Sacramento, California 95814-6240.

48. Larry Strasburger, Linda Jorgenson, and Rebecca Randles, "Criminalization of Psychotherapist-Patient Sex," *American Journal of Psychiatry* 148, no. 7 (1991): 859–63.

49. Ibid., 861.

50. *St. Paul Fire and Marine Insurance Co. v. Love*, 447 N.W. 2d 5 (Minn. Ct. App. 1989).

51. *Simmons v. United States*, 805 F. 2d 1363 (9th Cir. 1986).

52. Charitable immunity was a privilege granted the church, many hospitals, and institutions of social welfare that exempted them from numerous legal duties and obligations imposed by governments in recognition of their fundamental value and service to society. This doctrine has been all but abolished in twentieth-century America due to public policy favoring compensation to injured persons and the rise of the insurance industry to protect such institutions from dissolution when sued for injuries caused by their work.

53. *Jeffrey Scott E. v. Central Baptist Church*, 243 Cal. Rptr. 128, 197 Cal. App. 3d 718 (Cal. App.4 Dist. 1988).

54. In the case of *Carini v. Beaven*, 219 Mass. 117, 106 N.E. 589 (1914), the church was found not liable following a heinous rape in the parish vestry because it could not possibly have foreseen the commission of such a terrible act.

55. *Stevens v. Roman Catholic Bishop of Fresno*, 49 Cal. App. 3d 877, 123 Cal. Rptr. 171 (1975); and see Hotz, "Diocesan Liability for Negligence of a Priest," *Catholic Lawyer* 26 (1981), 228.

56. *Destefano v. Grabrian*, 763 P. 2d 275 (Colorado 1988).

57. Referred to in Giles, "Coping with Sexual Misconduct," 48–49.

58. Michael Smith, "Pastors Under Fire: A Personal Report," *Christian Century* (1994): 196–99.

PART VI

Turning the Tide
Against Sexual
Misconduct

Chapter Fourteen

Helping Sexual Violators: Restoration or Removal

*When a man of unusually fine organization . . . conscience
. . . reputation, and . . . ambition, suddenly, by one act, sacrifices the
slow honors of a lifetime, there is something in his self-destruction to ex-
cite the pity of mankind. . . . To such a man the agony is that there is no
restoration. The crime leaves an inefficable stain. He looks back upon a
violated ideal. He can never again be his former self. . . . [He is a] man
with a sword in his soul, giving him a wound that never heals, exciting in
him an agony that never sleeps, filling him with a despair that never takes
a ray of hope. . . .*[1]

WITHIN THE LAST TEN YEARS, MANY MEN with significant Christian
ministries have been exposed for yielding to the temptation of
sexual misconduct. Some of these individuals have become prominent examples to the world of all that is wrong with the church,
which has lead to the mockery of Christ and his people. The tragedy is not simply that many have fallen, but also that too many
have not responded to their exposure with genuine and deep repentance. Far too many who once stood as beacons leading people
to Christ have rejected the basic elements of being members of the
Body of Christ. Too many have gone their own way, and the damage to others within and outside the church is almost impossible
to estimate.

At present we lack clear data regarding outcomes of offender
rehabilitation over the lifespan and probably will not have conclusive

evidence for several decades. Nevertheless, cumulative clinical experience and the preliminary data we do have leads us to believe that a certain number of offenders are likely to be rehabilitated. We need to be able to assess and determine the difference between the restorable violator and the predator who must be barred from ministry. A crucial question for the future of the church is: Which offenders are likely candidates for successful rehabilitation and restoration, and which are not? We want to help churches face this question in spite of the chilling effect of current legal trends on the restoration of pastors and professional counselors.

In this chapter we address treatment issues for sexual violators. We then consider the recovery process for those who are likely to be restored and will present the case for assertive action against sexual predators in Christian counseling ministry. Since nearly nine of every ten incidents of sexual misconduct are perpetrated by men against women, we will focus on the characteristics of male violators.

SEXUAL OFFENDER ASSESSMENT

Sexual offender recidivism—the likelihood of offending again after being caught—is one of mental health's dirty little secrets. As we stated in chapter 7, apart from castration, recidivism rates are unacceptably high—in the 40 to 80 percent range.[2] Gonsiorek cites a study by Butler[3] indicating that 95 percent of offenders said they would never do it again, but 75 percent of those had violated someone more than once. Gartrell's study[4] revealed important information about the behavior and attitudes of psychiatrist offenders. When asked if sexual involvement harmed clients, only 39 percent of repeat offenders stated that it does, while 70 percent of one-time offenders and 88 percent of nonoffenders stated that clients are harmed. Furthermore, even though 100 percent of the repeat offenders had treated a victim of professional violation, not one had ever reported another professional who had offended.

These are the sobering facts of the professional offender profile. In spite of the offender's excellent education and greater likelihood than nonoffenders to have had psychotherapy, sexual abuse goes on. Clearly, repeat offenders are more dangerous than one-time offenders in the potential and degree of harm caused. This data supports the clear distinction, both in typology and in consequent action by authorities, between the vulnerable violator and the predatory offender.

We do not want to convey the idea that offender assessment and treatment is as simple as distinguishing predators from the rest of the field. The evaluation of sexual offenders for treatment and possible restoration is a difficult process because it involves a wide range of people with a great range of problems. "The fact that sexual misconduct is a complex problem involving a variety of different scenarios becomes apparent to anyone who studies a sufficient number of cases."[5] Those involved in the evaluation process must be careful not to do fact-finding outside their areas of competence. Also, to protect against conflict of interest, the offender should not be the evaluator's client for treatment.

PSYCHOSOCIAL ASSESSMENT

A proper offender assessment will yield a clear hypothesis of the causes of the misbehavior and will outline a concise rehabilitation plan, one that indicates whether ministry restoration is possible. This evaluation must highlight the difference between those who are on the vulnerable-but-restorable end of the offender continuum and those who are predatory in their sexual misconduct.

Key Principles for Offender Evaluation. The central aim of the evaluation is to determine (1) core offender typology, (2) the most appropriate form of treatment, and (3) whether or not this person is capable of rehabilitation, so that if the offender returns to human service, harm is not likely to occur to other counselees. It is important to remember that sexual offenders often lie to evaluators, thus the evaluation does not necessarily find the whole truth. The aim of the assessment is to construct a coherent scenario to explain the helper's behavior, including a judgment by the evaluator of the validity of the scenario presented by the violator.

Schoener and Gonsiorek[6] suggest a six-phase assessment process to determine eligibility for rehabilitation. A competent evaluation must include (1) an exact description of the offense(s); (2) personal adjustment, including the presence of psychopathology; (3) practice style, especially evaluating boundary issues; (4) practice setting and the nature of any supervision; (5) types of counselees served and the type the helper has boundary troubles with; and (6) any other pertinent factors in the helper's life. With information about the offender and about the offense, the assessment process can take place.

Interview Practices. Begin the interview by reviewing confidentiality and informed consent. The evaluator must have informed consent to investigate an offender. This form should include

1. statements that the subject will not hold the evaluator liable for outcomes;
2. statements that there will not be any off-the-record communication;
3. information regarding the evaluator's status as a mandatory reporter;
4. acknowledgment that the report could have major consequences, including possible loss of employment.

In addition, the evaluator should get signed releases in order to talk to anyone he or she deems necessary.

Develop and maintain an attitude of nonattachment. Remember, this is not counseling; in offender evaluation the focus must be on a clear, objective, and comprehensive assessment. Be prepared to do whatever is necessary to get a clear evaluation. Describe the events as you see them to the offender and challenge any discrepancies or puzzlements. Review the individual's life history, including sexual history, drug use, training, career, interpersonal, and marital history. Discuss his or her professional role and practice style, including boundary issues and violations.

Gathering Information. Gather detailed information from the victim or victims as to what occurred, including reports from police and legal filings. Schoener prefers to do this first, while Gonsiorek prefers to do it last or to have someone else do it and then to review that person's report.[7] At whichever point you do the interview(s), take time to prepare questions that are relevant to the critical issues in the case. ("What happened between you two toward the end of the counseling session on _____.") Challenge discrepancies by voicing your puzzlement. ("I am puzzled by the differences in your story on that point and what the victim reported to the police.")

In addition to victim interviews, review past treatment records, personnel records, and the offender's curriculum vitae to assess how the offender portrays himself or herself. If possible, interview the offender's spouse or partner, colleagues, supervisor, personal counselor, and other significant persons. These interviews may be carried out in person or on the telephone. (The information may or may not be useful for the final report.) It is wise to review the information gathered from each individual at the conclusion of the interview. Sometimes, people may decline to be interviewed.

Testing. Testing may or may not be part of the evaluation depending on the objectives and likely use of the evaluation. Testing should be done in cases where legal action is pending or contemplated. Three psychological batteries that are useful for the evaluation process are (1) the MMPI-II, (2) the CPI, and (3) the Rorschach. Each of these tests evaluates the person at different levels. We suggest that the assessor give the tests throughout the day interspersed with interview questions. If these batteries are used, they must be performed by a competent psychologist, preferably by someone trained in their use with this population.

Assessment of Offender Typology. Determining offender typology does not guarantee accuracy in assessment but does indicate some degree of likelihood of rehabilitation. Essentially, the purpose of the interviews with the offender and the victim(s) is to determine how the offense(s) occurred. Then, a determined judgment is made to categorize the offender within an area along the offender continuum. Following Gabbard's typology, there are four categories consistent with our continuum from predatory to mixed to vulnerable offenders:

1. psychotic disorders
2. predatory psychopathy and paraphilia
3. lovesickness
4. masochistic surrender[8]

While most counselors understand psychoses and paraphilias, Gabbard defines lovesickness as the compelling fantasy of curative love with the forbidden counselee. Masochistic surrender is essentially the seduction theory—the helper describes himself as having been the victim of the client's captivation.

If the offender is psychotic or within the predatory psychopathy and paraphilia categories, then the likelihood of restoration is highly unlikely. These individuals correspond to our predatory definition and are the poorest candidates for rehabilitation. They often show chronic personality disorders, have a history of substance abuse or other addictions, and have significant sexual or impulse control disorders. The most significant (and the most easily assessed) factor of predation is evidence of offense against more than one victim or the same victim many times.

Most helpers who become sexually involved with counselees fit in the lovesick category. Those in the categories of lovesick or masochistic surrender usually show a greater likelihood to benefit from rehabilitation and may even be able to return to counseling or pastoral ministry. Most of these individuals fit on the vulnerable end of the continuum, though some are in the mixed category and may be unlikely candidates for treatment. In all these cases, as Gabbard notes, "Even with successful treatment, [helpers] who have acted on sexual feelings with [counselees] should consider themselves at *high* risk for repeating the transgression"[9] (emphasis added).

Written Reports and Protection Against Misinterpretation and Misuse. The completed report should include

- a statement about the reason for the report;
- the methods used to gather information;
- a list of all documents provided in the report.

Summarize the interviews verbatim and interpret the psychological tests in detail. Then formulate the problem in a statement that pulls all the facts together into a coherent unit. Write a hypothesis or hypotheses explaining the offense and include a caveat regarding report limits. Finally, make recommendations about treatment and provide an estimate of rehabilitation and information regarding practice limitations. Do not be afraid to give unpopular recommendations if you believe they are warranted.

Offender reports are meant to assess the facts of the abuse and recommend treatment direction and the likelihood of rehabilitation. This document can be used in a variety of settings and can carry a great deal of weight to influence further action against an offender. As a result, there may be room for courts, licensing boards, associations, and church governments to misinterpret the intent, even to misuse the recommendations of the report. It is the responsibility of the evaluator to protect the report from such misuse (as much as possible) by clear and precise language. It is the court's, licensure board's, or governing body's responsibility to take action regarding the offender.

Sexual Offender Treatment

Sexual offender treatment needs to be grounded upon an experienced understanding of offending helpers—this is not the domain for ill-trained or novice counselors. It should be directed toward clearly specified and mutually understood outcome goals, rather than determined by relationships or time limits. Gonsiorek warns that, "One of the most regrettable and pernicious recent developments in this area has been the emergence of dogmatic, premature, and simplistic guidelines for the assessment and treatment of therapists who sexually exploit clients."[10]

Individual psychotherapy, especially a cognitive-behavioral approach, group therapy, and marital and family therapies are the treatment of choice with sexual offenders. Treatment for alcohol or drug abuse is crucial when needed. Involvement with a supportive social network is often necessary when violators lose regular family, work, and friendship networks. Psychiatric therapy and medication may be needed with multiple diagnoses or when significant mood disorders are also present. Further training and education ought to be considered, as well as changes in counseling style and possibly organizational style. Finally, vocational counseling may be necessary to assist the helper change vocations should it become evident that return to practice is not the best option.

Offender Treatment Process

To maintain objectivity, we recommend that offender treatment be done by someone without even the appearance of conflicting relations to the offender or the offender's church. Following evaluation, the treating therapist, offending helper, and the offender's church or organization should review the assessment and agree to a treatment plan based on the data, the typology of the offender, and the treatment recommendations.

Mandatory Treatment and Contracting. The treatment process does not occur in a vacuum, as the offending helper is usually responsible to a church denomination, licensing board, or professional association that is interested in the outcome of therapy. In fact, it is common for therapists working with this population to want mandatory treatment. Outside authority is often necessary as leverage to keep the offender engaged in serious treatment—purely voluntary therapy rarely works with sexual offenders. It must be made very clear to the offender that the therapist is also responsible to the court or other authoritative body. Confidentiality is limited by this fact, and the client must be apprised and consent to this limitation. It is normative to maintain this extra-therapeutic relationship, however, for victim justice and to keep the offender honest and committed to therapeutic change.

Whether or not the treating therapist is the assessment therapist, therapy begins with an agreement that the offending helper actually violated moral boundaries and ethical practice. If the offending helper remains rooted in denial of wrongdoing and does not agree to at least some violation, then therapy cannot proceed. If wrongdoing is acknowledged, have the offending helper sign a consent form agreeing to the nature and projected course of treatment.

There should also be strict practice limitations and close supervision if the offender has not been suspended. Other release forms may need to be signed that will allow the treating therapist to discuss the case with other professionals and relevant boards. It is also important to agree on a fee for service and to require prompt payment for services. Reluctance to pay promptly can be an indicator of a lack of ownership of the wrong and acknowledgement of the necessity for treatment.

Any authoritative board, including church councils, should wait on a report from the treating therapist before reinstatement. We agree with Gonsiorek that a "licensing board's decision to suspend a license on a temporary basis [should] not be viewed as a guarantee that the license will be reinstated."[11] Similarly, if the offending helper is not working with the plan, then recommendations should be made to the appropriate body indicating treatment and rehabilitative failure. The treating counselor should not hesitate to recommend a denial of reinstatement if there is any doubt regarding rehabilitation.

Beginning Phase of Treatment. Start with nonjudgmental acceptance in order to fully explore the issues and listen to what the offender identifies as the cause and motivation of the problem. Do not, however, allow the offender to project blame or deny fundamental wrongdoing. Striking this balance of empathic challenge requires clinical skill and, usually, some significant experience with this treatment population. Listen carefully and affirm the pain involved. It is extremely difficult for many men to allow themselves to be emotionally vulnerable and to work through the pain. Do not expect this to be easily or readily resolved.

Resistance to treatment is almost always present with sexual offenders. It will take much patience and encouragement to be able to change. The therapist must expect much work and some time to work through the offender's inherent resistance to change. Even when no apparent resistance exists, it is most often a case of optimistic zeal early in the process or a commitment to show authorities a willingness to work (some offenders are exhausted by their dark deeds and are truly ready to work). Make as much progress as you can with this attitude no matter the motivation, for you will eventually hit walls of resistance, but you may be able to move well into the change process before the struggle comes.

This can also be the most unpredictable period because of the uncertainties that surround the offending helper's life. He may be in the midst of criminal, civil, or licensing board proceedings. The spouse and family may be upset, with divorce or legal separation looming on the horizon. The offending helper may be intensely ashamed and possibly suicidal, afraid to face those who know about the offense(s). Most of the work in this initial phase needs to focus on steps of crisis intervention and methods to bring stability to the offending helper's life. The treating therapist may be able to bond with the offender—to form a therapeutic alliance early on— by assisting him or her in the resolution of crises and serving (in some ways) as an advocate for the offender's legitimate interests.

Core Treatment Principles and Process. In this longer phase of therapy, the primary goals of the treatment process are pursued. Often the most important objective is a dual focus on (1) identification and ownership of the impact of sexual exploitation on victims and (2) relapse prevention—effective control of wrongful sexual arousal and behavior. These goals include a careful exploration of underlying sexual and other boundary violations, denial and distortions of belief about sexual misconduct, and dealing honestly with any sexual or other addictive patterns. Cognitively, it is essential to challenge distortions and rationalizations and help restructure false beliefs around personal responsibility, blame projection, forgiveness and judgment, denial and minimization of harm, denial and management of anger and stress, "true love" with or sexual objectification of the victim, sexual neediness, and the impossibility of sexual self-control.

Often the offender's self-talk and imagery is saturated with obsessive fantasy that is secret, sexually arousing, and compulsively used as a distraction to avoid stress and to manage emotional discomfort. When coupled with overt offending behavior against another, or masturbation, it creates a self-rewarding, vicious cycle that reinforces both guilt and the sexual pleasure that temporarily overrides the guilt and shame. Therapists must get at and help pry open this secret world; directive and confrontational tactics are unavoidable here. Many offenders will deny or minimize the existence of this realm of the mind, and it is rare that the therapist will be invited or willingly allowed into its dark domain. Unless this fantasy world is altered, however, the risk of relapse remains high.

Once inside this secret world the therapist must challenge and assist in breaking and transforming powerful, dysfunctional thought and misbelief patterns that influence harmful behavior. Covert (mental) reconditioning and spiritual practices are most useful in changing arousing chains of fantasized thought. Teach the client to break the arousal chain—using fantasy as a cue—by thinking through an aversive consequence to the arousing cue (getting caught, imagining his family being told publicly, imagining front-page headlines of legal action, etc.). For some, sexual fantasy as a cue to confession, prayer, reciting Scripture, or journaling for later review with others is beneficial.

Similarly, have the client deliberately attach rewarding imagery and self-talk (thoughts that praise treatment success and positively communicate new marital and sexual messages) to thinking you want to reward but is not being experienced by the client. Remember, the counselor must return to this secret mental world constantly and deliberately monitor this area. The client must understand that the counselor will not relent and that the client's mental world can no longer be maintained as a dark, destructive secret. The client will often fight to protect this secret world and will grieve its loss even when it has been self-destructive.

Behaviorally, therapy is succeeding when verifiable control of aberrant sexual behavior is shown and an active commitment to victim restitution is being pursued. In addition, offender therapy must address and show resolution of power and control issues, current marriage and family issues, and vocational and financial concerns as they become appropriate. Treatment also involves overcoming any factors that led to isolated ministry and lack of accountability or supervision/consultation in counseling. Careful exploration of interpersonal competence, counseling practices, or ministry style is critical to help establish patterns that prevent rather than promote boundary violations.

The married offender is usually in marital and family crisis following disclosure, and significant attention must be given to these issues, starting with the critical question of reconciliation versus divorce. When reconciliation is possible, it is important to challenge and restructure the distorted mental contrasts between the offender's spouse (selectively negative and unattractive) and other sexual partner(s) (selectively positive and arousing). It is imperative to include the offender's spouse in the therapeutic process from time to time to address issues of intimacy in their relationship and to heal the wounds that contributed to crossing power and sexual boundaries.

If divorce is unavoidable, divorce counseling and mediation will need to be offered as part of the treatment regimen. There is often a powerful sense of loss and significant grief, even depression, that will need to be worked through. Again, we emphasize that some offenders will struggle with suicide; the shame of public disclosure coupled with loss of marriage, family, and ministry is too much for some. For many offenders, marital and family reconciliation is a most critical treatment issue and often determines the likelihood of offender rehabilitation and successful ministry restoration.

The therapeutic process must also help the Christian offender restore his or her relationship with God. There are often layers of confusing and contradictory attitudes, beliefs, failures, and fears toward God that must be sorted out, understood, and worked through. As Schaumburg states so clearly, "The essence of sin is *autonomy from God,* a failure to be dependent on Him. [Sexual addicts and offenders refuse] to cling to God as the only Person who can fill their deepest longings and ease relational pain."[12] Some of the most difficult issues of fear, shame, and resistance revolve around the challenge to become honest and more intimate with God Himself.

It is also true that some of the greatest breakthroughs come when a man admits, especially in the face of his "I am a good Christian" denial, his alienation from God and discovers the outpouring of God's redeeming love. This experience often yields fruit that overcomes a common lament of many clinicians working with offenders: the failure to show true remorse for wrongs and a genuine empathy for the victims. Reading assignments and personal prayer and meditation are also essential. We especially recommend Harry Schaumburg's *False Intimacy,* Robert Hicks' *The*

Masculine Journey, Larry Crabb's *Inside Out* and *Finding God,* and Dan Allender's *Bold Love.*

Concluding Treatment. The final phase of treatment should include plans either to re-enter marriage, family life, and professional counseling or ministry, or to begin a new life and a new career. This may mean that the offending therapist will not be able to return to the community where his or her practice was established.

The final elements focus on setting up a plan for follow-up processes, including assurance that such ethical violation will not happen again. (This process, including some related and overlapping issues with psychotherapy, are addressed in the next section on restoration.)

AVOIDING THE TROUBLES OF OFFENDER TREATMENT

Sexual offenders are considered by many mental health professionals to be among the most difficult treatment populations. Daniel Henderson, in an excellent article on offender treatment,[13] has outlined numerous pitfalls to be wary of when working with sex offenders.

1. *Over-Reacting to Sexual Deviance.* Some counselors become angry and disgusted by the graphic and often perverted descriptions of sexual wrongdoing. It is essential to maintain proper self-control in order not to punish offenders by allowing anger and disgust to rule the clinical interaction.

2. *Under-Reacting to Sexual Deviance.* The opposite problem is one of avoidance. It is easy to begin to gloss over or avoid honest discussion of sexual behavior, especially discussion of graphic material. "Effective counseling with these individuals requires a degree of comfort about matters that in most other contexts are unspeakable."[14]

3. *Jaded Desensitization.* Constant exposure to sexual deviancy can easily make one jaded—no longer sensitive to the awful harm that wrongful sex produces. Developing spiritual and mental means of washing away the dirt one regularly hears in this work is necessary for healthy self-care.

4. *Overidentification.* This is really a two-way problem. Overidentifying with offenders makes a helper vulnerable to be pulled into the subtle distortions that minimize the pain of abuse, deflect responsibility and true guilt, or blunt the moral acuity needed to challenge godly change. Overidentifying with victims can cause one to see violators as "subhuman monsters," rather than "persons in need of redemption."[15]

5. *Loss of Perspective.* In a similar way that persons in deliverance ministry can tend to see demons behind most sinful problems, sex offense counselors can become overly suspicious and read dark sexual intent into some behavior that is truly harmless.

6. *Isolated Practice.* One of the more subtle snares in offender treatment is something that got the offender in trouble: isolated work. Treatment of sexual offenders demands small group support and consultation with dedicated trust. Avoidance of burn-out and maintenance of professional skill and integrity requires, if at all possible, regular sharing with other helpers working with offender populations.

7. *The Paradox of Godly Change.* Christian therapists face a difficult paradox in offender treatment—what we call the "fox-hole conversion perversion." Some offenders genuinely use the crisis of disclosure to turn to God and begin redemptive change; others say all the right words but use religion as one more manipulative game. Either way, there is often a common presumption that repentance, forgiveness, and initial signs of redemptive healing are akin to a guarantee that there will be no repeated offense. Hence, requiring continued treatment is subtly perverted into unbelief—the onus is laid on the therapist for "doubting the power of God to change lives."[16] This dilemma descends to discord if the offender convinces a pastor, supervisor, or key supporters of the integrity of his change and enlists them to challenge continued therapy.

The Christian therapist must wisely resist this deceptive distortion, and challenge the charge that one is behaving no better than the secular therapist who might judge all religious change a sham. Instead, the counselor must affirm godly change—change as a process, not an event—while also challenging the lie that redemptive change is complete and no risk of repeated offense exists any longer. This is a continuing dilemma that is difficult to balance. It requires godly discernment and the wisdom of prayerful experience.

RECOVERY AND RESTORATION TO MINISTRY

When another person is overtaken in a fault or failure, you who are spiritual people will see to it that you graciously set about the extended task of seeing that person mended and returned to full fitness; doing it in a way that clearly indicates you do not hold yourself as superior to them for their having fallen and all the while remembering your own vulnerability.[17]

A PRESUMPTION FOR RESTORATION

Restoration is a biblical concept that forms the core of God's message to his people in both Old and New Testaments. There are many examples in the Bible of men and women who are brought to judgment for their wrongdoing, but who are consistently offered restoration. These violations cover the sins of adultery (David and Abraham), murder (Moses and David), and betrayal (Peter). These people suffered consequences for their sin—let there be no mistake about that—but they were also restored to positions of prestige, power, and service.

The final word of forgiveness and grace is Jesus Christ Himself, who came to redeem His enemies from the power and grasp of sin. This redemptive focus is central to the gospel message, both to humankind in general and to leaders within the community of Believers in particular. Therefore, any rehabilitation plan should stem from this foundation: redemption is always possible in Christ, *whether or not restoration to pastoral or counseling ministry takes place.*

Biblical Purposes for Restoration. The Bible gives three purposes for the discipline of recovery and restoration:

- to maintain the purity of the church (1 Cor. 5:1–13)

- to serve as a warning to others (1 Tim. 5:19–20)

- to restore the disciplined believer (2 Cor. 2:6–8, Philemon 10–12)

When we do not discipline in a serious manner, we reject justice; by not heeding the real harm of these activities, we undermine genuine healing grace.

When considering the restoration of offenders, we are confronted by those who doubt that offenders can ever change. These doubts are similar to those encountered when we consider homosexual change. Essentially there are four views regarding homosexuality: (1) it is normal and biologically-based, therefore homosexual behavior is acceptable (what we would call homoapologetic); (2) it is gross sin and homosexuals deserve hostile rejection as exceptional sinners (commonly called homophobic); (3) homosexual orientation and behavior are distinguishable and one ought to accept orientation as unchangeable and set clear limits on homosexual behavior; and (4) one ought to practice compassionate acceptance of the person regardless of his or her behavior, yet retain a fundamental belief in the potential and necessity for healing and change of orientation *and* behavior.

Many in the church would agree with one or more of the first three positions and hold little hope for fundamental change of homosexual persons. This is consistent with many outside the church who believe that sexually-offending beliefs and behavior are largely unchangeable. However, there are a number of Christian ministries that challenge this perception and hold to and practice the fourth approach to change of sexual identity and practice.[18] We join that group in making a similar proclamation to any sexually offending or addicted person: *IN CHRIST, there is always hope for fundamental change and redemption.*

RESTORATION OF THE VULNERABLE HELPER

Restoration is a demanding process; it cannot be entered into glibly or without an understanding of the serious harm that has been rendered. Frequently, people are anxious to forgive quickly and to restore a "gifted man of God" to ministry and service. Many Christians assume restoration to ministry is easy and inevitable— they deny or simply do not understand the devastating consequences of sexual misconduct. Though we challenge the belief that the fallen helper cannot be restored, we are chagrined by a contrary attitude of cheap grace that seems all too common within the church. Restoration does not come quickly or cheaply, and for many it does not, or at least should not, come at all. Restoration to ministry or counseling practice should come only to a portion of those who offend sexually.

We must also respect the time necessary for restoration to occur. This process usually takes from one to four years. Jack Hayford asserts that "'the discipline of time' is about healing and mending, not punishment. And the one who accepts that discipline becomes a disciple again, at a fresh point of beginning—forgiven and cleansed, and ready for the process of recovery."[19] It is clear that sexual sin is not the "fruit of a moment," and so the restoration process will also require time for the underlying issues to be fully resolved. Gordon McDonald, for one, has set an exemplary model for this process. His behavior and attitudes have demonstrated the best potential for a healing outcome: he repented deeply and has been restored.

The church has often failed to hold its leaders accountable for their moral failures, perhaps especially for their sexual sin. As one author observes, "Church professionals prefer to manage these situations from within. But our track record so far is not good, and victims, courts, and the public are impatient. If we wish to have responsibility for correcting this tragic condition, we must demonstrate integrity to the public and sensitive caring to victims, congregations, and perpetrators."[20]

The restoration process should also help protect potential victims from sexual violation. This protection is a fundamental responsibility of the Body of Christ to its members (see Matt. 18:1–9). When we do not discipline in a serious manner, we reject justice, and by not heeding the real harm of these activities, we undermine genuine healing grace.

Helping Sexual Violators. How should we approach the minister or counselor who has fallen sexually? To state it clearly: because of Christ, the church should assume restoration is possible, but because of sin and the dismal record of recovery, it should expect that full recovery and restoration to ministry will be rare. Tim LaHaye states,

> Since the Scripture gives no specific command prohibiting a fallen minister from returning to pastoral or public ministry, I would conclude that if over a period of time a minister faithfully meets the appropriate requirements for restoration, then he *gradually* should be allowed to assume whatever ministry the Holy Spirit opens to him—provided he submits to some form of accountability for the rest of his life.[21]

For those who would help sexual violators, the following commitments need to be made toward the goal of healing and restoring the offending counselor.[22] Help the violator find and pursue effective strategies for recovery. As much as possible, assist the offender to perceive and turn the experience into an opportunity for change, a challenge to growth.

The offender must be prepared to deal with the cost of treatment both in terms of professional counseling and by doing alternate work while not employed as a counselor or clergy member. Every crisis has two elements to it, danger and opportunity. In the light of eternal values, it is imperative to assess the opportunities for change and provide hope and help toward achieving that change. However, until all issues are resolved (personal, moral, legal, familial, and ministerial), the pastor or counselor should be

presumed to remain at risk to violate others again. Once these issues are resolved, then the gradual process of restoration to
counseling and other ministry can begin.

THE RESTORATIVE PROCESS

Ensure Accountability and Restitution. The offender who seeks restoration must show a commitment to continued accountability and
to restitution for the victims. A dedication to these principles reveals a changed heart—one that acknowledges personal weakness
and interpersonal needs and desires to make right the wrongs.
(This accountability/restitution process is outlined more closely
in chapter 11.)

Supervising Renewed Ministry. Supervision issues apply equally
to the counseling professional and the pastoral or ministerial
helper. Schoener[23] suggests that the term *practice monitor* may be a
more appropriate title than supervisor since the monitor should
act in a more intensive role to the rehabilitating helper. The monitor is advised not to undertake this role until it has been clearly
determined that the offender is truly eligible for recovery. Predators are bad candidates for restoration to helping roles and are a
high legal risk for the monitor.

The monitor must confirm with the offender in recovery the
purpose of close supervision and the limits to that role. The
monitor must be assured that the recovering offender understands and fully consents to these constraints. The monitor needs
to assist the offender in setting ministry limits, including the number and types of counseling cases that will be handled. Some
programs bar a recovering offender from working with women or
children altogether. If such contact is allowed, it should be done
progressively and with the strictest monitoring. In these cases,
a monitor should have access to the counselees in order to randomly interview them to assess compliance with supervision
goals.

The monitor should also have complete access to all evaluations,
reports, counseling records, and case notes belonging to the offender. These records, especially of current cases, are important
to review on a random basis as a source of assessment in addition to
self-reports. This step is especially important since crossing the
sexual boundary is related to the helper's ability to violate or
maintain other boundaries. The monitor should also be able to au-
diotape or videotape counseling sessions at random to obtain a

current picture of the helper's work as a counselor. This is preferred over direct observation because of the greater likelihood of compliance to fool the observer, the prohibitive costs, and the impeding dynamics of having a third party present who is neither a trained therapist nor a trained observer.

The monitor should document the supervision process, especially in view of the importance attached to his or her evaluation of the appropriateness of a fuller return to counseling or ministry. This documentation should include the name of the counselees that are seen, the dates seen, issues involved in counseling, tapes or notes reviewed, and contacts with any counselees. Documentation should also be presented to the offender as a means of ongoing periodic review of restoration progress.

Restoration in the Context of the Church. We suggest the following pattern for helping to restore a fallen pastor or staff member who admits to the sin, has quit the affair, respects suspension from ministry, and is willing to approach restoration in genuine repentance.

Most churches will want to distinguish between criminal and noncriminal proceedings. In those states where sexual misconduct has been criminalized and there is a high risk of prosecution, some churches may ask for the offender's resignation. Those who are criminally charged should probably be supported only in ways that do not jeopardize the church. This may mean receiving the kind of help outlined here once the criminal judgment has been determined. In the interim, especially when a clergy or staff is highly likely to be found guilty, the church should provide assistance to the spouse and children of the accused. However, it is vital to balance the support offered to the offender with sincere, active, and earnest support to any victims. (See the following section on sexual predators to consider those who molest minors.)

First of all, with the support of the church, organize a committee to oversee the restoration process. This committee should include both men and women and should be prepared to investigate any further accusations presented.[24] The committee needs to interview the accused minister or staff person to determine the facts from his or her perspective, weighing them against the larger mission of the church and determining how restoration fits into that mission. With this information, the group can establish clear ministry limits and determine treatment and personal growth objectives and reinstatement or termination options for the perpetrator. The goals should include efforts to help rebuild the offender's life and to restore the life of the church with the long-range desire to promote healing and growth beyond damage control—to emphasize forgiveness, accountability, grace, and prayer.

In addition to complying with the committee's restoration process, it is important for the offender to establish voluntary ongoing accountability with several people: his or her spouse, a spiritual leader from the committee, and a Christian friend in leadership. Such accountability indicates an offender who is making genuine progress toward healing and recovery. However, it is wise to heed Schaumburg's observation that, "True change in your inner being involves recognizing that it will be a lifelong process . . . [though] healing will never be complete, since we all live in a sinful world."[25]

The following steps are suggested to promote restoration within the context of regular meetings with the offender and spouse. It is vital to be certain that the offender is sincerely repenting, not simply offering a clergy person's lament—sexual sinners can be clever liars who demonstrate a shallow, albeit dramatic, repentance. There must be an uninhibited confession in which the person admits everything to someone and fully accepts all blame for the misconduct. Signs of true repentance will include brokenness, a spontaneous humility, and a total submission to Christ with a willingness to do anything God requires. Be wary of the offender who makes demands. The only acceptable demands from the offender are for due process.

1. Help rebuild the offender's spiritual life. The offender must be accountable to one member of the committee with whom he or she can share transparently. In addition to pursuing the five discipling habits of prayer, fellowship, study of God's Word, tithing, and evangelism, we believe it is essential to help the offender complete a thorough re-evaluation of his inner motives, since this is where all harm begins. Someone outside the church (perhaps a therapist) may be best qualified to do the in-depth work, but arrangements should be made for the therapist to report regularly to the committee. (It is wise to have the offender sign a release for this process.)

2. Help rebuild the offender's marriage. A pastor or staff member cannot fully recover unless there is also a renewal of marriage and family life. In fact, the quality of recovery to ministry often depends upon the outcome of the marriage following sexual betrayal: divorce

or unresolved marital/family trauma will preclude a successful return to ministry. It would be good, then, for the church to provide therapy with a Christian counselor, preferably one trained to do this work. Ideally, this process should begin with a one- to two-week marital retreat with intensive therapy. The pastor must also become *excessively* accountable to his or her spouse. After several months, the spouse should be interviewed by the restoration committee to assess progress.

3. Help the clerical offender find nonministerial work. Since it takes years for restoration to be complete, some churches will establish a minimum time frame (one to four years) before allowing the person to return to a ministry position. Even if closely supervised ministry is allowed (see the next section), this is usually done with little or no pay for the offender. Therefore, it is important for the offending minister who seeks restoration to be able to support himself and his family financially. While we make no case for the church to become a welfare resource for the offender, we do challenge the church that is willing to take restoration seriously to assist the recovering offender in finding appropriate work that will meet minimal financial needs and create no risk for further offense.

Recalled and Set Apart for Ministry. Once the restoration committee is assured that rehabilitation is fulfilled, it is good to consider convening a public restoration or recommissioning service—perhaps at the offender's former church. The focus should be on the restoration process and the offender's compliance with it. The committee might also consider an open door policy that would allow the offender to return to public ministry only in restrictive ways. Because of the danger of liability for any actions the person might take to violate others sexually, the committee needs to have great confidence in the completed restoration before taking this step.

BARRING SEXUAL PREDATORS

We have already discussed, from various vantage points, the high cost of sexual predators in Christian counseling and ministry. The church must confront this growing menace because of the poor prognosis for predatory change. Christ is able, but much research and pained experience show us that certain clergy and counseling professionals are not likely to respond well to the exposure of their sexual wrongdoing.²⁶ It is imperative that leaders in the church and the clinical professions learn to recognize predatory helpers and deal firmly and courageously with the moral, ministerial, legal, and therapeutic issues involved.

Styles of Predation. There are three primary predatory styles, all with overlapping features, that consistently demonstrate a poor prognosis for change. The first category involves those with impulse control problems and long-term personality or character disorders. Not only are sexual control problems evident, but problems of anger control, drug or alcohol abuse, excessive spending, and debt trouble are often present. The most problematic of these have histories of trouble with the law. Most of the others have a history of conflict with supervisors, employers, and other authority figures.

The second category includes those with sociopathic or narcissistic personality disorders. These have many characteristics of the preceding group, yet are normally more deliberate, socially sophisticated, and cunning. They are experts at seducing a wide range of counselees without discovery. These individuals are so smooth at their craft that they often fool colleagues, professional organizations, and state disciplinary groups. They appear to be genuinely remorseful if caught, but such remorse is often superficial and manipulative. They are not good candidates for change because they fundamentally deny that their behavior is wrong.

The third group includes borderline personality disorders and those who suffer occasional psychotic breaks. These people normally have poor social judgment and impaired reality testing. They have a wide variety of responses with respect to understanding the extent of their violation of others. This group may have periods of relative health and maturity of character but cannot sustain it and, over time, tend to re-enter periods of crisis and social instability. This chronic instability and cyclical disturbance makes restoration highly unlikely with this group.

Pedophile and Ephebophile Violators. As we stated in chapter 7, pedophile offenders are those who molest children under the age of twelve years old; ephobophiles molest children who are about twelve to seventeen years old. We include these violators here because the treatment necessary to recover from this level of offending is so complex and, as yet, remains unproven as an effective predictor against subsequent violation. Therefore, the continuing risk of sexual offense combined with the chilling legal environment makes it unlikely that these persons would ever be able to resume a counseling or pastoral ministry.

This is not to say that rehabilitation is impossible or always unlikely. Consistent with our model we believe there are nonpredatory molesters who are able to be restored to ministry. Based on the most critical criterion for predatory judgment (the number of molest incidents and/or victims), we would challenge the church to consider that the child molester with only one offense is presumptively restorable. In a review of the research on treatment for adult perpetrators of children, the authors stated that the "data indicate that [offender treatment] works for some in the short-run and for others in the long-run."[27]

What is not clear from the studies is how long child-abuse offenders remain free of sexual offense—the current legal, moral, and social environment nearly demands lifelong abstinence. Consequently, until we have more reliable and useful data—data that shows no recidivism over the long-term due to successful treatment, intensive aftercare, and significant restoration commitment by a congregation or parish—it is likely too risky to return child-abuse offenders to positions of influence with children. At this time it appears unlikely that an offender would be rehabilitated to the extent that churches and parishes could trust (or more to the point, would trust) an offender's return to a counseling or ministry position with minors.

One final point in defense of those who are accused of abuse of minors. It seems to us that accusations against people as child molesters is one of the most frequent areas of false allegations, especially if the accusation comes from a spouse engaged in divorce. Therefore, it is imperative that churches establish just and careful ways to evaluate for child sexual abuse in order to avoid the tragedy of false accusations. (Refer to chapter 6.)

Barring the Predator from Counseling and Ministry. The predatory counselor with a poor prognosis for recovery should be barred from further counseling practice and pastoral ministry. No matter what other good may come from that person's work, the risk that sexual abuse may recur is far too high. The price of suffering the predator to remain in ministry is obscene: more victims who could have been protected; incredible moneys extracted by lawyers and the courts through lawsuit; foolish, uncaring labels that are attached to the church for harboring a predator; and the incalculable stain to the name of Christ and the Christian witness of the church.

If we are to give every violator a second chance (a refutable but merciful presumption for sure), we must exercise strict control and set a maximum time by which full recovery must be demonstrated. Then we must help those who do not meet these standards to find another vocation.

CONCLUSION

Sex, as God created it to be, grows sweeter and richer when confined to one man and one woman in a healthy and growing marriage. Outside of this—in every way outside of this—sweet sex eventually sours and ultimately becomes toxic and deadly. Wrongful sex in the forbidden zone of Christian ministry is proving the high cost of deadly wages. The delusional intoxication of sexual lust and unrestrained fantasy quickly gives way to reveal the bitter onslaught of betrayal, horrific pain, and broken lives.

The future of sexual misconduct disclosure will bring not just disgrace and shame, it will also bring loss of marriage and family life, loss of ministry, even imprisonment. Even so, it is not too late to pull back from the moral precipice. Let the church show an exhausted and sex-saturated culture the way out of sexual slavery.

NOTES

1. Paxton Hibben, *Henry Ward Beecher: An American Portrait* (New York: The Press of the Readers Club, 1927; 1942), 200.

2. Studies of castrated men in Sweden, Holland, and Switzerland—a treatment not likely to be accepted in America due to various legal, ethical, and moral prohibitions—show recidivism rates of 1 to 3 percent, while recidivism for other forms of treatment fall in the 40 to 80 percent range. Reported in Fred Berlin and E. W. Krout, "Pedophilia: Diagnostic Concepts, Treatment, and Ethical Considerations," *American Journal of Forensic Psychiatry* 7 (1983): 13–30

3. S. Butler, "Sexual Contact Between Therapists and Patients," (Ph.D. diss., California School of Professional Psychology, 1975).

4. Nancy Gartrell et al., "Reporting Practices of Psychiatrists Who Knew of Sexual Misconduct of Colleagues," *American Journal of Orthopsychiatry* 57, no. 4 (1987): 287–95.

5. Glen O. Gabbard, "Psychotherapists Who Transgress Sexual Boundaries with Patients," *Bulletin of the Menninger Clinic*, (October 1992): 1–17. Handout from the Conference on Assessment, Treatment and Supervision of the Professional Who Has Engaged in Sexual Misconduct (Minneapolis, Minn. February 19, 1994).

6. Schoener et al., *Psychotherapist's Sexual Involvement*, 410.

7. Information shared at the Conference on Assessment, Treatment, and Supervision of the Professional Who Has Engaged in Sexual Misconduct, Minneapolis, Minn., February 19, 1994.

8. Gabbard, "Psychotherapists Who Transgress."

9. Ibid.

10. Schoener et al., *Psychotherapist's Sexual Involvement*, 421.

11. Ibid., 423.

12. Harry W. Schaumburg, *False Intimacy: Understanding the Struggle of Sexual Addiction*, (Colorado Springs, Colo.: NavPress, 1992), 54.

13. Daniel Henderson, "Breaking the Stranglehold: Treating Sex Offenders," *Christian Counseling Today* 2 (Summer 1994), 24–29.

14. Ibid., 28.

15. Ibid.

16. Ibid.

17. LaHaye, in getting at the true meaning of Galations 6:1 as it applies to the restoration of a fallen pastor, quotes Jack Hayford's paraphrase. *If Ministers Fall*, supra note 1, 140 quoting from Hayford, *Restoring Fallen Leaders*.

18. Two prominent examples of proponents of this fourth way are Desert Stream Ministries, 12488 Venice Blvd., Los Angeles, CA 90066–3804; and Exodus International, P.O. Box 2121, San Rafael, CA 94912.

19. LaHaye, *If Ministers Fall*, 141.

20. Rediger, *Ministry and Sexuality*, 116

21. LaHaye, *If Ministers Fall*, 161.

22. These ideas are adapted from Rediger, *Ministry and Sexuality*, 9–10.

23. See Schoener et al., *Psychotherapist's Sexual Involvement*, 436.

24. See chapter 11 for information on congregational healing processes. In some churches, the committee to restore the fallen pastor and heal the church may be one and the same, while in other churches the possible conflicting objectives may require two different groups.

25. Schaumburg, *False Intimacy*, 89.

26. See K. Callanan and T. O'Connor, *Staff Comments and Recommendations Regarding the Report of the Senate Task Force on Psychotherapist and Patient Sexual Relations* (Sacramento, Calif.: Board of Behavioral Science Examiners and Psychology Examining Committee [now Board of Psychology], 1988). After extensive review of rehabilitation programs, the heads of two of California's mental health licensing boards concluded regarding therapists who had committed sexual misconduct, "Prospects for rehabilitation are minimal and it is doubtful that they should be given the opportunity to ever practice psychotherapy again," 11.

27. Judith V. Becker and J. H. Hunter, "Evaluation of Treatment Outcome for Adult Perpetrators of Child Sexual Abuse," *Criminal Justice and Behavior* 19, no. 1 (March 1992): 74–92.

Chapter Fifteen

Before the Fall:
Prevention Guidelines

No matter how well I have learned to recognize and use sexual tensions in a therapeutic, nonphysical way, at times I still feel pulled in by the seductive intimacy of my work. There seems to be nothing I can do to prevent an occasional fantasy of sexual contact with a female patient. And although now I know how my struggle will be resolved, each time I must put forth deliberate effort to remember how and why I must resist the temptation to get out of my chair, traverse the short distance to my patient, and embrace her.[1]

THE PROBLEM OF SEXUAL EXPLOITATION must be resolved, as we argued in chapter 3, from two perspectives: inner transformation and outer control. The ideal constraint is by the transformation of the inner man's view of another. A transformed man can see and delight in the true woman within the beguiling sexual exterior. In Christ, a man is able to see a woman as one to be valued and not exploited. The female client—indeed, all women—can be prized and enjoyed in a mutual sharing of genuine Christian love. From this eternal and spiritual view, the greatest loss the woman suffers is not the sexual violation per se, as traumatic as that is, but the loss of dignity and personhood through the violation. She has also lost a man who could have helped heal her woundedness within and celebrated her as a unique person before God.

Men must understand and respect this spiritual foundation against forbidden sex: The "desired body belongs to the 'being' of a human being who [her] self belongs to another; a human being, that is, who has been bought with a price (1 Cor. 6:20; 7:23) and has a temporal and eternal destiny, a destiny in which one who claims this other person in his totality responsibly participates."[2] We should say to ourselves, "I must see the other person as one who belongs not just to herself or himself, or even possibly to me, but as one who is bought with a price and belongs to God. Inasmuch as I fail to include this relatedness to God when I look upon a person, I will fail to be protected from purely sexual temptation. My potential for failure stems from an unwillingness to see the person with dignity, as belonging to God."

A transformed view of women will help the counselor relinquish an attractive counselee as a potential sexual partner. If this is not done deliberately and frequently with some, then counseling will never help the woman grow as a person and can only undermine her faith and her self-esteem. This also challenges the helper to give up the fantasy that a sexual or dating relationship could occur once counseling is terminated. The counselor benefits by not violating the sexual boundary for love in his life, in his marriage and family, and in his ministry. The woman benefits because she is not abused and abandoned by yet another male, thus breaking the belief that she is somehow either toxic to men or useful only for sexual encounters. The healing power of this transformed view—of seeing the client through the eyes of Christ—is enormous.

Personal Prevention Guidelines

Safeguarding oneself from sexual involvement with counselees involves attending to seven areas of personal life and professional work:

1. assess personal well-being

2. provide services within areas of competence

3. maintain quality supervision and consultation

4. keep conservative touch limits;[3] limit contact with counselees in personal and social settings

5. sign counseling contracts and review them with counselees on a regular basis

6. maintain the professional demeanor of counseling by adhering to agreed appointment times, session limits, fees, and emergency contacts

7. be wary of excessive self-disclosure

Since temptation is inevitable, it is necessary to be prepared to deal with its potential dangers.[4] It is imperative to be on guard no matter how respected, how old, or how uninterested in sex you are!

PERSONAL BOUNDARIES

Grow in Christ and Practice Humility. As discussed in chapter 3, it is critical for helpers to maintain growth in Christian practices and principles; to maintain regular scripture reading, prayer, and meditation; and to maintain a deep personal relationship with God, one that transforms from the inside out throughout the lifespan. It is always important that helpers admit to themselves and to at least one other person who will hold them accountable, that they have limitations that could contribute to their downfall. When we understand that our power comes from admitting our weakness (2 Cor. 12:7–10), then God will lift us up (see 1 Pet. 5:6). As one author noted, "Your flesh will *always* serve the law of sin. And God never tries to fix it. It is dead. So Paul said his flesh was serving sin; he could not fix his flesh anymore than you can."[5]

Healing the Roots of Our Brokenness. A careful examination of basic spiritual and psychodynamic issues should be standard in the training process of every therapist and clergy person. For those who did not deal with these issues during preparation for ministry, it would be wise to address them even now. The roots of our brokenness—the awful depths of our sin nature—can be easily overlooked, especially by helpers who appear to be quite successful. A number of significant books written in recent years attempt to address the roots of this brokenness, encouraging people to make serious and dedicated efforts to heal the hurts and to take responsibility to become whole persons, especially as helpers.[6]

Ultimately, the protection of counselees from sexual misconduct comes down to the heart and actions of the individual counselor. As Bustanoby states so well, "All the safeguards in the world will not help the counselor who has not come to terms with his own sexuality, who does not loathe the idea of sex with a counselee, and who does not feel the terrible responsibility for helping, not hurting, that soul who comes for help."[7]

Committing to Excellence. The Christian helper is called by God and by the demands of living to a life of excellence. The excellent life can mean many things, with myriad applications, but is essentially an attitude. Excellence is a commitment to live and serve and enjoy the life given to the utmost of one's abilities, powers, and promises. It is a social life, one dedicated to rich relationships and to church and community, to serving others with integrity, and to fulfilling promises and commitments made to others. It is a learned life, not content with the status quo and maintenance of easy prejudice, but marked by disciplined study and exploration of the world close to home and across the globe. It is a spiritual life, growing in grace and knowledge of God, participating in the local and larger community of believers, and testifying boldly to the life and mission of Christ.

Cultivating an Excellent Marital Relationship. Helpers will find protection from misconduct by making their marriage a priority, maintaining emotional and sexual intimacy, and keeping their love life romantic. Tim LaHaye, who admits to having been tempted sexually from time to time in his ministry, suggests an idea that has been vital to his success in this area. He advocates that a couple pray together as part of the "fidelity insurance."[8] Specifically, he recommends that a couple pray four or five nights per week with each partner alternating in leading the prayer time while the other agrees in prayer. This allows each partner to share his or her burdens while the spouse participates in those burdens through prayer.

Committing to Accountability. Every Christian helper should evaluate his or her vulnerability with someone who is in a position to help without the threat of disclosure or abandonment. Admitting that sexual temptation is real and present is critical to the prevention of sexual misconduct. Every helper who discovers and keeps a walk in the Spirit (Gal. 5:16–18) will find it more difficult to fulfill the lusts of the flesh. Helpers must respect sexual temptation and honestly admit any inappropriate enjoyment of sexual fantasy—telling others defuses the power that secrecy inflames. No matter how stable, protected, and respected, every helper must be on guard.

We suggest that helpers meet with persons of accountability weekly or monthly. Such accountability to another believer should be frequent and ongoing for effective counseling and ministry. The days of Lone Ranger independence and unaccountable behavior are over. Growing numbers of men across the country are joining peer groups—in either personal or professional contexts—that consistently ask pointed questions of mutual accountability regarding sex, money, marriage, family life, professional integrity, abuse of power, and lying. Such groups not only keep one honest, but are there for support when crises come.

MAINTAINING PROFESSIONAL BOUNDARIES

A common problem among men in midlife ministry is the tendency to work too much and to skate on the edge of burnout. A general sense of burnout weakens one's ability to resist sexual temptation. Therefore, to avoid vulnerability to sexual violations, either in fantasy or in practice, it is vital to attend to the warning signs of burnout such as frequent exhaustion or boredom at work. Richard Exley states, "The first clue to burnout, and the spiritual and emotional exhaustion which accompanies it, is a lack of inner fulfillment."[9]

GENERAL PREVENTION PRINCIPLES

The Helper Must Recognize His or Her Limitations as a Helper. Increased success and influence—a common midlife development for many professionals—can also foster prideful illusions of power. Rutter has noted that "men in power encourage women to believe that they will help them toward leading meaningful, productive lives."[10] While this ability to encourage is central to effective helping, an important preventative step is for the helper to recognize his or her limitations and not promise more than can be delivered. It appears that some helpers become caught up in their *need* to help and begin to cross boundaries that must remain absolute. When helpers find themselves in a situation beyond their abilities to help, they need to remind themselves of their limitations and consult and refer carefully.

Assess and Respect Sexual Vulnerability. The helper must learn how to set and keep appropriate sexual boundaries within the professional context. Helpers must know what kind of woman most easily tempts them and must take precautionary action by letting their partners know when they are working with such a person. They also need to be aware that arranging house calls and other meetings increases sexual risks. It is critical that every helper heed Paul's warning: "So if you think you are standing firm, be careful that you don't fall. No temptation has seized you except what is common to man. And God is faithful; he will not let you be tempted beyond what you can bear. But when you are tempted, he will also provide a way out so that you can stand up under it" (1 Cor. 10:12).

In assessing sexual vulnerability, there are four signals of attitude and behavior to attend to carefully:

1. sustained self-reliance

2. compulsive behavior patterns

3. isolated and authoritarian leadership style

4. excessive pride

If these "early warning signals are taken seriously and reliable intervention, treatment, and furlough or career exit counseling are provided,"[11] then the risks of misconduct are greatly minimized. As might be expected, these issues may be especially difficult for helpers working in small, independent churches or solo counseling practices where isolation and the lack of connectedness and accountability with trusted colleagues can promote vulnerability.

Rehearse the Consequences. An idea we presented in the previous chapter and in *Law for the Christian Counselor*, is to challenge the denial of sexual fantasy by mentally reviewing the reality of the costs of participation.[12] When helpers are tempted by an arousing carnal thought, before giving way to the teasing fantasy, we suggest they stop the thought and deliberately and soberly tell themselves, "My sexual misconduct is a crime that will severely hurt my victim, cause me to lose my family and ministry, likely land me in prison with a massive fine, and expose me to hostile convicts with AIDS who sexually abuse sexual abusers . . . HELP ME, GOD!"

Alcorn[13] suggests that helpers develop a list of specific negative consequences that would result from sexual misconduct action and review the list on a regular basis, even adding to it as needed. It would be especially wise to read through the list during times of weakness or probable temptation. This can cut through the lies of denial and rationalization, keeping the helper and the counselee safe.

Managing Attraction and Sexual Feelings

There are various kinds of attraction that helpers may face in counseling relationships. As Rutter states, "Because sexuality is present in many situations whether or not we wish it, identifying its presence in oneself or in another *before* it gets acted upon, and then learning that there are other options, is of the utmost importance in preventing sexual violation."[14]

Control Fantasy. Fleeting sexual fantasies about counselees are common—one study suggests that between 80 to 90 percent of male therapists experience them on occasion.[15] However, self-permission to engage in uncontrolled fantasy about an attractive counselee is the gateway drug to sexual trouble. It is dangerous for the helper to give himself or herself permission to develop and expand sexual fantasies about a counselee. Fantasies—a form of covert or mental rehearsal—nearly always motivate or encourage sexual action, a slippery slope without effective limits. This mental rehearsal reinforces the denial process by desensitizing the helper to the error of fantasy while increasing the justification of inappropriate sex. It also tends to corrupt right judgment and promotes the acceptance of passionate misbeliefs such as "it's clear we both want to do this—why deny ourselves" or that falling in love with the forbidden person is a feeling that must be honored.

As denial, rationalization, and fantasy continue, the helper tends to ignore Christ-centered control or forget about Christian accountability. Saturated with unrestrained fantasy, the helper knows that he will not likely find peer acceptance for these thoughts and feelings. A man alone, hiding from his spouse, avoiding accountability, and nurturing secret and powerful fantasies is playing with an unquenchable fire—a fire that can burn up all that was once dear to him. *Purity in one's thought life is crucial to sexual self-control*, and it is basic evidence of a satisfying and mature spiritual life.

Attraction That Fosters Good Counseling. Counseling relationships customarily involve attraction as people who interact in close ways come to value and appreciate various qualities in one another. In addition to the conscious levels of attraction, we have also discussed the unconscious dynamics of transference and countertransference. Constructive transference is the natural relational process by which counselees develop affection for their helpers. This can influence them to grow and change through counseling. However, the helper cannot allow this affection or any countertransference (any aspect of the range of feelings felt for the counselee) to develop into harmful behavior. "To affirm the counselee involves affirming both personhood and gender. But—and this is crucial—gender can be affirmed in a way that acknowledges both the counselee's sexuality and biblical morality."[16]

Affirming the Counselee Without Violation. In some situations it can be beneficial for the helper to acknowledge that the counselee is an attractive person. However, helpers should never communicate their own attraction to the counselee but learn to interact with counselees in ways that redeem the feelings of attraction and do not put the counseling relationship at risk. Helpers can do this by verbally acknowledging the qualities and character traits that are attractive about the counselee while maintaining conduct that is respectful of the person's worth. This conduct affirms to the counselee two things: (1) that he or she is an attractive person who does not have to use sexuality to affirm self-worth, and (2) that there is a wider view of attractiveness beyond our cultural obsession with physical beauty—one grounded in the godly aspects of personality, character, service, spirituality, and social grace.

WHEN SEXUAL CONTROL BECOMES UNMANAGEABLE

We hope an alarm of warning will go off in a every helper's conscience who begins to cross the line of wrongful sexual behavior in counseling and ministerial work, and that the helper will immediately pull back and regain self-control. Helpers who reach this point need to get close consultation and assistance from a supervisor or an accountability group. The helper needs to disclose in detail the struggle and dangerous behavior, without hiding anything! As an added precaution, we suggest that the helper make a detailed plan for the next session with the client that will have built-in safeguards. Then ask an accountability group to pray during the session and follow up with accountability after the session is over. By agreeing to refuse to live in secrecy with this type of struggle, helpers will break the tempting power of misconduct.

If a male helper is unable to keep his sexual desires in control with a female client, he must immediately get supervisory or consultative help that can bolster his strength through accountability, proper case-planning, prayer, and renewal of humility and self-control. If this does not work, he must carefully and professionally refer the client to a more capable helper. He must convey the reality that this referral is not her fault, but stems from his own inability to help. There must be a commitment to not act-out sexually. If this step is violated, the nonsexual value of the helping relationship is lost forever to the woman.

In an emergency (or any at-risk situation), when the counselor senses that sexual violation is imminent, we suggest the following procedures.

- *Stop the session.* If you begin sexual action toward your client in session, *stop yourself before your harm escalates.* State your inability to respect the professional prohibition against sexual contact.

Call the session off with plans to follow up in the best interests of the counselee. Tell your client you will call to discuss the next appointment after you have discussed the situation with your supervisor or consultant. If you can deal with the issue and resolve it, then resume therapy. If you are not able to resolve in a reasonable time, inform the client that you will have to refer her to another professional.

- *If necessary, make an honorable termination.* If you have to terminate a relationship of trust, it must be done in a way that least injures the counselee. It is most harmful if the counselor terminates without an explanation, leaving the impression that it is the counselee's fault. Carefully and sensitively end the relationship with prayers that the termination is providing the counselee a chance to heal. When termination is necessary, the helper must make a responsible referral to another competent professional.

Counselee Seduction of the Helper. What does the helper do when the counselee tries to be seductive? "The true test of one's success at preparing to avoid sexual misconduct occurs at the point of stepping into the encounter. This focuses the absolute necessity to flee from sexual temptation, much as Joseph did from Potiphar's wife. If you have temptation thrown in your face, drop everything and run, *run*, RUN!"[17] If you sigh instead, say yes, and succumb to the sweet and momentary lust, you might as well put a gun to your head and pull the trigger. We must never forget the powerful impact of the choices made in the heat of passionate temptation. Rutter reveals and advocates the healing power of restraint:

> When a forbidden-zone relationship becomes erotically charged, several moments of decision inevitably occur that determine whether the sexuality will be contained psychologically or acted upon physically. Whenever a man relinquishes his sexual agenda toward his protege in order to preserve her right to a non-sexual relationship, a healing moment occurs. Because so many women have been previously injured by the uncontained sexuality of men who have had power over them, the potential healing power of restraint is enormous. Not only is the woman made safe from being exploited by this particular man, but the moment kindles the promise that she can be valued as a woman entirely apart from her sexual value to other men.[18]

EROTIC FEELINGS AND ETHICAL THERAPY

Most counselors and therapists will not—should not—have to take drastic action to control misconduct or to terminate therapy in the face of erotic feelings in the therapeutic interaction. While it is no doubt better to terminate and refer than to engage in wrongful sex, the mature therapist will be able to control his or her sexual feelings and help the client to identify and work through sexually-expressed issues. Not only does relinquishment of one's sexual agenda toward the client create a healing moment, but it opens the door to a healing journey that is otherwise lost either by sex or by ending therapy because the sexual feelings were unmanageable. Control of sexual feelings is preferable to termination and referral as most clients will be hurt and will leave counseling with some feelings of anger and abandonment.

The baseline therapeutic principle for work with erotic feelings is the same as that with the seductive client—the eroticism is an expression or cover of deeper wounds, needs, and patterns of dysfunctional living. This is true, for the most part, not only in the client transference but also in the countertransferent feelings of the counselor. Therefore, sexual feelings or expression is a signal to explore the deeper roots of the erotic manifestation, either with the client as a therapeutic issue or with a supervisor or consultant (never with the client!) when the counselor is aroused. As Rutter suggests, sexual restraint shown here promises not only to avoid exploitations but also to open doors to healing and redemption that go to the core of the promise of the counseling endeavor.

When a female client knows she will not be exploited by her male therapist, when she is genuinely safe from sexual wrongdoing, she becomes truly free and can take the risk to know and express her inner person. This client will often make herself deeply vulnerable to the helper and to God. Furthermore, she will face her deepest fears, express the pain and desire of her deepest longings about life, and explore options that are otherwise unavailable to her. This is true to some degree with all therapeutic encounters but seems especially so in the male therapist-female client dyad. This is when counseling around external change, important as that is in this era of managed care, can transform to a deep inner therapy where the Great Physician is invited to do wonders in the human heart.

Paradoxically, this dynamic can itself become a tempting fascination precisely because it is so increasingly rare in human relations. The emotional attraction and pull to relations that are this transparent and honest can become a backdoor trap that subtly erodes the boundaries of ethical counseling. It is not unusual for counselors to report in supervisory session about how overt sexual restraint early in counseling can lead to a depth of relationship that itself becomes attractive, even erotically charged. It is part of the wonder and fascination of the healing journey as well as a sober reminder that the ethical helper can never let down his or her sexual guard. Maintaining the call to sexual purity and respecting the difficulty of remaining emotionally and sexually safe for the client is an ethical constant for the effective Christian counselor.

ADMINISTRATIVE SAFEGUARDS

When hiring and supervising counselor or ministry staff, it is never wise to assume a person has no potential for sexual misconduct simply because that individual is a Christian. Unfortunately, it is not always possible to determine who is an offender, or even who may become an offender. One who is intent on hiding sexual sin can be highly deceptive. As Schoener so clearly states, "A very diverse group of therapists apparently engage in the sexual exploitation of clients [and] a large number of therapists, when distressed, may be capable of slipping into high-risk behaviors that lead to . . . sexual involvement with a client."[19] Nevertheless, it is possible to greatly minimize the likelihood that an offender will slip through the hiring process or that an otherwise good staff member will slip into sexual trouble.

HIRING COUNSELORS

The sexual misconduct epidemic in the church has made it necessary to screen applicants carefully for any job that will involve counseling as part of its activity. During the screening process ask direct questions about past misconduct and secure permission to contact previous employers, licensing boards, and past supervisors. The applicant should be willing to sign a broad release allowing the potential employer to make these contacts without incurring liability on behalf of former employers or supervisors. Texas, (you will recall from chapter 13) for example, has mandated employers to evaluate misconduct charges in the applicant's professional life for at least five previous years. Whether or not this reveals the trend of future law, each administrator must be thorough in the investigation and knowledgeable about the law in each respective state or province. Consider these additional suggestions:

1. *The Application.* Five categories of information to include on the application are (1) education, (2) degrees held, (3) licensure or certification status, (4) relevant training or experience, and (5) negative issues impacting licensure and certification, including any malpractice actions. The application should state clearly the agency's policies and expectations regarding ethical professional conduct. Require the applicant to sign the form in agreement with those policies.

When reviewing the application, carefully evaluate any degree program that does not bear recognized credentialing or certification. In addition, closely examine supervised training and experience as to the breadth and depth of counseling experience. Be careful not to take references at face value. Obtain unrestricted permission to interview previous supervisors or colleagues and during the course of these interviews be assertive in probing any incongruencies or hesitations to your questions.

2. *The Interview.* Prepare for the interview by reviewing the application and information gathered through contacts with references. In addition, determine what questions you need to ask the applicant in order to fill in the blanks and resolve discrepancies or inadequate information. Throughout the interview take time to evaluate sexual misconduct and any area of ethical concern; prepare several ethical issues for the applicant to address.

3. *Counseling Demonstration.* The final step in the hiring process is to observe the applicant in a counseling situation. This will enable you to determine how well the person would actually function with counseling cases typically seen by your agency or ministry. This demonstration can involve role-play, video or audio tapes, or an actual counseling session.

STAFF POLICIES

Counseling agencies, churches, and group practices must have written policies with detailed rules regarding sexual practices and consequences for failure to comply. These policies should address limits on sexual and romantic involvement with counselees, sexual harassment issues, the means by which complaints will be handled and adjudicated, and the process for filing a complaint against a supervisor or member of the administrative staff. In addition, the entire staff should review policy regularly and discuss actual situations that illustrate problems and pitfalls in sexual boundary violations. Revise and update staff policies annually and require that employees sign renewed policy statements as these are produced, indicating consent to abide by the rules.

Taking Complaints Seriously. Help your staff learn how to deal with complaints from counselees in constructive ways.[20] Complaints "must be treated as complaints and not as symptoms of a client's pathology, and they must be given some resolution."[21] Complainants must be treated with concern and respect—the lack of it or worse, when abusive behavior is shown, is a key motivator to lawsuit. We suggest a specific commitment to (1) resolve the complaint in an honorable way, (2) do so in a reasonable time, and (3) respond to the complainant about action taken in regards to the complaint.

Suspension of Alleged Violators. We strongly recommend a policy that suspends a minister or counselor in the face of serious charges of sexual or moral wrongdoing, especially when supported by two or more people or when admitted by the helper. Though this will be difficult and some exceptions may exist (each church and practice group must define the boundary between serious vs. less serious and frivolous charges), we recommend that the alleged violator be placed on temporary leave until the matter is resolved. (See appendix A for church policy examples.)

This policy, in place and practiced consistently, will protect the church or agency from further harm if the allegations are true; it also allows for the best return of the counselor to practice if they are not. Furthermore, such action will show the complainant—and the court should it go that far—that your organization is serious about such concerns, that you hold the interests of those served above the helper. It also increases the likelihood that the matter will be resolved in-house, without further legal or public action.

Though we empathize with and can understand the forces that lead churches and agencies to attempt to contain the damage and keep operations running normally, this action almost always backfires. Ministry leadership cannot escape this lesser-of-two-evils dilemma—one that forces costly choices at best. Most allegations are true to some extent, and some are only the tip of the iceberg. In these cases, containment begins to be perceived increasingly as unjust cover-up. Those wounded, whether real or perceived, will also persist in making noise and taking increasingly serious and public action until the church acts in their interest. Churches and agencies can either choose to do this when they still have control of those choices, or they can be forced to do it later by the media, or by the court and other authoritative bodies.

Supervision and Case Consultation

Supervision and consultation are advisable for every helper throughout the counseling career; these entail similar processes but have different elements.[22] Supervision involves a professional relationship in which the supervisor has control over and responsibility for the treatment provided. The supervisor should have complete access to the supervisee's notes and other materials and should determine (increasingly according to state law) the standards and ways in which the supervision will occur. Case consultation also includes case review and provision of another view of the casework, but it does not carry the same level of control or responsibility for treatment provided. Case consultation is normally voluntary while supervision is usually mandated to meet licensure, certification, and legal, association, agency, or ministry requirements. The case consultant should not use the term *supervisor* because of the legal implications of that term.[23]

Supervision for Clinical Excellence. Supervisors are not born, they are trained and molded by mentored experience. It is an increasingly negligent fact that most graduate training programs do not prepare helpers to do supervision.[24] The supervisor's role in helping to prevent sexual exploitation requires adequate training in supervision practices, experience with specific supervisory models and methods, and a clear picture of things to watch for that might indicate a supervisee's movement toward misconduct. The well-prepared supervisor is less likely to miss a supervisee's mistakes and will be able to assess and guide supervisees toward healthy reconciliation of issues that could lead to misconduct. This supervisor will also avoid suit for a supervisee's misconduct if trouble has been prevented or redirected early on.

There are a wide variety of models available for supervision, depending on one's theoretical orientation. Primary methods include self-reports by the supervisee, examining notes and treatment records, review of audio and video tapes, live observation, and co-therapy. The supervisor should carefully screen supervisees, have a clear contract that specifies each person's role and expectations, remain alert to misconduct signs, deal with countertransference issues, and discuss any signs of distress in supervisees. The supervisor should periodically review the supervision contract and evaluate treatment records on occasion.

It is crucial to identify risky counseling situations and at-risk supervisees. The supervisor must be familiar with the dynamics that lead to misconduct, alert both to vulnerable clients and features of risk in a supervisee. The attractive female with histrionic or borderline traits and the tired and chronically stressed helper are signal markers for closer review. Direct discussion about sexual temptations and concerns, and periodic and careful review of tapes and notes are viable methods to assess danger. Developing trust and encouraging honest risk-taking in the supervisory relationships will allow the supervisee to more seriously and deeply explore his or her fears, fantasies, frustrations, and self-demands in therapy.[25]

Supervisors should not let any counseling boundary violations occur without subsequent discussion—sexual misconduct often happens at the end of a long chain of milder ethical boundary violations. For the most part, supervisors must rely on the veracity of the self-reports of supervisees and their professional instincts for assessing trends toward trouble. However, the supervisor who never directly asks about sexual and other boundary violation issues in counseling is practicing poor supervision. We have found that carefully introducing our own sexual and moral struggles into supervisory discussion facilitates honest review of a subject that would otherwise be avoided and resisted.

Consultation for Christian Growth. The consultant should work with the consultee on the basis of a written contract. This is necessary because consultation is voluntary and advisory: the consultant does not have control of or responsibility for the treatment provided. However, since liability exists even with consultation, it is prudent to go through a similar screening process as was outlined above for supervisees. If you believe you know someone quite well, the screening may not seem necessary, but is probably still the wisest step to take.

Begin any new consultation with a short-term commitment (three or four sessions) to determine the appropriateness of mutual relations. If consulting with a group, it is important to delineate and clarify roles between education, administrative, and clinical consultation. Clarifying the boundaries of authority and the limits of your investment is essential when your consultation involves administrative leadership. The last thing you need is a power struggle with a pastor or agency head over the acceptance of your suggestions. If you do choose to consult, carefully respect the process, keep well-read and prepared, and be wary of getting in over your head.

Since sexual struggles in counseling are common (no counselor escapes them), we need to overcome our denial and demystify the fear of talking about them in the church. Sexual involvement occurs because "it is the result of either an intentional act by the therapist or an unintended consequence of the therapist's being unable to maintain proper professional boundaries . . . [resulting] from a personality flaw, the style of therapy, the unique challenges presented by the case, or the therapist's vulnerability that is generated by life events.[26] When a counselor or minister is slipping into unwise practices or struggling with personal issues that could lead to misconduct, the supervisor must not hesitate to help by requiring time off and providing personal counseling or any other remedial action to prevent misconduct.

SYSTEMIC PREVENTION: CHURCH AND PROFESSIONS

A variety of factors in the church, the counseling professions, and in society serve to maintain, even to foster the difficulty men have in dealing with sexual issues. One of these maddening issues is the fact that many men remain silent and paralyzed about their colleague's sexual misconduct. Consistent with the patriarchal criticisms of some feminists (see chapter 9), Rutter suggests that this trouble stems from men envying those who succeed in crossing the sexual boundaries.[27] It seems to be all too true that some men admire other men who succeed in sexual conquests; they are dazzled by the cultural icon of male sexual conquest of the prized female. Whatever the cause, this systemic dynamic of male denial and the minimization of sexual abuse gives as impression of approval to sexual misconduct.

Rutter asserts that *some* males (we reject the radical feminist assertion of universal male guilt) have accepted lying as normative when it comes to understanding women and relating to women. He states,

> The fact that lying has become an acceptable mode in the political arena is reflected in the way male-dominated institutions

deal with sexual misconduct by their own members, where truth is often a victim of political considerations. Professional organizations of doctors, therapists, lawyers, and clergy rarely make information about sexual misconduct available to the public for fear that the reputation of the profession itself will be damaged.[28]

Father Connors makes a similar assertion regarding the Roman Catholic Church by noting how abusive misconduct can be maintained only in environments where lies and secrecy are predominant.[29]

A prominent member of the American Psychiatric Association (APA) who openly fought to overcome sexual misconduct in the ranks of psychiatry stated, "I used to believe the [APA]. . . . They want to have one image publicly . . . [but] the way they act supports a completely different conclusion. I think the [APA] is not part of the solution . . . [but] is part of the problem."[30] Relatedly, the California Bar Association, after long and rancorous debate, only recently (April, 1991) voted to censure (a mild form of punishment) Bar Association lawyers who were found guilty of sexual misconduct.

In the church, it has been common practice for clergy to be transferred to another church or parish rather than dealt with publicly or therapeutically. This has fostered the dangerous communication of acceptance of wrongdoing, encouraging offenders to repeat their offense without significant consequence. When challenged in court, the church has been severely stung for this practice. We have already made the case for intensive treatment and recovery programs for which the church must assume the costs. In both the church and the clinical professions, systemic transformation that truly protects victims and helps or bars violators from professional practice can no longer be ignored.

CHRISTIAN HELPER SUPPORT NETWORKS

In confronting the problems of sexual misconduct, Rediger asserts that we must address the problem of the "half-intimacies of the clergy role."[31] People are encouraged to share their problems with the pastor or counselor, but the helper cannot reciprocate. These leaders are often isolated from help, without anyone in their denomination or region to whom they can talk. It seems that Christian clergy, especially, are expected to function essentially as loners. Yet this very isolation increases the risk of sexual misconduct.

Many Christian helpers are vulnerable because (1) they pay little attention to their own intimacy needs; (2) they have little direct accountability; and (3) they are frequently exposed to strong human needs and appetites.

Churches, pastoral colleagues, and lay people need to develop "systemic strategies for clergy development toward excellence . . . for the support of clergy in their lives and ministries."[32] Strategies of support can help prevent sexual misconduct and offer support to Christian helpers, particularly the clergy. Since healthy ministers provide good ministry, pastors and counselors must be encouraged to take their own needs seriously, to pursue spiritual disciplines, and to enjoy guarded time for rest and play.

Congregations and denominations must provide pastors with the resources for nurturance and support in ministry. Ministry to ministers must become a high priority throughout the Western church. There is tremendous wisdom in offering professional counseling and retreat resources not only to impaired ministers but, as a preventative goal, to all ministers. There is also a need for peer support groups, outside the bounds of ministerial associations, that are confidential, genuine, risk-taking, and honest about the pain and suffering of ministry.

Finally, churches must have clear ethical and procedural codes for ministry and counseling. Archibald Hart makes the point that even the moral, well-intentioned pastor can get in trouble by helpful action that did not adequately foresee troubling consequences.[33] Ethical codes that guide counselors and ministers through the many moral and legal dilemmas of ministry today are imperative. These codes must be grounded in Scripture, must challenge excellence and competence in ministry, and must be reviewed by and distributed among all church staff and leadership.

TRAINING AND EDUCATING FOR PREVENTION

Ultimately, the church and counseling professions must invest in remedial recovery and, beyond that, must emphasize the primacy of prevention. Helpers need training and education for sexual understanding and control; early assessment and intervention with at-risk counselors; development and maintenance of support systems; and sure, genuine accountability. Church leaders need to consider making sexual misconduct prevention programs a priority in the American church at all levels.

This work should become an integral core to ministry training in colleges, Bible schools, and seminaries and must be carried on in denominations, dioceses, and local churches and parishes. This training needs to include a comprehensive understanding of sexual dynamics in counseling and current law and ethics regarding sexual misconduct. We must also deal decisively with the high number of teachers and supervisors who require or pursue sexual favors from students and interns. Education programs need to incorporate more thorough testing and evaluation of potential pastors and therapists, screening and targeting those at risk for intensive prevention work.

Though not infallible, reliable tools for testing and assessing risk for sexual misconduct are available. Skilled Christian clinicians can reasonably predict those who have the character defects and psychological liabilities that will hinder their success in handling sexual temptations. Retreats and sabbaticals for the over-stressed minister should be made a high priority. Pastors and counselors need training on how to deal with sexual feelings aroused in the helping context. Men at risk should be challenged to explore unresolved parent/child relationships and how these relate to sexual and emotional relations with other women. Again, we advocate that careful examination of underlying psychodynamic issues should be a vital part of the training process of every therapist and minister. In addition, this work ought to emphasize the importance of quality marital and peer relationships as foundational to effective ministry.

CONCLUSION

In the previous chapter we stressed that rehabilitation and restoration of the sexually exploitive helper is a difficult, tenuous, and often treacherous road. While some people are certainly able to recover and return to helping ministry, many are not, and they face an uncertain future once their misconduct is uncovered. In this chapter we have emphasized the importance of preventing sexual exploitation. People at every level of preparing helpers for counseling work must do a much better job identifying at-risk helpers and trainees so they can receive appropriate help to change and become effective counselors. Those whose risk is too great must be transferred out of the counseling and ministerial professions. Clearly, there is much work yet to do to help prevent counselors and ministers from getting trapped in the beguiling web of sexual misconduct.

NOTES

1. Peter Rutter, *Sex in the Forbidden Zone* (Los Angeles: Jeremy P. Tarcher, 1989), 7.

2. Helmut Thielicke, *The Ethics of Sex*, trans. John W. Doberstein (Grand Rapids: Baker, 1964), 24–25.

3. See chapter 6.

4. For additional information on this point, see Henry Virkler, "When Temptation Knocks: Reducing Your Vulnerability," *Christian Counseling Today* 2, (Summer 1994): 39–43.

5. Jeff Harkin, *Grace Plus Nothing* (Wheaton: Tyndale, 1992), 61, emphasis in original.

6. For example, see Harry Schaumburg, *False Intimacy* (Colorado Springs, Colo.: NavPress, 1992); and Robert Hicks, *The Masculine Journey* (Colorado Springs, Colo.: NavPress, 1993). In addition, review chapters 2 and 3 of this book.

7. Andre Bustanoby, "Counseling the Seductive Female," *Leadership* 9, no. 1 (1988): 51.

8. LaHaye, *If Ministers Fall*.

9. Ibid. (54)

10. Rutter, *Sex Zone*, 54.

11. Rediger, *Ministry and Sexuality*, 122.

12. Ohlschlager and Mosgofian, *Law*, 74.

13. Randy Alcorn, "Strategies to Keep from Falling," *Leadership* 9, no. 1 (1988): 42–47.

14. Rutter, *Sex Zone*, 41.

15. See Sonne and Pope, "Treating Victims," 180.

16. Bustanoby, "Counseling the Seductive Female," 52.

17. Ohlschlager and Mosgofian, *Law*, 74.

18. Rutter, *Sex Zone*, 215.

19. Schoener, et al., *Psychotherapist's Sexual Involvement*, 469.

20. For a fuller treatment on this issue, see Schoener et al., *Psychotherapist's Sexual Involvement*, 462–464.

21. Ibid.

22. For a fuller treatment of the practice and legal dimensions of supervision and consultation see chapter 21 of Ohschlager and Mosgofian, *Law*.

23. See chapter 13 for further information regarding legal issues related to supervision.

24. For example, see C. Stoltenberg and U. Dalworth, *Supervising Counselors and Therapists* (San Francisco: Jossey-Bass, 1987); F. Kaslow, *Supervision and Training: Models, Dilemmas, and Challenges* (New York: Haworth Press, 1986); K. Hess and A. Hess, *Psychotherapy Supervision: Theory, Research, and Practice* (New York: John Wiley, 198; and Richard Leslie, *Practical Applications in Supervision* (San Diego: The California Association of Marriage and Family Therapists, 1990).

25. See J. Andrew Cole, "Eroticized Psychotherapy and Its Management: A Clinical Illustration," *Journal of Psychology and Christianity* 12, no. 3 (1993): 262–

67, who (except for use of a quote for our law book that is taken out of context and used poorly to make an otherwise good point) has written an excellent article on the clinical and supervisory aspects of this issue.

26. Gary Schoener, et al., *Psychotherapist's Sexual Involvement*, 487.

27. Rutter, *Sex Zone*, (62–63).

28. Ibid., 103.

29. Review chapter 10 and the comments of Howard Chua-Eoan, "After the Fall," *Time*, 9 May 1994, 58.

30. Quoted in Pope, "Therapist-Patient Sex," 229.

31. Rediger, *Ministry and Sexuality*, 82.

32. Ibid., 123.

33. Archibald Hart, "Being Moral Isn't Always Enough," *Leadership* 9, no. 2 (1988): 24–29.

Chapter Sixteen

Waging War on Sexual Abuse

You are the light of the world. A city on a hill cannot be hidden. Neither do people light a lamp and put it under a bowl. Instead they put it on its stand, and it gives light to everyone in the house. In the same way, let your light shine before men, that they may see your good deeds and praise your Father in Heaven.

Matthew 5:14–16

PEOPLE DWELL IN MANY TYPES OF PLACES, including houses of church and government. We are the light of the world, and we are called to bring the light into these houses—houses that need the light of good deeds, which will result in praise to our Father in Heaven. Jesus' words are a cry to boldly enter our worlds and our churches, to live the life of Christ, and to proclaim healing, renewal, and change.

We urge the church united—mainline and conservative, episcopal and congregational, Protestant and Catholic—to take assertive action against the agonies of sexual abuse within its pastoral, lay, and counseling leadership. We want the church universal to allow God to heal, redeem, and transform our sexuality. We hope this chapter helps individuals, churches, and organizations to envision a way to do this, united in common purpose and strong in the power of Christ.

LIGHT IN THE DARKNESS

We believe that sexual sin has been accepted, tolerated, and even embraced in Western culture and the church. We are a culture under serious sexual seduction and, as a result, we are bearing the awful fruit of sexual sin barely restrained. Canice Conners (author of chapter 10) said it succinctly, "You can't lie and expect change. This issue can't thrive without secrecy."[1]

We proclaimed in chapter 1 the need to blow the flickers of candlelight into a bright flame—light to drive out the sexual misconduct darkness. In this final chapter, we proclaim the light of Christ to a variety of arenas. First, this light must bring change to ourselves and to our families. Then we can best take it to the counseling professions, to the church, and to all the communities in which we live: church, town or city, county, state, and nation.

The war against sexual misconduct in the church and counseling ministry must be fought on multiple fronts. Evil structures and corrupted systems must be challenged systemically; new policies and remedial resources must be implemented and honorably practiced. Changing policy and battling unjust social structures (which seems to be the preferred approach of many mainline churches) is insufficient to win the war.

Challenging individual sin in perpetrators' lives and healing its evil impact on individuals must also be given high priority. An individualistic strategy by itself, however, which is the common preference of the evangelical and conservative church, is likewise deficient warfare. We proclaim the necessity of tying together both individual and systemic strategies to wage successful war. We believe even more is needed: spiritual warriors who, with the weapons of prayer, intercession, deliverance, networking, and community action, will do effective battle in the heavenly realms.

WILLIAM WILBERFORCE: THE POWER OF ONE LIFE IN CHRIST

William Wilberforce changed the course of history by his opposition to the English (and worldwide) slave trade in the eighteenth and nineteenth centuries. A Cambridge graduate, knowledgeable, well-spoken and witty, he was the only son in a prominent British merchant family. Twenty-one-year-old Wilberforce came to London in 1780 as a newly elected member of Parliament. His story is an example of what one person can do, in the power of Christ, to change a nation, to change the world.

London's high society—dynamic, decadent, full of intrigue, and fascinating to a young man—drew Wilberforce into its web. At the time, the international slave trade was a major source of wealth for the nation, as well as revenue for the government. The manifest horrors of this trade were far removed from London society, a community drunk on the considerable profits of an evil commerce that helped fuel the industrial revolution just beginning to take shape.

Young William's political career skyrocketed and by his mid-twenties Wilberforce was among the most influential leaders in England. On a trip to the European continent, he ran across his old schoolmaster, Isaac Milner, who challenged him with the claims of Christ. Wilberforce began reading the Bible and became confused and ill at ease in his soul. He sought the counsel of John Newton, Anglican cleric and former slaver who penned the famous hymn, "Amazing Grace." Young William heeded Newton's counsel to follow Christ and maintain his political career, which included opposition to slavery—a position his London contemporaries and law-making colleagues thought daft.

By 1787 Wilberforce, who had become a passionate slave trade abolitionist, began to introduce his abolitionist agenda into English Parliament. Initially introducing parliamentary resolutions for *discussion* of the trade, Wilberforce used these innocuous actions to rail at the horror and injustice of the trade. Opponents essentially denied the horrors of the trade and argued smugly that no action could ever be taken against an industry that undergirded over half the nation's economy (an argument not unlike that of the tobacco industry today).

For the next ten years Wilberforce submitted a bill for abolition into the English Parliament; every year it was defeated, sometimes by the slimmest of margins. During these years Wilberforce and the Clapham community (a group of fellow Christians and abolitionists) became a powerful force for moral, social, and political reform on a number of fronts in British society. At the death of his friend William Pitt, the dedicated abolitionist William Greenville became prime minister. This shifted the tensely balanced political equation in favor of abolition. Reversing the pattern of twenty years, Greenville and Wilberforce introduced the abolitionist bill first into the House of Lords and, after a month of bitter debate, it passed on February 4, 1807.

The House of Commons was primed and ready for historic action; stirring debate was climaxed by praise of Wilberforce and his

once-impossible cause. The entire House stood to cheer and applaud the now middle-aged man, later passing the resolution to
abolish slavery by a vote of 283 to 16. Wilberforce, realizing his
long battle was over, sat in his chair with head in hands, unable to
suppress the tears that streamed down his face.

It would take a quarter-century to dismantle the evil system in
England. Three days before his death in 1833, Wilberforce witnessed the final blow to the slave system in Parliament. As he lost
consciousness for the last time, he whispered, "Thank God that I
should have lived to witness a day in which England [gave up
millions of pounds] for the abolition of slavery."[2]

COMING FULL CIRCLE

As Christians, we need to openly challenge, even to tear down
the institutions that enslave people in sexual sin. This new slavery—truly a worldwide, multi-billion dollar commerce fueled by
lust, greed, and power—is promoted and protected under the seductive banners of sexual liberation and freedom of choice. The
rampant destruction to body, soul, and spirit of millions of sex-
enslaved people cries out for our involvement so that the liberating
grace of Jesus Christ can truly set people free.

As we argued in earlier chapters, the natural or carnal self (biblically speaking) is inherently polygamous (oriented toward and
pursuing sex with as many different women or men as possible).
This is the nature of the beast to be tamed at the Cross and con-
quered by the resurrection of Christ. Nothing short of this is truly
curative. Christ is also the King of kings over the systemic, patriarchal wickedness—the corporate counterpart of the individual sin.
He will conquer all that supports, justifies, rewards, hides, lies for,
and further abuses the victims of polygamous, patriarchal abuse.

Power over Patriarchy Protecting Polygamy. It is the power of sin
multiplied exponentially in the perpetuation of evil systems—
patriarchy protecting polygamy—that gives this sexual epidemic
such resiliant strength. We must soberly acknowledge these abusive power structures and how resistant they are to change exerted
by counter-forces, no matter how noble and right and necessary
those forces are for good. This acknowledgement will lead us all
to draw deeply from the only power that will overcome—the
power of Christ.

The power of God must be in the forefront of this war, for these
structures are not merely man-made nor can their power be

determined by purely quantitative analysis. They are also fueled by dark powers, the "spiritual forces of evil in the heavenly realms," (Eph. 6:12) under the leadership of the satanic ruler of this world. Churches and theologies that deny or underestimate the power of sin and the evil nature behind unjust structures will continue to experience sexual abuse in its worst forms, shattered and confused by its persistent presence.

THE COMPREHENSIVE NATURE OF THE BATTLE

Our primary goal in this book is to foster the abolition of sexual misconduct in the church and the helping professions—a battle that will likely rage the remainder of our lives. Comprehensive action involves four realms (four levels of personal and systemic intervention) that need the influence of Christ to redeem human sexuality and challenge the epidemic of sexual abuse. This comprehensive scope covers domains of influence from personal and family, to the community, to larger systems and, finally, to the universal or heavenly realm.

We address each of these in turn and challenge Christians in counseling professions and the church to prepare to do battle against the forces that seek to undermine the dominion of Christ, who alone is pre-eminent. We heartily agree with Colson's observation that, "Changing the habits of a darkening age may require something far grander than our individual efforts, something beyond the reach of most of us."[3] It is not an easy mission. Nevertheless we must press on, as Wilberforce did unrelentingly, to make this happen for the sake of Christ, for His church, for our nation, and for the redemption of those who are without Christ's love.

I. MICRO-SYSTEMS: THE PERSONAL AND FAMILY CHALLENGE

PERSONAL ASSESSMENT AND DEDICATION TO CHANGE

Before action in any of these realms, the Christian must first consider the redemptive work that God seeks in each heart. Dedication to moral purity, sexual healing, freedom from sexual sin, and the reshaping of personal priorities that puts God's Kingdom first must be an ongoing process in the life of the Believer. Compulsive sexual sin and sexual addiction are pervasive problems among many Believers—dark and shameful secrets that rob individuals and, ultimately, the church of the peace and power that God desires to pour forth. The Believer must be encouraged to challenge this double standard. The church must assist rather than punish and deny this essential work in order to know the creation of a pure heart and an empowered church.

The Christian must also seek to know and define the realm of service that gives life to others in need, including the challenge to redeem the institutions and systems of church and world government. Calling the church to clean up its act first has always been God's priority, then it is able to challenge the world in power. "The Church . . . does not leave the world to its own devices, but . . . summons it to submit to the dominion of Christ. [Therefore, the Church is concerned] with the secular institutions themselves in accordance with the will of God."[4] The goal is not to Christianize those worldly institutions, but to hold them accountable to the law of God in Christ: to confront evil and to stand against its power in the love of Christ.

TRANSFORMED FAMILY LIFE

We encourage helpers to let their lights shine before their children, to train their children to become the very best citizens of church and state. We need to challenge our children to be students and scholars that excel, not primarily to do well financially, but to change the world for good. We need to promote opportunities for sacrificial service (especially toward those less fortunate and in crisis) in our churches and communities. We can help our children create and join communities of young people who enjoy building relationships that are not obsessed with sexual contact but that emphasize worshiping, playing, serving, sharing, learning, suffering, and living together.

We must avoid buying into our materialistic, hedonistic culture—one that promotes adversarial parent-child relations. We must find ways to talk honestly to our pubescent sons and daughters about God's good sexual creation, while stopping any insidious collusion and unspoken communication that their sexiness is a means to power and the highest good. We need to focus a lot more of our attention toward equipping our children to be warriors for the Kingdom of God and peacemakers in the Body of Christ. It is not an easy task—in fact, it is neither desirable nor possible without the power of Christ—but it is an essential duty if our children will be saved from the darkness that is spreading across the world.

II. MID-LEVEL SYSTEMS: IMPACTING COMMUNITY INSTITUTIONS

COUNSELORS AND CHURCHES WORKING TOGETHER

As we mentioned earlier, some churches and denominations have been extremely neglectful in implementing sexual misconduct policy or have avoided it altogether. The net effect of this failure to promote healing and justice in the church is the perpetuation of great harm to many victims. This resistance to change by some is causing harm to the whole church, as the state takes an increasingly invasive role against all churches to stop harmful sexual practices.

Sexual abuse is a major contributor to personal moral failure and spiritual paralysis, marriage and family breakdown, social dysfunction, hidden pain and ministerial impotence in the church, and degradation in the life of the community. While many practices contain varied programs for victim's healing, few programs are comprehensive, especially in small town or rural practices where abuse rates are often as high as in cities.

We propose that local churches and counseling ministries develop and implement comprehensive sexual abuse treatment and recovery programs. In order to bring the gospel to the sexually broken, we must break the false sexual and doctrinal barriers and our pious inhibitions about talking honestly of sexual things (there is a Christ-honoring way to do this!). We must learn that sexual addicts (both heterosexual and homosexual) "can change, [and we must] deal with [our] own disgust and prejudice, befriend . . . sexual strugglers and stick with them through the change process."[5]

COMMUNITY PROGRAM FOR COMPREHENSIVE SEXUAL ABUSE TREATMENT

We outline below a developing model for community sexual abuse recovery services and challenge Christian counseling professions and the church to adopt and integrate this model in local communities.

Comprehensive Scope. We propose a program that offers a comprehensive scope of services applied to the special needs, resources, and limitations of the local community. It would network extensively with church and community services (including current intervention networks) and would honor victim protection as a primary objective throughout the process (especially in cases of family incest). This program would also include the integral goal of family reunification as a primary though selective outcome.

Quality and Comprehensive Evaluation. The service program should include accurate, comprehensive, and high-quality evaluation of sexual abuse—both current and past. The assessments must be comprehensive in scope, including psychosocial, medical, and spiritual elements. In addition, assessments should include play therapy and sand-tray for evaluation and treatment. Assessments need to include preparation for expert courtroom testimony and child/adult advocacy.

Multiple Modes of Victim Treatment. Victim treatment programs would cover many aspects, including structured ongoing treatment groups for women, children, adolescent, and male victims. Treatment programs need to integrate individual and group counseling and should aim toward justice, confrontation, and legal action assessment and advocacy. It is also necessary to plan toward intensive treatment and referral (day treatment and full or partial hospitalization) for severe dissociation (MPD) and other traumatic dysfunction. Finally, the program needs to be strongly linked to church and community support services for victims in separated families and for victims of Christian counselors, pastors, and workers.

Treatment of Sexual Offenders. Offender treatment programs should begin with a careful evaluation of the types of programs available, extensive training, and continuing education. In addition to individual counseling, there must be structured treatment groups for offenders. Training would also need to evaluate the use for polygraph assessment and training. This service would include coordinated relations with courts, district attorney's offices, and parole/probation. Offender treatment must distinguish predators from those who have or can develop victim empathy, remorse, and moral conscience. Consideration should be given to treatment, restoration, removal, and restraint of offenders in Christian ministry. The program must define and balance the tension between victim protection and offender restitution. Finally, it would be wise to consider joining the national professional group ATSA (Association for the Treatment of Sex Abusers).

Family Reunification. Family treatment and reunification issues must include assessing families for probability of successful reunification, accepting that some families cannot be reunited and be safe. Ancillary treatment and support for spouses and children of victims should be provided, including family counseling prior to and after reunification. Counselors need to understand and discern boundaries and timing in the role and limits of reconciliation, forgiveness, and intimacy dynamics between spouse and abuser. When appropriate, there should be integrated victim and offender reunification treatment plans. Finally, courts and public social services need to be challenged about their biases against reunification—in some programs the reunification goal has been all but abandoned by the state.

Community Policy and Practice Coordination. Systemic and policy issues to be addressed at the local level would include abuse prevention training in Christian families and churches as well as policy development on sexual abuse and misconduct for local churches. Such a program needs to encourage abuse reporting and offender screening by pastors and churches, and should seek to develop attitudes and ministries of redeeming human sexuality. Community service coordination between various service and ministry elements should be a high priority.

IMPROVING LOCAL GOVERNMENT

The struggle over allocating resources between prevention and remedial treatment is ongoing. Bonhoeffer asks poignantly whether the church's mission is to care for those who have been crushed by the institutions of our making, or should the church "prevent the wheel from crushing them" in the first place?[6] We believe this is not so much an either/or issue, but should elicit a both/and response.

There are many ways to influence local government and improve community institutions in their civil, professional, and sacred expressions, such as involvement with child and adult protective services, membership on boards and commissions, activity with court appointed special advocates, and election to seats on city councils, county seats, school boards, and the like. We can influence ministerial and denominational associations through prayer, service, and leadership. Community organizations need the salt and light of honorable Christian membership. If the conventional wisdom that "all politics are local" is true, then Christians need to be working at all levels to better their communities.

III. MACRO-SYSTEMS: NATIONAL AND GLOBAL POLICY

INVOLVEMENT VS. SEPARATION FROM THE WORLD

Scripture seems to give paradoxical directives to the Believer. On the one hand we are to expect that judgment will come on the earth for the increase of sin and rejection of God. On the other hand, even as the world suffers under the consequences of godly judgment, we are called to be light and salt, to influence the world with love and mercy toward wholeness in Christ. Christians throughout history have responded to the Scriptures either by forsaking all relations with a corrupt world or by being involved in the socio-political system as a loving witness and light-bearer to challenge its corruption. All too often, the conservative church has taken extreme approaches—either divorcing itself from involvement in the secular world or participating only in impossible, confrontational politics (supporting antiabortion violence for example) or attempts to build a theocratic Christian state.

Historically, Christians from Roman Catholic and mainline churches have become involved in politics within government and social change in the society—including at times being co-opted by it—while the conservative-evangelical Christian has shunned these areas. The Roman Catholic Church, a massive global government in its own right, and many Protestant denominations with episcopal and presbyterian forms of government, have made a fairly easy transition to be involved in national government and policy.

The Activist Christian. Today, much to the chagrin and annoyance of irreligious (and even some religious!) society, many conservative-evangelical Christians are beginning to engage dramatically with the social-political arena. Controversies about abortion, gay rights, humanistic education, integrity in government, assaults on the family and religious freedom, the decline of biblical morality, and the rise of drugs and violence are galvanizing Christians to act in the public sphere. While we sometimes wince at the positions and tactics of our brothers and sisters beginning to challenge the state and society, we applaud the involvement of Christians and religious peoples of all persuasions in this crucial sphere of life.

The separatist churches, however, which predominately are made up of conservative orthodox Christians, have especially divorced themselves from participation in the world system, seeing any such involvement as inherently evil. It seems that Christians who do not get involved in changing the political world because they have interpreted the Bible as denying such involvement, tend to denigrate education and intellectual pursuits. They forsake positions of social-political influence, and choose the more "spiritual" roads instead. These Christians have no belief system to support socio-political involvement nor the courage to get involved in these areas. All too often they are isolated in Christian ghettos, sometimes exacerbating the very problems we are challenging with this book—abuses of power, authority, and sexual boundaries. As best, they have little influence in the world that is having greater influence in determining the structures of how they will live.

Dr. Richard Mouw, the president of Fuller Theological Seminary, stated that he is "uneasy about our evangelical tendency to oversimplify complex issues, uneasy with our proclivities toward a pragmatic anti-intellectualism, and uneasy about our arrogant attitude—our *incivility*—toward others of God's children."[7] We see too many conservatives who hold similar views regarding engagement with the world and action in social politics. We are compelled to ask our separatist brothers and sisters to rethink their position toward civil government and the world at large, then make efforts to get involved to influence its direction in more godly ways.

IV. HEAVENLY SYSTEMS: SERVING IN THE KINGDOM OF GOD

The devil, and the fallen angels with him, have been relegated to live in darkness. This darkness does not simply mean "lightless regions" or areas void of visible light. The eternal darkness to which [the] Scripture refers is essentially a *moral* darkness . . . it is the absence of God, who is light. We are not trapped in darkness if we have been born of Light. But if we tolerate darkness through tolerance of sin, we leave ourselves vulnerable for satanic assault.[8]

In Romans, Paul writes that those who do not honor God become "futile in their thinking and their senseless minds [become] darkened" (Rom. 1:21 RSV) This darkness is moral darkness. Paul goes on to describe the digressive process—the spiritual and moral descent—that follows in minds that become so darkened.

> Therefore God *gave them up* in the lusts of their [own] hearts to sexual impurity, to the dishonoring of their bodies among themselves, abandoning them to the degrading power of sin. Because they exchanged the truth of God for a lie and

worshipped and served the creature rather than the Creator. . . . For this reason, *God gave them over* and abandoned them to vile affections and degrading passions. . . . And so, since they did not see fit to acknowledge God or approve of Him or consider Him worth the knowing, *God gave them over* to a base and condemned mind to do things not proper or decent but loathsome; until they were filled—permeated and saturated—with every kind of unrighteousness, iniquity, grasping and covetous greed, [and] malice. . . . They were without understanding, conscienceless and faithless, heartless, and loveless [and] merciless. Though they are fully aware of God's righteous decree that those who do such things deserve to die, they not only do them themselves but approve and applaud others who practice them (Rom, 1:24–32 AMB italics added).

These minds become darkened and God gives them over to progressive degradation as people choose to refuse His Grace. This degradation is primarily spiritual in nature and must be addressed spiritually if the darkness is to be overcome. In Paul's letter to the church in Ephesus, he declares that we do not "wrestle against flesh and blood, but against principalities, powers and rulers in high places" (Eph. 6:12).

SEXUAL SLAVERY PERSISTS THROUGH HISTORY

This pattern has existed through all ages and cultures. It persists today in Western culture as women and children are sacrificed on sexual altars for the sake of erotic pleasure and profit. It is an evil pattern that must be challenged and changed; one that requires battles in the heavenlies as much, if not more than, the battles outlined in the other areas.

Outrageous harm is perpetuated against young children and vulnerable adults for the sake of greed and pleasure, leaving millions scarred and severely harmed. Death, mutilation, trauma, degradation, depression, fears, broken marriages, psychoses, drugs, and pathological fear of God are all elements of the legacy of sexual abuse. Where does a man get the lust to fondle and sexually penetrate a one-year old baby? Where does the lust come from for a man to attack an elderly, disabled woman and brutally rape and murder her? Many factors weave together to shape this type of criminal lust, but one of the key factors flows from the evil power and God-hating rage of the prince of darkness.

Pornography is a worldwide industry involving mega-money. Reprobates with great cunning make incredible profits from the harm and degradation of women and children. This is a spiritual battle at the heart, as the wicked spiritual forces attempt to seduce the generations into their moral darkness. At the crux of the matter lies Satan's fierce hatred toward humans because they are able to procreate. Satan lacks the power of God to create as he wills, and lacks the privilege of man to procreate after his own kind. Since Satan cannot touch God, he seeks to rob God's created beings of life.

Breaking the Pattern of Denial. Too many citizens of the church deny both the power and pervasiveness of evil and its satanic origins. "Most Christians are quite familiar with basic factors such as regeneration, . . . the fruit of the Spirit, . . . but, it seems that relatively few are familiar with the mortal combat between light and darkness. . . . The Bible abounds in references to spiritual warfare. There is an Enemy. . . . We are warned not to be ignorant of his devices."[9] We are at war and war is never pleasant. People we love and treasure are the victims of great sexual harm. Many others we will never meet in this life have suffered greatly because of the wishes of the evil one.

We have, however, the power of Christ that enables us to thwart the forces of evil. Inviting the gifts and power of the Holy spirit, fueled by individual and corporate prayer, combined with individual and corporate action against evil incarnate is promised by God to overcome. In many cases, we even have the power to totally block the evil plans of the evil one and pull people back from the brink of total destruction. We must not faint, and we must continue to do good. If we stand, then our efforts will be redemptive. Every helper must become equipped to deal with spiritual warfare if he or she is to have maximum benefit in bringing change in the four areas of life.

FINAL CONCLUSION

We began this book by noting church leaders who have fallen prey to sexual misconduct within the last decade. Each of those men had significant ministries, many of them had led and fed thousands of Christians. They, and others like them, impacted millions of Christians and non-Christians alike. As a result of their fall to sexual pleasure, however, countless persons have been harmed and many ruined. The cost of sexual sin is high, the likelihood of rehabilitation is difficult, and the possibility of restoration to ministry is increasingly slim.

> *Gather together, gather together, O shameful nation,*
> *before the appointed time arrives and that day sweeps on like chaff,*
> *before the fierce anger of the Lord comes upon you.*
> *Seek the Lord, all you humble of the land,*
> *you who do what he commands.*
> *Seek righteousness, seek humility;*
> *perhaps you will be sheltered*
> *on the day of the Lord's wrath*
>
> *Zephaniah 2:1–3*

Our culture is in desperate need of godly lights—people who will make a difference for good. We need to petition God to renew His deeds and empower us to go forth and cleanse us from the sexual perversion of our lives and culture. We can make a difference!

NOTES

1. Chua-Eoan, "After the Fall," 5, quoting Father Canice Connors.

2. Quoted in Charles Colson, *Kingdoms in Conflict* (New York: William Morrow, 1987), 108.

3. Charles Colson, *Against the Night* (Ann Arbor, Mich.: Servant Publications, 1989): 172.

4. Dietrich Bonhoeffer, *Ethics*, ed. Eberhard Bethge (New York: MacMillan, 1965): 325.

5. Briar Whitehead, "A Better Response to Gay Activism," *The Standard* 11, no. 1 (1994): 8–9.

6. Bonhoeffer, *Ethics*, 321.

7. Richard J. Mouw, "Educating for the Kingdom," *Theology, News and Notes* 41, no. 1 (1994): 4–7.

8. Francis Frangipane, *The Three Battlegrounds* (Cedar Rapids, Iowa: Advancing Church Publications, 1989), 4.

9. From the foreword by V. Raymond Edman in Kurt E. Koch, *Christian Counseling and Occultism* (Grand Rapids: Kregel, 1965), 3.

Appendix A

Model Sexual Misconduct Policies

This Appendix contains documents regarding sexual misconduct policies developed by three different church denominations. The policies represent two possible ways to address sexual misconduct policy and reflect two different types of church government that influence the manner in which the policies are written and carried out. The first policy is authored by the Presbyterian Church of Canada and reflects the values of a presbyterian form of church government. The second policy statement was prepared by the Roman Catholic Archdiocese of St. Paul and Minneapolis and reflects the values of an episcopal form of church government. (These documents have received minor editing in order to prepare them for usefulness to a more general readership than the originally intended denominational audience.)

The Presbyterian Church in Canada

INTRODUCTION

This policy was written in response to the feed-back from presbyteries to the discussion paper on Sexual Ethics for Clergy and Other Professional Church Leaders. . . . Extensive legal counsel was necessary to make sure that the policy protected the Church as much as possible against civil legal proceedings. The policy is for all ministers, church leaders, staff, volunteers, sessions and congregations, and other groups using church space.

(Editor's note: The English spelling in this document adheres to the British style.)

Table of Contents

A. A complaint against a church leader under presbytery discipline.
Dealing with complaints promptly
Informing the accused
Pastoral and advisory care
Investigating the complaint
When investigation uncovers possible criminal complaint
Interviewing
Reporting to Presbytery
Records
Discipline

B. A complaint against a person not under presbytery discipline.

VII. DISCIPLINE
Disciplinary Procedures of Presbytery and Session
Admonition
Rebuke
Removal from Office or Position
Deposition from Ministerial Office

VIII. CONCLUSION

SECTION 1: THEOLOGICAL BASIS

The policy of The Presbyterian Church in Canada on sexual abuse is set in the framework of what it means to be a sexual person of Christian faith and a servant in the church. Our sexuality, as a dimension of our whole selves, is to be offered to God. In the expression of sexual desires we are called to holiness. God values sexuality as gcod, blessed, and purposeful, both as an expression of love and for the procreation of children. Sexuality is a gift to be celebrated. We are called to be responsible in the use of our sexuality and to respect each other as children, women, and men made in God's image. From this belief in the sacredness of our physical beings we understand and declare that every person has the right to sexual and bodily integrity.

All those who serve the Church, especially clergy, church leaders, staff, and volunteers, are expected to adhere to Christian ethical principles in their sexual conduct and in their exercise of authority and power. The Church and its extended ministries is to be seen as a safe place in the community; a place where it is known that sexual abuse is not tolerated. This is part of our Christian witness to the community. Therefore, the leadership of any group using church premises for its activities is also subject to this policy.

Our commitment is to model the example of Christ and to be rcoted in the love of Christ in all our relationships. For any Christian to betray trust by the grave ethical transgression of sexually abusing another, whether child or adult, is to deny his or her own Christian identity, as well as to deny to the one abused the witness to the risen Christ in the world. Such a betrayal will be a gross injury to the one abused and a violation of faithfulness to Christ. Because of the serious consequences of sexual abuse, the Church must make every effort to ensure that sexual abuse does not occur within its jurisdiction. When such abuse does occur, the Church must make a clear and just response.

It is, therefore, the policy of The Presbyterian Church in Canada that sexual abuse or harassment of any kind by any church leader, staff or volunteer will not be tolerated.

SECTION 2: GUIDING PRINCIPLES

All allegations of sexual abuse or harassment will be taken seriously. Every allegation will be received, investigated, and acted upon in accordance with the terms of this policy.

The accused person is always presumed innocent until proven guilty. In the context of this policy, no adverse finding will be made against an accused until a full investigation is completed and it has been determined that the complaint has been substantiated on a balance of probabilities.

The protection of children is a priority. In accordance with civil law, any allegation of sexual abuse of a child will be reported to the child protection agency immediately.

A person who is alleging to have been sexually harassed shall be informed of the right to seek assistance of and take his or her complaint to the appropriate Provincial Human Rights Commission.

SECTION 3: DEFINITIONS

What is sexual abuse?

Sexual abuse includes, but is not limited to, any unwanted sexual contact.

Sexual contact includes, but is not limited to, sexual intercourse, genital contact, petting, fondling, sexually suggestive language or the display of pornography.

Sexual abuse includes, but is not limited to, sexual assault and other sexual offenses involving children as defined in the Criminal Code of Canada.

Sexual abuse includes, but is not limited to, sexual harassment. Sexual harassment is defined as:

- a course of vexatious comment or conduct that is known or ought reasonably to have been known to be unwelcome, including repeated sexual remarks or physical contact that is degrading;
- a sexual advance or solicitation made by a person who is in a position to grant or deny a benefit to another;
- the threat of or an actual reprisal by a person in authority against a person who has rejected a sexual advance from that person in authority.

Sexual abuse is often accompanied by violence. Violence impairs or destroys mutual consent, which is needed to ensure that sexual activity is voluntary. Sexual abuse therefore includes spousal violence.

Consent

In order not to be abusive, any sexual act must be done by mutual consent of the parties involved. Mutual consent presumes that the parties are on an equal fcoting with each other, so that one person is not pressured by any consideration of the stature or position of the other person.

Clergy and all other church leaders are in a position of authority and trust, which makes the achievement of mutual consent difficult and increases the potential for harm and abuse of those whom they serve.

The pastoral counseling function creates a particular relationship of trust. Exploitation of the trust developed in the counseling relationship through sexual activity is considered to be abuse, and will not be tolerated.

In relationship of unequal power or trust, consent may not exist even when sexual activity has been initiated by the one who feels violated and alleges abuse has occurred. Therefore, the claim of mutually consensual or private sexual contact does not relieve the church leader of ethical responsibility. Sexual contact will normally be considered a serious breach of pastoral responsibility and subject to strict disciplinary action.

Sexual contact between a church leader and parishioner, counsellee, colleague, employee or any person over whom the church leader has pastoral oversight is fundamentally at odds with a pastoral relationship. It is one or more of the following:

- a breach of the trust placed in a spiritual leader;

- an abuse of the power of the minister over the vulnerability of the parishioner, counsellee, colleague or employee;

- a scandal to the Church;

- and a breaking of the vow taken "to conduct yourself in your public and private life as befits a minister of the gospel."

Acceptable Social Relationships

Sexual contact is not invariably defined as sexual abuse. The Church acknowledges that its leaders and members date, fall in love, and marry. The Church is the natural environment in which Christians can develop healthy relationships. Where there is pastoral responsibility, care must be taken not to exploit the pastoral trust while developing a private relationship. The minister or church leader who wishes to develop a mutually loving relationship that may eventually include sexual contact shall ensure that the pastoral needs of the other person will be met by another church leader. Within the bounds of private relationships the church leader is called to the highest standards of Christian ethics. Such relationship is not considered to fall into the category of sexual abuse. This does not imply that sexual abuse or harassment may not occur within such relationships.

Who Is Subject to this Policy?

The term *church leader* means any ordained or designated leader appointed, inducted, installed, or recognized by The Presbyterian Church in Canada or one of its agencies. The term includes ministers of Word and sacraments, diaconal ministers, ruling elders, and certified candidates for ministry. It also applies to all persons given positions of significant authority, power, or leadership within the agencies of the denomination, who are, by virtue of that position, accountable to the discipline of the Church. All people falling into these categories will normally be dealt with by the presbytery.

The term *staff members* refers to people working within the Church under contract or salary. These people may or may not be church members. The term *volunteers* refers to the many church members who donate their time to keep the work and ministry of the Church alive. People falling into these categories are often not subject to the discipline of presbytery but are accountable to the session.

SECTION 4: PREPARING TO IMPLEMENT THIS POLICY

Communication

1. This policy and process of response is to be clearly communicated to all ministers, church leaders, staff, volunteers, sessions and congregations and any other non-church group using church space.

Training

2. It is urgent that members of presbytery make themselves competent to deal with allegations of sexual abuse. The presbytery should arrange for appropriate training seminars as soon as possible for presbytery and session members within their bounds.

Structural Changes

3. A sexual abuse resource person or team, who can provide expert advice, information and support should be set up by synod and available to each presbytery. A network of such persons should be developed through, or in consultation with, the national Ministry and Church Vocations office.

4. A standing committee of presbytery should be appointed to receive, investigate, and recommend the action to be taken on allegations of sexual abuse or harassment. The committee should be not less than four people, with a balance of male and female representation, and should have the power to add. Members of the standing committee need not be members of the presbytery but will be responsible to the presbytery for this function and bound by the appropriate rules of conduct. A standing committee is needed so that, when necessary, allegations may be dealt with immediately.

SECTION 5: RECEIVING COMPLAINTS

1. Allegations of sexual abuse or harassment may be directed to the moderator or the clerk of presbytery, the minister or the clerk of session, or any other appropriate person. Any person who receives an allegation of abuse must direct it to the appropriate channel immediately. Presbytery is the appropriate body to receive allegations made against church leaders. The session is the appropriate body to deal with allegations made against those persons not under the discipline of presbytery. The session can request the standing committee of presbytery to conduct an investigation or to provide help and advice.

2. Any allegation that may involve criminal charges must be reported to the police.

3. In accordance with civil law, all cases of suspected abuse of a child must be reported immediately to the child protection agency. Once the child protection agency has been contacted, their staff will begin an investigation and contact the individuals as they see fit. Under the regulations, only the child

protection agency or the police may question the alleged victim or offender so the investigation may proceed unhindered. However, pastoral support is still appropriate.

4. If the person making the allegation is a third party to the complaint, the allegation may be dealt with by petition. The presbytery or session will investigate the complaint and lay the charges that arise from the incident.

COMPLAINT PROCEDURES: CRIMINAL AND NONCRIMINAL

Determining which procedure to follow.

Different procedures are required for criminal complaints (below) and noncriminal complaints.

1. In determining which procedure to follow, common sense can be a helpful guide: if the allegation seems like it might be criminal, it probably is.

2. The Criminal Code should be consulted. As the code is amended every year it is necessary to consult the current code. By and large, if the allegation involves minors or physical force, it will almost certainly be a criminal matter.

3. Before proceeding on the matter that the presbytery or session suspects might be criminal, it should check with the synod resource team.

4. In making the decision, it is better to err on the side of caution.

Criminal Complaint Procedures

A. A complaint against a church leader under presbytery discipline, requiring criminal investigation.

Who needs to be informed initially?

1. Upon receiving a complaint of a criminal nature the appropriate legal authorities must be informed immediately and section 5, paragraphs 1, 2, 3 and 4 complied with as necessary.

2. The standing committee of presbytery shall be informed as soon as possible that a criminal investigation of a church leader who comes under the discipline of presbytery is under way. The moderator and clerk of presbytery may call a pro re nata meeting of presbytery if they deem it necessary.

3. The committee will assist the child protection agency and/or the police in their investigations, and will approach the accused only on the advice of the police. Each presbytery should acquaint themselves with their local child protection agency at the first possible opportunity, pnor to any need of their services.

Pastoral and advisory support.

4. The committee arranges for a pastoral support structure to be put in place immediately, as follows:

(a) The committee will request the presbytery executive or equivalent to appoint a qualified person to offer pastoral support to the victim and family, if appropriate.

(b) Another person will be appointed to act as an advisor within the courts of the Church for the accused, if appropriate. Such advisor can be refused by the accused. Pastoral support for the accused should be offered.

It is not suggested that an advisor within the Church be a replacement for trained legal counsel within the criminal or civil court of law.

The accused should be cautioned that pastoral confidences may not be protected by the law in Canada, and that the pastoral counsellor or advisor could be required to testify in a court of law, as to matters disclosed by the accused person to him or her.

(c) A further person may be appointed to offer pastoral support to the family of the accused church leader.

(d) Those appointed in paragraphs 4 (a-c) need not be active members of presbytery, but they are responsible to presbytery in these functions.

Avoiding conflict of interest.

5. To avoid conflict of interest, those persons who offer either pastoral support or act as advisors cannot be a member of the standing committee, notwithstanding the limited resources of small presbyteries. If necessary they must withdraw from the committee.

Paid leave of absence while investigation proceeds.

6. During a criminal investigation the person who is the subject of the allegation will be placed on leave of absence with pay. This leave is without prejudice and does not imply the guilt or innocence of the person under investigation. In the case of a moderator of session, the presbytery will appoint an interim moderator for the congregation. During a criminal investigation the presbytery may in its discretion reinstate the accused into his or her position subject to whatever conditions may be appropriate, keeping in mind the possibility of the serious consequences if the accused should commit abuse during the investigation.

(a) A member of presbytery on a leave of absence retains the right to sit and correspond in presbytery, and in particular, has the right to directly address the presbytery on the issue of the allegation of sexual abuse against them.

Informing sessions and congregations.

7. Before the next Sunday service, the moderator of presbytery will meet with the session and inform them of the investigation and assure them of the support of presbytery. The moderator will advise them on the appointment of an interim moderator and make arrangements to conduct worship. Appropriate information should be offered to the congregation at the Sunday service respecting the confidentiality of the information, and having the goal of quelling rumour and speculation.

8. If the investigation lasts so long that financial hardship may result to the congregation, the presbytery must assume part of the financial burden of the salary of the accused.

(a) If a manse is involved, the accused and the accused's family continue to reside in it during the criminal investigation. If the presbytery deems that such close proximity is inappropriate, other suitable residence must be arranged during this time period. Should marital breakup ensue during this period, the presbytery must strive to respond in a supportive and just manner to both parties.

When there is conviction of a criminal offence.

9. A conviction of a criminal offence involving sexual abuse should be considered grounds to administer discipline as outlined in Section 7.

When there is no criminal conviction.

10. If the criminal investigation is inconclusive or the accused is not convicted, the standing committee shall conduct their own investigation in order to recommend appropriate action to the presbytery. (See paragraphs 4, 7, 8 and 9) If the committee finds that, on the balance of probabilities, the church leader has violated the Church policy on sexual abuse, it may recommend that the pastoral tie be severed or the accused person removed from the position held, or any other action it considers appropriate in the circumstances. (See Section VII)

Transfer during investigation.

11. [The accused shall not be transferred to another presbytery without the approval of the standing committee until such investigation and recommendations are completed. If such transfer should take place, the two presbyteries shall co-operate to complete the investigation. Full details of the events leading to the necessity of an investigation shall be disclosed in writing to the second presbytery. A written record of the events surrounding the transfer shall be maintained by both presbyteries. This transfer of information is of vital importance to prevent possible recurrence of abuse.] (Ministry and Church Vocations has asked the Clerks to consider paragraph 11 when they deal with the referral of paragraph 2[b] below.)

Records.

(a) If on a balance of probabilities, the accused is found to be innocent of the allegation, the files regarding the whole matter shall be forwarded to the Clerks of Assembly to be held *in retentis* according to The Book of Forms, section 31.

(b) [If on a balance of probabilities, the allegation is found to be substantiated, the record must be made known to those who might call or hire the church leader in the future. The record shall be noted on the Presbytery Certificate. General Assembly may choose to institute a process that would allow a convicted person to have the information removed from the Certificate after a significant period of time without further incident has elapsed.] (These procedures have not been approved. They were referred to the Clerks of Assembly for report to the 1994 General Assembly.)

Informing sessions and congregations of the result.

13. Presbytery should keep the session informed during the course of the investigation, and especially of any decision made by the presbytery that affects the ministry of the congregation. Session shall be informed of the result of the investigation. The session, in its discretion, may inform the congregation appropriately.

B. A complaint against a person not under presbytery discipline, requiring a criminal investigation.

1. The session must deal with complaints following the same general principles that guide the presbytery under similar circumstances.

2. The session must deal with the matter as soon as it is made known to them. The person accused must be presumed innocent until proven guilty, but may not continue in the position held while a criminal investigation is in process. Salaried staff must continue to be paid while the investigation is in process. Non-church groups may not use church space while being criminally investigated for allegations of sexual abuse. (When necessary services such as day care facilities, are threatened by this policy, the session has a positive duty to facilitate, as far as they are able, the continuation of the service under new leadership.)

3. During a criminal investigation the session may in its discretion reinstate the accused into his or her position subject to whatever conditions may be appropriate, keeping in mind the serious consequences if abuse should occur during the investigation.

4. The session should immediately inform the presbytery that a criminal investigation of sexual abuse is ongoing within the bounds of the congregation. The presbytery may require the session to consult with the standing committee, and/or the sexual abuse resource person or team. The session must not interfere with the police investigation. Pastoral support should be offered to all parties.

5. If the criminal investigation is inconclusive or the accused is not convicted, the session shall conduct its own investigation in order to determine the appropriate action to take. If the session finds that, on the balance of probabilities, the accused has violated the Church policy on sexual abuse, it may remove the person from the position held, or take any other action it considers appropriate in the circumstances.

6. The accused has the right to address session directly during the investigation and on the issue of any determination of discipline.

7. The paragraphs 1, 2, 3, 4, 5, 6, 9, 10, 11, 12, and 13 of Section 6 shall apply, with appropriate wording changes to indicate session instead of presbytery or standing committee.

NonCriminal Complaint Procedures

A. A complaint against a church leader under presbytery discipline, not requiring criminal investigation.

Dealing with complaints promptly.

1. The standing committee must act promptly on all sexual abuse allegations, whether written or verbal, that it receives against church leaders who are under the discipline of presbytery. Presbytery must use its discretion as to whether the person may continue in his or her position during the investigation, attaching any conditions considered appropriate, keeping in mind the serious consequences if abuse should occur during the investigation.

Informing the accused.
2. The accused person will be informed that a complaint has been received and an investigation will take place, whether the complaint has been made in writing or not.
Pastoral and advisory support.
3. The committee should follow the procedure outlined in Section 6, paragraphs 4 and 5.
Investigating the complaint.
4. The standing committee must investigate every allegation, interviewing all parties to the complaint. The sexual abuse resource person or team should be consulted to ensure that interviewing procedures are appropriate. Discretion shall be used to keep the identity of the accused confidential unless otherwise necessary. The committee will:

(a) Meet with the one(s) alleging sexual abuse to hear the accusation directly.

(b) Request a written statement along with any corroborating evidence for the allegations.

(c) Request permission to use the written statement in a meeting with the accused church leader.

(d) Explain the need for the complainant to appear before presbytery if requested.

(e) Explain in detail the process of presbytery investigation of complaints.

(f) Appoint, if required or requested, an advisor to provide pastoral care and advice during presbytery proceedings.

(g) Keep careful and complete written records of its meeting and treat proceedings as confidential.

(h) If the complainant refuses to allow the allegation to be put into writing, or refuses such written document to be used during the investigation, or refuses to appear before the presbytery, the investigation will be seriously hampered. The committee will still interview the accused person, but discipline cannot ordinarily be based on allegations upon which the complainant is not prepared to provide written or verbal testimony.

When investigation uncovers possible criminal complaint.
5. In the course of interviewing the complainant, the committee may discover that behaviour is being alleged which, if directed to the police, would warrant criminal charges being laid. The committee has the duty to inform the complainant that criminal charges may be warranted. If the complainant refuses to go to the police, the committee must seek the guidance of the police, before proceeding to interview the accused.
6. If the conclusion is reached that the police must be informed of the matter, the committee shall revert to the procedures appropriate to criminal investigations.

Interviewing.

7. If there is no suggestion of possible criminal charges, the accused person shall be interviewed. The committee shall:

(a) Meet directly with the accused as soon as possible. The committee has the right to compel an expeditious meeting, with right of appeal reserved for all parties.

(b) Present the complaint to the accused person, whether written or verbal.

(c) The complainant(s) shall not be present at this meeting.

(d) Outline the process followed by the presbytery in dealing with such matters, emphasizing the presumption of innocence and the right to due process.

(e) Hear the response to the complaint.

(f) Request a written statement of the response.

(g) Share the accused person's response with the complainant.

8. The committee shall interview any other party who they reasonably believe to have corroborative evidence or iniormation on the complaint.

Reporting to Presbytery.

9. The standing committee reports to presbytery in camera. The committee may make recommendations, but only the presbytery determines whether the allegation has been substantiated.

Records.

10. If, on a balance of probabilities, the accused is found to be innocent of the allegation, the files shall be forwarded to the Clerks of Assembly to be held *in retentis* according to The Book of Forms, section 31.

11. [If, on a balance of probabilities, the allegation is found to be substantiated, the record must be made known to those who might call or hire the church leader in the future. The record shall be noted on the Presbytery Certificate. General Assembly may choose to institute a process that would allow a convicted person to have the information removed from the file after a significant period of time without further incident has elapsed.] (These procedures have not been approved. They were referred to the Clerks of Assembly for report to the 1994 General Assembly.)

Discipline.

12. The presbytery shall determine what discipline is appropriate in the circumstances. (See Section 7)

B. A complaint against a person not under presbytery discipline, not requiring a criminal investigation.

1. The session must deal with complaints following the same general principles that guide the presbytery under similar circumstances.

2. The session must deal with the matter as soon as it is made known to them. The person accused must be presumed innocent until the allegation is substantiated on a balance of probabilities. Session must use its discretion as to whether the accused person may continue in the office held while the

investigation is in process, attaching any conditions considered appropriate. Salaried staff must continue to be paid while the investigation is in process, whether they continue in their position or not. Session should conduct its investigations promptly.

3. The session may, but is not required to, inform the presbytery of the investigation. Session is reminded that it is of the utmost importance that it become competent to deal with allegations of sexual abuse and harassment, and so is urged to consult with the standing committee, and/or the sexual abuse resource person or team, in order to educate itself at the earliest possible moment. If the session does not feel competent to conduct an investigation, it can request the standing committee of presbytery to do so. Pastoral support should be offered to all parties immediately, if appropriate. The accused person has the right to address the session directly.

4. Session investigates allegations in order to determine whether it is advisable for the accused person to continue in the position held. It may remove the accused from the position held, if deemed appropriate, and/or it may require counselling or other forms of therapy.

5. Session shall refer to paragraphs 1, 2, 3, 4, 5, 6, 7, 8, 10, 11, and 12 of Section 6, with appropriate wording changes to indicate session instead of presbytery or standing committee.

SECTION 7: DISCIPLINE

Presbytery administers discipline of ministers, diaconal ministers, and candidates for ministry. Session administers discipline to members in full communion and baptized adherents of the Church. Types of discipline are listed below.

For other staff members and volunteers who do not fit in the above categories, session can remove them from employment or office.

Disciplinary Procedures of Presbytery and Session

If the allegation of abuse is substantiated, the disciplinary body may invoke any of several sanctions, as deemed appropriate. The offender has the right to address the disciplinary body directly on the subject of the discipline to be administered.

If the offender is a moderator of session, or serving a congregation, the presbytery will inform the concerned session in writing of the action it has taken. A congregational meeting may be called in order that presbytery representatives may answer questions, with follow up visitation to occur within one year.

Admonition: If the abuse is considered isolated and relatively minor, such as a temporary lapse of judgement, then an admonition may be administered. An admonition may only be used if the accused displays remorse. Presbytery, or session must be satisfied that the abuse will not recur in order to use this level of discipline.

Rebuke: If the abuse shows a willful flouting of ethical sexual behaviour, or if the accused person shows an inadequate acknowledgement of the seriousness of the situation, a rebuke may be administered. The rebuke may include a temporary suspension from office without pay, a requirement to

enter therapy, or any other disciplinary task designed to prevent a recurrence
of the abuse. Evidence should be offered that the task has been undertaken.

Removal from Office or Position: If the disciplinary body considers the
abuse has been the cause of severe damage, or will recur in the future, or if
healing of professional relations is not possible, they may sever the pastoral
tie, or remove the accused person from his or her position. The ministerial
certificate shall not be released until the presbytery is satisfied that steps have
been completed to prevent future abuse. Such steps may include therapy,
withholding the certificate for a set period of time, spiritual direction or any
other task set by the presbytery or session.

Deposition from Ministerial Office: When the offender is an ordained or
designated church leader and if the abuse is substantial, involving criminal
acts, violence, abuse of minors, or repeated episodes of abuse, the abuse shall
be treated as gross immorality and the offender shall be deposed from the
ministerial office.

Section 8: Conclusion

Presbyterians must be willing to recognize that sexual abuse and harassment does occur within the Church. This policy is one step in preventing
that abuse and harassment. It should also be adapted for use by all church
agencies and colleges. We must do everything in our power to prevent further abuse by creating healthy environments and sound leadership.
Educational programmes are a necessity and must be initiated and supported
by both the national and local churches.

This policy is the first step in the ongoing process of formulating policy
and educating the Church on these issues.

The Archdiocese of St. Paul and Minneapolis of the Roman Catholic Church

SEXUAL MISCONDUCT BY CHURCH PERSONNEL: EDUCATION AND PREVENTION

The last decade has witnessed an enormous growth in understanding sexual misconduct[1] committed by persons working in the helping professions. Evidence about the long-term impact and the difficulty of detection of such misconduct has received new and much needed attention. Constructive attention has been given to resources for the healthy integration of sexuality into the life of the helping professional.

A traditional Roman Catholic approach to questions of sexuality emphasizes the importance of chastity. We believe that recent psychological and other insights can advance and complement this Gospel value. The intention of all that follows is to promote a ministerial environment in which those who receive the Church's services can expect to do so in safety. . . . This statement details our efforts at education and prevention.

GENERAL COMMUNITY EDUCATION

The Archdiocese of Saint Paul and Minneapolis makes an effort to respond fully to the news media both in answering questions about particular cases of alleged misconduct and in addressing the broader questions raised by such cases. We recognize that our Church has an accountability to the broader society and educative function toward it. We commit to continue this ccoperative effort.

Special efforts have been undertaken to inform and educate Catholics through channels of communication uniquely available to the Church. These include homiletic and other teaching material and the use of the Catholic Bulletin. We commit ourselves to continue to use these special forums.

Educational materials aimed at specific groups, such as clergy or lay ministers, sometimes have broader applicability to more general audiences as well. Our aim is to design materials so that they have broader applications. We encourage their use in parishes and other interested groups.

The publication of this statement, along with those on victim care, intervention with offenders, and the healing of communities, is intended to promote public awareness. This also signals our willingness to encourage responses and discussion in our parishes and other Catholic communities.

SCREENING, FORMATION, AND ONGOING EDUCATION FOR THE ORDAINED

Programs of clergy formation (seminaries and diaconate preparation) have included psychological screening and background checks of prospective candidates for decades. In recent years we have placed even greater emphasis on this screening. Although no perfect screening method exists, we are committed to using the current accepted methods and to continue working with competent professionals in strengthening that screening.

It has been our position that no candidate should be ordained unless he demonstrates the attitudes and behaviors necessary for living a celibate commitment, as a priest or unmarried deacon, or in a faithful marriage, as a married deacon. That position continues in force.

Local clergy formation programs all contain specific curriculum units or classes aimed at promoting positive sexual integration and establishing appropriate sexual boundaries in the practice of ministry. We commit ourselves to the ongoing review and strengthening of such curricula. Those in formation participate in internship programs. Those who know them in that setting are encouraged to comment on all aspects of their fitness for ministry, including their ability to maintain appropriate boundaries.

Seminary and deacon-formation spiritual directors are asked to pay particular attention to psychosexual development concerns. Because they have a confidential relationship with their directees, they cannot compromise that confidentiality in order to serve as a formal part of screening programs. Still, they have an important role in encouraging their directees to develop healthy personal boundaries for ministry or, if this is not possible, to reconsider their vocation.

For several years, the Archbishop has communicated with Archdiocesan clergy on various aspects of specific misconduct cases and changes in relevant laws. This important educational effort will continue.

Seminars and educational materials have been developed and are being developed for use by the clergy. We commit ourselves to make this an ongoing part of our continuing education efforts. Whenever appropriate, these same opportunities will be made available to other church personnel.

No clergy from outside the Archdiocese of Saint Paul and Minneapolis will be given the general faculties of this Archdiocese until we have received a thorough background reference from his religious superior or diocesan bishop. Such a reference must include information about any past allegations Of sexual misconduct, financial wrongdoing, and physical violence.

The Archbishop has encouraged priests for over a decade to participate in priest support groups. Such groups help to prevent misconduct by strengthening the positive supports for our clergy. We will continue to promote this and other encouragements to healthy living, including the use of a spiritual director, annual retreats, continuing education, and regular meetings with a vicar bishop.

SCREENING AND EDUCATION FOR PARISH PERSONNEL

Decisions about the employment of paid staff and the engagement of volunteers in parishes are made in the parishes themselves. Except as specifically stated below or in some other Archdiocesan publication, parishes remain free to establish their own criteria for the engagement and supervision of paid staff and volunteers. From time to time, the Archdiocese also will give suggested guidelines, which are offered to the parishes for their adoption or adaptation.

As an exception to this general principle of discretion, all parishes are required to perform background checks on certain personnel before engaging them in service. (A copy of the full Archdiocesan policy on background checks, by which the Archbishop makes this an Archdiocesan statute, is available from The Chancery', 226 Summit Avenue, Saint Paul, MN 55102).

Pastors and ministerial professional associations are encouraged to provide some form of regular education about sexual issues in ministry for their staffs, volunteers, and members. The Archdiocese will provide educational materials and forums from time to time. Pastors, groups of parishes, and professional organizations are also encouraged to seek out their own resources from among the many available in the Twin Cities. Archdiocesan officials, and especially the vicar bishops, vicar general, chancellor, and Center for Ministry are willing to assist in designing specific programs.

SERVICES TO PEOPLE HARMED BY THE
SEXUAL MISCONDUCT OF ROMAN CATHOLIC CLERGY

Catholic priests and deacons occupy important places of service in the life of our Church. We are proud that most do so with extraordinary generosity and care. In recent years, however, we have learned more about the misuse of position and power by some clergy. This statement is directed to people who believe they or someone close to them has been harmed by the sexual misconduct of the Roman Catholic clergy.

We are open to and respect your complaint.

Both justice and compassion call us to respond to the harm you have known. We are concerned to uphold the integrity of our Church's witness and ministry. The pastoral care of our community is aimed at the good of those who receive it. We want to correct the hurt that may occur when pastoral care is exercised improperly. Your complaint helps us to do so. Therefore, we respect the report you make.

Our Church law also protects the rights of those accused of misconduct. We ask you to understand that our immediate willingness to respond to your complaint and provide you assistance is not a "conviction" or judgment of the accused priest or deacon. The steps we will take with the accused are outlined in another statement that is usually attached to this statement. If you have not already received it, we will provide copies of that statement to you at your request.

We will respond to every complaint of sexual misconduct by clergy, insofar as we are able. As it is difficult and sometimes impossible to follow through on anonymous complaints, we will ask you to reveal your identity to Archdiocesan officials to assist our investigation. If you ask us to withhold your identity from the accused clergyman, this can severely limit the steps we can take.

We will provide an advisor/advocate if you so choose.

We recognize that bringing a complaint of misconduct to the Archdiocese can be a frightening process. It also can be time-consuming, since the questions involved are often complicated ones. Still, we want the process to move as rapidly as it reasonably can.

We have found that the process works best when the person bringing the complaint has the support of a knowledgeable companion, often referred to as an advisor/advocate. You may already have an advisor/advocate, such as a counselor, a Church staff member, an attorney, or a friend. We urge you to utilize their support throughout the process.

We want to make you aware of a special resource. A group of Protestant and Catholic churches across Minnesota has provided training to individuals who understand what support is available to you. They have been trained to promote your interests and direct you toward the services from the churches or other sources. A written statement of the advisor/advocate's responsibilities is available on request from the Chancery.

We will help you obtain counseling support.

Misconduct by a member of the clergy can cause deep hurt. This can be addressed through the assistance of skilled and reputable professional therapists.

We will try to help to make sure that financial restraints **do not** prevent you from receiving the competent therapeutic assistance of your choice. We will try to help you with insurance copayments for counseling or, where insurance is lacking or insufficient, with your therapy costs. From time to time, we will review with you the ongoing necessity **and** appropriateness of further assistance from the Archdiocese.

We will provide information about support groups.

As society's awareness of these problems grows, self-help and facilitated support groups are multiplying. We are fortunate to live in an area where such groups are respected and active. We make an effort to keep track of what may be available. Please ask, and we will provide the information we have.

We will help you obtain spiritual direction.

The damage caused by clergy misconduct is sometimes spiritual as well as psychological. We have learned from those who have been harmed that sometimes their relationship with God and with their faith community has been ruptured.

You may wish to address such a spiritual rupture. Generally this can only be done after other psychological issues have been addressed. When you are ready to do so, we can help you find competent spiritual help. Once again, we will try to ensure that financial constraints do not close this avenue for you.

There are several centers in the Twin Cities which are staffed by trained spiritual directors who understand the impact of sexual abuse on spiritual growth. Their staff members include women and men, lay people, religious and priests. Please speak with us if you need such help.

We will help you bring your concern to the proper church officials outside our Archdiocese.

Because of the mobility of our society, some people were hurt by clergy elsewhere before moving to the area of the Archdiocese. You may wish to pursue a complaint in another place, but do not know how to do so. We will assist you in contacting the leadership of other dioceses, religious orders, or denominations. If you were harmed by clergy elsewhere, we are unable to provide you with financial assistance for counseling or spiritual direction. We will assist you, however, in seeking such support from the diocese, religious community, or denomination from which the accused clergy came.

How to bring a complaint.
There are several ways to bring a complaint:
Write to the Archdiocese. Please mark your letter "Personal and Confidential." Please indicate by what means you would like a response (by phone, by letter, in a meeting).
Call the Chancery. You may also call our chancery (or archdiocesan administration) offices. Please ask to speak either with the vicar general or the chancellor [as they have been designated] to receive the initial reports of complaints.
Call the Advisor/Advocate Coordinator. You may also wish to speak first with our coordinator of advisor/advocacy services. . . . S/He will help you make further connections.
Make a confidential and preliminary call. You may be unsure about whether you wish to bring a complaint. You are welcome to make a confidential and preliminary phone call to the coordinator of advisor/advocates, the vicar general, or the chancellor. Without giving your name or the name of the clergyman in question, you can give a general description of your concern. The person you speak to will describe how the Archdiocese would be able to respond. You can then decide whether to make a formal complaint.
Once again, we want to indicate that we are open to and respect your complaint.

Sexual Misconduct by Religious and Lay Professional Employees, Independent Contractors, and Volunteers

The problem of ministry-related sexual misconduct can involve church personnel other than members of the clergy. The Archdiocese of Saint Paul and Minneapolis is concerned to address ministry-related sexual misconduct by religious and lay professional employees, independent contractors, or volunteers who provide services within parishes and other institutions of the Archdiocese.
When an accusation of ministry-related sexual misconduct is brought against a religious or lay professional employee, independent contractor, or volunteer serving in an Archdiocesan parish or institution, the Archdiocese stands ready to act as a resource to the parish or institution in responding to the matter. However, since our parishes and institutions function independently, they have the responsibility of putting in place adequate guidelines and procedures to address these accusations.
Parishes and institutions should see that those in supervisory positions are sufficiently trained to understand complaints of sexual misconduct and their investigation. If possible, professional counseling should be offered to the victim(s).

The following outlines the essential components that a parish or other institution in the Archdiocese should consider in responding to an allegation. A model parish policy follows at the end of this policy statement.

Receipt of the Allegation and Investigation

The person primarily responsible for investigating an allegation should be the pastor in the case of a parish, or the person who is in a major supervisory position in institutions where the accused is employed, contracted, or volunteering. Each parish or institution should designate and make known the person responsible for conducting an investigation should it be necessary. This person should take great care to see that allegations of sexual abuse of children or legally protected adults are referred to the proper civil authorities, insofar as this is required by the law. Every allegation is to be taken seriously. Upon receiving a complaint the pastor or supervisor immediately should begin an investigation. Early in this process the pastor or supervisor should contact the legal counsel of the parish or institution. The pastor or supervisor should also call the representative of the parish's or institution's insurer. It is in this phase that the relevant facts relating to the allegation are established. The pastor or supervisor should interview the person bringing the complaint. The pastor or supervisor should encourage the complainant to be accompanied by an advisor, friend, co-worker, or family member. Careful notes of the interview should be taken and maintained. In addition, the pastor or supervisor should interview others who may have knowledge of the accusation. If the accused is a member of a vowed-religious community, it is usually appropriate to involve the provincial superior of the accused early in the process.

Intervention

If the investigation establishes that there is substance to the allegation, the pastor or supervisor has the responsibility of meeting with the accused employee, independent contractor, or volunteer. For this meeting, the accused employee, independent contractor, or volunteer should be encouraged to have another person present. The purposes of this meeting are to present formally the allegation and to listen to the accused.

If the employee acknowledges that the allegation is true, then the supervisor should invoke the appropriate disciplinary procedures (including possible termination) as found in the parish or institutional employment guidelines. If the employee denies the allegation, then the pastor or supervisor should consider suspending the employee with pay, or taking some similar action, until a better understanding of the allegation can be gained. If a volunteer acknowledges the allegation as true, then his or her voluntary service with the parish or institution is to be reviewed by the pastor or supervisor; this review may indicate that the person's volunteer service should end. If the volunteer denies the allegation, then the pastor or supervisor should consider stopping the services they provide until a better understanding of the allegation can be attained.

In the event that the accused denies the allegation, the pastor or supervisor should seek assistance in investigating the matter further. Others who may be helpful at this stage include: an attorney, a trustee, Archdiocesan officials, fellow pastors or supervisors. Additional detailed information is gathered by further interviewing the victim, the accused and others who might have direct knowledge of the allegation. The person bringing the accusation and the accused at this stage should be assis~cd by an advisor or friend.

RESOLUTION

After sufficient information has been obtained, the supervisor must make a decision regarding the allegation and its impact upon the parish or institution. The supervisor must either invoke the appropriate termination procedure found in the parish employment guidelines for the suspended employee or volunteer, take some intermediate disciplinary action, or reinstate the individual's employment or service.

A parish or institution may choose to provide psychological assessments, treatment, or aftercare to religious or lay employees, independent contractors, or volunteers. It may be that insurance assistance is also available to pay for such care. This possibility should be reviewed carefully. The Archdiocese is ready and willing to offer the parish or institution's supervisor support and suggestions, but is not in a position to pay for these services.

In all cases, the procedure for discipline or termination of employment must follow the steps laid out by the parish or institution for other instances of discipline or termination. In addition, full cooperation with the civil authorities and adherence to reporting requirements, as determined by civil law, always must be rendered.

RESPONSE TO CLERGY WHO HAVE BEEN
ACCUSED OF SEXUAL MISCONDUCT

This statement is a description of how the Archdiocese of Saint Paul and Minneapolis will respond to those priests and deacons who are accused of engaging in sexual abuse, sexual exploitation, or sexual harassment.

RECEIPT OF ALLEGATION AND INVESTIGATION

The Archdiocese considers any allegation of sexual misconduct by its clergy to be a serious matter. When the Archdiocese receives such an allegation it will immediately begin an investigation and/or refer the matter to the proper civil authorities. The Archdiocese will help the alleged victim to obtain whatever assistance may be required. The Archdiocese is committed to working with the proper civil authorities such as the police and child protection agencies in its investigation of sexual misconduct allegations involving minors and legally protected adults.

Our Church law also protects the rights of those accused of misconduct. Because of the special difficulties surrounding ministry-related sexual misconduct, we must take some responsive~steps quickly. Still, our willingness to do so is not a "conviction" of the accused priest or deacon.

We will use every reasonable means to investigate any allegation of sexual misconduct. The first source of information for the investigation is the person making the allegation. The Archdiocese will ask the person bringing the allegation to allow his/her name to be used. With this permission, the Archdiocese will use this information as part of its investigation. If that person does not want his/her name used, the Archdiocese must discern whether it is possible to investigate without risking the disclosure of the person's identity. If no such investigation is possible, the Archdiocese will discuss that fact with the person, along with the danger that the alleged offender may pose to others. In some circumstances, the Archdiocese's responsibility to those who might be harmed if the activities of the alleged offender are not stopped may require it to conduct an investigation and risk disclosing the identity even of a person who wishes to remain anonymous.

Archdiocesan officials will carefully interview the alleged victim(s) and/or other persons who bring an allegation to gain as clear a picture as possible of the alleged misconduct. The Archdiocese will seek out corroborating witnesses and facts whenever possible. The purpose of the investigation is to get as complete a picture as possible of the nature and extent of the alleged inappropriate behavior; to identify other potential victims; and to make as strong a case as possible for an intervention with the accused if indicated. In certain circumstances when a complaint or claim is in litigation, the ability of Archdiocesan officials to investigate may be dependent on matters pertaining to the litigation.

The second source of information is the alleged offender. At some point in their investigation Archdiocesan officials will interview the priest or deacon, informing him of the allegation made against him and ask for his response (see next section on intervention).

If there is any major discrepancy between the accounts of the alleged victim and the accused, the Archdiocese will utilize whatever other sources of information it can identify. This may involve contacting those in a position to verify or challenge assertions made by the cleric or by the person making the complaint.

INTERVENTION

When there has been an allegation of sexual misconduct, officials of the Archdiocese will meet with the accused priest or deacon and inform him of the allegation. (If civil authorities are also investigating the accusation, we must and will respect their procedures.) The Archdiocesan officials will ask him for his response. Before he begins his response, he will be informed that we can give no assurance of confidentiality and that any information he offers may be used in the courts.

At the intervention the priest or deacon is offered the opportunity to have an advisor/advocate present. It is the cleric's choice whether he wishes to have an advisor/advocate present. The role of the advisor/advocate is to advise the accused on his rights and afterwards to help him review what was said in the interview. He may also wish to have an attorney present.

If the intervention interview raises serious doubts about the accuracy of the accusation, the Archdiocese will use as many resources as possible to investigate further.

One of the Archdiocesan officials in attendance will prepare a written summary of the intervention interview. The accused will have the opportunity to make a response to the summary. The Archbishop will review the summary and any response.

At the time of the interview appropriate restrictions on the ministry of the accused cleric may be imposed. These restrictions could include, but are not limited to: 1) prohibition from contact with the accuser and his or her family; 2) prohibition of or careful monitoring of any contact with persons who share characteristics of the alleged victim (e.g. children, vulnerable adults); 3) prohibition of any ministerial activity.

When a permanent deacon is accused of sexual misconduct the deacon's family will face tremendous strain and will likely be in need of assistance. The Archdiocese will work with the deacon and his family so that they can receive the pastoral and professional support they require.

The Archdiocesan official generally will inform selected co-workers or others in the place of work or residence that an accusation has been made and restrictions imposed. These persons will be instructed to report inappropriate behavior or violations of the imposed ministerial restrictions to a designated archdiocesan official.

Whenever indicated by the investigation, the Archdiocese will refer the accused to a qualified psychological center for an independent and objective assessment. The Archdiocese will require this assessment whether or not the accused admits to any wrongdoing. Agreement to participate in an assessment does not constitute an admission of guilt by the accused. If an accused refuses to be assessed, the Archdiocese will immediately impose restrictions on his ministry while making a decision as to the future of his ministry.

The investigation, intervention interview, and assessment will guide the Archdiocese in making a decision about the accused's continued ministry in the Archdiocese. Options available include: immediate resignation or removal, resolution of the complaint in favor of the accused with full restoration of ministry, or assignment to therapy.

THERAPY

The Archdiocese is committed to providing competent specialized therapy for any of its priests or deacons who engages in or appears to have engaged in ministry-related sexual misconduct.

First, the Archdiocese will share with the treatment provider the information that it has gained from its investigation that may be helpful in the therapy process.

Second, the Archdiocese, through an assigned official, will keep in regular contact with the therapeutic process. This may involve providing additional information about the cleric, restating to the priest or deacon the consequences of non-cooperation with therapy, and being available for a feedback session. This contact of Archdiocesan officials with the therapy process is designed so that it does not compromise the confidentiality of the therapist/patient relationship.

If a priest or deacon is being treated in an outpatient program the Archdiocese will provide that there is appropriate disclosure of the cleric's past behavior to selected co-workers and persons at his residence. These persons will be instructed to report inappropriate behavior or violations of the imposed ministerial restrictions to a designated Archdiocesan official.

The recommendation of the treatment center is essential to the discernment about the scope and nature of the priest or deacon's ongoing ministry. If the Archdiocese has concerns about the recommendation that the treatment center makes, we will review the recommendations with the aid of other competent professionals.

SHORT-TERM AFTERCARE (UP TO THREE YEARS AFTER PRIMARY THERAPY)

As the priest or deacon is preparing to complete primary therapy the Archdiocesan official who has been working with him will develop a behavior contract, in conjunction with the treatment provider and/or other competent professionals. The purpose of the contract is to make explicit what the Archdiocese expects of the cleric in terms of behavior, i.e. what is acceptable and what is not. It also helps to define appropriate boundaries in terms of which (if any) relationships from his former ministerial setting can be maintained and under what conditions. The contract also names members of the cleric's monitoring team and states explicit consequences if the priest or deacon does not adhere to the contract.

The diocesan official who has been the liaison to the priest or deacon will meet with him on a regular basis: at least quarterly during the first two years following therapy; at least semi-annually for the next three years; and, at least annually thereafter.

During the aftercare period there will be clear restrictions on what sort of ministry, if any, the priest or deacon can exercise. These restrictions are designed to prevent the repetition of sexual misconduct by the cleric. A plan of ongoing professional assistance may be established as needed for each individual. This plan could include elements such as ongoing professional counseling, spiritual direction, and the services of other helping professions. Some priests or deacons may be expected to participate in support groups and/or 12-step groups to provide support and peer accountability. Each individual's situation will be reviewed with one or more competent professionals and will be designed accordingly.

The Archdiocese will assign the priest to an appropriate residence. No one returning from treatment will be allowed to live alone or outside of a supervised setting. The residence will be safe both in terms of geography (distant from site of exploitation/abuse) and ministry (minimal contact with persons who share characteristics of victims, e.g. children, vulnerable adults, etc.).

REASSIGNMENT/OUTPLACEMENT

Upon the conclusion of therapy and aftercare a priest or deacon may be assigned to a parochial ministry, be assigned to a non-parochial ministry, or be assisted to resign from all clerical ministry. Some of the factors that will be considered in deciding to return a cleric to active ministry are: feelings of the victim(s), ability to assure the safety of the community or organization to be served, availability of an appropriate assignment.

If the priest or deacon is returned to active ministry the Archdiocese will see that there is a proper level of disclosure of the person's history in the ministerial setting. The cleric will continue to operate under the contract described above.

REVIEW OF PROCEDURES

It has been our practice for several years to review each individual case of an accused clergyman with objective outside assessors who are expert in appropriate responses to sexual misconduct. Recently other Catholic dioceses and other Christian judicatories have formalized their assessment processes by creating outside oversight committees. We hereby give notice of our intention to establish a committee representing various disciplines and perspectives to review the Archdiocese's handling of clergy sexual misconduct cases. The initial membership of the committee will include advocates for victims and clergy, as well as legally and psychologically trained members. The committee will be responsible for several tasks:

1. Reviewing the handling of past cases, paying particular attention to the appropriateness of the placement of the cleric and the response made to the direct victim(s). When the committee concludes there has been some inadequacy in the actions of the Archdiocese in the case they will suggest remedial action.

2. Review and advise about the handling of current cases.

3. Review and advise about the sexual misconduct policies of the Archdiocese to assure that they are realistic, accountable, and professional.

The membership of the committee, as well as its procedures and confidentiality issues, will be determined by the Archbishop.

RESPONSE TO PARISHES EXPERIENCING THE PAIN
OF CLERGY SEXUAL MISCONDUCT

When members of the clergy engage in sexual misconduct, many people may be harmed or affected. This is true not only of those directly involved in the misconduct, but also of the members of the parishes where the clergyman currently serves or served in the past. We outline here the key elements of the responses that we take to help heal this pain. These responses are guided by three key principles.

First, we acknowledge that parishes undergo a complex process of grieving. When people first learn that a respected leader has been accused, there is often a reluctance to believe that the report could be true. This denial is a reflection of our American belief that an accused person is innocent until proven guilty. But the same denial also can create a burden on those who, often after a long struggle, have found the ability to bring forth important information. Denial is usually followed by the other well-known steps in grieving a loss, including depression and significant anger against the accused, the accuser(s), the Archdiocese, and the whole Catholic Church. Only after time passes and the appropriate steps are taken can a congregation truly move on in the accomplishment of its mission.

Second, we also acknowledge that one of the most important elements in healing is that the parish receive information about what happened that is as full and accurate as possible. Information helps dispel the atmosphere of distrust that is fed by rumor, by the sudden departure of a clergyman assigned to the parish, and by the feeling that a "cover-up" is being imposed. Information also assists other victims to come forward, if there were any, and assures that the appropriate steps are taken so that a congregation can truly move ahead.

While committed to disclosure where possible, we also acknowledge that significant limitations on communication may exist. These limitations can include the concern of victims and their families for privacy as well as the need to protect the rights of the accused, especially when lawsuits or criminal action may be threatened. The fact that investigations often yield confusing, contradictory, or unsubstantiated conclusions, especially in their early stages, further limits disclosure.

Third and finally, we acknowledge that the healing of a parish is a multidisciplinary challenge. Our experience has taught us that neither Archdiocesan officials nor a new pastor alone can respond to all of the concerns and problems that arise in the aftermath of clergy misconduct. As a result, we usually involve teachers, therapists, lawyers, and communication experts in a team approach to specific parishes.

RESPONSE IN THE CURRENT PARISH OF THE ACCUSED CLERGYMAN

When a report of ministry-related sexual misconduct by a clergy member is received, Archdiocesan officials work with trained professionals to assess whether the accused priest or deacon can remain in his current assignment while the investigation progresses. If he remains, restrictions may or may not be imposed on his ministry. Whether he remains or leaves, there arc issues of communication to be faced in the parish.

When the Clergyman Is Removed

Credible accusations may result in removal of the accused clergyman from the parish. These steps follow:

a. If the accused is the pastor, a temporary administrator will be appointed in his place. The administrator is informed of the accusation and of the follow-up steps.

b. Key parish personnel will be informed as soon as possible. Depending on the organization of the particular parish, they may include the lay trustees, the professional staff, and the president of the parish council.

c. The pastor or administrator, after consulting with Archdiocesan staff and with the parish leadership, will notify the parishioners about the absence of the accused clergyman. This announcement can happen in several ways, including pulpit announcements, bulletin notices, or a parish mailing. Because the early stages of the investigation can be complex, the first announcement to the parish sometimes will include little information and may indicate only a temporary absence. It also includes, however, an indication that more information will be provided as it becomes available.

d. The investigation of the matter will proceed as quickly as possible, with the assistance of trained professionals, to a decision about the reliability of the accusation and its implications for the ministry of the accused. As soon as possible, the parish will receive a more comprehensive report about the reason for the absence of the clergyman. The parishioners will be told of his resignation, vindication, or other result. Along with this announcement, the parish members may be invited to a parish meeting within the following few days.

e. The meeting is a key step in the process of healing for the parish. It allows for a more complete discussion of the complaint, its investigation, and its implications for the parish. The meeting should include the participation of some or all of the following: archdiocesan official (usually the vicar bishop), pastor or temporary administrator, a facilitator, a therapist, an attorney, and a communications expert. Because it is a pastoral gathering of the parish, non-members are generally excluded.

f.   Following this meeting, a parish team will be formed to assess the immediate results of the meeting and the other issues of healing that arise in the parish. The team includes the pastor or administrator, some or all members of the professional staff, the trustees, and the parish council president. An outside expert usually should meet with the team. The team sets its own mode of operating. It should meet with the vicar bishop at least quarterly for the first year following the parish meeting.

g. In consultation with the vicar bishop, the team arranges for whatever further healing measures are needed in the parish. These may include: further general meetings, a small group process of reflection, a reconciliation service, a request for communication from the resigned clergyman.

When the Clergyman Remains in His Assignment

a. Key parish personnel (as above) are informed of the accusation, of the process of assessment, and of the restrictions that are in place. They are asked to report inappropriate behavior or violations of ministerial restrictions to a designated Archdiocesan official.

b. If there is reason to believe that the accusation will become public knowledge while an initial assessment is being performed, then steps e, f, and g, as above, will be implemented immediately. The accused clergyman will be offered the opportunity to resign rather than remain in his assignment through the assessment, but he will not be required to do so.

c. If the assessment suggests that the accused constitutes a risk for further misconduct, he will be required to resign. Then steps d through f, as above, will be implemented as fully as possible. As discussed above, however, only limited disclosure may be possible, even if the accused resigns.

d. If the assessment suggests that no current risk of misconduct exists, an Archdiocesan official will convene a meeting including the accused and the key parish personnel to whom disclosure was made earlier. They will assess the continued viability of the clergyman's ministry in the parish. Careful consideration should be given to disclosing fully the matter to the whole parish, as in steps d and e, above. This is not required in all cases, but can help avoid a subsequent sense of betrayal should the matter later become public knowledge.

Response in Former Parishes of the Accused Clergyman

Two reasons may cause the Archdiocese to inform members of former parishes of a priest or deacon that he has been accused of sexual misconduct.

The first and more pressing reason is so persons who may have been victims of misconduct in those other settings will know that they may come forward for assistance. The second is to encourage healing of the hurt and betrayal that can result from knowledge of the accusations. Archdiocesan officials will assess the applicability of each of these reasons to each former parish. Generally speaking, the current pastor of the parish will be consulted in making this determination. If disclosure is called for, then the fdlowing steps will be taken:

a. Key parish personnel will be informed of the accusation, the follow-up steps that are planned, and the potential impact of the news on their own parish. They will work with an Archdiocesan official to plan together for the best way to inform the parish as a whole, or at least those subgroups in the parish that may be affected by the news.

b. The pastor, after consulting with Archdiocesan officials and the parish leadership, will notify the parish of the accusation against their former clergyman. The announcement of disclosure also indicates that some process for immediate follow-up has been put in place. This is generally a parish meeting, but other options might be a parish "hot line," or opportunities for individual meetings with a counselor.

c. Key parish personnel will form a team to assess the ongoing impact of the disclosure in the parish. The team should meet at least once with the vicar bishop, about 3–6 weeks after the initial disclosure. More meetings can be scheduled if needed.

Continued Assessment of These Responses

The steps described above have emerged from our own experience with these questions and from the reflections of an ecumenical group concerned with the healing of congregations. We recognize that these steps leave wide latitude for implementation in different situations. Further experience and more study, by ourselves and others, will contribute to the formation of better response patterns. We pledge ourselves to find these.

NOTES

1. The terms "ministry-related sexual misconduct" and "sexual misconduct," as used throughout this statement, refer to three related forms of misconduct. The first, which is sexual contact between a church leader and a minor or vulnerable adult, is often called "sexual abuse." The second, which is sexual contact between a church leader and a person who is receiving pastoral care from the church leader, is often called "sexual exploitation." The third, which is unwanted sexualized conduct or language between co-workers in the church work setting, is often called "sexual harassment." All three are addressed here together because they have this in common: usually each involves an abuse of power or authority. State statutes give legal definitions of each of these. Such definitions either are appended to this statement or are available from the Archdiocese of Saint Paul and Minneapolis, 226 Summit Avenue, Saint Paul, Minnesota 55102.

Appendix B

The American Center for Peace and Justice: Proposal for a National Religious Court and Center for Alternative Dispute Resolution in the American and Worldwide Church

The strife is over, the battle is done,
the church is split, which side won?

Blessed are the peacemakers," said the King of Kings in his Sermon on the Mount. "For I, the Lord, love justice," declared the great prophet to Israel. These words of God, spoken by Jesus (Matt.5:9a) and through Isaiah (Is.61:8a), are the foundations of a proposal for 21st century ministry of peace and justice to the American and worldwide church.

We propose that the church of Jesus Christ—conservative and liberal, Catholic and Protestant, independant or denominational, large or small—yield its sexual misconduct (and eventually other) disputes to Christ-centered justice that seeks peaceful resolution of these conflicts. We further challenge the government, at both state and federal levels, and the insurance industry to recognize and support this action as a necessary first step in systemic transformation. If we as a modern American culture are to avoid a dangerous escalation of church/state conflict—an eventual "balkanization" and war over religious and cultural values—there may be no other way out.

The American Center for Peace and Justice (Center) is proposed as a national and global center for specialized ministry service, education, research, training, consulting, and dissemination of the peace and justice of Christ. We believe the submission of sexual misconduct (and eventually other church) disputes to a religious court and various kinds of non-litigated dispute resolution aligns the church with the biblical revelation of justice and reconciliation. We think such action will yield real justice for both victim and violator and a true peace for relations between church and state.

Approaching Deadlock

We confess to being distressed by the seriousness of the problem—at the no-win dilemma—the church faces in its relations with the state over the issue of sexual misconduct. The state, angered by growing misconduct reinforced by church ineptitude and resistance, begins to pass laws to force the church to protect its congregants or face severe state sanctions (like Texas has just done with its new criminal sexual exploitation law—see chapter 13). The church reacts to this state action as the aggrieved victim of secular state abuse, an argument with some (and only some) validity as the state overreaches unjustly into church affairs. Church-state "war" ensues and both church and state ultimately lose. This foreboding secenario seems to be advancing in our nation much more rapidly than we predicted in our law book.

Also distressing is the growing rate of suit between victims and perpetrators, including those employed in church ministry. The apostle Paul chided the Corinthian church for having lawsuits at all—charging them with defeat for having allowed their disputes to have gone so far and for resolving them publicly outside the Body of Christ. (1 Cor. 6:1-8) The world looks at the church and justifiably challenges, "So what's the difference Christ makes??" The Center, especially if geared initially to sexual misconduct dispute resolution, can provide church and state a powerful forum for lawsuit avoidance by the facilitation of true justice and real peace.

Hope in Christ. Christ, of course, does make a difference. Good misconduct policies honor Christ and are prevention-oriented. When the church is already in trouble, however, assertive remediation is needed guided by the Holy Spirit. We propose this Center as a national resource for remediation through a ministry of justice and reconciliation. The religious courts and dispute resolution programs of the Center could assist the just healing of victims, facilitate proper action toward offenders, and can save the church from the otherwise inevitable state legal oppression that will harm the entire church. Even more, as an intentional experiment in twenty-first century church-state harmony—serving the citizenry of both church and state—the Center could also assist the creation of true community that shows God's alternative to the failed and false ideologies of the world.

The Case for Church-State Harmony

Charles Colson has instructed Western culture about the proper relationship of church and state—and the vital need for both institutions:

". . . men and women need more than a religious value system. They need civic structures to prevent chaos and provide order. Religion is not intended or equipped to do this; when it has tried it has brought grief on itself and the political institutions it has attempted to control. An independent state is crucial to the commonweal. Both the City of God and the city of man are vital to society—and they must remain in delicate balance. "All human history and culture," one historian observed, "may be viewed as the interplay of the competing values of these . . . two cities;' and whenever they are out of balance, the public good suffers."[1]

There are two parallel governments ordained by God, one civil (Romans 13:1-5) and one ecclesial (Colossians 1: 13, 18; 1 Timothy 3:1-5). These two governments—both church and state—are accountable to God for their behavior, and ought to learn how to work in harmony in order to fulfill God's mandate. Government is ordained by God for specific purposes; primary is the power of the sword—the police power—in order to protect society from chaos. We agree with Bonhoefer who asserted that, "It was sin that made necessary the divine institution of government."[2] Paul's letter to the Roman church confirms this truth, "Everyone must submit himself to the governing authorities, for there is no authority except that which God has established. The authorities that exist have been established by God."[3] Government is from God and serves Christ by its very existence, either consciously or unconsciously, acknowledged or not.

The witness of church to state. Government must delicately balance and not abuse its enormous powers. The church is called to witness righteousness and justice and hold the government accountable to do what God intended. When salt and light withdraws from that mission, then it contributes to government dysfunction. Likewise the church will not be able to remake or control or, especially, replace government without abuse or injustice. That government is ordained for a future day and belongs in the fulfillment of God's Kingdom. Attempts to create or enforce that now, by promotion of a dominion theology and the creation of theocratic America, fail to acknowledge God's current ordination of dual governments and is doomed to failure.

The creative and power-contending tension existing between church and state is necessary in this world. It continually draws men and women to Christ and His life-changing solutions—the brokenness of the world and the personal and structural inability to fix it by human power alone causes the person to look toward the supernatural. If government does what God intended for it to do, then it fulfills its true purpose, the maintenance of order and the dispensing of justice. If it follows some other darker course, as it has in so many idolatrous varieties throughout the twentieth century, then the congregation of Christians are able to declare Christ through their suffering.

Using the state to discipline the church. As God uses the church to witness to government, He also uses government to check and challenge the church, especially when the church and its leaders becomes apathetic and lose their way. Without repentence and correction, which God will plead to the church and give many opportunities to turn, by default the government then becomes the instrument God uses to protect the innocent and impose justice on the church. We see this operating now in America as state governments increasingly impose justice on sexually wayward pastors and churches. "Through its service towards the Christ, government is ultimately linked with the Church. If it fulfills its mission as it should, the congregation can live in peace, for government and congregation serve the same Master."[4]

Protecting precious rights. Religious freedom and religious tolerance are fundamental both to democratic government and to a social order that supports the widest possible freedoms. Our First Amendment, separating and balancing the powers of church and state, has wonderfully protected religious

freedom from state power. This First Freedom also protects people and institutions from the imposition of a religion sanctioned by the state. Without
a renewed church and a revitalized government, it will be greatly strained in
the future to hold the delicate balance that has served this nation so powerfully for over two centuries. We hope the Center, by taking many disputes
out of the abusive arena of litigation, might serve the nation as one resource
that will maintain this dynamic balance and facilitate respectful church-state
realtions well into the twenty-first century.

ALTERNATIVE DISPUTE RESOLUTION

Little in life is more unpleasant than involvement in a lawsuit—even the
winners rarely experience the joyful fruits of victory. Alternatives to
adversarial litigation are advancing on many fronts in the legal world and
across the globe. In 1850, Abraham Lincoln instructed our American fore-
bears to "discourage litigation. Persuade your neighbors to compromise
whenever you can. Point out to them how the nominal winner is often a real
loser—in fees, expenses, and waste of time." Warren Burger, former Chief
Justice of the Untied States Supreme Court held that "the entire legal profession (lawyers, judges, and law school teachers) has become so mesmerized
with the stimulation of the courtroom contest, that we tend to forget that we
should be healers of conflict. For many claims, trial by adversarial contest
must, in time, go the way of the ancient trial by battle and blood. Our system is too costly, too painful, too destructive for a truly civilized people."
    Models of Ecclesial Dispute Resolution. Nearly five-hundred programs of
alternative dispute resolution (ADR) operate outside of or in conjunction with
the formal judiciary in the United States. These include church courts, community mediation programs, victim-offender reconciliation, legal mediation
and arbitration, and many other forms of conflict resolution.[5] The growing
and varied programs for Christ-centered peacemaking grounded in the
church are hopeful to us. Some of the best examples include:
    1. *The Christian Conciliation Service (CCS).* CCS is a growing nationwide
network of attorneys, pastors, and mental health profesionals trained in mediation and arbitration of church and community disputes. Disputants agree
to bring their matter to a panel of mediators trained in biblical conflict resolution and engage in a process of discussion and conciliation. If agreement
cannot be reached, disputants may elect arbitration, including legally binding arbitration, with agreement to abide by the panel's ruling. CCS stresses
forgiveness and reconciliation, while avoiding the high adversarial costs of
time, money, and unresolved feelings of hatred and victimization.
    2. *The Catholic Church Tribunal.* Every Catholic diocese has a formal tribu-
nal that hears cases on the nullity of marriage. For a thousand years these
tribunals have followed church (canon) law (which does not recognize civil
divorce). Tribunals are presided over by judicial vicars, aided by judges,
priests, and lay people with canon law training and degrees. Petitioners are
assigned lawyers to represent their interests and help guide the judicial process.
Annulment of marriage must be confirmed at the appellate level to be recognized—appeals are automatic to the archdiocesan court. The supreme court of

the Catholic Church is the Rota in Rome, where disputes and appeals that shape Catholic policy and influence canon law are heard.

3. The ecclesial courts of the Presbyterian Church. Presbyterian courts hear disputes brought as violations of the Presbyterian constitution, following the "Rules of Discipline." Cases fall under two broad categories: remedial or disciplinary actions. Remedial cases correct or order actions by a church body; discipline involves individual for violations of morals, ethics, or doctrinal error. The session of elders—the local governing body of a church—convenes at the reception of a complaint and seeks to resolve the matter at the local level. Higher courts at presbytery, synod, and general assembly levels hear appeals of continuing disputes. Decisions have less to do with precedent than with biblical principle, appeals to justice and reconciliation, and the rightness of the cause.

4. The Martin Luther King Dispute Resolution Center (MLK). MLK represents a different manner of biblical peace-making—one geared to stopping community violence in south-central Los Angeles by resolving neighborhood disputes and conflicts. Dedicated to the nonviolent legacy of Martin Luther King, MLK mediates a wide range of community disputes—family conflicts, landlord/ tenant disputes, disputes among neighbors, and consumer/merchant conflicts. Avoidance of court and police intervention is a major objective, with disputants given equal standing to have their concerns heard and respected.

5. The Alban Institute. Another unique form of Christian dispute resolution flows out of the Alban Institute in Washington, D.C. The Institute trains and consults with churches nationwide on issues of conflict management and mediation, long-range planning, team-building, and church growth. A central goal is to develop deep interventions in a church. These go beyond resolving the immediate problem to analyze deeper dispute patterns and give churches new structures and procedures to resolve conflicts and live together as Christ intends.

CENTER MISSION AND OPERATION

The Center would be empowered—by the church, the state, and the insurance industry—to hear cases, mediate disputes, and enact arbiter justice. The Center will help resolve sexual misconduct matters across the conservative Protestant, mainline Protestant, and Catholic church worlds. It will promote healing and restitution for victims, to punish or restore violators, and to promote healing and reconciliation in the church. Eventually, it would also serve as a national center for ADR training, research, and consulting across a wider range of church disputes and issues.

Created as a non-profit service institution and financed by development grants from major church denominations, major foundations, and interested governments, the Center would eventually be supported by a combination of fees for services, operations grants, and donations from nationwide sources. It could function as a free-standing Center or, ideally, as an administrative unit connected to a well-known graduate school or seminary or national service ministry. Accordingly, the Center should have broad and diverse support—cosponsored or endorsed by such major national groups as the Christian Conciliation Service, National Association of Evangelicals, National Conference of Catholic Bishops, National Council of Churches, American Association of Christian Counselors, American Association of Pastoral Counselors, Christian Legal Society, and major church denominations and other ministries. It should be staffed by a multi-disciplinary and theologically-diverse professional group—pastors, theologians, lawyers, judges, mental health professionals, researchers, policy analysts, academics on sabbatical, and administrators.

Dispute resolution process. As its first and foremost objective, the Center would be constructed to hear and resolve sexual misconduct complaints and disputes. These disputes would come from the church, parachurch ministries, the mental health and other professions, academia, and from business and government. Courts would refer matters to the Center, easing crushing court dockets and using court enforcement powers to assist action accountability. The Center would also seek involvement of the insurance industry, hoping to show them that justice of this sort, that victim restitution without exorbidant legal costs is good business and good national policy.

By themselves or through legal or other agreed representation, disputants would bring their cases to be heard by center panels, describing the alleged wrong and stating the relief sought. Panels would consist of no less than three or no more than five members, with sensitivity to the parties to the dispute, involving a mix of pastoral, legal, and mental health professionals specially trained in mediation and arbitration. Beginning with the least restrictive intervention, panels would be empowered to engage in mediation, then arbitration, or finally bindng arbitration to bring a dispute to just closure. The parties to the dispute would agree to abide by the decision, with denominations, local churches, and even local courts assisting the outworking and accountability to panel decisions.

Conclusion

Over time, the institute could expand the range of disputes it hears, eventually becoming an expert "court," a dispute resolution center of last resort before litigation, violence, and disollution of the church. It could also develop as a national information resource, research and training center, and advocate for peace-making alaternatives to violence and litigation. America, both its church, its federal government, and its state needs such a resource as we enter the 21st century.

NOTES

1. Charles Colson, *Kingdoms in Conflict* (New York: William Morrow/Zondervan, 1987), 47–48.
2. Dietrich Bonhoeffer, *Ethics,* ed. Eberhard Bethge (New York: MacMillan, 1965), 335.
3. Romans 13:1

4. Bonhoeffer, *Ethics*. 346.
5. See Sherrill Kushner, ed., "Divine Intervention," *Los Angeles Lawyer* (1988), 10–19, and related articles on "Catholicism," by Fr. Michael Moodie, and "Presbyterianism," by Daryl Fisher-Ogden; and L. Randolph Lowry, "Reconciliation: Both Sides Win," *Christian Legal Society Quarterly* 11 (Summer 1990), 4–8, and companion articles, "In Ethnic Neighborhoods," by Dennis Westbrook, and "In the Church," by Speed Leas.

Appendix C: Practice Forms

1. Disclosure/Consent Form for Homosexual Persons
(suggested with reference to Texas law)

A. Therapist Disclosure

As a Christian helper and licensed professional counselor (or _____)
I honor both the goals of Holy Scripture and Texas law in the delivery of
counseling services. No client is ever refused professional services based on
race, religion, gender, color, disability, national origin, socio-economic status,
or sexual orientation. This policy reflects my deep respect for the cardinal
professional ethic of client self-determination. I accept that the coercive
imposition of therapist values on a client is wrong, *including imposing one's belief
for or against homosexuality*. I also acknowledge the common reality that
homosexual clients come into therapy either confused and distressed or wanting to embrace or to change their homosexual behavior.
Therefore, I have a three-track counseling policy with homosexual persons:

1. I offer assessment and decision-making services to the homosexual
   person who presents with confusion and emotional distress about
   homosexuality.

2. I make professional referral to other licensed mental health professionals with persons who decide or desire—whether it be strong or
   weak—to affirm and assimilate his or her gay and lesbian practices.

3. I offer reparative therapy to the ego-dystonic homosexual who decides or seeks out counseling with a desire—strong or weak—to
   change or control his or her homosexuality.

This policy of therapeutic practice, respecting the differing client beliefs, desires, and goals about homosexuality, honorably fulfills both my duties to the Word of God and to Texas law. Assessment and decision-making services are an authorized form of "Counseling Methods and Practices" that integrate "individual counseling" and "assessing and appraising." (Rules of the Texas State Board of Examiners of Professional Counselors, [hereinafter stated as Rules], sect. 681.26 [1] and [16]). Referral is done according to the standards of "referral counseling." (Rules, sect. 681.26 [10]) Reparative therapy is an authorized, integrated form of "individual counseling," "rehabilitation counseling," and "sexual issues counseling." (Rules, sect. 681.26 [1], [6], and [9].) This policy fulfills my professional obligation to deliver "mental health services" that help clients in "resolving emotional, attitudinal, and relationship conflicts" and in "modifying feelings, attitudes, or behaviors that interfere with effective, emotional, social, or intellectual functioning." (Rules, sect. 681.33 [a] [1] [C] and [D].)

Lastly, but critically important, there is no practice by me nor can it be reasonably construed from this policy that I engage in any "sexual exploitation" or "sexual abuse" that "is offensive or creates a hostile environment" or "is sufficiently severe or intense to be abusive to a reasonable person in the context" by "making sexually demeaning comments to or about an individual's sexual orientation." (Rules, sect. 681.33 [g] [1] [A] [B] [4].)

B. Client Consent

As a prospective client of _____ I have read this disclosure, discussed it with this therapist, and understand its meaning and implications. I give my full consent to this policy and honor this practice as stated above. This therapist has respected my feelings and struggles around these issues and has honored my right to choose my goals and the best way of counseling to achieve them. My discussions about these issues with this therapist have proven that they honor this policy without violating the laws of God or the state of Texas.

Client Signature_____
Date_____

Therapist Signature_____
Date_____

2. Background Checks Regarding Sexual Abuse History

Employers of counselors, including churches, should screen prospective employees regarding previous acts of sexual exploitation. This implies the freedom to discuss the applicant's history with previous employers—a right inhibited by the fear of defamation suits if the prospect is not hired. Sexual abuse history screening is now mandatory in Texas (for previous five years) and Minnesota (for previous seven years), and other states will likely follow this pattern.

The recent explosion in sexual misconduct cases has brought focus to preventing continued abuse by offenders, especially those prone to re-offend in new job settings. Since offenders lie about and hide their abuse histories, careful screening of job applicants has become essential. Tragically, churches and ministries have become offender work targets because hiring procedures have been so lax. (If you have the skills and profess the right doctrine, you are often hired.)

PROTECTING YOURSELF FROM LIABILITY

We suggest the following steps for counselors to protect themselves and their agencies or churches from the legal consequences of inadequate hiring practices.

Application forms should include a request for valid licensure and relevant certification and list, with current addresses and phone numbers of all training and ministry experience. Inform applicants that previous supervisors and employers will be contacted and asked about the applicant's skills, abilities, limitations, professional judgment, ethics, sexual misconduct problems, or any concerns about their work. In addition, the applicants should answer the following questions:

1. Has disciplinary action ever been taken against you by a licensing board, professional association, or school?
2. Are there complaints pending against you before any of the above named bodies?
3. Has a civil lawsuit or criminal action ever been filed against you for your professional work or is any such action pending?
4. Have you ever been asked to resign or been terminated by a training program or employer?

If the applicant answers YES to any questions, require a detailed explanation, including evidence of the matter's disposition.

APPLICANT CONSENT STATEMENT

Close your application with the following consent statement:

"All information in this application is true to the best of my knowledge. I state and certify that I have not been convicted of a crime involving criminal sexual conduct, obscenity, or criminal assault nor have I been convicted of any such offenses in any other state or against the laws of the United States. I further state and certify that I have not been terminated from a former position nor have I been the subject of any disciplinary action or investigation because of sexual exploitation, sexual abuse, sexual harassment, or physical abuse by me with anyone. I understand that any misstatement, omission, or distortion may be cause for denial of appointment or for summary dismissal from this agency/church.

I authorize agency/church leadership to consult in detail with past and present employers, supervisors, and schools about my competence, character, and ethical qualifications. I further authorize agency/church leadership to conduct a criminal conviction records investigation, as may be required by the law of this state. I release from liability this agency and its duly authorized representatives for all actions performed in good faith in the evaluation of my application and background. I also hold harmless all individuals and organizations who provide information to this agency in good faith and without malice concerning my professional competence, ethics, character, and other qualifications.

I agree to notify this agency of any changes in my job or training status, licensure, censure or sanction by professional bodies, or any other information relating to my ability to perform my job at this agency/church."

Dated_____ Signed_____

Bibliography

Alcorn, Randy. "Strategies to Keep from Falling." *Leadership* 9, no. 1 (1988): 42–47.

Allender, Dan, and Tremper Longman III. *Bold Love.* Colorado Springs: NavPress, 1992.

American Association for Marriage and Family Therapy. AAMFT *Code of Ethical Principles for Marriage and Family Therapists.* Washington, D.C.: AAMFT, 1988.

American Association of Pastoral Counselors. *AAPC Handbook.* (Fairfax, Vir.: AAPC, 1991).

American Law Institute, *Restatement (Second) of Torts,* (St. Paul, Minn.: ALI, 1965), section 46, comments d–j.

American Psychiatric Association. "The Principles of Medical Ethics with Annotations Especially Applicable to Psychiatry," *American Journal of Psychiatry,* 130 (1985): 1057.

———. *Diagnostic and Statistical Manual of Mental Disorders.* 4th ed (DSM–IV) Washington, D. C.: American Psychiatric Association, 1994.

American Psychological Association, "Ethical Principles of Psychologists and Code of Conduct," *American Psychologist* 47 (1992): 1597–611.

Anderson, Ray. "A Theological Perspective on Human Personhood," Syllabus for the course Theology of Personhood. Fuller Theological Seminary, 1977.

Anderson, Theodore. "Psychotherapist-Patient Sexual Contact After Termination of Treatment: A Reply." *American Journal of Psychiatry* 149 (1992): 985.

Appelbaum, Paul, and Linda Jorgenson. "Psychotherapist-Patient Sexual Contact After Termination of Treatment: An Analysis and a Proposal." *American Journal of Psychiatry 148* (1991):1466–73.

————. "Dr. Appelbaum and Ms. Jorgenson Reply," *American Journal of Psychiatry* 149 (1992): 987–99.

Augustine, Bishop of Hippo. *The Confessions of St. Augustine.* Orleans, Mass.: Paraclete, 1986.

Auster, Simon. "Psychotherapist-Patient Sexual Contact After Termination of Treatment: A Reply." *American Journal of Psychiatry* 149 (1992): 986.

"Backlash Against Survivors: The False Memory Syndrome Foundation." *Off Our Backs* 24, no. 2 (1994): 10–13.

Baker, Anthony, and Sylvia Duncan. "Child Sexual Abuse: A Study of Prevalence in Great Britian." *International Journal of Child Abuse and Neglect* 9 (1985): 457–67.

Barker, Jeffrey. "Professional-Client Sex: Is Criminal Liability An Appropriate Means of Enforcing Professional Responsibility?" *UCLA Law Review* 40 (1993): 1275–340.

Barth, Karl. *Church Dogmatics,* III: 2, Edinburgh: T and T Clark, 1958.

Bates, Carolyn, and Annette Brodsky. *Sex In The Therapy Hour: A Case of Professional Incest.* New York: Guilford Press, 1989.

Becker, Judith V., and J. H. Hunter. "Evaluation of Treatment Outcome for Adult Perpetrators of Child Sexual Abuse." *Criminal Jusice and Behavior* 19, no. 1 (March 1992): 74–92.

Belser, E. "BBSE Joint Hearing with the Board of Psychology: Public Input Sought Regarding Dual Relationships." *NASW California News* 17, no. 5 (February 1991): 6.

Benetin, Juanita, and Mary Wilder. "Sexual Exploitation and Psychotherapy." *Women's Rights Law Reporter* 11, no. 2 (1989): 121–35.

Benowitz, Mindy. *Sexual Exploitation of Female Clients by Female Psychotherapists: Interviews with Clients and a Comparison to Women Exploited by Male Psychotherapists.* Unpublished Doctoral Dissertation, University of Minnesota, Minneapolis.

————. "Comparing the Experiences of Women Clients Sexually Exploited by Female versus Male Psychotherapists." *Women and Therapy* 15, no. 1 (1994): special issue.

Bera, Walter. "Betrayal: Clergy Sexual Abuse and Male Survivors." *Dulwich Centre Newsletter* 3, no. 4 (1993): 62–75.

Berlin, Fred, and E. W. Krout. "Pedophilia: Diagnostic Concepts, Treatment, and Ethical Considerations." *American Journal of Forensic Psychiatry* 7 (1983): 13–30.

Berliner, Lucy, and J. R. Conte. "Sexual Abuse Evaluations: Conceptual and Empirical Obstacles." *Child Abuse and Neglect* 17 (1993): 111–25.

Berry, Jason. *Lead Us Not Into Temptation.* New York: Doubleday, 1992.

Besharov, Douglas. "Doing Something about Child Abuse." *Harvard Journal of Law and Public Policy* 8 (1985): 539–89.

Bess, B., and Y. Janssen. "Incest: A Pilot Study." *Hillside Journal of Clinical Psychiatry* 4 (1982): 39–52.

Black, Henry C., et. al. *Black's Law Dictionary.* 5th ed. St. Paul: West Publishing, 1979.

Blume, E. Sue. *Secret Survivors: Uncovering Incest and Its After Effects.* New York: John Wiley and Sons, 1990.

Bonhoeffer, Dietrich. *Ethics*. Ed. Eberhard Bethge. New York: The MacMillan Co., 1965.

Bouhoutsos, J. C., J. Holroyd, H. Lerman, B. R. Forer, and M. Greenberg. "Sexual Intimacy Between Psychotherapists and Patients." *Professional Psychology: Research and Practice* 14, no. 2 (1983): 185–96.

Bowman, Jim. "Cardinal Joseph Bernardin: Shepherd Enfolded by His Flock." *Commonweal* 20, no. 22 (1993): 6.

Braceland, F. "Historical Perspectives on the Ethical Practice of Psychiatry." *American Journal of Psychiatry* 126 (1969): 230–37.

Brock, Raymond T., and H. C. Lukens. "Affair Prevention in the Ministry." *Journal of Psychology and Christianity* 8, no. 4 (1989): 44–55.

Brown, Laura, Debra Borys, Anette Brodsky, Nannete Gartrell, Jacqueline Bouhoutos, Virginia Davidson, Shirley Feldman-Summers, Glen Gabbard, Judith Herman, Silvia Olarte, Kenneth Pope, Melba Vasquez, Rina Folman, Joseph George, Hannah Lerman, Peter Olsson, and Janet Sonne. "Psychotherapist-Patient Sexual Contact After Termination of Treatment: A Reply." *American Journal of Psychiatry* 149 (1992): 979–80.

Brubaker, David R. "Secret Sins in the Church Closet." *Christianity Today* 36, no. 1 (1992): 30–32.

Bustanoby, Andre. "Counseling the Seductive Female." *Leadership* 9, no. 1 (1988): 48–54.

Butler, S. "Sexual Contact Between Therapists and Patients." Unpublished doctoral dissertation, California School of Professional Psychology, 1975.

California Association of Marriage and Family Therapists. *Practical Applications in Supervision*. San Diego: CAMFT, 1990.

Callanan, K., and T. O'Connor. *Staff Comments and Recommendations Regarding the Report of the Senate Task Force on Psychotherapist and Patient Sexual Relations*. Sacramento, Calif.: Board of Behavioral Science Examiners and Psychology Examining Committee (now Board of Psychology), 1988.

Callahan, Sidney. "Memory Can Play Tricks and So Can Therapists." *Commonweal* 120, no. 22 (1993): 6–7.

Canadian Council of Catholic Bishops. *From Pain to Hope*. Ottawa: CCCB, 1992.

Canadian National Population Survey. *Sexual Offences Against Children: Report of the Committee on Sexual Offences Against Children and Youth*. Ottawa: Canadian Government Publishing Centre, 1984.

Carlson, Margaret. "Full of Grace." *Time* 143, no. 11 (1994): 37.

Carotenuto, Aldo. *A Secret Symmetry: Sebina Spielrein Between Jung and Freud*. New York: Pantheon Books, 1982.

Carr, Melanie L., G. E. Robinson, S. E. Stewart, and D. Kussin. "A Survey of Canadian Psychiatric Residents Regarding Resident-Educator Sexual Contact." *American Journal of Psychiatry* 148, no. 2 (1991): 216–20.

Chesler, Phyllis. *Women and Madness*. San Diego, Calif.: Harcourt Brace, 1989.

Christian Association for Psychological Studies. *Ethical Guidelines for the Christian Association for Psychological Studies*. Temecula, Calif.: CAPS, June 1992.

Chua-Eoan, Howard. "After the Fall." *Time* 9 May 1994, 56–58.

Cole, J. Andrew. "Eroticized Psychotherapy and Its Management: A Clinical Illustration." *Journal of Psychology and Christianity* 12, no. 3 (1993): 262–67.

Colson, Charles. *Kingdoms in Conflict*. New York: William Morrow/Zondervan, 1987.

————. *Against the Night*. Ann Arbor, Mich.: Servant Publications, 1989.

Comiskey, Andrew. *Pursuing Sexual Wholeness*. Lake Mary, Fl.: Creation House, 1989.

Committee on Women in Psychology of the American Psychological Association. "If Sex Enters Into the Psychotherapy Relationship." *Professional Psychology* 20 (1989): 112–15.

Conte, Jon R., Steven Wolf, and Tim Smith. "What Sexual Offenders Tell Us about Prevention Strategies." *Child Abuse and Neglect* 13 (1989): 293–301.

Crabb, Larry. *Inside Out*. Colorado Springs, Colo.:NavPress, 1988.

Crewdson, John. *By Silence Betrayed: Sexual Abuse of Children in America*. Boston: Little-Brown, 1988.

Davies, Bob, and Lori Rentzel. *Coming Out of Homosexuality: New Freedom for Men and Women*. Downers Grove, Ill.: InterVarsity Press, 1993.

DeDomenico, Gisela S. "Sand Tray World Play: A Psychotherapeutic Technique for Individuals, Couples, and Families." *The California Therapist* 5, no. 1 (1993): 57.

Driese, John J. "A Priest Looks at Priest Pedophilia." *Commonweal* 121 (April 1994): 13.

Drummond, Edward. "Psychotherapist-Patient Sexual Contact After Termination of Treatment: A Reply." *American Journal of Psychiatry* 149 (1992): 983.

Duhl, Bunny, and Frederick Duhl. "Integrative Family Therapy." In *Handbook of Family Therapy*. Vol. 1, ed. A. Gurman and D. Kniskern. New York: Bruner/Mazel, 1981.

Edman, V. Raymond. Foreword in Kurt E. Koch, *Christian Counseling and Occultism*. Grand Rapids: Kregel Publications, 1965.

Eliot, Diana M. "The Impact of Conservative Christian Faith on the Prevalence and Sequelae of Sexual Abuse." Paper presented at the Christian Association for Psychological Studies, 1991.

Eysenck, Hans J., and D. K. B. Nias. *Sex, Violence and the Media*. New York: St. Martins Press, 1978.

Feldman-Summers, S., and G. Jones. "Psychological Impact of Sexual Contact Between Therapists or Other Health Care Practitioners and Their Clients." *Journal of Consulting and Clinical Psychology* 52, no. 6 (1984): 1054–61.

Finkelhor, David. *Sexually Victimized Children*. New York: Free Press, 1979.

————. *Child Sexual Abuse: New Theory and Research*. New York: Free Press, 1984.

Fischer, J. "State Regulation of Psychologists." *Washington University Law Quarterly* 58, (1980): 639.

Fisher-Ogden, Daryl. "Presbyterianism." *Los Angeles Lawyer* (1988): 10–19.

Forer, B. R. "The Taboo Against Touching in Psychotherapy." *Psychotherapy: Theory, Research and Practice* 6 (1969): 229–31.

Fortune, Marie. *Is Nothing Sacred? When Sex Invades the Pastoral Relationship.* San Francisco: HarperCollins, 1989.

————. "Betrayal of the Pastoral Relationship: Sexual Contact by Pastors and Pastoral Counselors." In *Psychotherapists' Sexual Involvement with Clients: Intervention and Prevention.* Ed. G. R. Schoener, et.al. Minneapolis: Walk-In Counseling Center, 1989.

Frangipane, Francis. *The Three Battlegrounds.* Cedar Rapids, Iowa: Advancing Church Publications, 1989.

Frankel, T. "Fiduciary Law." *California Law Review* 71 (1983): 795–836.

Freud, Sigmund. "Observations on Transference-Love: Further Recommendations on the Technique of Psychoanalysis." In *The Standard Edition of the Complete Psychological Works of Sigmund Freud.* Vol. 12., ed. and trans. J. Strachey. London: Hogarth Press, 1958.

Friedrich, William. "Sexual Victimization and Sexual Behavior in Children: A Review of Recent Literature." *International Journal of Child Abuse and Neglect* 17 (1993): 59–66.

Friesen, James. *Uncovering the Mystery of MPD: Its Shocking Origins . . . Its Surprising Cure.* San Bernardino, Calif.: Here's Life Publishers, 1991.

Froula, Christine. "The Daughter's Seduction: Sexual Violence and Literary History." *Signs: Journal of Women in Culture and Society* 11, no. 4 (1986): 621–44.

Fulero, S. "Insurance Trust Releases Malpractice Statistics." *State Psychological Association Affairs* 19, no. 1 (1987): 4–5.

Gabbard, Glen O. "Psychotherapists Who Transgress Sexual Boundaries with Patients," prepared for the *Bulletin of the Menninger Clinic,* October 1992. Presented at the conference on "Assessment, Treatment and Supervison of the Professional Who Has Engaged in Sexual Misconduct," Minneapolis, Minnesota, February 19, 1994.

Gardner, Richard. *Sex Abuse Hysteria: Salem Witch Trials Revisited.* Cresskill, N.J.: Creative Theraputics, 1991.

Gartrell, Nancy, J. Herman, S. Olarte, M. Feldstein, and R. Localio. "Psychiatrist-Patient Sexual Contact: Results of a National Survey, I: Prevalence." *American Journal of Psychiatry* 143, no. 9 (1986): 1126–31.

————. "Reporting Practices of Psychiatrists Who Knew of Sexual Misconduct of Colleagues." *American Journal of Orthopsychiatry* 57 (1987): 287–95.

"Gays Look for Mr. HIV." *Citizen* 7, no. 9 (September 1993): 8.

Gibson, Janice T., and Mika Haritos-Fatouros. "The Education of a Torturer." *Psychology Today* 20, no. 11 (1986): 50–58.

Giles, Thomas. "Coping with Sexual Misconduct in the Church." *Christianity Today* 37, no. 1 (1993): 48–49.

Gonsiorek, J. C. "Sexual Exploitation by Psychotherapists: Some Observations on Male Victims and Sexual Orientation Issues." In *Psychotherapists' Sexual Involvement with Clients: Intervention and Prevention.* Ed. G. R. Schoener, et. al. Minneapolis: Walk-In Counseling Center, 1989.

Goodwin, J., T. McCarthy, and P. DiVasto. "Prior Incest in Mothers of Abused Children." *International Journal of Child Abuse and Neglect* 5 (1981): 87–96.

Groth, A. Nicholas. *Men Who Rape.* New York: Plenum, 1979.

Groth, A. Nicholas, and R. C. Birnbaum. "Adult Sexual Orientation and Attraction to Underage Persons." *Archives of Sexual Behavior* 7 (1978): 175–81.

Gutheil, Thomas. "Borderline Personality Disorder, Boundary Violations, adn Patient-Therapist Sex: Mediolegal Pitfalls." *American Journal of Psychiatry* 146, no. 5 (1989): 597–602.

Gutheil, Thomas, and Glen Gabbard. "The Concept of Boundaries in Clinical Practice: Theoretical and Risk-Management Dimensions." *American Journal of Psychiatry* 150, no. 2 (1993): 188–96.

Hardcastle, D. A. "Certification, Licensure and Other Forms of Regulation." In *Handbook of Clinical Social Work*. Ed. A. Rosenblatt and D. Waldfogel. San Francisco: Jossey-Bass, 1983.

Hardman-Cromwell, Youtha C. "Power and Sexual Abuse in Ministry." *The Journal of Religious Thought* 48, no. 1 (1991): 65–72

Harkin, Jeff. *Grace Plus Nothing*. Wheaton: Tyndale House, 1992.

Hart, Archibald. "Being Moral Isn't Always Enough." *Leadership* 9, no. 2 (1988): 24–29.

Haugaard, Jeffrey J. and N. Dickon Reppucci. *The Sexual Abuse of Children*. San Francisco: Jossey-Bass, 1988.

Hawkins, Russell. "An Analysis of Hypnotherapist-Client Sexual Intimacy." *The International Journal of Clinical and Experimental Hypnosis* 41, no. 4 (1993): 272–86.

Hayford, Jack. *Restoring Fallen Leaders*. Ventura, Calif.: Regal Books, 1988.

Heggen, Carolyn Holderread. *Sexual Abuse in Christian Homes and Churches*. Scottsdale, Penn.: Herald Press, 1993.

Heise, Lori. "Violence Against Women is Global." *Church and Society* 82, no. 4 (1992): 50–55.

Henderson, Daniel. "Breaking the Stranglehold: Treating Sex Offenders." *Christian Counseling Today* 2 (Summer 1994): 24–29.

Hess, K., and A. Hess. *Psychotherapy Supervision: Theory, Research, and Practice*. New York: John Wiley, 198[date?].

Hibben, Paxton. *Henry Ward Beecher: An American Portrait*. New York: The Press of the Readers Club, 1927, 1942.

Hicks, Robert. *The Masculine Journey: Understanding the Six Stages of Manhood*. Colorado Springs, Colo.: NavPress, 1993.

Hogan, Daniel. *The Regulation of Psychotherapists: A Review of Malpractice Suits in the United States*. Vol. 3. Cambridge, Mass.: Ballinger, 1979.

Hotz, Edward. "Diocesan Liability for Negligence of a Priest." *Catholic Lawyer* 26 (1981): 228.

"Imagined Abuse: No Thanks for the Memories." *Psychology Today* 26, no. 1 (1993): 14.

Jones, W. H. S. "Selections from the Hippocratic Corpus." In *Ethics in Medicine: Historical Perspectives and Contemporary Concerns*. Eds. S. J. Reiser, A. J. Dyck, and W. J. Curran. Cambridge, Mass.: MIT Press, 1977.

Jordan-Lake, Joy. "Conduct Unbecoming a Preacher." *Christianity Today* 36, no. 1 (1992): 26–30.

Kaslow, F. *Supervision and Training: Models, Dilemmas, and Challenges*. New York: Haworth Press, 1986.

Kertay, Les, and Susan L. Reviere. "The Use of Touch in Psychotherapy: Theoretical and Ethical Considerations." *Psychotherapy* 30, no. 1 (1993): 32–40.

Kinsley, Mike, and John Sununu. "Memories, Real or Not?" *CNN Crossfire*, transcript #1039. Denver, Colo.: Journal Graphics, Inc. Air Date: March 1, 1994.

Koch, Kurt E. *Christian Counseling and Occultism*. Grand Rapids: Kregel, 1965.

Kushner, Sherrill. "Divine Intervention." *Los Angeles Lawyer* (1988): 10–19.

Kutchins, Herb. "The Fiduciary Relationship: The Legal Basis for Social Workers' Responsibilities to Clients." *Social Work* 36, no. 2 (1991): 106–13.

Last, Helen and Jan Tully. "Churches Against Violence to Women." *Compass Theology Review* 25, (Autumn 1991): 26–28.

LaHaye, Tim. *If Ministers Fall, Can They Be Restored?* Grand Rapids: Zondervan, 1990.

Laswell, Harold. *A Preview of the Policy Sciences*. New York: Elsevier, 1971.

Lazarus, Jeremy. "Sex With Former Patients Almost Always Unethical." *American Journal of Psychiatry* 149 (1992): 855–57.

Leas, Speed. "In the Church." *Christian Legal Society Quarterly* 11 (Summer 1990).

Leo, John. "Who Gets Invited to the Table." *U.S. News and World Report* 117, no. 3 (1994): 18.

Leslie, Richard S. "Child and Sexual Abuse Repressed Memories: Real or Imagined? Staying Clear of Unethical Behavior." *The California Therapist* 6, no. 1 (1994): 22–25.

Leupker, Ellen. "Clinical Assessment by Clients Who Have Been Sexually Exploited by Their Therapists and Development of Differential Treatment Plans." In *Psychotherapists' Sexual Involvement with Clients: Intervention and Prevention*. Ed. G. R. Schoener, et.al. Minneapolis: Walk-In Counseling Center, 1989.

Lewis, C. S. *The Four Loves*. San Diego, Calif.: Harcourt Brace, 1971.

Lisak, David. "Sexual Aggression, Masculinity, and Fathers." *Signs: Journal of Women in Culture and Society* 16, no. 2 (1991): 238–62.

Loftus, Elizabeth F. "The Reality of Repressed Memories." *The American Psychologist* 48, no. 5 (1993): 518–37.

Lothstein, L. M. "Can a Sexually Addicted Priest Return to Ministry After Treatment? Psychological Issues and Possible Forensic Solutions." *Catholic Lawyer* 1 (1991): 107.

Lottes, Ilsa. "Sexual Socialization and Attitudes Toward Rape." In *Rape and Sexual Assault*. Vol. 2, ed. Ann Wolbert Burgess. New York: Garland, 1988.

Lowry, L. Randolph. "Reconciliation: Both Sides Win." *Christian Legal Society Quarterly* 11 (Summer 1990): 4–8.

Lynn, S. J., J. W. Rhue, B. P. Myers, and J. R. Weekes. "Pseudomemory in Hypnotized and Simulating Subjects." *The International Journal of Clinical and Experimental Hypnosis* 42, no. 2 (1994): 118–29.

MacCormack, A., M. Janus, and A. Burgess. "Runaway Youths and Sexual Victimization: Gender Differences in an Adolescent Runaway Population." *International Journal of Child Abuse and Neglect* 10 (1986): 387–95.

Madanes, Cloé. *Sex, Love, and Violence*. New York: Norton, 1990.

Malony, H. Newton, Thomas Needham, and Samuel Southard, eds. *Clergy Malpractice*. Philadelphia: Westminster, 1986.

SEXUAL MISCONDUCT IN COUNSELING

Markowitz, Laura. "Crossing the Line: Who Protects Clients from Their Protectors." *The Family Therapy Networker.* (Nov/Dec 1992): 25–31.

Marmor, Judd. "Some Psychodynamic Aspects of the Seduction of Patients in Psychotherapy. *The American Journal of Psychoanalysis* 36, (1976): 319–23.

Martin, Grant L. *Critical Problems in Children and Youth.* Dallas: Word, Inc., 1992.

Martinez, Demetria. "Parish Wants a Town Meeting Before Bailing out Santa Fe See." *National Catholic Reporter* 30, no. 14 (1994): 5.

Masters, William, and Virginia Johnson. "Principles of the New Sex Therapy." *American Journal of Psychiatry* 133 (1976): 548–53.

Maslow, Abraham. *Eupsychian Management: A Journal.* Homewood, Ill.: R. D. Irwin, 1965.

McCartney, J. L. "Overt Transference." *Journal of Sex Research* 2 (1966): 227–37.

McDonald, Gordon. *Rebuilding Your Broken World.* Nashville: Oliver Nelson, 1988.

McKee, Kathleen. "The Napa Repressed Memory Case." *The California Therapist* 6, no. 4 (1994): 24–26.

Minnesota Interfaith Committee on Sexual Exploitation by Clergy. *Sexual Exploitation by Clergy: Reflections and Guidelines for Religious Leaders.* Minneapolis: Minnesota Interfaith Committee, 1989.

Moberly, Elizabeth. *Homosexuality: A New Christian Ethic.* Greenwood: Attic Press, 1983.

Moodie, Fr. Michael. "Catholicism." *Los Angeles Lawyer* (1988).

Mouw, Richard J. "Educating for the Kingdom." *Theology, News and Notes* 41, no. 1 (1994): 47.

NASW Task Force on Ethics. "Ethics Analysis: Conduct and Responsibility to Clients." *NASW News* (May 1980): 12.

National Association of Social Workers, *NASW Code of Ethics.* Washington, D.C.: NASW, 1993.

National Conference of Catholic Bishops. *Recommendations of the Think Tank on Child Sexual Abuse.* Washington, D.C.; NCCB, 1992.

O'Brien, Raymond C. "Pedophilia: The Legal Predicament of Clergy." *Journal of Contemporary Health Law and Policy* 4, (1988): 91–154.

Ohlschlager, George, and Peter Mosgofian. *Law for the Christian Counselor: A Guidebook for Clinicians and Pastors.* Dallas: Word, Inc., 1992.

————. "Sex Therapy in the Body: A Roadmap to Christian Sexual Treatment." *Christian Counseling Today* 2 (Summer 1994): 9–13.

Olio, Karen, and W. F. Cornell. "The Therapeutic Relationship as the Foundation for Treatment with Adult Survivors of Sexual Abuse." *Psychotherapy* 30, no. 3 (1993): 512–23.

"Painful Pastoral Question: Sexual Abuse of Minors." *Origins* 22 (1992): 177–78.

Pateman, Carole. "Sex and Power." *Ethics* 100, no. 2 (1990): 398–407.

Payne, Leanne. *The Broken Image: Restoring Personal Wholeness Through Healing Prayer.* Westchester: Crossway, 1981.

"People and Events," *Christianity Today* 36, no. 10 (1992): 63

Peters, Noel Benedict. "Relationships as a Determinant of Stress Among Catholic Religious Professionals in the United States and South Africa." *Journal of Psychology and Christianity* 12, no. 2 (1993): 117–29.

Petersen, J. Allan. *The Myth of the Greener Grass.* Wheaton: Tyndale, 1983.

Plummer, Kenneth. "Pedophilia: Constructing a Sociological Baseline." In *Adult Sexual Interest in Children: Personality and Psychopathy.* Ed. Mark Cook and Kevin Howells. London: Academic Press, 1981.

Pope, Kenneth S. "Ethical and Malpractice Issues in Hospital Practice." *American Psychologist* 45, no. 9 (1990): l066–70.

————. "Therapist-Patient Sex as Sex Abuse: Six Scientific, Professional, and Practical Dilemmas in Addressing Victimization and Rehabilitation." *Professional Psychology: Research and Practice* 21, no. 4 (1990): 227–39.

————. "Sexual Involvement Between Therapists and Patients." *The Harvard Mental Health Letter* 11, no. 8 (1994): 25–31.

————. *Sexual Involvement with Therapists: Patient Assessment, Subsequent Therapy, Forensics.* Washington, D.C.: American Psychological Association Press, 1984.

Pope, Kenneth S., and Jacqueline C. Bouhoutsos. *Sexual Intimacy Between Therapists and Patients.* New York: Praeger, 1986.

Pope, Kenneth S., P. Keith-Spiegel, and B. G . Tabachnick. "Sexual Attraction to Clients: The Human Therapist and the (Sometimes) Inhuman Training System." *American Psychologist* 41, no. 2 (1986): 147–58.

Press, Aric, and Carolyn Friday. "Priests and Abuse." *Newsweek,* 16 August 1993.

Putnam, Frank. *Diagnosis and Treatment of Multiple Personality Disorder.* New York: The Guilford Press, 1989.

Rambo, Lewis. "Interview with Reverend Marie Fortune, August 8, 1990." *Pastoral Psychology* 39, no. 5 (1991): 305–19.

Raven, Robert. "Disciplinary Enforcement: Time for Re-examination." *American Bar Association Journal* (May 1989): 8.

Reardon, Katherine Ann. "The Theology of the Body in the Thought of Pope John Paul II." Masters of Theology Thesis, Dominican School of Philosophy and Theology, Berkeley, California, 1986.

Rediger, G. Lloyd. *Ministry and Sexuality: Cases, Counseling and Care.* Minneapolis: Fortress Press, 1990.

Rigali, Norbert J. "Note on Pedophilia." *Theological Studies* 55 (1994): 139.

Rinck, Margaret. *Christian Men Who Hate Women: Healing Hurting Relationships.* Grand Rapids: Zondervan, 1990.

Robertiello, R. "Introgenic Psychiatric Illness." *Journal of Contemporary Psychotherapy* 7 (1975): 3–8.

Roberts, Tom. "Bernardin Sex Abuse Charges Dropped." *National Catholic Reporter* 30, no. 19 (1994): 3–5

Rossetti, Stephen. "Parishes as Victims of Abuse." *Human Development* (Winter 1993): 15–17.

Russell, Diana. "The Incidence and Prevalence of Intrafamilial and Extrafamilial Sexual Abuse of Female Children." *International Journal of Child Abuse and Neglect* 7 (1983): 133–39.

Rutter, Peter. *Sex in the Forbidden Zone*. Los Angeles: Jeremy P. Tarcher, Inc., 1989.

Rutzky, Jaques. "Leading the Witness: Countertransference in Treating Adult Incest Survivors. *The California Therapist* 6, no. 4 (1994): 27–29.

"Satanic Ritual Abuse: The Current State of Knowledge." *Journal of Psychology and Theology* 20, no. 3 (fall 1992).

Schaumburg, Harry. *False Intimacy: Understanding the Struggle of Sexual Addiction*. Colorado Springs, Colo.: NavPress, 1992.

Schmucker, Jane. "Sex Suit Against Cardinal Dropped." *USA Today*, 1 March 1994.

Schoener, Gary. "Common Errors in Treatment of Victims/Survivors of Sexual Misconduct by Professionals." Paper presented at the seminar, Intervention with Victim/Survivors of Sexual Misconduct by Professionals, Minneapolis, Minnesota, February 18, 1994.

————. "Rehabilitation of Professionals Who Have Sexually Touched Clients." In *Assisting Impaired Psychologists*. Rev. ed., ed. M. Schwebel, J. Skorina and G. Schoener. Washington, D.C.: American Psychological Association, 1994..

Schoener, Gary, J. H. Milgrom, J. C. Gonsiorek, E. T. Luepker, R. M. Conroe. Eds. *Psychotherapist's Sexual Involvement with Clients: Intervention and Prevention*. Minneapolis: Walk-In Counseling Center, 1989.

Schultz, L. G. "Survey of Social Workers' Attitudes and Use of Body and Sexual Psychotherapies." *Clinical Social Work Journal* 3 (September 1975): 90–99.

Serban, G. "Sexual Activity in Therapy." *American Journal of Psychotherapy* 35 (1981): 81.

Shepard, M. *The Love Treatment: Sexual Intimacy Between Patients and Psychotherapists*. New York: Peter H. Wyden, 1971.

Silbert, M., and A. Pines. "Sexual Abuse as an Antecedent to Prostitution." *International Journal of Child Abuse and Neglect* 5 (1981): 407–11.

Sipe, A. W. Richard. *A Secret World*. New York: Brunner/Mazel, 1990.

————. "Sexual Abuse of Clergy: Who and Why." Testimony at the Governor's Conference on Child Abuse and Neglect, Baltimore, Maryland, 1993.

Smith, Michael. "Pastors Under Fire: A Personal Report." *Christian Century* (1994): 196–99.

Smolowe, Jill. "Dubious Memories: A Father Accused of Sexual Abuse Wins a Malpractice Judgment Against His Daughter's Therapists" *Time* 23 May 1994.

Sonenschein, David. *How to Have Sex with Kids*, Austin Pedophile Study Group II. Pamplet presented by R. P. Toby Tyler of the San Bernardino Sheriff's Crimes Against Children Detail, 655 East Third Street, San Bernardino, California, 92415.

Sonne, Janet, and Kenneth S. Pope. "Treating Victims of Therapist-Patient Sexual Involvement." *Psychotherapy* 28, no. 1 (1991): 183.

"Special Report: How Common Is Pastoral Indiscretion? Results of a Leadership Survey." *Leadership* 9, no. 1 (1988): 12–13.

Spurgeon, C. H. *The Metropolitan Tabernacle Pulpit*. Vol. 23. Pasadena, Tex.: Pilgrim Publications, 1974.

Stahel, Thomas H. "One Pastoral Response to Abuse: Interview with Joseph P. Chinnici." *America* 170, no. 2 (1994): 48).

Stake, Jayne E., and Joan Oliver. "Sexual Contact and Touching Between Therapist and Client: A Survey of Psychololgists' Attitudes and Behavior." *Professional Psychology: Research and Practice* 22, no. 2 (1991): 297–307.

Stark, Kathe. "Child Sexual Abuse Within the Catholic Church." In *Psychotherapists' Sexual Involvement with Clients: Intervention and Prevention.* Ed. Gary Schoener, et al. Minneapolis: Walk-in Counseling Center, 1989.

"Statement on Priests and Child Abuse." *Origins* 19 (1989): 395.

Stoltenberg, C., and U. Dalworth. *Supervising Counselors and Therapists.* San Francisco: Jossey-Bass, 1987.

Strasburger, Larry, Linda Jorgenson, and Rebecca Randles. "Criminalization of Psychotherapist-Patient Sex." *American Journal of Psychiatry* 148, no. 7 (1991): 859–63.

Summit, Roland. "The Child Abuse Accommodation Syndrome." *International Journal of Child Abuse and Neglect* 7 (1983): 177–93.

The Offbeat. "Reagan's Pastor Stepped Over the Line." *Times-Standard,* Eureka California, 22 February 1993.

Thielicke, Helmut. *The Ethics of Sex.* Trans. John W. Doberstein. Grand Rapids: Baker, 1964.

Thomas, Gordon. *Desire and Denial: Celibacy and the Church.* Boston: Little, Brown and Co., 1986.

Thoreson, R. W., P. Shaughnessy, P. P. Heppner, and S. W. Cook. "Sexual Contact During and After the Professional Relationship: Attitudes and Practices of Male Counselors." *Journal of Counseling and Development* 71, no. 4 (1993): 429–34.

"USCC Pedophilia Statement." *Origins* 17 (1988): 624.

Vinyard Ministries International. *Equipping the Saints* 4 (1992).

Virkler, Henry. *Broken Promises.* Dallas: Word, 1992.

————. "When Temptation Knocks: Reducing Your Vulnerability." *Christian Counseling Today* 2 (Summer 1994): 39–43.

Wall, James M. "The Bernardin Factor." *Christian Century* 110, no. 34 (1993): 1195–96.

Webster's New World Dictionary, Second College Edition. Cleveland, Ohio: Prentice Hall Press, 1986.

White, John. *Eros Redeemed: Breaking the Stranglehold of Sexual Sin.* Downers Grove: InterVarsity, 1993.

White, William L. *The Image of Man in C. S. Lewis.* New York: Abingdon Press, 1969.

Whitehead, Briar. "A Better Response to Gay Activism." *The Standard* 11, no. 1 (1994): 8–9.

Wilkes, Paul. "Unholy Acts." *New Yorker* 7 June 1993.

Wilkins, David. "Who Should Regulate Lawyers?" *Harvard Law Review* 105 (1992): 799.

Zimmerman, Anthony. "Naked But Not Ashamed." *The Priest* 48, no. 9 (1992): 47–54.

Cases, Constitutions, and Statutes

California Business and Professions Code, section 729 (West Supp. 1990).

California Civil Code, section 43.93 (West 1993).

Carini v. Beaven, 219 Mass. 117, 106 N.E. 589 (1914).

Colorado Revised Statutes, section 18-3-405.5 (Supp 1992).

Cotton v. Kambly, 101 Mich. App. 537, 300 N.W. 2d 627 (1980).

Decker v. Fink, 47 Md. App. 202, 422 A. 2d 389 (1980).

Destefano v. Grabrian, 763 P. 2d 275 (Colorado 1988).

Erickson v. Christenson, 99 Or. App. 104 (1989).

Florida Statutes Annotated, section 491.0112 (West 1991).

Greenberg v. McCabe, 453 F. Supp. 765 (E.D. Penn. 1978), affirmed 594 F. 2d 854 (3d Cir. 1979), cert. denied 444 U.S. 840.

Horak v. Biris, 130 Ill. App. 3d 140, 474 N.E. 2d 13 (1985).

Jeffrey Scott E. v. Central Baptist Church, 243 Cal. Rptr. 128, 197 Cal. App. 3d 718 (Cal. App. 4 Dist. 1988).

Maine Revised Statutes Annotated, title 17-A, section 253(2) (West Supp. 1992).

Michigan Laws Annotated, sections 750.90, 520b (1) (f) (West 1991).

Minnesota Statutes Annotated, sections 148A.01–06, 609.341, subd. (19) and (20), and 609.344, h-j. (West 1993); section 609.341–.345 (West Supp. 1993).

Moxon v. County of Kern, 233 Cal. App. 2d 393, 43 Cal. Rptr. 481 (1965).

New Hampshire Revised Statutes Annotated, section 632-A.2 (Supp 1992).

North Dakota Revised Statutes Annotated, section 12.1-20-06.1 (Supp 1991).

People v. Bernstein, 340 P. 2d 299 (Cal. Ct. App. 1959).

People V. Middleton, 350 N.E. 2d 223 (Ill. App. Ct. 1976).

Rhode Island General Laws, section 11-37-2(C) (Supp. 1992).

Rowe v. Bennett, 514 A. 2d 802 (Me. 1986).

Roy V. Hartogs, 85 Misc. 2d 891, 381 N.Y.S. 2d 587 (Sup. Ct. 1976).

Schultz v. Roman Catholic Archdiocese of Newark, 95 N.J. 530, 472 A. 2d 531 (1984).

Seymour v. Lofgreen, 209 Kan. 72, 495 p. 2d 969 (1972).

Simmons v. United States, 805 F. 2d 1363 (9th Cir. 1986), at 1364–65.

St. Paul Fire and Marine Insurance Co. v. Love, 447 N.W. 2d 5 (Minn. Ct. App. 1989).

State v. Ely, 194 P. 988 (Wash. 1921).

Stevens v. Roman Catholic Bishop of Fresno, 49 Cal. App. 3d 877, 123 Cal. Rptr. 171 (1975).

Strock v. Presnell, 527 N.E. 2d 1235, at 1238 (Ohio 1988).

Texas State Board of Examiners of Professional Counselors' Rules, sections 681.33 (g)(1)(A)and (B), (1994), 6–7.

Wisconsin Statutes Annotated, section 940.22 (West Supp. 1992).

Wisconsin Statutes Annotated, sections 895.70 and 940.22(1)(i) (West 1993).

Wyoming Statutes, section 6-2-303 (a) (1988).

Zipkin v. Freeman, 436 S.W. 2d 753 (Missouri 1968).

INDEX

350   SEXUAL MISCONDUCT IN COUNSELING

format, 149–51
Minnesota-St. Paul diocese, 169,
     309–27
no policy, 157–59
policy in place, 155–57
Presbyterian Church of Canada,
     293–308
Roman Catholic, 173–78
Memory
     repressed, 105–8
     recovered, 105–8
MPD (Multiple Personality Disor-
     der), 81–83

National Association of Social
     Workers, 196
National Council of Catholic
     Bishops, 168–70, 178, 337

Partializing, 42–43
Patriarchy, 159–62
Pedophiles, 123–25, 170–71
Polygamous, 32, 285–86
PTSD (Post Traumatic Stress
     Disorder), 81–83
Power, 18–20, 24–26
Prevention guidelines
     administrative, 271
     personal, 262–64
     professional, 265–71
     systemic, 276–78, 288
     training/education, 278–79

Ramona case, 108, 109
Rape, 21–23
Religious courts, 328
Religious rights, 332

Seductive clients, 100–103, 269–70
Sexual addiction, 16–17
Sexual ethics, principles, 194–95
Sexual misconduct
     incidence, 6–7
Sexual misconduct law
     breach of contract, 215–16

civil lawsuits, 211–16
corporate/institutional liablility,
     226–28
criminal liability, 220–23
fiduciary duty, 215, 216
infliction of emotional distress,
     214–15
license revocation, 217–20
reporting duties, 223–25
Texas statute, 222–23
Sexual offender
     restoration, 249–56
     treatment, 243–49
Sexual policies (staff), 272–74
Sexual vulnerability, 265–66
Sex with former clients, 198–203
Spiritual warfare, 292–94
Star factor, 66
Supervision, 274–75

Theological anthropology, 29–30
Touch, 103–105
Transference, 26, 63
Transformation, 41–44, 261–62
Trust, 64

Victims, Adult
     evaluation, 80–81
     harm, 78–79
     legal action, 93–94
     profile, 52
     spiritual issues, 92–93
     treatment, 84–93
Victims, Children
     (also see Child Sexual Abuse)
     counseling environment, 134–37
     treatment, 137–44
     treatment issues, 140–42
     treatment options, 142–44
Violators
     borderline, 57
     predatory, 59–60
     vulnerable, 55–57

Wilberforce, W., 283–85

CPSIA information can be obtained
at www.ICGtesting.com
Printed in the USA
LVHW080820220720
661149LV00018BA/1518